MW00777707

FACES ON SCREEN

FACES ON SCREEN

New Approaches

Edited by Alice Maurice

EDINBURGH
University Press

Edinburgh University Press is one of the leading university presses in the UK. We publish academic books and journals in our selected subject areas across the humanities and social sciences, combining cutting-edge scholarship with high editorial and production values to produce academic works of lasting importance. For more information visit our website: edinburghuniversitypress.com

Edinburgh University Press Ltd
The Tun – Holyrood Road
12 (2f) Jackson's Entry
Edinburgh EH8 8PJ

Typeset in 10/12.5 pt Sabon
by IDSUK (DataConnection) Ltd,

A CIP record for this book is available from the British Library

ISBN 978 1 4744 9378 9 (hardback)
ISBN 978 1 4744 9380 2 (webready PDF)
ISBN 978 1 4744 9381 9 (epub)

CONTENTS

FIGURES

ACKNOWLEDGEMENTS

I wish to thank all those who helped make this collection possible. Research for this collection was supported in part by an Insight Grant from Canada's Social Sciences and Humanities Research Council (SSHRC). Thanks also to the English Department at the University of Toronto Scarborough and to the Cinema Studies Institute at the University of Toronto for their collegial support. Ideas for this collection were informed by presentations and audience feedback from conferences including the Society for Cinema and Media Studies (SCMS), Domitor and the Modernist Studies Association. Thanks to my colleagues at University of Toronto and elsewhere for their input – especially Sara Saljoughi, James Cahill, Karen Redrobe, Maggie Hennefeld, Noa Steimatsky, Genevieve Love and Angelica Fenner. I am thankful to my undergraduate and graduate students at the University of Toronto, with whom I discussed many ideas related to this volume. Thanks especially to my research assistant, Jillian Vasko, and to editorial assistant Emma W. Johnson.

I wish to thank Gillian Leslie at Edinburgh University Press for her enthusiastic support of this project from its early stages. Thanks also to Sam Johnson, Eddie Clark, Caitlin Murphy and the entire staff of EUP, and Lel Gillingwater and Jo Penning, for all their incredible work in guiding this book to publication. I also wish to thank the anonymous readers of the manuscript for their comments and advice.

Most of all, thank you to all of the authors who contributed their exciting work to this collection – I am so happy to be able to bring this work together here.

Finally, thank you to Mark Rigby, for his critical insights and support while I was editing this collection. And to my son, Oscar, for being amazing.

NOTES ON CONTRIBUTORS

Tanine Allison is Associate Professor of Film and Media Studies at Emory University and author of *Destructive Sublime: World War II in American Film and Media* (2018). Her essays on war media, visual effects and video games have appeared in *New Review of Film and Television Studies*, *Quarterly Review of Film and Video*, *Journal of Popular Film and Television*, and other journals and anthologies. She is currently writing a book about performance capture and visual effects.

Koel Banerjee is a Visiting Postdoctoral Fellow of English at Carnegie Mellon University. Her current research focuses on South Asian film and popular culture, postcolonial studies, consumer culture and critical theory. Her writing has appeared in *Studies in South Asian Film and Media* and *Cultural Critique*. She has also contributed chapters to several forthcoming edited anthologies, including *Third Cinema, World Cinema and Marxism*; *The Oxford Handbook of Children's Film*; *Bollywood's New Woman: Liberalization, Liberation, and Contested Bodies*; and *The Cold War in South Asia*.

Lisa Bode is Senior Lecturer in Film and Television Studies at The University of Queensland, Brisbane, Australia. She is the author of *Making Believe: Screen Performance and Special Effects in Popular Cinema* (2017) and has published elsewhere on digital actors, the digital resurrection of dead actors, motion capture, prosthetic makeup and the uncanny valley. Her work has appeared in *Cinema Journal*, *Animation: An Interdisciplinary Journal* and various edited collections. She is currently working on a history of digital visual effects.

Iggy Cortez is Mellon Assistant Professor in Cinema and Media Arts at Vanderbilt University. He is currently at work on a book on night-time and world cinema, and his articles have appeared or are forthcoming in *The Journal of Cinema and Media Studies* (formerly *Cinema Journal*) and *Camera Obscura*. With Ian Fleishman, he is also co-editing a volume of essays on the relationship between negative affect, cultural politics and acting through the lens of Isabelle Huppert's performances.

Zara Dinnen is Senior Lecturer in Contemporary Literature at Queen Mary University of London. She is author of *The Digital Banal: New Media and American Literature and Culture* (2018) and co-editor of *The Edinburgh Companion to Contemporary Narrative Theories* (Edinburgh University Press, 2018).

Angelica Fenner is Associate Professor cross-appointed in the Cinema Studies Institute and the Department of Germanic Languages and Literatures at the University of Toronto. She is author of *Race Under Reconstruction in German Cinema* (2011), co-editor of *The Autobiographical Turn in Germanophone Documentary and Experimental Film* (2014), guest editor of special issues of the journals *Transit*, *Camera Obscura* and *German Feminist Studies*, and contributor to various edited collections. Her research interests encompass but are not limited to diaspora and migration in European cinemas, women's film authorship and first-person documentary.

Jenny Gunn is an instructor in the Department of Film and Media at Emory University and the School of Film, Media and Theatre at Georgia State University. She completed her doctorate in Moving Image Studies at Georgia State University in 2019. Her book project analyses the impact of the forward-facing camera and the emergence of practices of digital self-mediation on contemporary visual culture and historical understandings of the cinema and the self. She is an ongoing contributor to the liquid blackness research group and social media strategist for *liquid blackness: journal of aesthetics and black studies*. Her writing has been published in *Film-Philosophy*, *Black Camera*, *Cinephile*, *Mediascape* and in *JCMS*.

Andrea Gyenge is a scholar of the critical humanities. Her research focuses on themes of orality and the mouth in continental philosophy and visual culture. Her essays have appeared in *New German Critique*, *Angelaki: A Journal of the Theoretical Humanities*, *Cultural Critique* and *Free Associations*. Her work on the philosophy of Jean-Luc Nancy is forthcoming in Nancy's *Corpus* III (with John Paul Ricco) and an edited collection (*Understanding Nancy, Understanding Modernism*). She recently completed a postdoctoral fellowship in the Department of Visual Studies at the University of Toronto Mississauga.

Stefka Hristova is Associate Professor of Digital Media at Michigan Technological University. She holds a PhD in Visual Studies with emphasis on Critical Theory from the University of California, Irvine. Her research analyses the digital visual cultures of difference and displacement. Hristova's work has been published in journals such as *Transnational Subjects Journal*, *Visual Anthropology*, *Radical History Review*, *TripleC*, *Surveillance and Security*, *Interstitial*, *Cultural Studies* and *Transformations*. She is a member of the Executive Committee at the Institute for Policy, Ethics and Culture.

Delia Malia Konzett is Professor of English, Cinema and Women's Studies at the University of New Hampshire in Durham. She is the author of *Ethnic Modernisms* (2002) and *Hollywood's Hawaii: Race, Nation, and War* (2017). She is also the editor of *Hollywood at the Intersection of Race and Identity* (2019). She has published in numerous critical journals on film, focusing on race, imperialism and aesthetics. Her present work discusses race in Hollywood and its representation in mass culture.

Alice Maurice is Associate Professor of English and Cinema Studies at the University of Toronto. She is the author of *The Cinema and Its Shadow: Race and Technology in Early Cinema* (2013). Her work has appeared in journals including *Camera Obscura, Cinema Journal, The Moving Image, New Review of Film and Television Studies*, and a number of anthologies. Her current research focuses on the face, identity and transformation in American cinema.

Sam McBean is Senior Lecturer in Gender, Sexuality and Contemporary Culture at Queen Mary University of London. She is the author of *Feminism's Queer Temporalities* (2016) and has published on contemporary literature and culture, new media and affect, and queer and feminist theory in journals including *Feminist Review, Camera Obscura* and the *Journal of Lesbian Studies*.

Adrienne L. McLean has been Professor of Film Studies at the University of Texas at Dallas since 1998 and is the editor of several anthologies as well as the author of *Being Rita Hayworth: Labor, Identity, and Hollywood Stardom* (2004), *Dying Swans and Madmen: Ballet, the Body, and Narrative Cinema* (2008) and *All For Beauty* (2022), along with a number of journal articles and book chapters on stardom, dance, and the body. She is currently working on a project about film dancer and choreographer Eleanor Powell.

Hannah Parlett is a PhD candidate at the Centre of Film and Screen, University of Cambridge. Her current doctoral research examines maternity and transgression in contemporary art film, drawing on the work of Andrea Arnold, Lynne Ramsay, Claire Denis and Barry Jenkins. Her broader research interests include moving-image art, the politics of gesture on screen and theories of stardom. She completed her undergraduate degree in History at Gonville and Caius College in 2016, before receiving an MPhil in Film and Screen Studies in 2018.

Paula Quigley is Assistant Professor in Film at the Department of Film, School of Creative Arts, Trinity College Dublin. She has published on a wide range of topics in film studies, including the work of Sergei Eisenstein and André Bazin, the impact of psychoanalysis on film theory, and studies of the short film. In addition, she has published on issues of genre and gender in relation to American and European film and filmmakers, with a focus on iterations of the 'woman's film' in diverse cinematic and cultural contexts.

Sara Saljoughi is Assistant Professor of English and Cinema Studies at the University of Toronto. Her essays have been published in *Camera Obscura*, *Feminist Media Histories*, *Iranian Studies* and *Film International*. She is co-editor of *1968 and Global Cinema* (2018).

Elyse Singer is a PhD candidate in Theatre and Performance, with Film Studies Certificate, at the Graduate Center, City University of New York (CUNY). Her work has been published in *PAJ: A Journal of Performance and Art*, *Studies in Musical Theatre* and the *New England Theater Journal*. She received the 2020 Graduate Student Writing Prize from the SCMS Women's Caucus and the Special Commendation, 2018 Domitor Student Essay Contest. She teaches at the Feirstein Graduate School of Cinema and New York University's Tisch Department of Dramatic Writing. A Yale graduate, she is a theatre director and playwright and Artistic Director of the Obie-winning Hourglass Group.

Aaron Tucker is an Elia Scholar and VISTA Doctoral Scholar in the Cinema and Media Studies Department at York University (Toronto, Canada) where he is studying the moving images of facial recognition software. In addition, he is the author of a novel, two books of poetry and two scholarly cinema studies monographs, *Interfacing with the Internet in Popular Cinema* (2014) and *Virtual Weaponry: The Militarized Internet in Hollywood War Films* (2017).

Brenda R. Weber is Provost Professor and Jean C. Robinson Scholar in the Department of Gender Studies at Indiana University. Her books include *Makeover TV: Selfhood, Citizenship, and Celebrity* (2009), *Women and Literary*

Celebrity in the Nineteenth Century (2012), *Reality Gendervision: Gender and Sexuality on Transatlantic Reality Television* (2014), *Latter-day Screens: Sexuality, Gender, and Mediated Mormonism* (2019) and *Ryan Murphy's Queer America* (2022).

Genevieve Yue is Assistant Professor of Culture and Media and Director of the Screen Studies Program at the New School. She is also a film critic and programmer of experimental film, and she serves as the chair of the programming committee on the Flaherty Board of Trustees. She is the author of *Girl Head: Feminism and Film Materiality* (2020).

INTRODUCTION: FACING FORWARD, FACING BACK

Alice Maurice

In *Visible Man* (1924), early film theorist Béla Balázs predicted that the cinema would rescue the face from illegibility. Through the close-up, people would 'relear[n] the long-forgotten language of gestures and facial expressions' and man would 'become visible once again'.[1] Now, nearly a century later, it would seem we have learned this language too well. Whether we consider the digitally created and manipulated faces of Hollywood cinema or the social media filters, 'face apps' and surveillance software of everyday life, reading 'face language' has become the seemingly endless task of humans and machines alike. For his part, Balázs dreamed of a time when 'academics [would] perhaps realise that we should turn to the cinema so as to compile a lexicon of gestures and facial expressions on a par with our dictionaries of words', adding that academics would in fact be unnecessary for the project of compiling this 'new grammar' because audiences would 'go to the cinema and learn it themselves'.[2] Indeed, as we trade animated GIFs of expressive faces and punctuate our sentences with emoji, we seem to have become fluent in the face language that Balázs imagined. Or have we? With faces flying across our screens as a form of communicative currency, we find ourselves not in a utopian Esperanto of gesture, but rather in a kind of facial alphabet soup. Is this what all our cinema-face training has come to? This collection seeks to contextualise and decode the many 'face languages' that have proliferated on screens and, in so doing, to rethink the meaning of the face in film and media.

This is an odd moment for faces. With the world having recently emerged from the deadly COVID-19 pandemic, it might seem that the face is also emerging – coming out from under the mandatory medical masks that became the norm around the globe in 2020. And yet, in many ways, the face became even more prominent during the pandemic. Very early on, as the virus spread, we were told to 'stop touching our faces', which of course only made us more aware of the desire to do so. The masks, too, only made the face more visible – increasing the obsession with the face (through its denial), but also bringing to the surface, quite literally, the 'face politics' (to use Jenny Edkins's term) of our contemporary moment.[3] Wearing (or not wearing) masks became a political statement for many, rather than merely an issue of public health, especially in the US, where Trump-induced mask hysteria reached absurd heights. Not wearing a mask became a badge of personal freedom for some and a denial of the virus's existence. In a seeming literalisation of toxic masculinity, men (at least in the US context) were less likely than women to wear masks, viewing them as what one commentator called 'emasculating face condoms'.[4] But it was more complicated than that, and the mask only underlined the fact that facial politics are always also racial politics: as the deadly nature of anti-Black racism and police violence was laid bare once again in the George Floyd murder in Minneapolis in May 2020, many Black men were reticent about masks, as they feared that covering their faces would lead to more harassment and racial profiling by police.[5] If there is privilege in being able to show one's face, there is also privilege in who gets to hide it with impunity. Right on cue, the producers of facial recognition technologies ramped up their efforts, and we were assured (warned?) that those technologies could 'crack masked faces' and 'beat the Covid mask challenge'.[6] As Hans Belting reminds us, mask and face are not opposing terms; rather, the face and the mask have always been closely entwined 'operative concepts' that form a 'single theme in the organizing principle of a "history of the face"'.[7] That has perhaps never been more clear, as the COVID-19 mask simply added one more layer to the fraught territory of the face.

The face on screen didn't disappear during COVID-19 – it only proliferated. Even as the face was masked in public, the face on screen became ever-present and ubiquitous, as many of us – those fortunate enough to work from home, those with technology at hand – were reduced to the telepresence of faces on screens. Zoom, a company founded in 2011, suddenly became the most popular video-calling platform during the pandemic, so much a part of people's lives – for online meetings, online classes, family group calls and so on – that 'zooming' became a verb with a new meaning, signalling its arrival as a 'cultural phenomenon'.[8] And while the company's name implies the speed and ease with which we can virtually 'zoom' from our homes to anywhere in the world to meet with virtually anyone, the name also of course references a zoom lens – aptly capturing the feeling of being 'zoomed-in-on' and framed for others' consumption. Ready or not, we were all getting our close-ups. With most of us denied the 'big-screen' experience of movie theatres during the pandemic, the face on screen became an intimate affair.

In many ways, then, this is an important and opportune moment from which to survey the past, present and future of the face on screen. This collection takes the face as its subject, considered primarily in cinema but also broadly across various visual technologies and screen practices. The face – in particular the face in close-up – has been a central concern of film and media studies since the invention of the cinema. From Sergei Eisenstein, Jean Epstein and Béla Balázs writing in the silent era to Gilles Deleuze and beyond, one might say it has almost been an obsession. Indeed, Mary Ann Doane has argued just that, noting that the history of 'excessiveness, even hysteria' in responses to the close-up only testifies to its ideological function – the way it seems to marry the fantasy of overwhelming totality with the graspable, attainable fragment, offering a salve to the disintegration and 'strongly felt loss specific to modernity':[9]

> This confusion, and the apparent collapse of the oppositions between detail and totality, part and whole, microcosm and macrocosm, the miniature and the gigantic, is crucial to the ideological operation of the close-up, that which makes it one of our most potent memories of the cinema.[10]

If we are mesmerised by the face in close-up, if we have been under its spell, then in order to break the spell, we must look beyond the close-up; we must widen our lens, if you will, to look at the screen face in historical, material, technological and cultural context. *Faces on Screen* aims to do just that – going beyond the close-up and beyond a singular methodology, putting work on early and classic iterations of the screen face in conversation with work on the face in contemporary media. The authors in this collection take a number of different and complementary approaches: from close readings of films to historical analyses of analogue and digital 'face reading practices'; from practical accounts of technology, performance modes and digital imaging to a variety of theoretical approaches to the screen face. The essays range across different time periods, topics and media – from *photogénie* and silent cinema to facial recognition, digital creatures and deepfakes – offering a way to think about the way our current 'face culture' follows from what came before and where and how technological, aesthetic and epistemological shifts have changed the way we think about – and look at – the face on screen. In short, these essays examine how we make and consume faces, offering a multifaceted and historicised look at the roots of our current, ever-multiplying entanglements with the face on screen.

On screens big and small, the face has become modular, digital, swappable and frangible, and our relationship to it is increasingly kaleidoscopic and vertiginous. Whether we are looking at the vaguely uncanny, de-aged faces of Robert De Niro and Al Pacino on movie screens, or at the everyday faces (including our own), manipulated, stretched, emoji-fied and commodified online, we are confronted with the face as a site of transformation, modification, masking and exchange. Socially directed as they are, our faces are never fully 'our own', but contemporary culture speeds up and literalises the alienation of the face. In 2019, when FaceApp offered users the ability to age their own faces and share them online in the 'FaceApp challenge', it seemed like good, clean internet fun (if there is such a thing), but of course this was quickly revealed to be just another platform for data mining and face collection (for purposes including training facial recognition technology).[11] Only a few years later, that technology already seems archaic, as improvements now allow other 'face-swap' apps (such as ReFace) to offer more, with users now able to seamlessly insert their faces into videos, replacing celebrity faces with their own. The app's promise (as expressed in its slogan) is both simple and expansive: 'Reface. Be anyone.'[12] The promise of irresistible interchangeability obscures (indeed, masks) the true aspiration (and real moneymaking potential) of these technologies powered by AI and machine learning. The company's CEO identified the future of this technology in 'synthetic ads' and personalised marketing: targeted ads featuring the consumer's own face.[13]

For all its fragmentation, modification and reduplication, the face on screen still has the power to command our attention, even our reverence – or perhaps we simply hope it does. In her *New York Times* review of the domestic violence-themed update of *The Invisible Man* (Leigh Whannell, 2020), for example, Manhola Dargis gives much of the credit for the film's success to Elizabeth Moss's face:

> Moss's full-bore performance – anchored by her extraordinarily supple face – gives the movie its emotional stakes . . . With her high forehead, prominent jawline and eyes that can pop or menacingly narrow, Moss has an ideal big-screen canvas, one she fills with subtle fluctuations that let you follow Cecilia's inner states even when she goes quiet. Directors like to over-pump Moss's tears (she's a real sob sister), but here the waterworks don't gush, which complicates the idea of Cecilia as a hapless victim.[14]

Note here the combination of the physical qualities of Moss's 'supple' face – just the physical facts of her features, her jawline, forehead and so on – and what she can do *with* them. Dargis's ode to the face as 'big-screen canvas' hearkens back to the silent cinema and the faces that inspired early film theorists like Jean Epstein and Béla Balázs to wax poetic about the film face, and to identify the close-up as 'the film's true terrain'.[15] While Dargis seems thankful here that Moss can do so much with her face, she also seems relieved that

Moss doesn't do *too* much – that her emoting doesn't end up in 'waterworks', that she doesn't become a 'sob sister', which would signal her demotion to a 'hapless victim'. The face must be 'supple', plastic and pliable, with eyes that can 'pop' on the one hand but limited to 'subtle fluctuations' on the other – a long tradition of asking the face on film to be expressive without toppling over into melodrama or grotesquerie. This is an extension of the limited range within which the face must act even off the screen – as sociologist Georg Simmel put it in 1901, the 'aesthetic unity' of the face can only be maintained 'if the spatial relation among the facial elements be allowed to shift only within very narrow limits'.[16] It is perhaps no coincidence that the face would come to prominence in a film about invisibility: when one is playing leading lady to an invisible man, the pressure to make the face speak is great and the need to make emotions 'visible' redounds even more onto the woman's face – already the site of emotional excess in the history of cinema.[17]

This play of visibility and invisibility, revelation and concealment, has always been a part of the face's allure. That sense of being out there for all to see, 'naked' and vulnerable, exists in tension with the idea that there is a truer face 'behind the mask'.[18] This tension is just one of the many oppositions that the face mediates, as it stands at and for the boundary between self and other, internal and external, subjectivity and signification.[19] These tensions are key not only to the power of the face on screen but also to the face's 'haunting significance and political consequence', what Edkins calls 'the paradox of the face': the contradiction between the sense that 'the face is disappearing, with a shift from the modern episteme to a world of digital images and the post-human, and what seems to be happening – that the face endures as an emblem of political personhood'.[20] Each new effort to pin down the face – to fix and codify its meaning through visual media – seems only to reveal the political and aesthetic stakes of the face: the way it enflames our desire and eludes our grasp. *Faces on Screen* explores how screen culture builds on and complicates our urge to search the face for answers to our most intractable questions.

Part I of this volume, 'The Sum of Its Parts: Features, Codes, Practices', brings together essays on early cinema, photography, and historical and contemporary practices for codifying and reading faces. The authors in this section dig deeper into what Tom Gunning has called the 'gnostic mission of cinema': the 'role that capturing the face played in tracing a saraband between seeing and knowing within the new visual terrain opened up by photographic technology, which could not only reproduce human eyesight, but exceed it'.[21] The essays in this section, taken together, put contemporary facial recognition and related technologies in historical context, showing how these digital technologies reach back to the analogue history of anthropometrics, photography, face reading practices and early cinema. The opening essay, 'The Generic Face: Galton, Muybridge and the Photographic Proof of Race' by Genevieve Yue, suggests a connection between Eadweard Muybridge's photographic motion studies and Francis Galton's project of using composite photographs to picture and codify racial, ethnic and moral 'types'. Yue argues that 'Muybridge's photographic evidence of a galloping horse's simultaneously lifted legs demonstrated for Galton that race, which he took to be a similarly obscure visual phenomenon, could likewise be verified through photographic means'. In 'Mad Faces: Coding Features and Expressions of Female Madness in Physiognomy Texts, Asylum Photographs and Early Cinema', Elyse Singer decodes the performance of madness on stage and screen. Singer demonstrates how the codes for 'theatricalising mental distress' were 'rooted in white supremacy'. These essays remind us of the facial coding that existed long before digital codes, neural networks and AI – and that the racialising, physiognomic imagination remains the ghost in the cinema's facial machine. Andrea Gyenge turns our attention to the mouth in 'Elastics of the Film Mouth'. While priority has typically been given to the eyes as 'windows of the soul', Gyenge suggests another access point for entering the filmic image: the mouth. The essay offers both a rereading of Michel Chion's *The Voice in Cinema* and a re-viewing of the 1901 James Williamson film *The Big Swallow*, ultimately suggesting the mouth as a neglected but privileged site of the cinema. Turning to our contemporary moment as the logical extension of the various face-practices and face-theories of early cinema, Aaron Tucker traces a clear through line between early theories of *photogénie*, the origins of facial recognition technology and our contemporary moment in 'The Problem of Recognition: Celebrity Faces, *Photogénie* and Facial Recognition Technologies'. Tucker focuses on the fundamental role that celebrity faces have played in facial recognition technologies from its very beginning and demonstrates the dire consequences of this connection, as the use of celebrity faces 'amplifies' the racist and gendered logics of these technologies. Finally, Stefka Hristova's essay, 'Emptied Faces: In Search of an Algorithmic Punctum', considers the harvesting of facial portraits across the Internet and 'the politics of emptying photographed faces of meaning and their rearticulation into data-driven predictive landscapes'. Taking an archaeological approach to facial data sets (such as UTKFace) and engaging in a new way with Roland Barthes's concept of the punctum, Hristova suggests that affective connections and new sets of relations might offer a way to return these emptied faces to social context and to resist the voraciousness of ever-expanding 'faciality machines'.

The essays in Part II, 'Reframing the Close-up', feature close readings of films, offering ways to rethink the shot that has been synonymous with the face in cinema. Rather than just accepting Deleuze's dictum that '*the close-up is the face*',[22] these authors find various ways to ask: is it? Considering questions of affect, shot composition, and the formal and symbolic functions of the face in these contemporary films, the authors get 'beyond the close-up' to the resistances enacted at the site of the face. In his essay, '"A Landscape of Faces":

The Farewell and Ecologies of the Face in Independent Asian-American Film', Iggy Cortez discusses the aesthetic strategies of Lulu Wang's film – in particular the way Wang uses wide framings and other techniques to link face and place. Discussing the film in the fraught context of 'Asian-American cinema', Cortez argues that in *The Farewell*, the face 'serves as a locus that links cinema's imbrication of the virtual and the real to how Asian-American subjects have been coded as unintelligible or unassimilable to the US national body'. Jenny Gunn proposes the notion of a 'post-cinematic' close-up in her essay 'The New Transactional Face: Rethinking Post-cinematic Aesthetics through *The Neon Demon*'. Through a close reading of Winding Refn's film, Gunn explores the way contemporary film negotiates and remediates the face-as-currency of social media, and what this means for cinema. In her essay 'Black Faces Matter: Close-ups in *Selma*, *Fruitvale Station* and *Moonlight*', Delia Konzett takes us through close analyses of these three works by contemporary African American filmmakers, examining how these filmmakers rethink the treatment of the face on screen, combatting a history of stereotype and neglect and also the long-standing equation of the 'Hollywood close-up' with whiteness. Konzett shows how these filmmakers' very different aesthetics are nonetheless connected in their re-imaginings of Black faces on film. Combining an auteurist approach with a consideration of the politics and aesthetics of the face on film, Paula Quigley's essay, '"Sheer Epidermis": "Face Politics" and the Films of Lynne Ramsay', offers an analysis of Ramsay's *oeuvre*, exploring the way her films 'recalibrate our existing relationship to the face on film through a reimagining of its role in the *mise-en-scène*'. Discussions of the face, in film and in life, almost always hinge on the question of 'what it means to be human'; the face is inextricably bound to the very category of the human, especially as it has been distinguished from the (non-human) animal. And yet, animal faces have provided a repository of metaphorical, anatomical and aesthetic references for our understandings of the human face and the concepts of humanity and animality more generally. In 'Facing Life in the Open: The (Post)human Worldmaking of *My Octopus Teacher*', Angelica Fenner explores the 2020 Netflix sensation and the way it might shift the anthropocentrism of the filmic fascination with the face. My own essay, '*Bête Noir(e)*: Animality, Genre and the Face in *Border*', examines Ali Abbasi's 2018 film, exploring the way the face functions in negotiating proliferating boundaries: between animal and human, male and female, legal and criminal, moral and immoral. Finally, Sara Saljoughi's essay, '*Hejab* as Frame in *Ten* and Beyond', analyses moments from Kiarostami's *Ten* – alongside other films by Kiarostami and Iranian cinema more generally – to explore how we might 'conceptualise the (cinematic) aesthetics of the veil as an aesthetics of the face'.

In Part III, 'Making Faces: Celebrity, Performance, Self', authors consider the way faces are made – and in particular how acting, celebrity and identity are connected, consumed and reproduced via the face on screen. The essays in this section remind us that there is 'no such thing as an uncontrived face in the movies'[23] (as James Naremore put it), and indeed that every face is 'made', whether through makeup, gesture, publicity or, increasingly, through digital animation techniques. In 'The Faces of Ginger: Beauty Makeup, Facial Acting and Hollywood Stardom', Adrienne McLean takes Ginger Rogers as a case study in how Hollywood star faces (especially female ones) were made and unmade. McLean shows how Rogers's career – so often understood solely by her collaborations with Fred Astaire, was itself a kind of 'dance' between expressivity and class-based limitations on facial movement and variation in acting style. In her essay, 'At Face Value: Consuming the Star Image', Koel Banerjee examines the consumption of stardom in India by looking at *Fan* (Maneesh Sharma, 2016) and the 'paradigmatic star of Bollywood cinema', Shah Rukh Khan. Looking at the film in the context of neo-liberal market reforms in India, Banerjee argues that *Fan* 'highlights the cinematic and extra-cinematic ways in which the star image is desired and consumed by the fans . . . ultimately present[ing] a cautionary tale about the limits of such consumption, and more importantly, of such desire'. Continuing the exploration of the value of the star's face as it is consumed and exchanged in celebrity culture, Brenda R. Weber traces the twisted tale of Renée Zellweger's face. In her essay 'The Face is the Lie that Tells the Truth: Renée Zellweger and the Mediated Politics of Age, Self and Celebrity', Weber explores the notion of the 'surgical self' and unpacks the combination of celebrity gossip, fan recrimination and feminist discourse launched by the 'did she or didn't she' reactions to what were seen as startling changes to Zellweger's face in 2014. Taking another approach to the question of ageing on screen, Tanine Allison traces the recent history and rhetoric of performance capture and related technologies, with a special focus on digital de-ageing. Her essay, 'Mediating the Human in Facial Performance Capture', identifies the tension between the goals of 'capture' and 'simulation', exploring how the dual strategies 'reflec[t] competing visions of human inte-riority and the role of the face in expressing it'. We move from one kind of face-making to another, as Hannah Parlett examines the work of South African, Berlin-based artist Candice Breitz, particularly her 2003 video instal-lation, *Becoming*, in which she mimics the facial gestures of well-known Hollywood actresses (including Zellweger). In her essay, '*Becoming* a Woman: The Many Faces of Candice Breitz', Parlett suggests the iterative nature of (white) Hollywood femininity and how in the 'close interrogation of corporeal performance in *Becoming*, Breitz proffers a reflection on the role of the (white, female) human face on screen and its complex encounter with the film spectator'. In 'The Face as Technology', Zara Dinnen and Sam McBean take up another star image – Scarlett Johansson's – and the sci-fi films that exploit it in order to 'tell stories about the face as made by and in relation to digital technology, but also in relation to discourses of celebrity, whiteness and femininity'. Dinnen and McBean show how the genre's exploitation of Johansson's image reveals the face as 'primarily a gendered and raced technology in the making'. And in the final essay of the collection, 'From Holy Grail to Deepfake: The Evolving Digital Face on Screen', Lisa Bode offers a deft rethinking of the contemporary history of the digital face in cinema. Bode traces the discourses and shifting paradigms that have guided the quest for the ever-more photo-realistic digital face in cinema, asking where we have been and where we are going, and 'to what extent . . . the recent emergence of machine learning generated deepfake videos indicate a continuity or break with older understandings'.

Collectively, the essays in this volume look forward by looking back – at the way faces have been made from photography and proto-cinematic techniques to our contemporary face fabrication machines. As Noa Steimatsky has argued, the face is 'both a compelling iconographic and discursive nexus and a way of see-ing, a critical lens, a mode of thought'.[24] Thinking about the 'myths of the face' that have guided the cinema, that have functioned as a '*dispositif*' or set of ideas 'comprising the very consciousness of the medium',[25] Steimatsky suggests that we might see the cinema most clearly (or at least most revealingly) through the face. The authors in this collection look at film and other visual media through this lens, but they also look at the lens itself, refracting and reframing the screen face. This collection brings forward essays that connect the theoretical to the historical, highlighting points of contact between old and new, early and late conceptions of the face in film and media. In so doing, these essays bring us back from the brink of the screen face, rethinking our relationship to it, putting it in perspective, fleshing it out – bringing us face to face with the image that has defined (and will likely continue to define) our relationship to screen culture.

NOTES

1. Béla Balázs, *Visible Man* in *Béla Balázs: Early Film Theory*, ed. Erica Carter, trans. Rodney Livingstone (New York: Berghahn Books, 2010), 10.
2. Balázs, *Early Film Theory*, 12.
3. Jenny Edkins, *Face Politics* (Abingdon and New York: Routledge, 2015).
4. Emily Willingham, 'The Condoms of the Face: Why Some Men Refuse to Wear Masks', *Scientific American*, 29 June 2020. Available at <https://www.scientificamerican.com/article/the-condoms-of-the-face-why-some-men-refuse-to-wear-masks/> (last accessed 20 September 2021).
5. Derrick Bryson Taylor, 'For Black Men, Fear that Masks Will Invite Racial Profiling', *The New York Times*, 14 April 2020. Available at <https://www.nytimes.com/2020/04/14/us/coronavirus-masks-racism-african-americans.html> (last accessed 20 September 2021).
6. Jane Li, 'China's Facial Recognition Giant Says It Can Crack Masked Faces During the Coronavirus', *Quartz*, 18 February 2020. Available at <https://qz.com/1803737/

chinas-facial-recognition-tech-can-crack-masked-faces-amid-coronavirus/> (last accessed 20 September 2021).

7. Hans Belting, *Face and Mask: A Double History*, trans. Thomas S. Hansen and Abby J. Hansen (Princeton, NJ: Princeton University Press, 2017), 18.

8. Pilita Clark, 'Year in a Word – Zoom', *Financial Times*, 21 December 2020. Available at <https://www.ft.com/content/170649d0-4cdf-454b-a4ec-e28d130974cd> (last accessed 20 September 2021).

9. Mary Ann Doane, 'The Close-up: Scale and Detail in the Cinema', *differences* 14:3 (2003), 93.

10. Doane, 'The Close-up', 108.

11. Ashley Hoffman and Josiah Bates, 'FaceApp is Getting People to Age Overnight. Here's What You Should Know About Its Security Concerns', *Time*, 17 July 2019.

12. This is the company's marketing slogan. Available at <https://hey.reface.ai> (last accessed 20 September 2021).

13. Dima Shvets, 'Changing the Face of Marketing with Synthetic Personalized Ads', *Forbes*, 18 June 2018. Available at <https://www.forbes.com/sites/forbesbusiness-council/2021/06/18/changing-the-face-of-marketing-with-synthetic-personalized-ads/?sh=5548a48e5106> (last accessed 20 September 2021).

14. Manhola Dargis, "The Invisible Man' Review: Gaslight Nation, Domestic Edition', *The New York Times*, 26 February 2020. Available at <https://www.nytimes.com/2020/02/26/movies/the-invisible-man-review.html> (last accessed 20 September 2021).

15. Béla Balázs, *Visible Man, Or, The Culture of Film* (1924), in *Early Film Theory*, ed. Erica Carter, trans. Rodney Livingstone (New York: Berghahn Books, 2010), 28.

16. Georg Simmel, 'The Aesthetic Significance of the Face', in Kurt Wolff (ed.), *Georg Simmel: 1858–1918: A Collection of Essays* (Columbus: Ohio State University Press, 1959), 276. Gunning discusses the way early facial expression films played with the grotesque by exceeding precisely these limits. See 'In Your Face: Physiognomy, Photography, and the Gnostic Mission of Early Film', *Modernism/modernity* 1, 4:1 (January 1997): 1–29.

17. For an account of women's bodies and emotional excess, especially in 'body genres' like horror, see Linda Williams, 'Film Bodies: Gender, Genre, and Excess', *Film Quarterly* 44:4 (Summer 1991), 2–13.

18. Emmanuel Levinas, for example, stresses the 'nudity' and vulnerability of the face in his ethical philosophy and theory of the 'face to face'. For a good, condensed summary of this idea, see Emmanuel Levinas, *Ethics and Infinity: Conversations with Philippe Nemo*, trans. Richard A. Cohen (Pittsburgh: Duquesne University Press, 1985), 85–92.

19. On the face is the site of subjectification and signification (the formation of subjectivity on the one hand and expression/meaning on the other), see Gilles Deleuze and Felix Guattari, *A Thousand Plateaus: Capitalism and Schizophrenia*, trans. Brian Massumi (Minneapolis: University of Minnesota Press, 1987), 167–92. See also Jacques Aumont, 'The Face in Close-up', in Anita Dalle Vacche (ed.), *The Visual Turn: Classical Film Theory and Art History* (New Brunswick, NJ: Rutgers University Press, 2003), 127–51.

20. Edkins, *Face Politics*, 3.
21. Gunning, 'In Your Face', 2.
22. Gilles Deleuze, *Cinema 1: The Movement-Image*, trans. Hugh Tomlinson and Barbara Habberjam (Minneapolis, University of Minnesota Press, 1986), 87.
23. James Naremore, *Acting in the Cinema* (Berkeley: University of California Press, 1988), 96.
24. Noa Steimatsky, *The Face on Film* (New York: Oxford University Press, 2017), 4.
25. Steimatsky, *The Face on Film*, 3.

PART I

THE SUM OF ITS PARTS:
FEATURES, CODES, PRACTICES

1. THE GENERIC FACE: GALTON, MUYBRIDGE AND THE PHOTOGRAPHIC PROOF OF RACE

Genevieve Yue

How to describe a generic face? The issue that had once been resolved by painting and drawing in rendering ideal 'types' was opened again by the arrival of photography in the mid-nineteenth century. The mechanical technology of photography afforded a precision unavailable to the human hand, with the result orienting towards the specific and idiosyncratic. If a photograph was always of an individual, the project of the generic face, if rendered photographically, had to be reconceived. In what follows, I examine the practice of composite photography proposed by statistician and pioneering eugenicist Francis Galton, a method of overlaying multiple exposures onto a single frame. On his own terms, Galton achieved a generic face which had significant bearing on later institutional uses of the photographic camera especially where it concerned the identification of racialised subjects. What is less known is what Galton learned from the motion studies of Eadweard Muybridge, namely the use of the medium to produce positive proof of a hitherto invisible phenomenon.[1] Muybridge's photographic evidence of a galloping horse's simultaneously lifted legs demonstrated for Galton that race, which he took to be a similarly obscure visual phenomenon, could likewise be verified through photographic means. Though Galton was not the only person that produced photographic studies of racialised subjects, he was the first to attempt to provide visual and quantifiable form for previously invisible racial markers within the face, thereby 'proving' the existence of race.

The entry of photography into scientific research in the nineteenth century had far-reaching implications for the study of the face. The fields of physiognomy and phrenology had long been practised for determining a person's character from their physical attributes, and the new medium revitalised both. Photography offered what appeared to be a rigorous, scientific basis that would dispense with the occultist connotations of each, which were then taken as popular science. The acute study of the face, in turn, profoundly affected the development of the medium itself. As Tom Gunning notes, both the study of the face and the development of photography were driven by a 'gnostic mission', which was a desire to *see*, and by extension to *know*, the face in its slightest and most fleeting expressions.[2] The capability of the photographic apparatus to see in more detail and precision than the human eye, and thus to present a better instrument of knowledge, was crucial to the development of both film and photographic media, as evident in the writings of Dziga Vertov, Jean Epstein and especially Béla Balázs.[3]

Much of the research in nineteenth-century physiognomy employed photography to confirm and identify the visual markers of specific populations. Like many others, G. B. Duchenne de Boulogne and Jean-Martin Charcot incorporated photography into the treatment of mental illness, using photographs to render diagnoses and make scientific demonstrations. For these researchers, the precision one could obtain through photography meant that the face and its expressions could be examined in unprecedented detail. For Duchenne, seeing through the lens of the camera, the face became a surface onto which expressions were 'written', in effect, a medium.[4] Charcot, meanwhile, applied photography in his studies of hysteria to produce what he called a '*facies*' or general picture of the disease. Meanwhile, Paris police clerk Alphonse Bertillon began using photography to devise a more practical and comprehensive system for identifying criminals, including, in addition to the now standard mugshot, measurements and written descriptions of the body. Bertillon's system was anthropometric, designed to identify individual faces, particularly those of repeat offenders, using a vast filing system to sort and retrieve them. It aimed at verification and was complemented by records of fingerprint variation. Bertillon was not concerned, as Duchenne and Charcot were, with identifying general types with photography, though his methods amounted to what Allan Sekula described in his landmark essay 'The Body and the Archive' as a similarly large database of images.[5]

In 1877, Galton began experimenting with what he called 'generic images' in a study of criminal populations, done in collaboration with Edmund Du Cane, director general of the British penal system.[6] Du Cane had provided Galton photographs of criminals sorted by their crimes: murder and violent crime, felony and forgery, and sexual crimes. Galton sought to demonstrate what he and Du Cane thought they could already perceive just by looking at photographs of criminals. They assumed that genres of crimes could be identified by distinguishing facial features, or what amounted to what Galton termed the 'felon face'.[7] In an address to the Anthropological Subsection of the British

Association at Plymouth in 1877, Galton described the impetus for composite photography, which was to test out this theory. The formation of the generic image was based on a conversation he had with Herbert Spencer, in which they discussed drawing multiple portraits on layered sheets of transparent paper.[8] His composite photographs realised what had previously only been accomplished as a composite drawing, or what Bertillon called the 'memory image', a type of image drawn from witness accounts for the purpose of identifying possible suspects. Galton's originality came from the photographic application of the composite method to quantitatively determine visible attributes among common populations. Using a device similar to an optical printer for film, each image would be proportionally underexposed and rephotographed so that only the most salient characteristics would become visible in the final, singular image. Galton was not the first to use a method of multiple or composite exposure, but he saw its potential for elaborating a statistical programme. Previously, Julia Margaret Cameron had employed the technique in her pictorialist photography, and the practice was widespread in spirit photography, which was widely popular at the time.[9]

The results of Galton's prison photographs were inconclusive, though Du Cane was satisfied; in justifying the pictures he said, 'I should anticipate that a great number of those who commit certain classes of crimes would be found to show an entirely inferior mental and bodily organisation.'[10] For Galton, the criminal photographs failed to show 'special villainous irregularities' as sorted by crime. Instead, he observed, they revealed a 'common humanity that underlies them' in the men who committed the crimes.[11] These images did not discourage Galton; rather they demonstrated the potential of the technique for other applications.

Galton went on to apply his method to identify different populations, including the sick, different professions, portraits on coins and, finally, racial types.[12] For him, composite photographs offered a statistical basis to support his project of eugenics, a field Galton named in 1883. Galton was close to his half-cousin Charles Darwin, and he sought to apply composite photography as a tool to describe the process of and factors in evolution. This eventually would guide a positive eugenics project of genetic engineering and a negative one aimed at steering away from the blight of 'racial degeneration' festering among Britain's urban slums, which then were largely associated with Jewish and Irish communities. Instead of survival of the fittest, racial degeneration saw the survival of the poorest – those with the deleterious attributes of criminality, low intelligence, and ill health – which had actually been promoted by government welfare programmes.[13]

Composite photography could aid a eugenics project by determining essential types or races at a granular level. Historian Theodore Porter observes: '[Galton] aimed to divide humanity into an array of discrete types, then photograph in a single image the members of a particular type to reveal racial or

Figure 1.1   Francis Galton, 'The Jewish Type', in Karl Pearson, *The Life, Letters and Labours of Sir Francis Galton*, vol. 2, pl. 35 (1883).

collective characteristics that no individual can display to the same extent.'[14] Galton was the most successful in identifying racial characteristics. In 1883, he was approached by Joseph Jacobs, an anthropologist and literary critic interested in establishing a Jewish race-science, to produce composite photographs of pictures of Jewish schoolboys. Jacobs, inspired by the depiction of Jews in George Eliot's *Daniel Deronda*, asked Galton to make composite photographs of men and boys at the Jewish Working Men's Club and the Jews' Free School in London.

The result, 'The Jewish Type', was Galton's most successful study; he called it 'the best specimens of composites I have ever produced'.[15] Jacobs was also pleased with the results and agreed that Galton's photography furnished 'averages which no measurements can supply'.[16] The positive identification of a Jewish 'type' was at that time highly contested. There was considerable debate as to whether Jews were an ethnic or racial formation. Jacobs, a proponent of a pure Jewish type, assumed the latter, and found visual confirmation in Galton's method. He wrote:

> Most people can tell a Jew when they see one. There is a certain expression in Jewish faces which causes them to be identified as such in almost every instance. Being engaged in some investigations into Jewish characteristics

generally, I was anxious to discover in what this 'Jewish expression' consists. It occurred to me that Mr Galton's method of composite portraiture would enable me to answer this question with some degree of exactitude.[17]

Galton's contemporary and biographer Karl Pearson, writing in 1924, confirmed Jacobs's view: 'We all know the Jewish boy, and Galton's portraiture brings him before us in a way that only a great work of art could equal – scarcely excel, for the artist would only idealise from one model.'[18] With the 'Jewish boy' already widely known and recognised, Galton's project, and the terms of its success, were shaped by his ability to statistically and photographically confirm this underlying assumption. Hence Galton and Jacobs believed their composites, with their strong and distinctive features, settled the question firmly on the side of a racial type.[19]

Even for the purposes of race science, the Jewish face, however, was hardly a stable set of attributes. Jacobs admitted that the vast Jewish diaspora contained numerous variations owing to intermarriage and environmental conditions across different countries, though he did not believe these were significant enough to dilute the evidentiary purity of a Jewish racial type.[20] He turned to Galton, who offered a method that could synthesise and accentuate 'essential' characteristics. Just as importantly, it could minimise variation. It is telling that none of the subjects are named, as their anonymity is another way of collapsing them into generality. Instead they are called 'components', already understood as the discrete parts that go into making the composite whole. If Galton had been supplied any names, he did not use them, unlike Phryne, the horse Muybridge photographed and whose name makes its way into Galton's 1882 creation of a 'hybrid monster'. Galton's composite photograph was more than an 'idealised model' drawn by an artist, but a wholly new and previously impossible image: the generic face of the Jew. For Jacobs, this face was more expressive than any individual representative could be. He observed, the original 'portraits [were] less Jewish than the composites'.[21]

Daniel Novak has called the generic Jew of Galton a 'phantasmatic figure', an abstraction made out of the attributes of multiple individuals.[22] The Jewish type had an appearance of reality but existed nowhere but in the image. Galton himself remarked on the 'surprising air of reality' of his composite portraits, and Jacobs contended that the Jewish face was 'more ghostly than a ghost, more spiritual than a spirit . . . [because] [t]he thing, person, spirit, ghost, idea, type, or what you will that looks at us . . . has no bodily existence; and yet there is life in its eyes'.[23] Though imaginary, this image was produced by a photographic apparatus that was specifically utilised to furnish evidence in identifying and determining an appearance of race. 'The Jewish Type' not only apparently proved the existence of a pure Jewish race, but by extension, it could verify the existence of *any* race.

Figure 1.2   Francis Galton, 'Conventional Representation of the Horse in Motion', *Nature* (6 July 1882).

Galton's faith in photography's ability to provide proof of a previously unavailable or invisible phenomenon was influenced, if not learned, from Eadweard Muybridge. Galton was well aware of the pioneering motion studies of both Muybridge and Etienne-Jules Marey, both of whom he mentions in his memoir and various research publications from the early 1880s to 1905. He was particularly drawn to Muybridge's study of the galloping horse as a demonstration of the superiority of the photographic instrument over the mental image of conventional, artistic representation. As is well known, Muybridge was commissioned by Leland Stanford to decisively prove whether a horse's legs completely leave the ground during a gallop. The resulting twenty photographs in Muybridge's *The Attitudes of Animals in Motion* (1881) fascinated Galton. The following year, he produced his own composites of Muybridge's images. It is unknown whether Galton corresponded directly with Muybridge, but he was unable to gain access to the original photographs, suggesting that the interest between the two men was only one-sided. Galton proceeded undeterred, using the plates and working with a wood engraver to make his reproductions. He published his findings along with his composites in 'Conventional Representation of the Horse in Motion' (1882).

Galton demonstrated that photography was about to convey 'real attitudes' about phenomena where conventional visual art fell prey to misjudgements.[24]

By extension, he also demonstrated the superiority of the composite photography method. The former is the proof that Muybridge provides. On Galton's account, when confronted with something outside ready visual apprehension, such as the rapid movement of a galloping horse, the mind filled the gap by forming an image. Such imaginings were natural aspects of perception, which was riddled with 'prevalent errors of conception which govern the judgment in its interpretation of a movement that is hard to follow'.[25] Muybridge exposed this error in the precision of his method, as each of the individually exposed frames arrest the movement of the horse in a way unavailable to the human eye. The horse's legs not only lifted off the ground, but the position and 'real attitude' of its entire body is newly available for scrutiny.

Galton used composite photography to demonstrate the way in which mental images misrepresented their subjects. Muybridge's chronophotographs proved that the mental image was distorted and Galton's composite renderings of those same images explained why and how. He grouped his composites by various measures, then compared them to what he took to be conventional renderings in painting and sculpture of horses with all four legs splayed out. First, in collapsing all twenty images together, he notes that 'In the general composite the blur somewhat justifies the conventional representation, because though the lower parts of the limbs leave no definite image at all . . . the upper portions have a distinctly outflung look . . .'[26] Next, Galton broke up the images into four different sets arranged by 'momentary attitudes', namely the position of the legs ('A' includes the legs tucked in, 'B' with front legs tucked and lifted and hind legs touching the ground, and so on.) Finally, Galton combined the positions into two aspects: Figure 1 showed front legs lifted, and Figure 2 with hind legs lifted. He then took half of each composite so that his new, Frankensteined composite, Figure 3, showed a horse with all legs lifted. This new creation arrived at the conventional representation, providing a 'very fair correspondence with a not uncommon representation in sculpture'.[27] This confirmed for Galton that the mistake in apprehension comes from the human eye only being able to perceive the legs of a horse one side at a time, front or back. Galton thus improved on Muybridge's method by not only providing positive proof, but also reproducing the error in unmediated perception. Through precise photographic means, Galton reconstructed the way that art 'seizes the most characteristic attitudes of each [part of the horse], and combines them into a *hybrid monster*'.[28] Granted, such proof rested on Galton's ability to discern what groupings were useful to composite, and how to read areas of indistinction in the image. Galton was convinced he possessed these powers, just as he was certain of his ability to recognise the essential Jewish type in the composite studies he produced just a few years later.

The lessons Galton learned from Muybridge distinguish him from other nineteenth-century figures who photographed race under quasi-scientific premises. Muybridge used photography not only to describe but to prove, and Galton extended this proof to verify in exacting visual detail the existence of something that had only previously been assumed, namely the existence of race. While anthropometric photographers like Louis Agassiz, John Lamprey, Thomas Henry Huxley and Rudolf Martin drew on phrenology to emphasise alterity and animality of non-white peoples in their anthropological research, none went as far as Galton to provide visual, quantitative evidence of race.[29] His method was taken up in the US by Henry Bowditch, who in 1888 used composite photography to describe the features of exemplar populations by occupation and class.[30] The closest would likely be Félix-Louis Regnault, a student of Etienne-Jules Marey, who in 1895 applied Marey's chronophotographic method to a study of Wolof people brought to Paris. Using Marey's camera-gun, he recorded their gaits, gestures and physiognomies in often fleeting movement. As Catherine Russell has argued, Regnault's work produced a 'visual *proof* of racial difference', evidence that would prove important in the development of biometric technologies.[31]

Galton's two projects on criminals and Jews offer insight into his working assumptions. The criminal study was undefined insofar as he did not begin from assuming a physical type. Rather, Galton could only proceed in an experimental fashion, searching for an as yet unknown correlation between behaviour and physiology which, unsurprisingly, did not exist. As a population, murderers or thieves proved to be indistinguishable from the 'common humanity' underlying them. Galton's work on the Jewish type, however, was tautological, as the set of common characteristics with which he began his study functioned to produce what he was seeking. In ostensibly scientific – but no less imaginary – terms, he produced the object he had already imagined. Furthermore, the relative indeterminacy of the Jewish subject provided all the more confirmation for Galton's method: if a subject as contested as the purity of Jewish racial identity could be settled, then this was owing to the superior ability of the composite photographic method. Ironically a correlation does arise from the two best-known studies by Galton, namely the prevailing intertwining of non-white race and criminality. Novak observes, 'Because more easily arrested by science, race is more criminal than the fugitive essence of criminality.'[32]

Galton aimed to make the photograph of the face the statistical basis for expressing an average. He understood his composite photographs as visual expressions of statistical quantification and directly referenced the work of statistician Adolphe Quetelet who in the 1830s theorised the 'average man' in his study of populations. Galton's composite photograph was an attempt at producing a visual equivalent of Quetelet's average man, and he saw it as an improvement on Quetelet because he produced not an outline of this figure, but a detailed picture:

> Composite pictures are . . . much more than averages . . . They are real generalisations, because they include the whole of the material under consideration. The blur of their outlines, which is never great in truly generic composites, except in unimportant details, measures the tendency of individuals to deviate from the central type.[33]

The immediate problem of Galton's method was in the blurring that occurred, most prominently around the edges of the face. He dismissed this as falling within the acceptable margin of error: the 'unimportant details'. Such details were the marks of individuals who vanished in the blurred portions: 'the peculiarities' of individual subjects.[34] The individual is abstracted in favour of the mass, and the idiosyncratic is sacrificed as such. Moreover, these minor drawbacks were compensated for by the photographic method. Like many early practitioners of photography, Galton maintained considerable faith in the objective nature of the machine: 'The merit of the photographic composite is its mechanical precision, being subject to no errors beyond those incidental to all photographic productions.'[35]

There is also a methodological problem: the discernment of what details were important or unimportant.[36] Galton, for example, focused primarily on the eyes, and ignored other features such as the ears. This was based on backward reasoning. He selected that which photographed well; what was blurred became unimportant as a result of that selection. Galton re-encountered the problem of the blur that previously appeared in his composites of Muybridge's galloping horse, but here again, instead of casting doubt over his method, it serves to confirm his operating assumptions. At each step of the photographic procedure, the apparatus already presumes what it purports to discover. What we might call 'precognition' is not only the stuff of a dystopian science fiction film like *Minority Report*, but a circular form of logic central to biometric practices. This is a system that already associates criminality with racialised bodies, so its machines accordingly search for and 'see' crimes that conform to this assumption.[37] The blurriness that emerged in the composite photograph – which was exacerbated by the size of the sample population – undermined Galton's aim of producing a coherent typology, though ironically, he himself could not see this. Instead, as Ciara Ambrosio observes, Galton sought in the composite photograph an 'ideal form of empiricism, one in which observable evidence gathered through the photographic process answered the question of what makes (inductive) generalisations reliable'.[38] In this he represented the awkward conjunction between a nineteenth-century mechanical method to accomplish an eighteenth-century project of producing ideal types.[39]

A single composite photograph contains an archive. It is not a representative sampling, but an image of a collapsed populace. One can imagine a composite photograph that holds within it an entire social order.[40] This is a social order that, in the mid-nineteenth century, was already conceived in photographic terms. As Walter Benjamin notes in 'Little History of Photography', the photographic image of a face 'was no longer a portrait', but pointed instead to a vast and imaginary archive by which a social order could be conjured photographically.[41] In other words, photography transformed the face into a social sign. Photography had so permeated the nineteenth-century imaginary that inscription into a photographic logic became largely involuntary. Benjamin continues:

> Sudden shifts of power such as are now overdue in our society can make the ability to read facial types a matter of vital importance. Whether one is of the left or right, one will have to get used to being looked at in terms of one's provenance. And one will have to look at others in the same way.[42]

This imaginary archive was undergirded by an expectation in which, as Benjamin describes, 'one will have to get used' to a photographically derived form of sociality. A person's social existence, then, became a matter of mediation via the photographic apparatus. Photography additionally inscribed the face, the individual, within a social matrix. As Allan Sekula argues, photography has an 'unavoidable social referentiality, [a] way of describing . . . a world of social institutions, gestures, manners, relationships'.[43] These social institutions can also turn back on the individual, as correspondingly, the development of photographic practices has been attended by a history of institutional uses of identifying and sorting people. Unsurprisingly, photography was instrumental in identifying and sorting 'fit' faces and bodies – namely those who were white, male and bourgeois – from the non-white, female, diseased, debilitated, criminal or poor.[44]

This photographically mediated sociality occurs in Galton's work as well. In describing the process for making 'The Jewish Type', he provides an account of a visit he made to the Jewish quarter:

> The feature that struck me the most, as I drove through the adjacent Jewish quarter, was the cold scanning gaze of man, woman and child, and this was no less conspicuous among the schoolboys . . . I felt, rightly or wrongly, that every one of them was coolly appraising me at market value, without the slightest interest of any other kind.[45]

The anecdote is curious, not least because Galton made his composites from photographs provided by Jacobs.[46] There was no ostensible need for Galton to visit the Jewish quarter, or to mention it in his article. But Galton devotes some space to describing the way the Jewish residents look at *him*. They 'coolly appraise' him, as if anticipating his own look of detachment and abstraction in the compositing process. This expresses the situation Benjamin describes, though Galton reverses the terms, feeling *himself* regarded 'at market value', perhaps a reference to stereotypes of rapacious Jewish moneylenders. The anecdote presents an opportunity for Galton to reflect on his method's own cool appraisal of others and the discomfort it may cause. But the spectre of race refuses the 'common humanity' Galton and his subjects might otherwise share. In his composite photographs, Jewishness can only confirm its own alterity, and Galton did not aim to rescue Jews for any kind of shared condition. This was the gaze of what Jacobs called the 'ghetto expression', a look characterised not only by physiognomy but by its alienating effect on Galton.[47]

Galton, of course, gets the last look. In describing the difference between the appearance of the Jewish boys in the original photographs and their later composited forms, he evokes the transformative powers of his method: 'They were children of poor parents, dirty little fellows individually, but wonderfully beautiful, as I think, in these composites.'[48] The photographic composites transform the Jewish face into an object for public consumption, scrubbed and cleansed for institutional purposes. In this his process mirrors that of Mordecai in *Daniel Deronda*, a Kabbalist in search of a man who 'must glorify the possibilities of the Jew'.[49] Mordecai has for years been 'measure[ing] men with a keen glance',[50] and his quest takes him to the National Gallery where he looked into paintings for glimpses of this idealised Jew:

> But in the inevitable progress of his imagination toward fuller detail, he ceased to see the figure with its back toward him. It began to advance, and a face became discernible; the words youth, beauty, refinement, Jewish birth, noble gravity, turned into hardly individual but typical form and colour: gathered from his memory of faces seen among the Jews of Holland and Bohemia, and from the paintings which revived that memory.[51]

Mordecai finds this idealised type in Deronda, a young man initially unaware of his Jewish origins, living among the landed English elite, far from the squalid conditions of the Jewish quarter. Given the strong impression the novel left on Jacobs, it is unsurprising that Jacobs conducted his search in terms of finding his own Deronda, an ideal type. (To be sure, he ignores the way this ideal could 'pass' as English.) His collaboration with Galton, and the use of the composite photograph to reveal a hidden and racialised face already presumed to exist, indicates the tremendous authority invested in photography at the time, not to mention the conjuring powers to provide visible form to what could only previously be imagined.

Galton's method, however flawed it may now appear, offered quantitative confirmation for a social order organised by racial and photographically visible difference. Though the techniques and capacities of contemporary biometric technologies are dramatically different from those of the nineteenth century, the fundaments for their current uses in policing and military applications remain remarkably unchanged from their origins.[52] Much of this can be traced directly to Galton, and, perhaps, a walk that discomfited him. Strolling through the Jewish quarter, Galton might well have imagined a vast photographic archive of faces, and the *need* for such an archive, all the while averting his eyes from the people staring back at him.

NOTES

1. Scholarship on Francis Galton tends to occur within disciplinary boundaries, and surprisingly little addresses his photographic and statistical methods as applied to race, much less to his connection to Muybridge. Those whose primary focus is race mention Galton chiefly in the context of his work on statistics (Zuberi, Muhammad) and eugenics (Shawn Michelle Smith). See Tukufu Zuberi, *Thicker than Blood: How Racial Statistics Lie* (Minneapolis: University of Minnesota Press, 2001); Khalil Gibran Muhammad, *The Condemnation of Blackness: Race, Crime, and the Making of Modern Urban America* (Cambridge, MA: Harvard University Press, 2010) and Shawn Michelle Smith, *At the Edge of Sight: Photography and the Unseen* (Durham, NC, and London: Duke University Press, 2013). Those who work on the history of photography tend not to take up race (Daston and Galison), though Josh Ellenbogen does provide comparative analysis of Muybridge and Galton. See Lorraine Daston and Peter Galison, *Objectivity* (Brooklyn, NY: Zone Books, 2007) and Josh Ellenbogen, *Reasoned and Unreasoned Images: The Photography of Bertillon, Galton, and Marey* (University Park, PA: Penn State University Press, 2012). Wendy Hui Kyong Chun, Daniel Novak, Anne Maxwell and Allan Sekula address Galton's photographic methods and its racial implications but without mentioning Muybridge. Fred Moten, meanwhile, provides a parenthetical linkage between Galton and Muybridge in a broader discussion of race and photography. See Wendy Hui Kyong Chun, *Discriminating Data: Correlation, Neighborhoods, and the New Politics of Recognition* (Cambridge, MA: MIT Press, 2021); Daniel Akiva Novak, *Realism, Photography, and Nineteenth-century Fiction* (Cambridge: Cambridge University Press, 2008); Anne Maxwell, *Picture Imperfect: Photography and Eugenics, 1870–1940* (Brighton: Sussex Academic Press, 2008); Allan Sekula, 'The Body and the Archive', *October* 39:1 (Winter 1986), 3–64; and Fred Moten, *Black and Blur* (Durham, NC: Duke University Press, 2017). The conceptual implications of Galton's composite photography, meanwhile, has been important to the thinking of major intellectual figures including Sigmund Freud, Roland Barthes, Charles Sanders Peirce and Ludwig Wittgeinstein.

2. 'The desire to know the face in its most transitory and bizarre manifestations was stimulated by the use of photography, but that desire, in turn, also stimulated the development of photography itself, spurring it to increasing technical mastery over time and motion, prodding it toward the actual invention of motion pictures.' Tom Gunning, 'In Your Face: Physiognomy, Photography, and the Gnostic Mission of Early Film', *Modernism/modernity* 4:1 (1997), 1–29, citation on 25.

3. See Dziga Vertov, *Kino-Eye: The Writings of Dziga Vertov*, trans. Kevin O'Brien (Berkeley: University of California Press, 1985); Sarah Keller and Jason N. Paul (eds), *Jean Epstein: Critical Essays and New Translations* (Amsterdam: Amsterdam University Press, 2012); and Béla Balázs, *Theory of the Film: Character and Growth of a New Art*, trans. Edith Bone (London: Dennis Dobson, 1952).
4. G. B. Duchenne de Boulogne, cited in Gunning, 'In Your Face', 8; G. B. Duchenne du Boulogne, *The Mechanism of Human Facial Expression*, ed. and trans. R. Andrew Cuthbertson (Cambridge: Cambridge University Press, 1990), 19.
5. Sekula, 'The Body and the Archive', 3–64.
6. Francis Galton presented his work at the Anthropological Institute of Great Britain in 1877 and his remarks were subsequently published in multiple venues, including, first, 'Composite Portraits', *Nature* 18 (May 1878), 97–100, and 'Composite Portraits, Made by Combining Those of Many Different Persons into a Single Resultant Figure', *Journal of the Anthropological Institute* 8 (1879), 132–44. The term 'generic images' comes from two nearly identical publications Galton published in 1879: 'Generic Images,' *Nineteenth Century* 6:29 (July 1879), 157–69 and 'On Generic Images', *Notices of the Proceedings at the Meetings of the Members of the Royal Institution of Great Britain* 9 (25 April 1879), 161–70.
7. Francis Galton, *Narrative of an Explorer in Tropical South Africa: Being an Account of a Visit to Damaraland in 1851* (London: Ward, Lock, 1854), 75.
8. Galton, 'Composite Portraits', *Nature*, 97.
9. See Julian Cox and Colin Ford (eds), *Julia Margaret Cameron: The Complete Photographs* (Los Angeles: Getty Publications, 2003).
10. Du Cane in discussion, Francis Galton, 'Composite Portraits', *Journal of the Anthropological Institute*, 133.
11. Galton, 'Composite Portraits', *Journal of the Anthropological Institute*, 135.
12. Du Cane was satisfied; in justifying the pictures he said, 'I should anticipate that a great number of those who commit certain classes of crimes would be found to show an entirely inferior mental and bodily organisation.' Du Cane cited in Galton, 'Composite Portraits', *Journal of the Anthropological Institute*, 133.
13. See Maxwell, *Picture Imperfect*, 79–96.
14. Theodore Porter, in Paul Fleming and Theodore Porter, 'Life on the Bell Curve: An Interview with Theodore Porter', *Cabinet Magazine* 15 (Fall 2004). Available at <http://cabinetmagazine.org/issues/15/fleming2.php> (last accessed 20 September 2021).
15. Galton, 'Photographic Composites', *The Photographic News* (17 April 1885), 243–5, citation on 243.
16. Joseph Jacobs, 'On the Racial Characteristics of Modern Jews', *The Journal of the Anthropological Institute of Great Britain and Ireland* 15 (London: Trübner & Co., 1885–6), 23–62, citation on 38.
17. Joseph Jacobs, 'The Jewish Type and Galton's Composite Photographs', *The Photographic News* 29:1390 (24 April 1885), 268–9 citation on 268.
18. Karl Pearson, *Researches of Middle Life*, Vol. 2 of *The Life, Letters and Labours of Sir Francis Galton*, 3 vols (New York: Cambridge University Press, 1924), 293.

19. 'The Jewish Type' was Galton's most successful study; he called it 'the best speci-mens of composites I have ever produced'. Galton, 'Photographic Composites', 243. Galton believed that statistically establishing a Jewish racial identity would help in rescuing Jews from the anti-Semitism of the day. In an 1884 letter he writes, 'It strikes me that the Jews are specialised for a parasitical existence upon other nations, and that there is need of evidence that they are capable of fulfilling the varied duties of a civilised nation by themselves.' Francis Galton, letter to Alphonse de Candolle, 27 October 1884, cited in Pearson, *Researches of Middle Life*, 209.

20. 'If these Jewish lads, selected almost at random, and with parents from opposite parts of Europe, yield so markedly individual a type, it can only be because there actually exists a definite and well-defined organic type of modern Jews. Photo-graphic science thus seems to confirm the conclusion I have drawn from history, that, owing to social isolation and other causes, there has been scarcely any admix-ture of alien blood amongst the Jews since their dispersion.' Jacobs, 'The Jewish Type', 268. Anne Maxwell notes that Jacbos's understanding of the Jewish type as a result of social conditions differed from Galton's biological essentialism. See Maxwell, *Picture Imperfect*, 90–2 and Novak, *Realism*, 100–5.

21. Jacobs, 'The Jewish Type', 268.

22. Novak writes: 'the equivocal and phantasmagoric figure of the Jew operated as an Ur-race for Galton'. Novak, *Realism*, 99.

23. Galton, 'Composite Portraits', 132–3, and Jacobs, 'The Jewish Type', 269.

24. Francis Galton, 'Conventional Representation of the Horse in Motion', *Nature* (6 July 1882), 228–9, citation on 228. See also Ellenbogen, *Reasoned and Unreasoned Images*, 81–3.

25. Galton, 'Conventional Representation', 228.

26. Galton, 'Conventional Representation', 228.

27. Galton, 'Conventional Representation', 229.

28. Galton, 'Conventional Representation', 229, emphasis added.

29. For Louis Agassiz, see Brian Wallis, 'Black Bodies, White Science: Louis Agassiz's Slave Daguerrotypes', *American Art* 9:2 (Summer 1995), 39–61. For John Lam-prey and Thomas Henry Huxley, see Maxwell, *Picture Imperfect*, 34–5. For Rudolf Martin, see Amos Morris-Reich, 'Anthropology, Standardization and Measure-ment: Rudolf Martin and Anthropometric Photography', *British Journal for the History of Science* 46 (2013), 487–516.

30. See Maxwell, *Picture Imperfect*, 109–11.

31. See Fatimah Tobing Rony, *The Third Eye: Race, Cinema, and Ethnographic Spec-tacle* (Durham, NC: Duke University Press, 1996), 21–76, and Catherine Russell, *Experimental Ethnography: The Work of Film in the Age of Video* (Durham, NC: Duke University Press, 1999), 55–6.

32. Novak, *Realism*, 100.

33. Galton, 'On Generic Images', 166.

34. Galton, 'Composite Portraits', *Journal of the Anthropological Institute*, 134.

35. Galton, 'Composite Portraits', *Nature*, 97.

36. Sekula notes of Galton's method that there is 'an unacknowledged presupposition: only the gross features of the head mattered', rather than, to take another method of facial analysis, the measurement of the ears. Sekula, 'The Body and the Archive', 48.

37. The wider the range in Galton's sampling, the hazier the images, not just in locating distinct outlines of the face, but the foggy appearance overall. This is a problem similar to the one Etienne-Jules Marey encountered in his multiple exposure method of motion studies: the more slight the interval between exposures, that is, the more precise the measurement, the muddier the resulting image would be. Mary Ann Doane observes: 'For Marey, time was an objective plenitude that always seemed to escape the grasp of his differential photographic technique. It could be adequately "represented" only at the risk of illegibility.' Mary Ann Doane, *The Emergence of Cinematic Time: Modernity, Contingency, the Archive* (Cambridge, MA: Harvard University Press, 2002), 26.

38. Ciara Ambrosio, 'Composite Photographs and the Quest for Generality: Themes from Peirce and Galton', *Critical Inquiry* 42:3 (Spring 2016), 547–79, citation on 555–6.

39. See Ambrosio, 'Composite Photographs', 557.

40. See Sekula, 'The Body and the Archive', 19. On page 54, Sekula notes the similarities between Bertillon and Galton, and describes Galton's composite photograph as a 'collapsed version of the archive'.

41. Walter Benjamin, 'Little History of Photography', in Walter Benjamin, *The Work of Art in the Age of Its Technological Reproducibility and Other Writings on Media* (Cambridge, MA: Harvard University Press, 2008), 274–98, citation on 286.

42. Benjamin, 'Little History of Photography', 287.

43. Allan Sekula, *Photography Against the Grain: Essays and Photo Works 1973–1983* (Halifax, Nova Scotia: The Press of the Nova Scotia College of Art and Design, 1984), ix.

44. 'The general, all-inclusive archive necessarily contains both the traces of the visible bodies of heroes, leaders, moral exemplars, celebrities, and those of the poor, the diseased, the insane, the criminal, the nonwhite, the female, and all other embodiments of the unworthy'. Sekula, 'The Body and the Archive', 10.

45. Galton, 'Photographic Composites', 243.

46. Jacobs, 'The Jewish Type', 268.

47. Jacobs, 'On the Racial Characteristics of Modern Jews', 51.

48. Galton, 'Photographic Composites', 243.

49. George Eliot, *Daniel Deronda* (New York: Penguin Classics, 1995), 472.

50. Ibid., 472.

51. Ibid., 474.

52. As Sarah Kember argues, much of photography's authority derives from its development within these institutional frameworks. She writes: 'This is partly because the underlying principle of the system is photographic, and historically, the authority of photography derives not only from its strong claim to indexicality, but from its development and use in the very institutions in which it continues to be deployed.' Sarah Kember, 'Face Recognition and the Emergence of Smart Photography', *Journal of Visual Culture* 13:2 (2014), 187.

2. MAD FACES: CODING FEATURES AND EXPRESSIONS OF FEMALE MADNESS IN PHYSIOGNOMY TEXTS, ASYLUM PHOTOGRAPHS AND EARLY CINEMA

Elyse Singer

Deciphering historical rules for performing female madness on screen requires a bit of cryptography. While the gestures and expressions associated with imitating hysteria in early cinema may be especially legible, the coded meanings are also more fluid, as approaches to screen acting were in flux.[1] Actors in silent film utilised embodied practices to represent mental distress that referenced networks of meaning. Unravelling these threads reveals a residue of centuries-old connections between madness and the savage that glazes a racialised lexicon of emotional gesture imagery, coding certain expressions and parts of the body as excess, animalistic and heathen. In this essay, I examine some of the facial codes expressing female madness in their transition from texts featuring medical or pseudo-scientific illustrations and photography, through embodiment on theatrical stages, to early cinema featuring 'madwomen'. Across the long nineteenth century in the US, representations of mad faces intersected with racialised tropes rooted in subjugation. As Therí Alyce Pickens argues in *Black Madness :: Mad Blackness*: 'In an ideological construct of white supremacy, Blackness is considered synonymous with madness or the prerequisite for creating madness.'[2] Enacting white female hysteria on stage and in early cinema required the player to follow different but overlapping rules of expression. The actor was expected to resist 'melodramatic ranting', while theatricalising mental distress enough to demonstrate and preserve the actor's sanity.[3] These gestures made it possible for the spectator to decipher codes rooted in white supremacy that preserved the whiteness, sexual purity and reason of the mad heroine.

Curiosity surrounding historical representations of female hysteria sprouted in the late 1970s – a century after neurologist Dr Jean-Martin Charcot's notorious lecture-demonstrations at the Salpêtrière Hospital in Paris. Scholars in fields including cinema studies, feminist history and psychology embraced the symbolically fertile photographs of the performing hysterics.[4] An urgency to decode the meaning of these images and gestures persists. In the 2020 volume *Performing Hysteria: Images and Imaginations of Hysteria*, editor Johanna Braun frames her analysis within the mission of the 'New Hystorians': scholars engaged in 'coaxing out the representations of hysteria, rhetorically searching for its metaphors and metonymies, visually following its iconographic relations and imagery – all this out of a belief in the significance of the cultural representations of illness within society'.[5] To examine iconography of madwomen in the late nineteenth and early twentieth centuries, I utilise an intermedial approach, with a special eye towards the convergence and unarticulated frictions between the discources of race and mental distress. Pickens proposes that 'relationships between Blackness and madness (and race and disability more generally) are constituted within the fissures, breaks, and gaps in critical and literary texts'.[6] Such a fissure exists in the evolution of film art between 1908 and 1913, what some early cinema scholars have termed the 'transitional period' of the silent era. Rules guiding screen acting shifted radically at this time, from a theatrically rooted pantomimic style of 'histrionically coded acting' to what Roberta Pearson identifies as a 'verisimilar' form of performance.[7] My question is: how did racialised representations of mental distress operate across this transition and how did they intersect with white women's performative expression of hysteria?

Physiognomic Coding

As early as the fifth century BCE, physiognomonia studies attempted to identify, measure and decipher facial attributes scientifically.[8] Physiognomy met visual art during the Renaissance, when artists and physicians produced illustrated studies of the passions. This literature provided a visual glossary of expressions and gestures, including faces of madness. Actors, painters and doctors thereafter consulted the same sources, such as those by physician and philosopher Marin Cureau de la Chambre (1594–1669) and painter Charles Le Brun (1619–90). Theatre scholar Joseph R. Roach explains that these materials 'helped to foster the idea, later abetted by the acting textbooks of the eighteenth century, that the study of the passions involves contemplating graphic representations of idealized characters'.[9] For example, the figure representing 'Désespoir' (despair) in Le Brun's *Expressions des passions de l'âme* (1727) shows a bearded man with long hair extending upwards in tendrils as if a lion's mane. The lines from the hair extend into the furrows of the forehead. His lips and nose are large, and the pervasive cross-hatching gives his skin a darker tone. A woman's face represents the passion of 'Desir' (desire) with protruding eyes and flaring nostrils.[10] Pre-Enlightenment, bulging eyes and dishevelled hair were seen as signs of pathological bodily fluids such as black bile.[11] For actors, this meant keeping extreme emotions 'down', lest potentially lethal bodily forces and fluids rise up in the body.[12] Blood-filled 'extended eyes' also suggest racialised bodily excess or spillage, rooted in what Rizvana Bradley notes are 'Eurocentric assumptions about the body and embodied expression'.[13] While the figures in these French illustrated texts are almost uniformly white, the faces representing mental distress appear to have exaggerated features that code them as monstrous, animalistic or other.

Renderings of stereotypically racialised mad faces circulated across texts, time and geographic borders. By the late nineteenth century, pseudo-scientific reference texts such as Mary Olmstead Stanton's two-volume and 'profusely illustrated' *A System of Practical and Scientific Physiognomy; Or, How to Read Faces* (1890) served as a form of *fin de siècle* facial recognition software. Stanton identified what was 'normal' or 'abnormal' in the physical features and expressions of the face. An eyelid that did not form a '*true curve*' [*sic*] or a narrow chin, for example, were said to be signs of a morally defective character; racial and ethnic groups were aligned with criminal and mentally ill populations on the basis of these physiognomic and phrenological theories.[14] Stanton, moreover, neatly aligned physiognomy and race-based typecasting with eugenics:

> That the time will come when we shall all be judged and understood by our faces is not, I am convinced, far distant, and herein lies the opportunity for race-improvement by design; for, when men have learned to recognize the criminal or insane neuroses, as exhibited in the face, they will undoubtedly refrain from intermarrying with those who would be sure to curse instead of bless posterity by reproducing their own weaknesses.[15]

Stanton expresses her white supremacism and classism unapologetically in her writings about reading the face. Even when not promoting race-based population control, nineteenth-century British and North American physiognomy texts tended to illustrate mental anguish or melancholy using white figures with 'African' facial features.[16] Representations of madness that focused on engorged eyes and excessive hair connoted wildness, unreason, as if a revisionist take on medieval illustrations that aligned mental illness with demonic possession. This is seen clearly in *The Expression of the Emotions in Man and Animals* (1872), where Darwin purports that 'paroxysms of violence' cause the hair of the insane to rise up, just as may be seen in 'lower animals'.[17] The section on 'Surprise–Astonishment–Fear–Horror', is illustrated with an image

Fig. 19.—From a photograph of an insane woman, to show the condition of her hair.

Figure 2.1   The hair of a madwoman, as illustrated in Charles Darwin's *The Expression of the Emotions in Man and Animals* (1872).

of an older white 'insane woman', shown facing front from the waist up, her face accented with lines and shadows, whose dark hair extends more than a head's width in both directions (Figure 2.1).[18] While the chioruscuro effect may have been utilised to convey a realistic impression of shadows in this engraving, the volume of the insane woman's hair suggests an overlap of madness and Africanisation.[19]

Printed works from this period comparing humans to animals appear to have perpetuated an alternative form of racist coding. For example, Dr James W. Redfield's 1866 *Comparative Physiognomy* features illustrations that compare black men to fish, because 'the caught are stowed away on board vessels like codfish and whale-oil'.[20] Citing Harriet Beecher Stowe for context, Redfield's second model for Black physiognomy is that of the docile elephant. He describes a 'negro-looking female' as having features that are 'elephantine', so that one might 'ascribe to her all the docility, faithfulness, caution, substitution, and love of children, that are characteristic of the elephant' (Figure 2.2).[21] This suggests 'plantation nostalgia', what Saidiya V. Hartman calls the 'contending variants of racism' and the historical romanticisation that 'constituted the African as childish, primitive, contented, and endowed with great mimetic capacities'.[22] Ascribing a physiognomic marker for docility was the flip-side of savagery, but both denotations were forms of race-based subjugation.

Figure 2.2   'Elephantine features' from James W. Redfield's *Comparative Physiognomy* (1866).

FACE-MAKING IN ASYLUM PHOTOGRAPHY AND ON THE SCREEN

Visual metrics for identifying white female hysteria became more widely system-ised across the nineteenth century in correlation to developments in photography.[23] Starting mid-century, the camera entered hospitals in England, France and the US, and photographic studies of mentally ill and disabled patients circulated across media, coding which corporeal expressions were healthy and which were not. At the Salpêtrière, Charcot's studies emphasised clinical observation of seizure disor-ders and hypnosis which, enhanced by the production and circulation of print and photographic media, led to a panoptic enterprise that was both sensationalist and visuality-centric. Charcot aimed to make mental distress legible to the observer by labelling poses expressing female hysteria according to four sequential phases. At the same time, the 'contagious' nature of hysteria was amplified by Parisian cabaret performers who, according to Rae Beth Gordon, purposely imitated and 'borrowed' the celebrated hysterics' nervous twitches and glitches on the café-cabaret stages. The 'phenomenon and enormous popularity of epileptic performers and of songs about nervous pathologies in the *caf'conc'* contributed to the furor of attention to nervous disorders in the 1880s and 1890s'.[24] Actors animated coded madness. This, in turn, perpetuated more interest in female hysterics.

Facial expression or 'grimace films' were a sub-genre of early cinema. As Tom Gunning explains in his influential 1997 essay 'In Your Face: Physiognomy, Photography, and the Gnostic Mission of Early Film', extreme close-ups of faces in single-shot non-fiction 'actualities' or within narrative shorts may have been motivated by a desire to uncover visual knowledge – to see the human face 'categorized, investigated, and visualized' through cinema – but these films emphasised the grotesque.[25] Gunning observes that some of the first and most well-known moving pictures, including Thomas Edison's 1894 kinetoscope *Fred Ott's Sneeze* as well as the extremely popular 1896 *The May Irwin Kiss* showcase faces-in-action – notably, mouths 'eating, slobbering, kissing, guffawing and generally partaking of the carnivalesque pleasure of the open orifice in a most unseemly manner'.[26] Recognisable biological activities and gestures became spectacle when magnified on the screen.

Recent scholarship has provided additional intermedial lenses for looking at the racialisation of expression in early grimace films. A vivid example of this is film historian Allyson Nadia Field's assertion that *The May Irwin Kiss* must be contextualised within the minstrel tradition due to race-based codes associated with Irwin's face itself:

> She was known for popularizing what were called 'coon songs' where she would – dressed as a woman and without blackface – adopt the persona of a 'threatening black man'. If you're a turn-of-the-century spectator, you know May Irwin is very famous and you know you're looking at a minstrel.[27]

In this example, the performer's identity in itself referenced minstrelsy. Yet, the spectacularly exaggerated grimaces may also be seen within the tradition, dating back to the 1830s, of white male performers using burnt cork to exaggerate their facial features such as their mouths and eyes to outrageous proportions while performing racist songs, comedy sketches and dances for white audiences. In 'blacking up', minstrels affirmed whiteness. As Douglas A. Jones, Jr explains: 'Simply put, blackface minstrelsy was for, by, and about the white community.'[28] Hartman speaks of the embodied 'excess' of blackness in nineteenth-century minstrelsy, and its correlative, violence: 'If grotesque bodily acts like rolling eyes, lolling tongues, obscene gestures, shuffling, and the like animated the body, blows invested it with meaning.'[29] These stage blows may have been farcical, but they mimicked the brutal physical abuse used against Black and brown bodies to keep them in check; the grotesque and unrestrained gestures of minstrelsy carry this affective connotation even in comedic contexts. Black subjectivity in early facial expression films, however, was not necessarily framed as mad. For example, *Something Good, Negro Kiss* (William Selig, 1898) clearly quotes, even satirises, *The May Irwin Kiss*, but the performances by dancers Suttle and Brown as they swing hands and kiss are affectionate and natural. There are no excessive gestures or facial expressions.[30] Carnivalesque grimaces in early cinema overlapped with tropes from minstrelsy, but we see many examples of Black performers who resisted perpetuating these mad associations.

FUNNY MAD FACES

The grimaces, obscene gestures and rolling eyes of the comic madwoman in early cinema are another form of embodied mad excess. In the British comedy short *Mary Jane's Mishap* (1903), actor Laura Bayley looks directly at the camera and crosses her eyes, acknowledging the soot on her face (a possible nod to blackface minstrelsy) before pouring paraffin into the stove and causing an explosion. Close-up cut-ins of the heavily pregnant 'Madame' in Alice Guy Blaché's *Madame a des envies* (1907) show her ravenously enjoying a stolen lollipop, a glass of absinthe, a herring sandwich and a cigar; the sexualised oral consummation of the desired objects is embellished by raised eyebrows and silly blinking. Pregnancy is hysterical here, but Blaché uses satire to frame the excess. The 1903 Edison short *Goo Goo Eyes*, featuring Gilbert Sarony cross-dressed as the 'Old Maid' (an 'ugly woman'), is an example where the grimaces of the comic madwoman intersected with traces of minstrelsy.[31] The catalogue describes the actor as grimacing and contorting his face while speaking rapidly: 'In order to better illustrate the story, he crosses his eyes and twists his mouth until the film ends.'[32] Sarony here is parodying female madness with grotesque expressions and crossed eyes, while simultaneously alluding to the popular 'minstrel ballad' *Just Because She Made Dem Goo-Goo Eyes* (1900) recorded by numerous singers in the early 1900s.[33] Maggie Hennefeld suggests that vaudeville-trained performers such as Florence Turner utilised face-making as a subversive and 'alternative means for unleashing their comedic mayhem'.[34] Several Turner shorts from the 1910s use 'funny faces' as a plot device, including *Hypnotizing the Hypnotist* (1911) and *Daisy Doodad's Dial* (1914). Ridiculous madwomen in early cinema theatricalised unreason in the act of contorting their facial features in proximity to the camera or participating in what Hennefeld has identified as a recurring trope of hysterical and contagious laughter. Such expressions alluded to nineteenth-century hysterics 'characterized as repressed women who spoke with their bodies, representing unrepresentable ideas and desires through a vast array of somatic complaints'.[35] By the mid-1910s, however, Alice Maurice argues, with the emergence of identifiable film stars, the abnormally contorting 'body-face' film had fallen from favour. Critics pathologised and racialised the face-makers as unnatural and carrying residue from working-class entertainment:

> These cinema faces stand in synecdochically for the 'burlesque' body – vaudevillian, freakish, and unrestrained. This new creature, which we might call the 'body-face', threatens early cinema's vulnerable status as art by recalling vaudeville and other 'low' popular forms.[36]

The shift to naturalism in US film acting in the mid-1910s, however, did not completely eliminate this often minstrelised 'body-face', as highly gestural expressions of madness persisted into the sound era.

SAVAGE HAIR

Loose or wild hair has long stood as a code for female madness in the visual, literary and performing arts. Mad Ophelia enters 'with her haire downe singing' (G4v) in the First Quarto of *Hamlet* (1603), and Maurice and Hanna Charney assert that loose hair as representative of melancholy or excessive grief was 'virtually an emblem of feminine madness on the Elizabethan stage'.[37] In late nineteenth-century imagery, when a white woman let down her hair, it connoted different degrees of psychosis, sexual promiscuity and otherness. Untamed hair was the go-to visual marker for madwomen in early cinema. I would argue, however, that the savage or sexualised symbolism of the hair correlated to the perceived curability of the woman. In Louis Feuillade's short melodrama *Le violon* (1907), the mother character goes mad when she almost loses her child in a fire. Prior to the mother's hospitalisation, her hair is pinned up. Once she enters the asylum itself, it hangs down to her waist. In the medium shot establishing the hospital's space and culture, the other female mental patients, some playing with dolls, also have loose hair; the child-women, moreover, suggest the iconic images of Charcot's female hysterics posing suggestively in their nightgowns. In contrast, the hair of the nurses is pinned under their caps. Notably, in this scene, an older white woman with dark frizzy hair crouches on the ground in the corner of the frame, baring her teeth and clawing the air like a rabid animal. She tries to swipe at the mother and is removed quickly from the room by attendants. This suggests that the savage and the psychotic are incurable; they must be confined and punished – even within the asylum. When the mother recovers her reason in the final scene of *Le violon*, her hair is neatly braided.

Wild hair denotes both female madness and class in the Pathé melodrama *Pauvre mère* (Albert Capellani, 1906). In this short, a working-class single woman is despondent with guilt after her young daughter falls to her death while the mother was at her sewing machine. A year later, she is shown – wine bottle in hand – with what the scenario describes as 'mad eyes' (*des yeux fous*).[38] In the next shot, she stumbles drunkenly into a park, her hair now undone. Grabbing and embracing a child that looks like her daughter, the madwoman pulls her to her lap. Magically, through trick film technology, the little girl with the white hat becomes the mother's dead child in a simple dress. They hug tenderly. The melodramatic trope of a mother's excessive grief over a deceased child merges here with what Tom Gunning calls the 'impossible body'; through cinema, we experience 'fantasies of impossible bodies that could be experienced through technology'.[39] We see and long for what the hysterical mother wishes. The superimposed beloved daughter fades away and the madwoman creates a near riot, engaging in an aggressive tug-of-war over the white-hatted girl with a group of bourgeoise mothers. Upon losing the fight, the 'poor mother' with the patched dress and unkempt hair raises her hands to her head, faces the camera, laughs broadly and then faints to the ground. Two police officers appear and drag her limp body out of the frame. This woman is not recuperable; her mad body must be confined, out of view, away from polite society. In the final scene, set in a Catholic hospital, she reaches with open hands towards a final vision of her ghost-child before dying of excessive grief, surrounded by Sister Nurses. This tableau, as Richard Abel has noted, is ambiguous; it may be read as a religious 'reward' for suffering, or a social critique of the conditions faced by poor single mothers.[40] But I would argue that, in the film's denouement, the affective excess triggered by the woman's psychotic projections overwhelms her mad gestures. The spillage overloads the symbolic circuit, and she succumbs to unreason. Both of the mothers in these early French melodramas go mad due to maternal guilt, but only the married one whose child survived is cured of her madness.

A more overtly minstrelised variation of mad hair is seen in the Lumières's *Le Cake-Walk au Nouveau Cirque* (1902). This short showcases dancers from Les Joyeux Nègres (The Joyous Negroes), a US troupe that was appearing at the Nouveau Cirque in Paris. The elegantly dressed Black male, female and cross-dressed dancers perform variations of the cakewalk, followed by a white couple, who launch into an exaggerated parodic version of the dance.[41] While the Black dancers watch, the white woman begins to move so wildly and out-of-control that her thick dark hair comes loose from its bun, and swings violently about her head as she dances (Figure 2.3). What stands out in this film is the ferocity and loss of control in the white woman's imitation of the cakewalk. In her mimicry of the Black dancers, she clearly elides Black dance – and Black female sexuality – with madness. Her flying long hair in itself would be read as a double sign suggesting sexual and primal desires.[42] This is mimetic appropriation, but rather than imitating specific gestures, the white female dancer nearly goes 'wild', embracing animalistic or primal mania.[43] Moreover, while

Figure 2.3   Imitating Black dance through wild hair in *Le Cake-Walk au Nouveau Cirque* (1902).

the white female dancer in *Le Cake-Walk au Nouveau Cirque* is not literally in blackface, her flying-hair dance may be compared with the performance of the raging figure of Topsy, the actor in blackface dancing wildly and head-butting Miss Ophelia, in the 1903 film version of *Uncle Tom's Cabin*; it is mad minstrelsy without the comic gloss.

METHODS FOR MADNESS

The mad mothers in both *Pauvre mère* and *Le violon* use identical gestures to express their grief. They raise their hands above their heads, chins up, fingers spread apart (Figures 2.4 and 2.5). And while the actors are unidentified in these shorts from 1906–7, the gestures are not. These poses are rooted in centuries of Western theatrical conventions around expression of extreme emotions. Influential French acting instructor François Delsarte (1811–71) identified the gesture of raising one's hands by or above the head to represent 'Anguish: Strongest Form'.[44] In *Gestures and Attitudes: An Exposition of the Delsarte Philosophy of Expression* (1892), Edward B. Warman explains that the actor doing this pose should 'Clasp the hands still more tightly, and drop the head

Figures 2.4 and 2.5   Hands-up gesture to indicate female madness in two French melodramas. Left: *Pauvre mère* (Albert Capellani, Pathé Frères production, 1906). ©Fondation Jérôme Seydoux-Pathé. Right: *Le violon* (Louis Feuillade, 1907). A Gaumont production. Reproduced by permission of Gaumont-Pathé Archives.

still lower as the hands are raised higher. Make sure that the movement of the head is simultaneous with the movement of the hands'[45] (Figure 2.6). Pearson argues that Delsarte, who believed that emotions could be codified in poses, is inextricably linked to the style of 'histrionic acting' seen in pre-1915 silent cinema. She explains that, as time went on, Delsarte's disciples focused more on the physical posing than finding truthful emotional expression: 'His system, in its debased form, became emblematic of histrionically coded performances. His followers forgot about following "nature sufficiently close" in their enthusiastic determination to "idealize nature".'[46] Holding a gesture freezes a moment of spectacle as embodied allegory.

The hands-up gesture to illustrate white female madness has proven to be especially resilient across time. Moreover, in early French cinema, it appears to have been a convention to accompany the anguished gesture of raising the hands with a title card to corroborate the character's mental breakdown with words such as 'Pauvre Folle!' (poor madwoman!) in *Le violon* and, in *Angélus de la victoire* (1916), 'Jacqueline avait perdu la raison' (Jacqueline had lost her mind). The text plus the gesture dually signified to the silent film spectator that the character was – internally – in mental distress. A variation on this gestural coding of madness is the hand-to-forehead pose. In *Amour et science* (1912), Max, the inventor, goes mad when he sees (through his futuristic video-telephone screen) his fiancée kissing what appears to be another man. As he aims his pistol at the kissing couple on the monitor, he raises his left hand to his forehead, palm out. In a moment of meta-filmic madness, he shoots, destroying the screen. This scene is followed by a title card that reads 'Max is insane'.[47] Sarah Bernhardt uses this same hand-to-head gesture in *Le duel d'Hamlet* (1900) after being stabbed, right

Figure 2.6   Delsartian Anguish (left), a Salpêtrière hysteric (centre), Sarah Bernhardt c. 1905 (right).

before collapsing to the ground. It is an expression of mad excess and, while she is playing a male role, this moment stands out as being more feminine and rooted in theatrical melodrama than the rest of her choreography in the film. The gesture of placing one's hand upon the forehead, with the other hand on the heart, is recommended for imitating 'mental pain' according to Edmund Shaftesbury in *Lessons in the Art of Acting* (1889): 'This attitude is made by the weight on the right foot, placing the left hand upon the heart, the right upon the forehead, inclining the head backward, the eyes looking upward.'[48] Nineteenth-century stage audiences knew how to read these symbolic postures of madness and early film actors continued to utilise them even as screen acting became more nuanced.

Visual representations of embodied emotions in nineteenth-century gestural handbooks tend to focus on those that would occur in the most dramatic or conflict-filled moments. Of the nearly seventy figures in the stage acting theory book *Practical Illustrations of Rhetorical Gesture and Action* – adapted by the English actor-manager Henry Siddons in 1807 from Johann Jakob Engel's *Ideer Zu Einer Mimik* (1795) – only two or three represent subdued sensations. The rest of the illustrations show people in heightened emotional states such as 'Jealous Rage' and 'Despondency'.[49] It recalls the propensity for nineteenth-century Western actors including Sarah Bernhardt to incorporate multiple opportunities to faint into their performances, as if hysterical histrionics and white women's acting were inextricable. Mad scenes or death scenes provided opportunities to showcase athleticism at the same time as raising melodramatic stakes. These handbooks perpetuated a tension; they emphasised and codified extreme expressions while advocating for propriety and restraint. Siddons, for example, stressed that, in playing a mad rage, an actor should avoid '*disgusting*' [sic] forms of imitation.[50] Specifically, he decries actors for making 'abominable grimaces and unnatural distortions', and accuses women 'acting Juliet, or any other character of that description' of a propensity to exaggerate performances of grief or heartbreak through slamming their bodies to the floor: [the actress] 'will sometimes fall on the boards with such violence, when she hears of the death or banishment of her lover, that we are really alarmed, lest her poor skull should be fractured by the violence of the concussion'.[51] Audiences rewarded the spectacle of extreme emotions such as lovesickness and madness, but critics urged verisimilitude.

The authors of the first film acting handbooks to emerge in the US and England in the mid-1910s borrowed extensively from earlier acting and gestural handbooks, while stressing decorum in performing madness using modern terms. 'Don't overact!' Frances Agnew exhorted in 1913. A columnist for *Motion Picture Magazine* in 1916 proclaimed that the photoplayer 'must be able to depict the emotions without "ranting", and this requires the highest art of this nature possible to obtain'.[52] The predominant acting method prescribed is to practise expressions in front of a mirror, not simply to assume postures to denote emotions. Agnew advised finding motivations 'impelled by intense feeling' for signifying gestures.[53] She claims: 'Natural actions and expressions are the secret of success on the screen.'[54] Hugo Münsterberg allows in *The Photoplay: A Psychological Study* (1916) that the silent film actor may need to exaggerate expression to some degree to compensate for the lack of speech; he contrasts this with the mime who demonstrates or 'exhibits' emotion, pointing to it, and warns the photoplayer against such self-referentiality.[55] The screen acting guides focus on practising nuanced expression using the eyes, yet concede that film casting directors may be looking foremost for certain physical types and that no prior acting experience is required for many roles. Typecasting unapologetically reverted to physiognomic stereotypes.

CONCLUSION

A 1914 magazine series by Eugene Brewster on 'Expression of the Emotions' encapsulates the challenges of performing madness on screen. Published at the cusp of a new style of film acting rooted in naturalism, Brewster's essays are tainted with the residue of white supremacist iconography in their physiognomic illustrations and ideologies.[56] He praises D. W. Griffith for the 'trick', where one might 'read the whole story' in the eyes of the actor: 'For you will remember that he seldom allows his players to rant. He makes them turn toward the camera and tell the story with faces almost serene.'[57] This is exemplified in Griffith's 1912 *The Painted Lady*, where a medium close-up shows Blanche Sweet's mental unravelling in her father's arms after she shoots her lover. The gestures of madness had moved from the full body to a more interior, immobile perfor-mance. It is evident from the look in her eyes that Sweet's character has lost her hold on reality. Yet, the 'mulatto housekeeper' Lydia Brown in *The Birth of a Nation*, performed by Mary Alden in blackface, spits on the floor and then fills the frame with motion in a sex-crazed rage before ripping her dress, grabbing her breast and collapsing to the floor, panting. Linda Williams contends that the 'racialized villains' in Griffith's films, which he refused to integrate 'could be played only by whites in (various degrees of) blackface, thus undercutting the "realism" of the sexual-racial threat they supposedly depicted'.[58] Lydia is a minstrel figure, like the Topsy earlier in the century, but in 1915, Griffith balances this spontaneous lack of control by the shot focusing on her 'crazy' eyes. The exaggerated 'ranting' discouraged by critics for being 'ridiculous' and 'more burlesque than physical expression' did not apply to performing charac-ters coded as both mad and Black.[59] While expressions of mental distress do find their way into early screen acting literature in the menu of emotions to practise, the emphasis on making feelings visible-yet-decorous served to perpetuate very old beliefs in what madness looks like without addressing methods for how an actor might ethically or truthfully enact such distress.

NOTES

1. On the evolution of acting methods across the transitional period of early cinema, see: Victoria Duckett, 'Acting', in Claudia Springer and Julie Levinson (eds), *The Silent Screen, 1895–1927* (New Brunswick, NJ: Rutgers University Press, 2015); Charles O'Brien, 'Camera Distance and Acting in Griffith Biographs', in Kaveh Askari et al. (eds), *Performing New Media, 1890–1915* (Bloomington: Indiana University Press, 2015); Roberta Pearson, *Eloquent Gestures: The Transformation of Performance Style in the Griffith Biograph Films* (Berkeley: University of California Press, 1992); and Pamela Robertson Wojcik (ed.), *Movie Acting, The Film Reader* (New York: Routledge, 2004).
2. Therí Alyce Pickens, *Black Madness :: Mad Blackness* (Durham, NC: Duke University Press, 2019), 4.
3. The phrase 'melodramatic ranting' is taken from Eugene V. Brewster, 'Expression of the Emotions (Part 2) ', *Motion Picture Magazine* (August 1914), 107.
4. The scholarship around Charcot's hysterics is ever-expanding. Important works include: Georges Didi-Huberman, *Invention of Hysteria Charcot and the Photographic Iconography of the Salpêtrière*, trans. Alisa Hartz, originally published as *Invention de l'hysterie*, Paris: Éditions Macula, 1982 (Cambridge, MA: MIT Press, 2003); Sander L. Gilman, *Seeing the Insane* (Ithaca: Cornell University Press, 1982); Rae Beth Gordon, 'From Charcot to Charlot: Unconscious Imitation and Spectatorship in French Cabaret and Early Cinema', *Critical Inquiry* 27:3 (Spring 2001), 515–49; Maggie Hennefeld, 'Death from Laughter, Female Hys-teria, and Early Cinema', *differences* (December, 2016), 45–92; Asti Hustvedt, *Medical Muses: Hysteria in Nineteenth-century Paris* (New York: W. W. Norton

& Co., 2011); Elaine Showalter, *Hystories: Hysterical Epidemics and Modern Culture* (New York: Columbia University Press, 1997); and Temenuga Trifonova, *Warped Minds: Cinema and Psychopathology* (Amsterdam: Amsterdam University Press, 2014).

5. Johanna Braun, 'Hysterical Cure: Performing Disability in the Possession Film', in Johanna Braun (ed.), *Performing Hysteria: Images and Imaginations of Hysteria* (Leuven: Leuven University Press, 2020), 210.

6. Pickens, *Black Madness*, 3.

7. Pearson, *Eloquent Gestures*, 23.

8. Mariska Leunissen, 'Physiognomy', in Paul T. Keyser and John Scarborough (eds), *Oxford Handbook of Science and Medicine in the Classical World* (New York: Oxford University Press 2018), 743–64. DOI: 10.1093/oxfordhb/9780199734146.013.36

9. Joseph R. Roach, *The Player's Passion: Studies in the Science of Acting* (Ann Arbor: University of Michigan Press, 1993), 67.

10. 'Les expressions des passions de l'âme. Par Charles Le Brun, 1727'. Available at <http://www.histoiredelafolie.fr/psychiatrie-neurologie/les-expressions-des-passions-de-lame-par-charles-le-brun-1727> (last accessed 21 September 2021).

11. Sander Gilman, *Seeing the Insane* (Lincoln: Univeristy of Nebraska Press, 1982). See especially Chapter 7, 'The Physiognomy of Madness', 58–71.

12. Roach, *The Player's Passion*, 48.

13. Rizvana Bradley, 'Black Cinematic Gesture and the Aesthetics of Contagion', *TDR: The Drama Review* 62:1 (Spring 2018), 23.

14. Mary Olmstead Stanton, *A System of Practical and Scientific Physiognomy; Or, How to Read Faces* (Philadelphia: F. A. Davis, 1890), 161. The 'abnormal eye' and '*true curve*' may be found in Stanton's *The Encyclopedia of Face and Form* (Philadelphia: F. A. Davis, 1900), 953.

15. Stanton, *System*, 161.

16. A notable example may be found in Rosa Baughan's *Physiognomy: The Handbook* (London: George Redway, 1885).

17. Charles Darwin, *The Expression of the Emotions in Man and Animals* (London: John Murray, 1872), 296. Darwin emphasises the connection between hair and psychosis: 'The state of her hair is a sure and convenient criterion of her mental condition.'

18. A Google image search of the plate on 5 April 2021 produced 'visually similar images' that include drawings of Nina Simone, Jimi Hendrix and Prince.

19. Darwin quibbles that 'the hair appears rather too coarse and too much curled' (viii). This is one of the few plates representing a woman in the entire nearly 400-page volume on emotional expression.

20. James W. Redfield, MD, *Comparative Physiognomy or Resemblances Between Men and Animals* (Clifton Hall, NY: Redfield, 1866), 82.

21. Ibid., 53.

22. Saidiya V. Hartman, *Scenes of Subjection: Terror, Slavery and Self-Making in Nineteenth-century America* (Oxford: Oxford University Press, 1997), 23, 29.

23. Didi-Huberman, *Invention of Hysteria Charcot*, 34.

24. Gordon, 'From Charcot to Charlot', 517.

25. Tom Gunning, 'In Your Face: Physiognomy, Photography, and the Gnostic Mission of Early Film', *Modernism/modernity* 4:1 (January 1997): 3.
26. Ibid., 23.
27. Nina Metz, 'How America's Earliest Films Were Based in Minstrelsy', *chicagotribune.com* (19 June 2019). Field helped to identify stage performers Saint Suttle and Gertie Brown in the recently rediscovered *Something Good, Negro Kiss*.
28. Douglas A. Jones, 'Black Politics but Not Black People: Rethinking the Social and "Racial" History of Early Minstrelsy', *TDR* 57:2 (2013), 22.
29. Hartman, *Scenes of Subjection*, 30.
30. Field suggests that this 'resistance was able to burst through that framing', and, while it is not a 'a corrective' to racialised misrepresentation in early cinema, 'it shows us that that's not the only thing that was going on'. Jack Wang, 'Silent Film of Black Couple's Kiss Discovered, Added to National Film Registry', *UChicagoNews.com* (12 December 2018). Available at <https://news.uchicago.edu/story/silent-film-black-couples-kiss-discovered-added-national-film-registry> (last accessed 21 September 2021).
31. *Motion Pictures from The Library of Congress Paper Print Collection 1894–1912* (Berkeley: University of California Press, n.d.), 123.
32. Ibid.
33. John Queen and Hughie L. Cannon, 'Just Because She Made Dem Goo-goo Eyes' (1900), New York Public Library Digital Collections. Available at <https://digitalcollections.nypl.org/items/853b76bb-efb1-9410-e040-e00a180610c4> (last accessed 21 September 2021).
34. Maggie Hennefeld, *Specters of Slapstick and Silent Film Comediennes* (New York: Columbia University Press, 2018), 107–8.
35. Hennefeld, 'Death from Laughter', 46.
36. Alice Maurice, 'The Essence of Motion: Figure, Frame, and the Racial Body in Early Silent Cinema', *The Moving Image: The Journal of the Asssociation of Moving Image Archivists* 1:2 (Fall 2001), 129.
37. Maurice Charney and Hanna Charney, 'The Language of Madwomen in Shakespeare and His Fellow Dramatists', *Signs* 3:2 (1977), 452.
38. 'Pauvre mère – Albert Capellani – 1906', *Filmographie Pathé*. Available at <http://filmographie.fondation-jeromeseydoux-pathe.com/6296-pauvre-mere> (last accessed 21 September 2021).
39. Tom Gunning, 'The Impossible Body of Early Film', in Marina Dahlquist et al. (eds), *Corporeality in Early Cinema: Viscera, Skin, and Physical Form* (Bloomington: Indiana University Press, 2018), 19.
40. Richard Abel, *The Ciné Goes to Town: French Cinema, 1896–1914* (Berkeley: University of California Press, 1998), 136.
41. 'Le Cake-Walk au Nouveau Cirque', in *Dances with Darwin, 1875–1910: Vernacular Modernity in France*. Rae Beth Gordon identifies the white couple as 'Mr and Mrs Elks'. The troupe including the young brother-and-sister team, Rudy and Fredy Walker ('Les Enfants Nègres').
42. As Daphne A. Brooks notes, the 'semiotics of race and hair' are especially 'loaded'. See Brooks, *Bodies in Dissent: Spectacular Performances of Race and Freedom, 1850–1910* (Durham, NC: Duke University Press, 2006), 229.

43. Also see Diana Taylor, 'A Savage Performance: Guillermo Gómez-Peña and Coco Fusco's "Couple in the Cage"', *TDR* 42:2 (1998), 160–75.

44. Edward B. Warman, *Gestures and Attitudes: An Exposition of the Delsarte Philosophy of Expression* (Boston: Lee and Shepard, 1892), 205.

45. Ibid., 204.

46. Pearson, *Eloquent Gestures*, 22.

47. The Eye Filmmuseum (Amsterdam) version of *Amour et science* features title cards in Dutch; the card at 9:55 begins 'Max is krankzinnig . . .'

48. Edmund Shaftesbury, *Lessons in the Art of Acting* (Washington, DC: Martyn College Press, 1889), xxxiii.

49. Subdued examples include: 'Tranquil Joy' or 'Quietude', while the dramatic include 'Despair', 'Vulgar Triumph' or 'Jealous Rage'. Henry Siddons, *Practical Illustrations of Rhetorical Gesture and Action; Adapted to the English Drama from a Work on the Subject by M. Engel* (London: Sherwood, Neely and Jones, 1822), vii–viii.

50. Siddons, *Practical Illustrations*, 45. Henry Siddons was the son of the legendary tragedienne Sarah Siddons (1755–1831). He discourages tearing 'the hair in a frightful manner, which throws the whole visage into the distortions of grimace, which pants till every muscle swells, and the blood gushes up to the extended eyes'.

51. Ibid., 16–17.

52. Sam Schlappich, 'Expressing Emotions on the Screen', *Motion Picture Magazine* (August 1916), 46.

53. Frances Agnew, *Motion Picture Acting: How to Prepare for Photoplaying, What Qualifications Are Necessary, How to Secure an Engagement, Salaries Paid to Photoplayers* (Reliance Newspaper Syndicate, 1913), 40.

54. Ibid., 66.

55. Hugo Münsterberg, *The Photoplay: A Psychological Study* (New York: D. Appleton and Company, 1916), 177–8.

56. As Alice Maurice has observed, Brewster's use of 'racial taxonomies is no coincidence'. Alice Maurice, 'Making Faces: Character and Makeup in Early Cinema', in Marina Dahlquist et al. (eds), *Corporeality in Early Cinema* (Bloomington: Indiana University Press, 2018), 214.

57. Brewster, 'Expression of the Emotions (Part 2)', 107.

58. Linda Williams, 'Surprised by Blackface: D. W. Griffith and One Exciting Night', in Stephen Johnson (ed.), *Burnt Cork: Traditions and Legacies of Blackface Minstrelsy* (Amherst: University of Massachusetts Press, 2012), 136.

59. Schlappich, 'Expressing Emotions on the Screen', 47. Agnes Platt, *Practical Hints on Acting for the Cinema* (New York: E. P. Dutton, 1921), 40–1.

3. ELASTICS OF THE FILM MOUTH

Andrea Gyenge

While Michel Chion was not the first to theorise the film voice, he was perhaps the first to invest it with a kind of theoretical mystique.[1] Published in 1982, *The Voice in Cinema* not only de-naturalised a seemingly banal technical effect of sound cinema, it was also wildly faithful to its object. From the start, Chion identified the voice as fundamentally strange – 'what grist for poetic outpourings' – and even stranger yet when it came from the cinema, which had chattered relentlessly in the ear of its audiences for over fifty years.[2] That it took that long to articulate a full theory of the film voice was a testament to Chion's conviction that film theory had forgotten the voice: 'By what incomprehensible thoughtlessness can we, in considering what after all is called the talking picture, "forget" the voice? Because we confuse it with speech.'[3] Once Chion liberated the voice from the spoken, the film voice emerged as essentially bodiless, or perhaps more accurately, it acquired its most potent effects when it seemingly came from 'nowhere'. When the voice is heard but not seen, it becomes a filmic god: it sees, knows and hears all.[4] But the effect is fragile. If the voice is returned to the body, its power falters and breaks. The *acousmêtre* is thus by nature incorporeal; it is a voice without a mouth. In Chion's reading, the mouth is a terminal point, an inferior space of negative materiality, and so subordinate to the more critically significant work of the film voice, which seduces both viewer and theorist.

The cover of the English edition of *The Voice in Cinema*, however, suggests a rather different story. Four vertical stills from Hans-Jürgen Syberberg's Wagner film, *Parsifal* (1982), show an actress (Karen Krick) first in shadow, then progressively more visible in proportion to her open mouth. In the last frame, we assume that she's singing: a voice surely rings out from the void of her black throat. In Chion's Prologue, a still from Fritz Lang's *The Testament of Dr. Mabuse* (1933) serves as a frontispiece. Karl Meixner holds a phone with frantic urgency; he's leaning over the desk; his right hand is caught in mid-gesture and his eyes bulge out with desperate force. And his mouth is open – something is coming out. Is it a voice? On the next page, a still from Sergei Eisenstein's *Strike* (1925) shows the police chief with his mouth open as superimposed images flow out of the cavity. A still of a screaming mouth supports the opening of the fifth chapter, 'The Screaming Point'. Jennifer Salt in a slasher film (*Sisters*, 1972) screams an abyss into the left page. A smaller still below shows John Travolta holding a listening device to his ear in a different film (*Blow Out*, 1981), but his urgent expression offers a pedagogical instruction to hear Salt's scream. A few pages later, a close-up of Charles Foster Kane's mouth serves as the counterpoint for a chapter on auteur greats. The caption states that the mouth is saying 'Rosebud', but this mouth, bristled with moustache, is closed at the source. We are left to explore its tactile geography: trace the shape of the lips, count the facial hairs, feel the rough, shaved terrain. The four stills from *Parsifal* later reappear as a two-page spread: an ode to the mouth.

These images of the mouth appear among many other stills, including several from Alfred Hitchcock, Stanley Kubrick and Marguerite Duras. Film stills, though often unremarked upon, constitute something of a method for Chion. They function as emblems, or icons, of his cinematic interlocuters and so slices of their visual potency. All the same, the images of the mouth independently possess a kind of theoretical obviousness. A book on the voice filled with images of the mouth requires little open reflection. This is because, to paraphrase Chion, we proceed by a similar (if no less thoughtless) mistake: we confuse the voice with the mouth. We stuff every kind of sound and stutter into its open spaces. But the stills are not so easily mastered. Even as they strain to pass from image to sound – from our eyes to our ears – the mouth's specific geography, which is to say, its unique heterogeneity appears both alien and interminable. Even as an operatic signifier, Krick's open mouth solicits a chain of art historical associations cut from stone, not celluloid: Daphne's gasp (Bernini), or Laocoön's tormented sigh – both open mouths that depict sound but at the risk of letting the mouth deform vision. A second still of Meixner features a spotlight on another phone call. The open mouth and the circular lens mirror each other like a secret passageway – here cinema is more digestive than aural. Indeed, almost all the mouths reveal strings of teeth. Salt's scream is a savage bite (an animal muzzle, not a human jaw) while Meixner's anxious phone calls twist his body with the frenzy of appetite and drive.

That these images are meant to signify the voice is more an effect of Chion's theoretical logic than it is of the images themselves, which threaten to supplant the voice by unleashing the mouth's full material and visual cacophony. For every association with life and communicative power, the mouth is also a monstrous figure of excess and grotesquerie. It balloons (or shrinks) in proportion to its desires and so with it, the expanses of corporeality. Think of the Rabelaisian body, enormous and rotten with gluttonous feast. Or the mouth that gives fleshy support for the force of vomit. Pleasure becomes death: sour, acidic, guilty. Or those Freudian nightmares of missing teeth and diseases of the inner cheeks – anxieties that stay caught, literally, in the paralysis of the throat. A seemingly infinite object – never itself, always other – the mouth is thus more befitting to 'delirium' than acousmatics, more kindred to an infinite recital of its manic forms than sober, systematic reflection.[5] As such, even as Chion offers a highly idiosyncratic and playful meditation on the *acousmêtre*, which moves from high auteur cinemas to low-brow horror films with ease, the mouth still ultimately suggest something unthought in his contribution. That these polyphonous images of the mouth appear as film images, moreover, allow that the mouth might constitute something entirely different in the history of the cinema, something even more strange and elusive than that of the voice. In fact, I want to argue that *The Voice in Cinema* is a theory of the mouth, or at least, if not yet a theory, a text that keeps silent counsel with the mouth's allure. By any stretch of the imagination, 'La bouche au cinéma' would constitute an entirely legible theoretical sequel. Even without the overdetermined images of open mouths, Chion's text is suffused with trace marks, clues or otherwise notable 'oral' inflections. In early pages, Chion likens a film's visual power to an oral cavity: 'Certain audio elements (essentially those referred to as synchronous, i.e., whose apparent source is visible onscreen) can be immediately "swallowed" up in the image's false depth.'[6] Later, filmic narrative offers another opportunity for oral metaphor: 'The proof is that so-called synchronous sounds are most often forgotten as such, being "swallowed up" by the fiction.'[7] Elsewhere, a film scream violently 'gobbles everything up into itself'.[8] In Chion, cinema has an appetite for its own formal power. Sometimes sound, sometimes image, but always a force best likened to a mouth.[9] Perhaps the oceanic liquefaction that so horrified Barthes (that is, cinema as cocoon) isn't the best metaphor for cinema's particular kind of singular seduction.[10] Chion, for his part, seems to prefer orality for describing the vast reach of cinema's aesthetic power: 'this omnivorous and diverse art'.[11]

Chion's preference, this subterranean strand of mouth metaphors, is never fully squared with the more official theoretical account of the *acousmêtre*, which positions the mouth as form of suffocating materiality. Indeed, it's not only that the *acousmêtre* is a voice without a mouth, it's a voice that's broken free from its earthly counterpart, a counterpart that threatens to unseat its transcendent twin by returning the voice to the body. For Chion, the cinematic example par excellence is Fritz Lang's aforementioned *The Testament to Dr Mabuse* (1933), which presents a formal lesson in acousmatic logics: a voice terrifies and seduces, until its origin (a machine and a man) is revealed. The *acousmêtre*, therefore, is only as secure as the image that refuses to show its source. The mouth becomes a site of erotic speculation and wonder – most itself when it is not seen. Waiting to see the mouth from which this unholy voice originates finds comparison with the striptease: 'The process doesn't necessarily happen all at once; it can be progressive. In much the same way that the female genitals are the end point revealed by undressing . . . there is an end point of de-acousmatization – the mouth from which the voice issues.'[12] Later, the voice returning to the body is likened to sexual penetration: sound enters the mouth and becomes impure and adulterated. As soon as the body of a voice appears on screen, '*de-acousmatization*, which results from finally showing the person speaking, is always like a defloration. For at that point, the voice loses its virginal-acousmatic powers.'[13] Once captured by the mouth, the *acousmêtre* goes limp in a disappointing body, the dull specificity of this body here. No amount of bodily strangeness or narrative twist can compete against the fermenting fantasies of an unseen mouth. Between seduction and disappointment, searching for the film mouth always has the air of a psycho-sexual drama. Ironically, and so counter to nearly every association, Chion thus proposes that where there is the mouth, there can be no *acousmêtre*, or put differently, there can be no desire. The mouth is poor but lethal – it is where the voice goes to die.

If the mouth is the death of desire, at least from the point of view of any film whose logic depends on the *acousmêtre*, Chion's own use of mouth stills (and metaphors) appears clearly unresolved. These images are not masters of desire; they are open, potent catalysts. They are equal parts silent and raucous, empty and full. They carve a void into the celluloid that solicits the eye to an otherwise, an elsewhere. The open mouth promises unseen interiority but refuses entry. It keeps vigil at a threshold and so tempts the gaze. The eye burns out in search; the eye flares up and sees brightly. Cinema erupts out from the centre of the face: open mouth or black celluloid, open mouth or the black screen, open mouth or the dark of the theatre. Is there any other part of the body filmed that resembles cinematic space so intimately and without metaphor? All the same, the mouth is always shut, agape or not. It's the home of a secret – where desire takes germ and flowers. Chion notes that before the advent of sound cinema, cinema's relationship to the imaginary hung on its power to generate fantasies of sound. In the age of silent cinema, when voices were nothing more than echoes of imagined things, the mouth thus nourished the pleasures of dreams, an oneiric sensibility.[14] The arrival of sound put an end to this desiring intimacy, this dream-like stance: 'We're no longer allowed to dream the voices – in fact, *to dream period*: according to Marguerite Duras, the cinema has "closed off" the imaginary' [his emphasis].[15] What if this relation to dreams was not a matter of unheard voices or sonic longing but of the mouth's own polyphony as an image of cinema's relation to the imaginary?

As if to confirm the strange potency of his film stills, Chion realises late that a return to the mouth actually guarantees nothing, least of all the surety of the voice: 'If talking cinema has shown anything by restoring voices to bodies, it's precisely that it doesn't hang together; it's decidedly not a seamless match.'[16] Moreover, this alienation between the voice and the body opens a cinematic aporia, which is to say, opens the question of cinema's limit: 'If there is a *somewhere* of the voice, a place that is the place of vocal production, is the cinema capable of filming it?'[17] In offering the mouth as a question for cinematic representation, Chion first confirms what his film stills have suggested from the beginning: that the link between the voice and the mouth is indeed symbolic. Chion repeats his thesis – that the *acousmêtre* functions most powerfully 'it can't be strictly localized to the symbolic place of vocal production . . . when the mouth isn't visible' – but acknowledges that the mouth is really a matter of cinematic convention.[18] He offers a chain of body parts and functions that participate in vocality as demonstration that the mouth is but one of many bodily organs that produce vocal sounds.[19] In fact, Chion argues that 'one could reasonably contest the idea that the mouth is the sole place to film as the source of vocal production' but finally decides that the mouth is chosen because it 'affords the more precise cues for synchronization'.[20] Its appearance on screen is thus both a psychic and technical effect. It dampens the voice and its spectral powers while simultaneously 'authoriz[ing] belief' in the film apparatus itself.[21] If the acousmatic voice is a fantasy of omnipotent power, the mouth only destroys it so as to launch a greater power: that of the cinema itself, which presents moving images to our eyes and ears with an existential veracity.

This would place the mouth at the forefront of sound cinema as its technical and symbolic foundation were not for the fact that Chion speculates whether cinema is even 'capable of filming it'.[22] At first, it seems as if the question is merely a technical one. If body and voice cannot fully merge together, even with the best equipment, then perhaps it's just a problem of history. Eventually some telos will perfect the technology. But Chion is clear. It's not a failure of the apparatus; it's an ontological problem. Cinema *is* the separation of voice and body, even as it tries to force their mutual appearance. This separation, however, is as rooted in the mouth's relationship to cinematic representation as it is to cinema's own formal structure. Indeed, as Chion discovers, the mouth has a history in the cinema that long predates the advances of sound. In fact, the mouth is a singular figure, an *originary* image of unrepresentability: 'It's as if one of the first challenges of the movies was to film this black hole, this dispenser of life, this cavity which threatens to devour everything.'[23] It's no surprise then that 'the mouth may well be the first part of the human body ever shot in close-up'.[24] For his part, Chion attributes the mouth's early history in silent cinema to an 'oral fixation' rooted in our originary bond with the mother.[25] While this reading suits Chion's inventive psychoanalytic method, which inserts Freudian nuance wherever the voice seems stubbornly resistant to interpretation, it offers a rather unsatisfying account of the mouth's historical 'challenge' to the cinema.[26] If the mouth is a focal point of obsession in early cinema, one which has its psychic roots in infantile drives shaped by oral pleasure, it doesn't explain why the mouth poses a problem for filmic representation nor indeed why Chion himself fills his own text with cinematic mouths. It does, however, suggest that Chion has no more a precise explanation for the mouth's strangeness on screen than Freud's attribution of oral obsessions to the earliest forms of auto-erotism and infantile desire. While I am sympathetic to Chion's Freudian hermeneutics, in this case, the Freudian landing ultimately serves to obfuscate Chion's original question: 'If there is a *somewhere* of the voice, a place that is the place of vocal production, is the cinema capable of filming it?'[27]

Even though he ultimately turns to Freud, Chion does leave us with one other provocative clue. Book-ended by his comments on the close-up and the mouth's devouring force, Chion cites James Williamson's *The Big Swallow* as the origin for his reflections on the mouth in cinema:

> The mouth may well be the first part of the human body that the movies ever shot in closeup. In a 1901 short by the British photographer James A. Williamson, *The Big Swallow*, the person who is the 'big swallower' approaches the camera threateningly. His mouth opens as wide as a house to swallow up the camera, the cameraman, the image (which goes totally dark) and in a way, the spectator too. It's as if one of the first challenges for the movies was to film this black hole, this dispenser of life, this cavity that threatens to devour everything.[28]

In attempting to account for the mouth's relationship to filmic representation, it's not surprising that Chion finds inspiration in Williamson's meditation on orality. An early innovator of the silent era and a member of the Brighton School, Williamson produced nearly 200 films during his lifetime. Of these, *The Big Swallow* is the most famous, especially for its use of trick effects and its humorous (if slightly sinister) offering of cinema's elasticity of perspective. Even by 1912, the film had struck early film critics as an 'extraordinary film . . . which created no little amount of astonishment . . . and was decidedly startling in its effect'.[29] Nearly a century later, *The Big Swallow* found new company in theorists of the 'cinema of attraction'. In this context *The Big Swallow* is a kind of a lubricant for early film historiography, a film that easily confirms the thesis of show as early cinema's essential spectatorial draw and boldness of invention.[30] In *Cinema of*

Attractions: Reloaded, Wanda Strauven, for example, lists as *The Big Swallow* as the earliest film in a canonised list of 'most cited "attractions"' while Tom Gunning himself takes up the film in detail in a recent essay.[31] Notably, however, Chion makes little of the film's trick history or its historiographical significance. He stays close to the mouth – as if to suggest that the theoretical power of *The Big Swallow* originates wholly in the mouth's inviolable status as a material force that provokes a specific visual disturbance or impossibility. Indeed, if something attracts Chion here, which is to say, if something calls vision into a field of potency and impact, it's seemingly the oral cavity itself now spectacularly brought to the film screen while menacing the spectator – and cinema itself – with disappearance and death. Art history readers will recall that the mouth was also fodder for controversy long before Williamson thought to film it. The German Enlightenment, among other things, was galvanised by a debate over the Laocoön statue's mouth, which exchanged the expected scream for a softened sigh, even though the statue depicted explicit pain through muscle and pose. Gotthold Ephraim Lessing, perhaps the debate's most famous representative, insisted that the mouth is a stain on the visible that mars an artwork beyond recuperation.[32] His stated distaste for the mouth, however, never fully succeeded in hiding his fascination for a statue that might have violently screamed in the end. Showing the full force of an open mouth thus remained a tantalising image for figural art, one which also threatened to drive aesthetic thought to ruin by tempting it towards a hole that snuffed out meaning in exchange for visceral encounter. As such, an open mouth often comes with the whiff of aesthetic scandal and its appearance in *The Big Swallow* belies a much older history, if not also a kind of indecent inheritance. If cinema was a nascent art capable of 'magical possibilities', what better image than that of a 'big swallow' to mark its power to attract?[33] If Laocoön wants to scream, cinema will not just film it, it will follow the scream, camera and all, to the abyss – quite literally. Thomas Elsaesser's account of the history of 3D technology, for instance, situates *The Big Swallow* as one of several early films that contested Renaissance perspective, which cinema had already begun to reinforce by treating the screen, in effect, as a canvas and frame.[34] *The Big Swallow* entered the canon only by virtue of this violation of perspectival norms – what Elsaesser calls the film's 'impossible spaces'.[35] Given the mouth's abundant visual history, especially as a candidate for all things repulsive, it's no surprise that Williamson saw the mouth, even unconsciously, as *the* vehicle for an experiment in spatial arrangement. Chion's clandestine sense, however, is that this willingness to fall into the mouth is not so much a question of cinema's technical agility or its iconoclastic verve as it is a question of the film's speculative gesture towards its own threshold of visibility.

Even though it is barely a minute long, *The Big Swallow* can be divided into two parts. The first part stages the ethical problem that ostensibly shapes the action of the entire film. The camera is stationary; it captures a man reading on the street. The threat of surveillance lurks: an impassive technological gaze is met with anger and suspicion. The camera's presence is a disruption of the right to be private in public – the right *not* to be watched. After politely refusing the camera's intrusion, the man delivers an increasingly vociferous speech. Anticipating a fight, he removes his glasses and starts waving his cane around, a pantomime of the violence to come, if the filming continues. History tells us this rage was portrayed by an actor (Sam Dalton), and not an actual passerby, but its authenticity is not lessened by its fiction. Almost 120 years later, the body's filmic movements are still entirely transparent. The immediate legibility of his irritation, the deep familiarity of anger on camera all coalesce around a body that broadcasts meaning through kinetic dynamism. His body thus performs its submission to a new technological and social order precisely by expressing its antagonism as something visible. It's the trap of the camera: the more he refuses, the more *cinematic* he becomes. At this point in the film, the mouth is a driver of gesture. The rapid movements of Dalton's mouth are matched with a whole catalogue of movements that function like words, as if his mouth has overtaken his body and captured it for its own signifying purposes.[36] This tendency in silent cinema is usually read as a function of vocal lack.[37] If the voice cannot be heard, then the body's physical intensity will 'shout' so as to fill the silence with visual sound. We thus hear the body rather than see it, which accounts for the sense that *The Big Swallow* is a loud film, even though it is silent. What is interesting about the film, however, is that it's not quite obeying the silent cinema script that subordinates everything to the missing voice and imagined sound. Verbal threats, wild gestures, body dramas – nothing works like it should. The camera doesn't move, the spectator is still the giggling and disobedient voyeur, and the frustrated man is now stuck in front of the camera.

But as the film continues, his body and mouth undergo a transformation. Instead of stepping out of the frame, the man inexplicably begins to move *closer* to the camera he despises. As he comes forward, his mouth begins to affect a strange, oral performance. What we might have recognised as a mouth issuing words becomes a hole opening, closing, pursing, inflating – all in rapid, if fragmented, succession. It seems less a mouth than a machine, less a face than a geography of buccal flow. The jaw yammers up and down; it moves to the side; it stops or starts; it contorts and expands. It feels as if the camera can barely keep up with the performance on his face. The mouth, now the author of *illegible* movements, threatens to overtake the camera with both speed and elasticity. As the man's face finally arrives at the front edge of the camera, the screen blurs and the scene is wrecked. But while one power recedes; another arrives. The man's facial hair suddenly sharpens, comes into focus. A detail (his mouth) appears. The world at a distance becomes a different world unveiled. As if to mark this transformation, the man's mouth yawns open and reveals a massive, abyssal hole. It fills the screen entirely: the black nothing of the throat becomes the black nothing of the screen. Flat distance becomes intimate interiority. If the spectator felt assured of their superior position relative to the man captured by the camera, this security is violently dismantled. His experimental mouth is now a camera, its throat is the aperture of the lens. It wants to see and eat *all*. Immediately, we realise that *we* have been subject to the same technological gaze all along – it orders the very space we occupy. Cinematic space is now the space around us – it envelops us completely; 3D vision indeed. It sees us from behind, from the side, from every possible vantage point. The solution to surveillance becomes, in short, its ultimate confirmation. As if he too recognises the truth of this structural gesture, the cameraman, suddenly faced with the void of Dalton's mouth in the horizon of his vision, panics and falls into its pit. Unmoored from the world, he loses all sense of direction and placement. The shot then reverses and the man chews as he recedes into the distance. The gestures are exaggerated, muscular and like a child proving he has taken his medicine, he opens his mouth to confirm the camera's disappearance into the path of digestion. The film's thesis is thus both simple and disturbing: cinema is not just an eye; it's a *mouth*. And this mouth never closes, its throat never sleeps. Always another shot, another image, to infinity.

In *The Big Swallow*, therefore, the mouth is not a metaphor; it literally expresses the aperture of the lens as the unveiling of the world as an image. As the object of filmic vision, the mouth *shows* the cinema's capacity to show: it goes where the human eye cannot, and so becomes a technology of immeasurable power. Under the gaze of the camera, the mouth is a seemingly endless architecture of possible knowledge and an entrance to the body's secret spaces. Here, the cinema is the mouth's revelation: its induction into the realm of both scientific and aesthetic truth. But as a visible limit to the body's interiority, the open mouth and its receding throat also hold out the promise of images to come – a vision beyond vision. If Descartes's telescope opened the distant world to close knowledge, then Williamson's mouth opens the *unseen* as cinema's essential identity. It's not only just what comes to sight; it's what remains at the edge of visibility like a glowing horizon, or in this case, a black screen that communicates nothing but its power to bring appearance into being. The threshold of the mouth, therefore, functions as a threshold of visual history. As such, everything is anticipated here: the advent of endoscopic imaging, dental photographs, ultrasounds and CT scans but perhaps also deep-sea imaging or the live feed of the Mars Rover. In this sense, *The Big Swallow* inaugurates what Elsaesser calls 'technologies of probing and penetration'.[38] By advancing towards the throat, its camera might be closer to something like a tactical camera meant to penetrate 'enemy' tunnels or a drone camera floating above treacherous spaces of pollution than it is to panoptic vision or narrative storytelling.[39] Even though it is Dalton's mouth, this mouth proposes a posthuman sight beyond history, technical meaning or aesthetic truth. For as soon as the mouth opens into a black screen, empty of content, it takes leave of the face and becomes an image born of a machine. Divorced from faciality, *The Big Swallow* thus liberates the mouth from its subjectivised container and by extension, cinematic perception.[40] After all, for Chion, *The Big Swallow* is not a film of triumphant technological advance that upholds an Enlightenment imaginary of optics, power and subjectivity. Rather, it poses cinema's representational limit as an essential formal question. The mouth, which 'threatens to devour everything', never ceases to resist cinema's claim to presenting reality to our eyes and ears.[41] The film's technical gaze is always bound up in its own impossibility. It's as if the film's representational power paradoxically hinges on its relationship to nothingness: cinema as a place of neutrality or imagelessness. There where it sees maximally, it also sees and films nothing. The mouth thus animates filmic representation with extreme dialectical force – across genre, history and form.

Even before Chion arrives to his reflection on Williamson's film, he identifies the film scream as posing modern variants of this problem. As he argues, a film scream, most often uttered by a woman, unleashes more than the force of sound: 'it becomes a sort of an ineffable black hole' that eats the entire narrative apparatus, as if it was 'made in order to be consumed and dissipated, in the unthinkableness and instantaneity of this scream'.[42] The oral metaphors are again notable – the scream is, first and foremost, a *mouth*, but a mouth that evades identity or representation. The scream is a visceral, material power but its explosive force is not due to its sonic violence. In fact, a film scream is silent at its terminal 'point', akin to the peaceful eye of a hurricane, where time, duration and sense suspend themselves in a space of absolute nothing.[43] For Chion, 'the screaming point is a point of the unthinkable inside the thought, of the indeterminate inside the spoken, of unrepresentability inside representation'.[44] Its power rests less on audible sound as it does on its existence as a mouth that confounds the very terrain of representation: '[t]he screaming point is where speech is suddenly extinct, a black hole, the exit of being.'[45] Over and over, therefore, Chion points us back to the mouth as some inexplicable foundation of cinematic imaging – its testing of the visible and perhaps too of the human. His turn to *The Big Swallow* as the last example of this oral thread keeps us likewise attuned to the critical importance of the mouth in the film. In his reading of Williamson, Tom Gunning argues that the film organises the creation of what he calls 'film's impossible body' by birthing new forms of corporeality that are beyond the limits of human embodiment.[46] Early cinema, by adventuring into bodily space, produced 'a flexible, polymorphic body that could turn itself out, engulfing the world, even as it projected its gaze beyond itself'.[47] Later, Gunning emphasises that '[c]inema technology creates a body we could never have, but one that, like technological prothesis, extends and transforms the affordances of our natural body'.[48] But Gunning, oddly enough, makes little of the fact that such an imaginary rests on filming a bodily organ that is itself the domain of impossible and infinitely contradictory events. When the body convulses and throws food out, is this not itself a kind of organic impossibility? Or when the same space that chews food like an animal uses its erogenous sensitivity to lovingly (or aggressively) taste the body of another, is it not also suddenly flexible and projective? Is the mouth not itself *already* a space where all things 'human' expand and move beyond a physical limit? What is the mouth if not *the* image of an elasticity of being and body that throws itself, constantly, into an otherwise?

This is not to return cinema, as Gunning himself warns, to some notion of an organic totality or bodily origin that might orient cinema in a kind of vital, naturalism.[49] On the contrary, I want to argue that the mouth, especially the mouth in cinema, is a kind of 'non-fact' that refuses to conform to a single, still body – to some tranquility of being or representation. Yes, the mouth is obviously material, but its materiality is kaleidoscopic and virtual. *The Big Swallow* is thus rather *plural* than singular. It's the mouth that speaks, then the mouth that jabbers strangely, then the mouth that swallows, chews, spits and laughs. Recall, for instance, Jean-Luc Nancy's description of the oral cavity in his reading of Descartes, which reads indeed as if he is thinking instead of *The Big Swallow*. He writes:

> [t]he mouth: the orifice the elastic pulped edge of which draw the mobile contours of the opening of a sense that is each time other, singular, thrown and suspended in various ways, interrupted, without accomplishment, so it can better retain in suspense the force of its impulse.[50]

Scattered across Chion's text as silent supports to his meditation on Williamson, the film stills now perhaps read as so many slices of this anonymous and open impulse – singular, thrown and suspended across Chion's text as a cinematic experiment in orality.[51] There is sounding here, yes, but not only. The film mouth might let loose keening voices, but domesticate them it does not. On the contrary, it offers sound as one of its generous intimacies, its solicitation to a thought (Chion's) that cannot but wander toward its filmic origins in 'this black hole, this dispenser of life, this cavity that threatens to devour everything'.[52] If the film mouth was once, as Chion teaches us, the domain of something like a dream, where spectators, theorists and filmmakers came to wander the expanse of the imaginary, it has, in truth, never lost that power. There is no singular mouth, only an opening that draws us, and the world, into a cinematic ecstasy at the limit – an image of the edge, split wide.

NOTES

1. See, for example, Mary Ann Doane's 'The Voice in the Cinema: The Articulation of Body and Space', in Philip Rosen (ed.), *Narrative, Apparatus, Ideology: A Film Theory Reader* (New York: Columbia University Press, 1986), 335–48; and Pascal

Bonitzer's 'The Silences of the Voice', trans. Philip Rosen and Marcia Butzel, in Philip Rosen (ed.), *Narrative, Apparatus, Ideology: A Film Theory Reader* (New York: Columbia University Press, 1986), 319–34.

2. Michel Chion, *The Voice in Cinema*, trans. Claudia Gorbman (New York: Columbia University Press, 1999), 1.

3. Chion, *Voice in Cinema*, 1.

4. Ibid., 24.

5. Brandon LaBelle, *Lexicon of the Mouth: Poetics and Politics of Voice and the Oral Imaginary* (London: Bloomsbury Publishing, 2014), 2.

6. Chion, *Voice in Cinema*, 3.

7. Ibid., 3.

8. Ibid., 79.

9. Ibid., 79.

10. Roland Barthes, 'Leaving the Movie Theatre', in *The Rustle of Language*, trans. Richard Howard (New York: Hill and Wang, 1986), 346.

11. Chion, *Voice in Cinema*, 79.

12. Ibid., 28.

13. Ibid., 23.

14. Ibid., 8.

15. Ibid., 9.

16. Ibid., 125.

17. Ibid., 127.

18. Ibid., 127.

19. Ibid., 127.

20. Ibid., 128.

21. Ibid., 127.

22. Ibid., 127.

23. Ibid., 127.

24. Ibid., 127.

25. Ibid., 128.

26. Ibid., 127.

27. Ibid., 127.

28. Ibid., 127.

29. Frederick Talbot, *Moving Pictures: How They Are Made and Worked* (London: William Heinemann, 1912), 254. See also Frank Gray's commentary on Talbot and pre-war criticism re. Williamson in *The Brighton School and the Birth of British Film* (Cham: Springer International Publishing AG, 2019), 17–38.

30. Tom Gunning, 'The Cinema of Attraction[s]: Early Film, Its Spectator and the Avant-Garde', in Wanda Strauven (ed.), *The Cinema of Attractions Reloaded* (Amsterdam: Amsterdam University Press, 2006), 381–2.

31. Wanda Strauven, 'Introduction to an Attractive Concept', in Wanda Strauven (ed.), *The Cinema of Attractions Reloaded* (Amsterdam: Amsterdam University Press, 2006), 24.

32. Gotthold Ephraim Lessing, *Laocoön: An Essay Upon the Limits of Painting and Poetry*, trans. Ellen Frothingham (Mineola, NY: Dover Publications, 2005), 14.

For an extended discussion of the importance of the mouth to German aesthetics, especially Lessing's *Laocoön*, see my essay, 'Laocoön's Scream; or Lessing Redux', *New German Critique* 48:1 (142) (2021), 41–70.

33. Gunning, 'Cinema of Attractions', 383.
34. Thomas Elsaesser, 'The "Return" of 3-D: On Some of the Logics and Genealogies of the Image in the Twenty-first Century', *Critical Inquiry* 39:2 (2013), 231.
35. Ibid., 231.
36. Doane, 'The Voice in the Cinema', 335.
37. Ibid., 335.
38. Elsaesser, 'The "Return" of 3-D', 242.
39. Ibid., 242.
40. See Deleuze and Guattari's chapter 'Year Zero: Faciality', in *A Thousand Plateaus*, trans. Brian Massumi (Minneapolis: University of Minnesota Press, 1987).
41. Chion, *Voice in Cinema*, 128.
42. Ibid., 76.
43. Ibid., 76–7, 79.
44. Ibid., 77.
45. Ibid., 79.
46. Tom Gunning, 'The Impossible Body of Early Film', in Marina Dahlquist et al. (eds), *Corporeality in Early Cinema: Viscera, Skin, and Physical Form* (Bloomington: Indiana University Press, 2018), 18–19. Gunning draws his analysis, among other things, from Jennifer Barker's comments on *The Big Swallow*, which are rooted in a phenomenological approach to touch and cinematic perception. See Barker's 'Conclusion' from *The Tactile Eye: Touch and Cinematic Experience* (Berkeley: University of California Press, 2009), 157–60. See also Akira Mizuta Lippit's comments in *Atomic Light: Shadow Optics* (Minneapolis: University of Minnesota Press, 2005), 73, where he identifies the film as producing a form of 'film psychology, a deep interiority'.
47. Gunning, 'The Impossible Body of Early Film', 19.
48. Ibid., 22.
49. Ibid., 18.
50. Jean-Luc Nancy, *Ego Sum: Corpus, Anima, Fabula*, trans. Marie-Eve Morin (New York: Fordham University Press, 2016), xi.
51. Ibid., xi.
52. Chion, *Voice in Cinema*, 127.

4. THE PROBLEM OF RECOGNITION: CELEBRITY FACES, *PHOTOGÉNIE* AND FACIAL RECOGNITION TECHNOLOGIES

Aaron Tucker

INTRODUCTION

Clare Garvie's Georgetown Law Center on Privacy and Technology 2019 report 'Garbage In, Garbage Out' begins by detailing the problematic use of celebrity headshots as 'probe images' within law enforcement use of facial recognition technologies (FRTs): after unsuccessfully processing grainy footage through their FRT, the New York Police Department officers noticed that the suspect resembled movie star Woody Harrelson; they then used Google image search results of Harrelson within their FRT to identify their shoplifting suspect. This practice is not uncommon as the report also recounts prior incidents where photos of famous basketball players were utilised in a similar manner. Within these instances, the famous faces' public circulation, combined with the recognisability of celebrities' faces, made the images of the celebrities' faces useful strategic materials within the apparatus of FRT.[1]

The examples outlined by Garvie are a reminder that famous faces have been central to the development, application and improvement of FRT from the beginnings of its history. Under the theme of 'Progress and Harmony for Mankind', the 1970 World Expo in Osaka, Japan and the Nippon Electric Company (NEC) Pavilion hosted a piece titled 'Computer Physiognomy'. As described within Takeo Kanade's *Computer Recognition of Human Faces*, the exhibit was the first public demonstration of a FRT in which 'a person sits before a Picamera, the picture of [their] face is digitised and fed into the computer . . . [and their] face is classified into one of seven categories, each of which is represented by a very famous person'.[2] A full list of the included celebrity faces is not provided in the text; however, in a 2015 talk, Kanade details how it required the person to stay exactly still for three seconds while their face was digitised, after which their face would be matched to one of faces such as 'Marilyn Monroe, Winston Churchill, John F. Kennedy'.[3] From the engineers' perspectives, the exhibit was a relatively straight-forward tech-demo that leveraged both the spectacle of celebrity faces and emerging computational wizardry.

The NEC described its 'Computer Physiognomy' as a 'magnifying glass' and billed it as a well-received wonder that was actually quite intimate in how it 'connected image processing technology with personality analysis'.[4] Yet, the inclusion of images of celebrity faces within the NEC's exhibit, in particular that of movie stars like Marilyn Monroe, links this early tech-demo to 2021 instances of FRT where many machine learning facial databases utilise celebrity faces as training materials; the more well-known databases include: YouTube Faces in the Wild, CelebA, MS-Celeb-1M, and ibug but many others exist on sites like Kaggle.[5] 'Computer Physiognomy' anticipates and/or creates the desire to utilise famous faces within its data practices, using celebrity faces' recognisable qualities alongside the readily available and public-facing wealth of facial image data (in the form of headshots, interviews, film stills) to prototype, train and improve FRT.

This phenomenon of famous faces in FRT can be better understood by examining the technology in relation to notions of faces that are photogenic. Stemming from the straightforward definitions of photogenic as describing those who are attractive in photos or on film, this basic notion has been extrapolated further by thinkers like Jean Epstein and Roland Barthes.[6] However, 'Computer Physiognomy' did not display such faces at a movie theatre-sized scale but rather at the scales of a TV screen and computer monitor. The intense multiplication and extreme distribution of famous faces on a more life-sized scale within 'Computer Physiognomy' reflects changing attitudes towards the recognisable spectacle of technologically mediated famous faces and how such faces circulate freely and deliberately as public commodities. When such logics are co-opted into a contemporary FRT, those under the gaze of FRT, famous and not, become subject to the same principles of public circulation, producing data practices where individuals, and their facial data, are also viewed as public commodities. FRTs instrumentalise the faces under its gaze, effectively deploying the power of the photogenic from the movie-theatre screen at the level of individual body.

Kelly Gates voices a similar sentiment on her reflection on the NEC exhibition: 'Imagine that in 1970, the experience of having a computer scan and analyse one's own face might have impressed upon the sitter a powerful sense of her own future subjection to information processing machines.'[7] Extending from Gates, not only are nearly half of American citizens already enrolled in a government facial database, but FRTs are rationalised as objective machines capable of efficiently categorising and sorting individuals and populations.[8] Dovetailing with the use of famous faces in FRT, such thinking is compounded further by considerations of Jean Epstein's concept of *photogénie*, a quasi-spiritual conviction in the supreme power of cinema's abilities to capture time and movement; the quality of *photogénie* is exemplified by the cinematic face in close-up. However, Epstein goes further in tying *photogénie*'s functioning to moral judgements; recalling the NEC's description of 'Computer Physiognomy', *photogénie* reveals the 'truth' underneath the face, and, for those captured on film, wherein 'their heredity [is] made evident, their past [becomes] unforgettable, their future [is] already present'.[9] That a person's moral standing is a combination of their hereditary elements as well as their behaviour aligns *photogénie* with physiognomic logics. Yet, as the chapter will detail, Epstein does not frame *photogénie* in the scientific discourses that nineteenth-century advocates of physiognomy did, but rather as a potential interrogatory tactic, separating the guilty from the innocent and thereby providing the machinery for a media capable of automated decision making. Following this trajectory, FRTs require a re-examination of *photogénie* in the current moment: contemporary computer vision, in particular FRTs, encompasses much of what Epstein admires, but enhances analogue film's abilities to splice images of the face into minute fractions of movement and time in order to computationally process those under the apparatus's gaze; those fractions are then tied into other algorithmic non-human (visual) systems of computerised categorisation and identification that act as automated and decentralised decision makers. This does not eradicate the racist and gendered vision of physiognomic vision but rather more deeply inscribes such biases into the operation of FRTs, with the reliance on famous faces amplifying such logics.

The problems of celebrity faces and *photogénie* within FRTs are therefore threefold: the use of famous faces within database and AI training normalises the face as an open source of data to be freely used; that once those faces are enrolled in a database, the instrumentalised facial data is used to sort and categorise individuals and populations under the guise of a superior and transcendent vision that echoes much of the description of Epstein's *photogénie*; and finally, FRT results are not in fact objective but are shaped by the over-inclusion of white faces within training facial databases, activating what Simone Browne flags as a 'white prototypicality'.[10] One should not ignore the dominance of white, Hollywood, and Western-centric celebrity faces in 'Computer Physiognomy', which is particularly jarring when placed within the setting of a World Fair. The disproportionate inclusion of white, often male faces within Hollywood culture, as reflected within 'Computer Physiognomy', is also reflected within the composition of current facial data sets composed of celebrity faces.

When the *photogénie* of FRTs is paired with such data practices, the technology becomes a prime illustration of the white default body in the design and implementation of digital technologies. Utilising celebrity faces as normalised templates of facial data reifies the cultural bias present in spaces like Hollywood cinema and popular culture, optimising for the subjective qualities of the photogenic face. When such practices are combined within a media, like FRT, that houses an evolutionary form of *photogénie*, there is the real risk that the subjective construction of the photogenic is potentially equated to subjective moral qualities and alleged hereditary history recalling the racist and eugenic logics underlying nineteenth-century physiognomy.

THE CULTURAL CIRCULATION OF THE FAMOUS FACE

The cropped facial images that populate FRT databases and training materials owe a great debt to the visual language of the cinematic face in close-up: the central framing of the face, made its most visible by light and pose, may not be borrowed directly from cinema, but the close-up was instrumental in making such treatments of the face normalised; Mary Ann Doane contends that the close-up, in particular that of a face, is part of cinema's 'universal language' and acts as its 'most recognisable unit[s] of cinematic discourse'.[11] More than that, the close-up was built for the most photogenic of faces: as Béla Balázs argues, 'A film star has to be beautiful. This requirement, one that is never made of stage actors in so absolute and unqualified a manner, is a further feature of film';[12] further, Barthes, in 'The Face of Garbo', says that the close-up of the human face is a sort of 'philtre', a love potion that makes the drinker fall in love with whoever gave it to them.[13] From this, celebrity faces are produced to be beautiful and mesmerising, and their cultural and material circulation reinforces the famous face as magnetic and spectacular, fulfilling desires for both beauty and renown. These magical qualities, when combined with the proliferation of images of famous faces make the inclusion of faces like Monroe's and Kennedy's seem like a natural fit within the NEC's exhibit.

However, in contrast to 'Computer Physiognomy', a large part of the cinematic close-up's appeal is its massive scale. Doane argues that the close-up's oscillation between the extreme detail in diegesis and its gigantic impact from the spectator's perceptive state creates an important tension between the face's individuality and its generalisability.[14] Indeed, as the 1970 World Fair was also the debut of the first IMAX film, cinema technology was also expanding at the moment of the NEC exhibition to include even larger images of the face.[15] By contrast, the use of the close-up within 'Computer Physiognomy' shrinks this scale to life-sized and smaller: when they appear as human-viewable images, they are on computer monitors and TV screens; the faces, when digitised for computational processing, are even smaller and more ephemeral, reduced to data patterns for more effective and efficient processing.[16] The tensions that Doane points out are transformed: the face on screen in 'Computer Physiognomy' and the datafied faces undergo similar oscillations of scale, but substitute the spectacle of the movie-screen-sized face for the wonder attached to the FRT's technological prowess. In the way, the dynamics within Doane's thinking are reversed, wherein the datafied faces are the generalised but spectacular versions that are polar to the individualised life-sized faces being captured by the technology.

This rescaling makes the cinematic face less spectacular; further, matching those famous faces to the general public further equates the two, normalising the production and wide circulation of all faces as if they were celebrities for public consumption. While outside the scope of this paper, it is worth stating that FRT's treatment of the famous face perhaps has more in common with Pop Art sensibilities than it does Hollywood cinema; for example, Andy Warhol's treatment of famous faces foregrounded those faces' – and the promotional materials used for the circulation of those faces' – existence as public goods, to be used and manipulated as needed.[17] There is no sense in the documentation of 'Computer Physiognomy' that the designers and engineers thought any differently: the famous faces were a readily available data set that would provide an engaging hook to demonstrate their biometric. There is a similar absence of reflection upon the choices of faces in the internal documents of the aforementioned examples of contemporary facial databases that utilise celebrity faces: there is no need to ask permission to use such faces as the materials exist in the public sphere and are therefore freely available to adapt into various stages of an FRT.

The problem is then that this attitude about the use of famous faces is transferred to non-public faces, wherein any face under the gaze of a FRT is available to be used freely. This extends further to the composition of data sets: as just one example, IBM's Diversity in Faces data set was discontinued in part after it was revealed that the data set was composed of faces taken without direct consent from Flickr accounts that had made their photos available under a Creative Commons licence. Returning to Kanade's description of 'Computer Physiognomy', he states that 688 public faces from the exhibition were harvested for later FRT experimentation, mentioning nothing about whether it was consensual or if the public even knew such faces were being kept for later databases; he laments not having better protocols, as he claims they could have collected thousands of faces instead. It is not only about quantity: in *Picture Processing System by Computer Complex and Recognition of Human Faces*, he states the exhibit was especially effective at gathering a wide variety of faces (bearded and with glasses as two examples) that would make further improvements and FRT experiments more effective.[18] This extractive attitude has reigned supreme through the development of FRTs, and lingers in examples

such as the establishment and use of entities like Clearview AI.[19] The early con-
flation of celebrity faces with the faces of the general public within 'Computer
Physiognomy' makes every face potential materials for biometrics and other
computational tactics and strategies, setting the stage for the contemporary
moment's predominate data practices.

PHOTOGÉNIE AND THE TECHNICAL CIRCULATION OF THE FAMOUS FACE

While 'Computer Physiognomy' presented FRT as a relatively light-hearted
technology, it also shows the central desires of the technology: to separate and
categorise those under its gaze. As Tom Gunning writes, both photography
and film's early histories contain instances where the technology's mechanical
vision was utilised to provide allegedly objective visions of the face.[20] Acting as
a self-proclaimed microscope, the FRT within the NEC exhibit's utilisation of
celebrity faces demonstrates that the technology can amplify *photogénie* so that
it can sort each person by their face's correspondence to its 'true' type.

The basis for Epstein's concept of *photogénie* is outlined in the much-
cited passage: 'We have discovered the cinematic property of things, a new
and exciting sort of potential: *photogénie . . . photogénie* [is] any aspect whose
moral character is enhanced by filmic reproduction.'[21] The use of 'enhanced'
does not mean to increase, but rather to make more clear to the viewer. These
thoughts are expanded in other essays by Epstein, including 'Photogénie and
the Imponderable', 'Magnification', and 'L'Ame au Ralenti' wherein *photogénie* is described as the manifestation of cinema's quasi-spiritual abilities to
manipulate and display beyond-human depictions of movement and time.[22]
Epstein repeatedly describes such abilities as acting as a microscope and/or a
magnifying glass, with the face in close-up being 'the soul of cinema' and the
maximum expression of *photogénie*.[23] *Photogénie* is explained as human-tran-
scendent technical ability to reveal the invisible nature of an object or person,
a type of vision that extends beyond human capabilities to show the world in
its most objective form.

In contrast to this argument, scholars like Christophe Wall-Romana see
photogénie as a corporeal vision, one that focuses upon the extreme details of
the body, and should not be 'reduced to denote an exalted but now obsolete
technical aestheticism, a naive fetishism for the filmic shot'.[24] Doane, in 'Facing
a Universal Language', points out that *photogénie* captures an affective bond
between the image and the spectator, with the close-up erasing the space between
object-on-screen and spectator to the point of maximum intensity.[25] However,
FRTs, as the previous section mentions, rescales the images, and the action of
those images, to scales closer to that of the body. Instead of the viewer 'losing
themselves' in the image of the large-scale cinematic face, bodies like those captured within 'Computer Physiognomy' becomes the site of technological spec-

tacle, wherein their faces, through mechanics invisible to those under its gaze, is transformed into data patterns and incorporated into the apparatus. Unlike the watching movie-going spectator, those captured by FRTs become the raw materials, or raw footage: their movements over time are captured, then spliced into computer-readable instances of data patterns, then computationally resurfaced for human viewership. Compared to film, an FRT's technical capabilities are denser and intensified, including those tethered to notions of *photogénie*. An FRT can capture and scrutinise faces as a camera does but is enhanced by computational mechanisms that allow the apparatus to view such faces in even more slow motion, with greater magnification, in near real-time.

Further, like tactical use of FRTs, Epstein argues that *photogénie* can function as a 'refractive moral index'. In the first instance, he argues

> if a high-speed film were made of an accused person during [their] interrogation, then from beyond his words, the truth would appear, unique, evident, written out, that there would no longer be any need of indictment, or of lawyers' speeches, or of any other proof than that provided by the deep images.[26]

Further, in 'Photogénie and the Imponderable' he gives the example of an American judge watching and rewatching the film of two different women claiming to be a girl's mother in order to accurately discern which was telling the truth. Empowered by *photogénie*, cinema is 'a machine that would confess souls', one potentially 'capable of baring the most secret thoughts'.[27] In Richard Abel's footnote following this quote, he explains that Epstein 'inadvertently . . . attributes to cinema a unique power of rational analysis that could extend – and has extended – the Panopticon-like surveillance system of the modern state';[28] one can see the echoes of Paul Ekman's neo-Darwinian work, described in Gates's chapter 'Automated Facial Expression Analysis and the Mobilization of Affect', in classifying and analysing facial expressions as a means to judge the interior emotional state of a person, including guilt.[29] Indeed, it is Epstein's repeated insistence that cinema can be used to come to accurate judgements on people's morality that links into a contemporary FRT, even when it is cloaked in the carnivalesque wonder of the technology's operation, such as within 'Computer Physiognomy'. Much like Hollywood cinema popularised and de-fanged the more dangerous potential functioning of *photogénie*, the NEC exhibition acted much like contemporary social media filters that use FRTs in that it normalised the functioning and existence of the technology, enabling a feature-creep into a wide range of everyday activities. In all such cases, the logics of identification and categorisation, by way of a more objectively 'clear' vision, is provided by the media's operation and rationalised by its purported abilities to do so accurately and efficiently.

Such thinking requires putting aside the well-documented false-positives and biases of FRTs towards non-white faces and imagining a world where the technology instead functions perfectly. Even then, the use of FRTs in 2021 as a plagiarism detector within test-taking environments and/or the use of the technology within job applications and mortgage applications operate to interrogate and sort the moral qualities and financial potentials of individuals.[30]

PHOTOGÉNIE AND WHITE PROTOTYPICALITY

Importantly, *photogénie*'s potential within interrogations is not objective but is tied to underpinnings of racial differentiation and physiognomy wherein the hereditary that Epstein flags as present within *photogénie* is tied to objects, and faces in particular, whose moral character are targeted by their portrayal on film. Doane sees such sentiments as demonstrative of the fact that 'cinematic technology is . . . haunted and possessed by a primitive and animistic past', tethering Epstein's treatment of the face to the more overt language of Balázs in his *Visible Man*.[31] For Balázs, the machine vision the cinematic camera presents as 'microphysiologies' can operate physiogometrically to reveal a great deal about 'alien races':

> Simply looking is not enough for us to distinguish those aspects of our face that are the common property of our family, race and class . . . In this respect film has a mission that transcends the realm of art and can provide invaluable material for both anthropology and psychology.[32]

Balázs's treatment of faces on film mirrors larger societal desires for scientific logics of cause and effect wherein the face could function as a deterministic site of knowledge revealed by the camera's beyond-human abilities. Such logics then allowed faces to be categorised effectively, with positivist impulses linked to atavistic ideologies that defined populations of faces as normal or deviant depending upon their traits.

Vision technologies like film, possessing and demonstrating *photogénie*, provide clear precedents for the interrogation and categorisation of faces within contemporary FRTs. From this perspective, *photogénie* has the potential to be an effective rationale for objectively judging and categorising within larger political strategies. The faces captured within an FRT's enhanced *photogénie* are even more susceptible to the technology's alleged truth telling, with FRTs being a powerful machine for differentiating and categorising faces. Within the 'Computer Physiognomy' exhibit there is the more innocent assertion that each face could be categorised into one of seven types of celebrity faces, but underlying this is the same categorising function that Balázs sees in cinema's potential; when that categorising potential is combined with a machine that confesses souls, there is a tethering of moral characters to certain types of faces that would underline the troubling eugenic insistences from photography and cinema's early histories. Aided by computational powers and AI training, a contemporary FRT's expanded capabilities carries out such tasks in an automated and decentralised manner, in real time.

However, FRT's automated decision making is not truth telling or a confessing of souls but a probabilistic system defined by its detection, identification and verification mechanisms; such mechanisms are built from machine learning techniques, artificial intelligence, and the databases used within the construction and application of an FRT. No element of an FRT's operation is free from the potential inscription of subjectively defined categories of race, gender or class (to name only three). In this way, the machine-training and facial databases within FRTs are especially important events wherein the technology learns different categories of faces and the qualities attached to those different types of faces. The over-representation of white Western faces in 'Computer Physiognomy' is indicative of the history of data practices within FRTs, and internet technology design, including the use of celebrity facial databases in the contemporary moment. As an example case study, the ibug data set, used for detecting facial landmarks, houses 119 images of various types of images, with the majority being famous faces either in a headshot or a film or television still; within the database, only seventeen are of medium to darker skin tones with the majority of the darker-skinned faces being shown in group photos or the rare candid or documentary photograph.[33]

These data practices have direct impacts on the technologies they are incorporated into. Broadly speaking, Beth E. Kolko insists that the Internet is a place that further deepens social constructions of race; categories of racial difference, often drawn along lines of biological features, are increasingly generated in step with digital media technologies. Further, the notion of self-representation and construction is then undermined by an assumed homogeneity and a default 'white male body' that structures the mechanisms and 'communicative possibilities' used as protocols for digital technologies.[34] Bridging these arguments to FRTs more specifically, Joy Buolamwini argues that

> Given the convenience and reusability of libraries, over time many programmers use popular code libraries to do common tasks. If the code being reused has bias, this bias will be reproduced by whoever uses the code for a new project or research endeavour.

She calls the specific vision of an FRT a coded gaze, wherein the uncritical reuse of code libraries and databases ignore the fact that 'embedded views are propagated by those who have the power to code systems'. The use of celebrity faces within FRTs are a prime example of when the default white male body combines with the coded gaze, promoting what Simone Browne contends is 'a certain white normativity, meaning that whiteness is made normative'; Browne argues that 'this prototypical whiteness is one facet of the cultural and technological logic that informs many instances of the practices of biometrics and the visual economy of recognition and verification that accompanies these practices'.[35] Browne argues that this destructive logic stems in part from schools of thought like eugenics and physiognomy that view the white (male) body as normal and any deviations from this body to be seen as abnormal.[36]

Using celebrity faces in machine learning training materials are a good example of how this default white body then becomes embedded into the code and logic structures of biometric software like FRTs. When the default white body is integrated into the enhanced *photogénie* that an FRT provides, faces outside of the unifying standards provided by the photogenic faces of celebrities run the real risk of being associated with 'lesser' moral qualities that fall outside the norms of the faces the technology has been optimised for; in extreme cases, such faces are simply unrecognisable.

Conclusion – the Political Problem of Recognition within FRT

Taken superficially, one might make the argument that instances of white prototypicality may work to cloak certain faces from surveillance and that the ability to remain unrecognised by systems like FRTs is actually beneficial. If such logics are true, they are only within in a very small set of FRT use cases; the historical reality is that those outside of a white prototypicality have historically been under- and/or misrecognised, to greatly damaging effects. Further, the fact remains that FRTs are increasingly ubiquitous and utilised in everyday decisions, to say nothing of the expansive law enforcement and border security usages of the technologies. This is the exact demonstration of how problematic the mechanisms of 'recognition' are within a facial recognition technology; power within FRTs is not centralised but rather dispersed through many different sites, from the formation and annotation of the facial data sets to the writing and functioning of its code and algorithms, to the protocols of its material deployment as part of larger political infrastructures. The functionality of a tactic like an FRT is secondary to the power it serves: when it functions perfectly it recognises one population over others; when it malfunctions, it also recognises specific populations over others. FRT is a dangerous technology not because it 'malfunctions' and demonstrates bias, but because it is wildly flexible at many levels of its operation, making it an extremely powerful and nimble tactic within applications of asymmetrical power and for gatekeeping tactics resources attached to citizenship. Complicating typical discourses about biometrics which tend to revolve around surveillance and securitisation, power within FRTs is not distributed in a top-down manner but rather circulates through the material and immaterial components of the technology and the bodies under observation. Knowing this, solutions and/or improvements to FRTs based on diversity are half-measures at best: while diverse coding teams and data sets are a positive step forward, they do not address the fact that the core problem of recognition within a FRT is not technical nor cultural, but political.

Judith Butler draws from Emmanuel Levinas in order to flag the face as the main site of recognition. As she explains, the problematic dependence on another self-consciousness to both see and acknowledge the life of another is reappropriated into biopolitical strategies to reinforce strategies of larger domination; a person is not allowed to self-determine their personhood but instead relies upon another entity granting it through recognition. Swerts and Oosterlynck define recognition as 'a state of mutual understanding between actors engaged in meaningful interaction in civil society about the cultural worth of their participation in and the legitimacy of their civic membership of that society'.[37] The tension around the application of recognition is in the performative elements of citizenship wherein citizenship is tied to moral and/ or performance-based metrics. These dynamics replicate the tensions within a *photogénie*-enhanced FRT described earlier in this chapter, which are then further exacerbated by the inscription of white prototypicality into the technology.

In the end, the use of famous faces within FRT, including 'Computer Physiognomy', frame 'recognition' not as political but as primarily technical and/ or cultural: the ability for a face to be deemed recognisable is dependent on either how much that face circulates within the larger culture or how well a face can be identified and verified within an automatic and decentralised technical environment. However, the use of recognisable celebrity faces within biopolitical tactics, such as FRTs, distracts from the fact that a person subjected to biopolitical strategies is not allowed to self-determine their personhood but instead relies upon another entity granting it through an act of recognition. These acts of legitimation, especially when outsourced to automated tactical assemblages like FRTs, are what needs to be grappled with when effectively auditing, restricting and potentially abolishing such technologies.

NOTES

1. Clare Garvie, 'Garbage In, Garbage Out', *Georgetown Law Center on Privacy and Technology*, 16 May 2019. Available at <https://www.flawedfacedata.com/> (last accessed 22 September 2021).
2. Takeo Kanade, *Computer Recognition of Human Faces* (Basel and Stuttgart: Birkhauser Verlag, 1977), 33–4.
3. Takeo Kanade, 'Takeo Kanade: Computer Face Recognition in Its Beginning', *MITCBMM*, 22 April 2016, Video, 25:10. Available at <https://www.youtube.com/watch?v=fY98kQWxJQc&t=5s> (last accessed 22 September 2021).

4. Due to the COVID-19 pandemic, I was unable to access the physical copy of issue 100 of the NEC Technical Journal which describes 'Computer Physiognomy' in more detail; future research will include a translation of the article. Basic information can be found at <https://www.nec.com/en/global/techrep/journal/history/index02.html> (last accessed 20 February 2021).

5. The YouTube Faces in the Wild data set, with accompanying methodology, can be found at <https://www.cs.tau.ac.il/~wolf/ytfaces/> (last accessed 20 February 2021). The CelebA data set can be found at <http://mmlab.ie.cuhk.edu.hk/projects/CelebA.html> (last accessed 20 February 2021); although the original MS-Celeb-1M data set found at <https://msceleb.org/> has since been discontinued, further information about the MS-Celeb-1M data set can be found at <https://www.microsoft.com/en-us/research/project/ms-celeb-1m-challenge-recognizing-one-million-celebrities-real-world/> (last accessed 20 February 2021). The Celebrities Images data set is one example of those that can be found at kaggle.com, <https://www.kaggle.com/greg115/celebrities-100k> (last accessed 20 February 2021).

6. Jean Epstein, 'On Certain Characteristics of Photogénie', in Richard Abel (ed.), *French Film Theory and Criticism: A History/Anthology*, Vol. 1 (Princeton: Princeton University Press, 1988); Roland Barthes, 'The Face of Garbo', *Mythologies* (New York: Hill and Wang, 2013), 73–5.

7. Kelly Gates, *Our Biometric Future* (New York: New York University Press, 2011), 26.

8. Further information about enrolment in facial databases can be found at 'The Perpetual Line-Up' (Clare Garvie, Alvaro M. Bedoya and Jonathan Frankle, *Georgetown Law Center on Privacy and Technology*, 18 October 2016. Available at <https://www.perpetuallineup.org/> (last accessed 22 September 2021)).

9. Epstein, 'On Certain Characteristics of Photogénie', 317.

10. Simone Browne, *Dark Matters: On the Surveillance of Blackness* (Durham, NC: Duke University Press, 2015).

11. Mary Ann Doane. 'The Close-up: Scale and Detail in the Cinema', *differences: A Journal of Feminist Cultural Studies* 14:3 (2003), 90.

12. Béla Balázs, *Béla Balázs: Early Film Theory: Visible Man and the Spirit of Film*, ed. Erica Carter, trans. Rodney Livingstone (New York: Berghahn Books, 2010), 29–30.

13. Barthes, 'The Face of Garbo', 75.

14. Doane, 'The Close-up', 107–9.

15. *Tiger Child* was screened at the Fuji Pavilion as the world's first IMAX film: the nine non-linear simultaneous screens that made up *Tiger Child* were made possible by a projector prototyped for the event and a rotating viewing space within the two-storey inflatable pavilion. Seth Feldman describes one of the piece's most direct legacies as the ability to 'produce a single image filling the viewer's entire field of vision', a moving image of such massive scale that its content becomes secondary to the immersive, bodily effect it has on its audience. Seth Feldman, '*Tiger Child*: IMAX and Donald Brittain Times Nine', in Zoë Druick and Gerda Cammaer (eds), *Cinephemera: Archives, Ephemeral Cinema, and New Screen Histories in Canada* (Montreal: McGill-Queen's University Press, 2014), 160.

16. Barthes, for all of his rhapsodic treatment of Garbo's face, is also lamenting the cinematic images of her face as a cinematic face of the past; instead of the mythically iconic cinematic face, faces like Audrey Hepburn's face are individualised, unique and singular.

17. While there is no direct evidence of inspiration from Andy Warhol's 1960s *oeuvre* on the 1970 NEC exhibit, the export of Western culture and Hollywood in post-World War II Japan and globally is present in the exhibit's choices of faces. The straightest line between the two is the inclusion of Marilyn Monroe within 'Computer Physiognomy', with Warhol's technologically reproduced portraits of the movie star speaking to the digitalising and distribution of Monroe's face within 'Computer Physiognomy'; also, both the artist and the exhibition are trafficking on how cross-culturally recognisable Monroe is, leveraging her famous face as a publicly circulated commodity. There is further research to be done linking Warhol's industrial-style production of technologically mediated faces in his portraits, as well as his treatment of famous faces in his *Screen Tests* (1964–6); such exploration would also include Warhol's *13 Most Wanted Men*, a series of replicated mugshots first presented at the 1964 World Fair.

18. Takeo Kanade, *Picture Processing System by Computer Complex and Recognition of Human Faces*, Department of Information Science (Kyoto: Kyoto University, 1973), 61–2.

19. Clearview AI is a facial recognition company that, in many ways, encapsulates contemporary Big Data practices, boasting of a facial database of three billion images scrapped from various sites on the Internet. Companies like Twitter and Google have taken legal action against Clearview AI demanding they stop such indiscriminate extractive practices. See Alfred Ng and Steven Musil, 'Clearview AI Hit with Cease-and-Desist from Google, Facebook over Facial Recognition Collection', *CNET*, 5 February 2020. Available at <https://www.cnet.com/news/clearview-ai-hit-with-cease-and-desist-from-google-over-facial-recognition-collection/> (last accessed 22 September 2021).

20. Tom Gunning, 'In Your Face: Physiognomy, Photography, and the Gnostic Mission of Early Film', *Modernism/modernity*, 4:1 (1997), 1–29.

21. Epstein 'On Certain Characteristics of Photogénie', 315.

22. Jean Epstein, 'L'Ame au Ralenti', *Écrits sur le cinéma: tome 1* (Paris: Editions Seghers, 1974), 191; Jean Epstein, 'Magnification', in Richard Abel (ed.), *French Film Theory and Criticism: A History/Anthology*, Vol. 1 (Princeton: Princeton University Press, 1988), 235–40; Epstein, Jean. 'Photogénie and the Imponderable', in Richard Abel (ed.), *French Film Theory and Criticism: A History/Anthology*, Vol. 1 (Princeton: Princeton University Press, 1988), 188–92.

23. Epstein, 'Magnification', 238; Epstein, 'Photogénie and the Imponderable', 192.

24. Christophe Wall-Romana, 'Epstein's Photogénie as Corporeal Vision: Inner Sensation, Queer Embodiment, and Ethics', in Sarah Keller and Jason N. Paul (eds), *Jean Epstein: Critical Essays and New Translations* (Amsterdam: Amsterdam University Press, 2012), 52.

25. Mary Ann Doane, 'Facing a Universal Language', *New German Critique* 41:2 (Summer 2014), 118.

26. Tom Gunning, in 'In Your Face', attributes this quote to Epstein's 'The Soul in Slow Motion' but an inspection of Epstein's essay in the original French shows no such quote. Instead, Annette Michelson, in 'Reading Eisenstein Reading "Capital"' (*October* 2 (Summer, 1976), 33) cites the quote as coming from 'A Conversation with Jean Epstein', *L'Ami du Peuple*, 11 May 1928, Lamberton, New York, Anthology Film Archives. I, however, was unable to find this original text, and am relying on the Michelson citation.

27. Epstein, 'Photogénie and the Imponderable', 192.

28. Ibid., 192.

29. Gates, *Our Biometric Future*, 161–2.

30. Anushka Patil and Jonah Engel Bromwich, 'How It Feels When Software Watches You Take Tests', *The New York Times*, 29 September 2020. Available at <https://www.nytimes.com/2020/09/29/style/testing-schools-proctorio.html> (last accessed 22 September 2021); Ginia Bellafante, 'The Landlord Wants Facial Recognition in Its Rent-Stabilized Buildings. Why?' *The New York Times*, 28 March 2019. Available at <https://www.nytimes.com/2019/03/28/nyregion/rent-stabilized-buildings-facial-recognition.html> (last accessed 22 September 2021); 'What Your Face May Tell Lenders About Whether You're Creditworthy', *The Wall Street Journal*, 10 June 2019. Available at <https://www.wsj.com/articles/what-your-face-may-tell-lenders-about-whether-youre-creditworthy-11560218700> (last accessed 22 September 2021); Charles Hymas, 'AI Used for First Time in Job Interviews in UK to Find Best Applicants', *The Telegraph*, 27 September 2019. Available at <https://www.telegraph.co.uk/news/2019/09/27/ai-facial-recognition-used-first-time-job-interviews-uk-find/> (last accessed 22 September 2021).

31. Doane, 'Facing a Universal Language', 119.

32. Balázs, *Early Film Theory*, 30.

33. This cataloguing of the ibug database is part of an ongoing research project auditing facial databases and presenting the results in transparent and public-facing manners. Doing so, however, still means relying on the potential biases within human data annotation and so the figures here should understood as a rough picture of the database's contents.

34. Beth E. Kolko, 'Erasing @race: Going White in the (Inter)Face', in Beth E. Kolko et al. (eds), *Race in Cyberspace* (London: Routledge, 2000), 216–17.

35. Browne, *Dark Matters*, 110.

36. Further discussion of the impacts of white prototypicality, in particular within biometrics, can be found in Joseph Pugliese, *Biometrics: Bodies, Technologies, Biopolitics* (London: Routledge, 2010). While ultimately outside the scope of this chapter, I found Simone Browne's discussion of the overlap between race and cinematic representations of biometrics very compelling (Browne, *Dark Matters*, 119–23).

37. Thomas Swerts and Stijn Oosterlynck, 'In Search of Recognition: The Political Ambiguities of Undocumented Migrants' Active Citizenship', *Journal of Ethnic and Migration Studies* 47:3 (2020), 668–85. My research current expands on the use of FRTs as a gatekeeping technology tasked with monitoring and controlling access to different resources attached to citizenship. My work also considers indigenous scholars who are taking up this problem, in particular in contrasting the right to

self-determination against state recognition; political acts of recognition are key to the continued structural existence of settler colonialism, reinforcing rule by forcing or enticing groups to be defined in relation to the colonial state as subordinate and Other subject-citizens. See *Red Skins White Masks* by Glen Sean Coulthard (Minneapolis: University of Minnesota Press, 2014) and Mark Rifkin's 'Indigenizing Agamben: Rethinking Sovereignty in Light of the "Peculiar" Status of Native Peoples', *Cultural Critique* 73 (2009), 88–124, as just two examples.

5. EMPTIED FACES: IN SEARCH OF AN ALGORITHMIC PUNCTUM

Stefka Hristova

INTRODUCTION

File 28_0_3_20170119194439188.jpg presented a familiar face in a new context. Reading the nomenclature of the file, I was to encounter the face of a twenty-eight-year-old Asian male as part of the UTKFace dataset. Yet, upon looking at the image, I encountered a familiar face – namely that of the infamous Afghan girl Sharbat Gula who graced the cover of *National Geographic*, inspired support for Afghan refugees and became the hallmark of the difficulties of migration, war and displacement.[1] Reduced to a data-point, Steven McCurry's photograph of Gula and Gula's face itself were to be emptied of any prior cultural meaning and rearticulated in a study about the ability of algorithms to predict ageing patterns. Gula's face was now to serve as nothing more than a set of facial landmarks.

In thinking about how the face becomes reconfigured in the context of algorithmic culture, this chapter engages with the politics of emptying photographed faces of meaning and their rearticulation into data-driven predictive landscapes. More specifically, it explores how photographic portraits have been scraped from the World Wide Web and further reduced and classified by what Deleuze and Guattari call 'faciality machines'.[2] In the aftermath of this classification, the images themselves emerge as what Mitra Azar has called the 'algorithmic facial image'[3] and faces are further reduced into facial parts or facial attributes. I trace the life of the face as raw data in the context of the UTKFace dataset by deploying the methodology of 'archaeology of data'

```
●  ●  ●    landmark_list_part1.txt
1_0_2_20161219140530307.jpg -4 71 -4 96 -3
120 -1 144 9 166 28 179 53 186 77 192 100 194
121 191 142 183 161 174 180 161 192 142 195
120 194 97 192 74 16 53 29 39 48 33 68 34 86
40 113 39 129 33 148 32 164 37 175 49 100 59
101 72 101 85 101 99 78 112 89 113 100 116
110 114 120 111 39 62 51 61 61 60 71 65 60 63
50 62 124 64 134 59 144 59 155 62 144 62 134
62 55 137 72 134 87 132 97 133 107 131 120
132 136 133 121 143 109 146 98 147 88 146 72
145 61 138 87 137 97 138 107 136 130 135 108
139 98 140 88 139 |
```

Figure 5.1   A sample photograph from the UTKFace dataset.

articulated by Kate Crawford and Trevor Paglen in their project 'Excavating AI'. Further, I argue that the decomposition of the face in the context of big data and machine learning algorithms has led to two distinct rearticulations: one linked to predictive algorithms and the other linked to the generation of deepfake portraits. Last, but not least, I argue that 'faciality machines' might be resisted by thinking about the face in relation to what Roland Barthes calls its unanalysable air – air that could prick us, and therefore has the potential to act as a punctum, by prompting an affective relationship to the images, faces and people that stand before us.[4]

Kate Crawford and Trevor Paglen's project 'Excavating AI' has provided a powerful methodology for understanding the origins of visual data used to train algorithms. Crawford and Paglen propose 'archaeology of data' as a new way of thinking about how data sets have been compiled and harnessed. In excavating the data behind facial recognition technology, they provide a powerful genealogy of the ways in which humans have been historically as well as currently algorithmically reduced to raw data via distillation of personhood to facial features. More specifically, the researchers point to two databases that house thousands of images that were classified by Amazon Turk workers and subsequently used for the development of facial recognition technology: ImageNet and UTKFace. Taking on the method of 'archaeology of data' outlined by Crawford and Paglen, I focus on the UTKFace data set consisting of 20,000 photographs.[5]

UTKFace is only one example among many data sets that have collected people's faces by obtaining photographic portraits without much consideration or consent from the World Wide Web. Indeed, as Karen Hao has illustrated, there are 'over 130 facial-recognition data sets compiled over 43 years'.[6] I focus here on UTKFace, as this dataset has been heavily utilised for the purposes of predictive identification and ageing: 'UTKFace dataset is a large-scale face dataset with long age span (range from 0 to 116 years old). The UTKFace dataset consists of over 20,000 face images with annotations of age, gender, and ethnicity.'[7] I want to address how the UTKFace data set as established by Yang Song and Zhifei Zhang configures faces into data in a bit more detail here. This data set labelled 20,000 portraits containing people and thus faces into 'raw' material classified by age from zero to 116, gender (0 for male and 1 for female), and race (0 for White, 1 for Black, 2 for Asian, 3 for Indian, 4 for Other (Hispanic, Latino, Middle Eastern)). The databases are heteronormative in that they articulate only two gender options and further display the bias of the algorithmic developers and data gatherers here as Indian stands for its own category. Faces are isolated from bodies through alignment and crop and further distilled into a set of 'landmarks'. The landmarks include the following parameters: around chin, line on top of nose, left eyebrow, right eyebrow, bottom part of the nose, line from the nose to the bottom part above, left eye, right eye, lips outer part, lips inner part. In order to show what portraits reduced to data look like, I took the first photograph listed as data and am including the image and the landmark data as reference below (Figure 5.1). This portrait of a sleeping baby is classified as age one, gender – male, race – Asian. His/their closed eyes, button nose and smirky little smile are listed through semantics understandable by an algorithm.

MULTITUDE OF FACES

As I was looking through the photographs that constitute the UTKFace data set, I was captivated by the photographs and the people whom they represented. I want to take a moment and note a couple of the portraits and people I encountered. First, I will focus on the photograph of an elderly woman, maybe someone's grandmother, wearing a black headscarf. Her image bears the watermark 'shutterstock' and a Shutterstock number: #38261362. In the UTKFace database she is labelled as 100_1_0 meaning that she is assessed to be 100 years old, female and white. On the Shutterstock database, she is labelled as '[v]ery old hoary woman face close up portrait against light background'.[8] The image was taken by Magomed Magmegadaev, who on the Shutterstock database identifies as a photographer from Moscow. The data set includes numerous photographs from Shuttersock and Getty Images, as well as Almy Stock Photo. The old woman in the photograph reminded me of my own grandmother. I grew up in Bulgaria and dark headscarves are common attire for women as they age. I wanted to find out more about her. I used the Google search with image function, where one can upload an image and see where it appears on the Internet. The photograph in question also stars in a prominent HR meme. Her face is listed under the questions 'What do you mean? We get a solid two hours of sleep every night.' In response, the meme argues 'Who Said Recruitment was stressful I am 25 and look great.'[9] In the world of satire, this woman is twenty-five and sleep-deprived. The photograph in question was thus part of a multiplicity of archives: a commercial photographic one, a cultural meme one and an algorithmic one. All of these images exploited her portrait for its semantics, embedding her face in a myriad of contexts without giving us access to knowing her. Photographs as symbolic, iconic images in digital and algorithmic media contexts have been emptied of meaning in order to be introduced into a new semantic order. As have been faces. Faces had already been transformed into an empty signified even before they entered the semantics of algorithmic coding, one that was invested in social bias, agism, gender and sexuality bias, as well as outright anti-Blackness. There have been numerous studies that have articulated the social bias encoded in algorithms, especially in the context of facial recognition. Notable here is the work of Joy Buolamwini and Timnit Gebru,[10] and Ruha Benjamin.[11] This bias is manifest in the inability of facial recognition technology to recognise Black faces as well as the inaccuracy of the algorithm when identifying Black and brown faces.

In another photograph that I pulled from the data set, we encounter a Black man: most photographs of Black men and women in this data-set feature prominent athletes or represent mugshots from the crime section of online news sources. According to the algorithmic evaluation, he is fifty-three, male and Black. The image looks like a mugshot as the subject is wearing a blue prison uniform. My Google search confirmed my suspicion. This photograph is indeed the intake photo taken of Johnnie Pulley. Behind this face, there was a story of an alleged beating and a revenge murder.[12] Johnnie Pulley's face looks sombre, his eyes looking down. An article from the *Riverfront Times* identifies Pulley as a sixty-year-old man who thought 'he'd identified a teenager who had beaten him on a Metro bus weeks earlier' and thus followed and shot a teenager.[13] A sombre story of abuse was obscured by a set of coordinates useful for algorithmic training and subsequent facial recognition. Pulley's mugshot is indeed exemplary of a growing trend of research that has harnessed algorithmic measurement in predictive crime analytics and thus revived racist theories of criminality via the work of Cesare Lombroso. Lombroso's work in criminal anthropology posited that one's criminal character can be derived based on the measurements and proportions of one's skull.[14] His theories were further connected with the development of eugenics. As Carl Bergstrom and Jevin West demonstrate, projects such as Xiaolin Wo and Xi Zhang's 'Automated Interference on Criminality Using Face Images' is exemplary of this new technocratic quest for truth. Emptied faces have been summoned once again as testaments to one's criminal inclination: 'Wu and Zhang claim that based on a simple headshot, their programs can distinguish criminal from noncriminal faces with nearly 90 percent accuracy.'[15] The probability of facial traits continues to be anchored in landscapes of surveillance and predictive policing. The UTKFace data set does not discriminate between historic photographs, public portraits, selfies and mugshots. Everyone is given the same treatment and everyone's face is subjected to the same algorithmic processing. Faces no more, these images were presented as empty vessels for new meanings. They were the supposed perfect subjects for an algorithmic faciality machine.

FACIALITY MACHINE

Algorithmic facial recognition and recombination algorithms, as well as data sets of faces such as UTKFace, are thus part of a larger historical trajectory of the quantification of the face and its distillation into a set of elements that on one hand can be mapped onto human traits through a variety of facial recognition algorithms and on the other hand recombined as deepfake human portraits through the TensorFlow machine learning platform. These processes of distilling people into faces and further faces into maps is precisely what Deleuze and Guattari call 'an abstract machine of faciality'. Deleuze and Guattari make several important points here that resonate deeply with the contemporary landscape of AI facial recognition and deepfake generation as well as with the history of anthropometrics and photographic composites more broadly. First, they point to how 'signifying traits are indexed to specific faciality traits'. In other words, measuring and evaluating facial traits has de facto been seen as a way of measuring and evaluating human character. Second, they argue that '[f]aces are not basically individual: they define zones of frequency or probability, delimit a field that neutralises in advance any expression or connections unamenable to the appropriate signification'.[16] In other words, faces signal the frequency and probability of facial traits and their seemingly correlating human cultural traits. Faces, for Deleuze and Guattari, emerge as non-human calculations, as surfaces that indeed ellipse the messy and unamenable human.

The mapping of facial traits into signifying traits in the context of AI is linked to anthropometrics or the direct measurement of one's face on one hand, and the use of photography in physiognomy, phrenology, craniology and so on, on the other. As Crawford and Paglen write, the distillation of faces into data for the purposes of algorithmic processing is part of a larger history of datafication. They have explicitly identified the UTKFace data set as an extension of the work of

> [p]hysiognomists such as Francis Galton and Cesare Lombroso [who] created composite images of criminals, studied the feet of prostitutes, measured skulls, and compiled meticulous archives of labelled images and measurements, all in an effort to use 'mechanical' processes to detect visual signals in classifications of race, criminality, and deviance from bourgeois ideals.[17]

The UTKFace data set, as well as ImageNet, are thus examples par excellence of the ways in which algorithms have harnessed the duality of photography: its honorific and repressive capacities, as the prominent photographer and photographic critic Allan Sekula wrote.[18]

Historically, the individual human body, as a site of truth, has been identified and classified in relation to the 'truth-apparatus'[19] constituted by the archive as theorised by Michel Foucault[20] and the database as conceptualised by Mark Poster.[21] Sekula has eloquently argued that in the nineteenth century, photographic portraiture came to 'establish and delimit the terrain of the other, to define both the generalised look – the typology – and the contingent instance of deviance and social pathology'.[22] These processes were made possible by the linkage of photography to a 'truth-apparatus' as the 'camera is integrated into a larger ensemble: a bureaucratic clerical-statistic form of "intelligence"'. In other words, photography became meaningful as intelligence only when accompanied by data. As Sekula illustrates, Bertillon's system of policing as well as Galton's anthropometric eugenic human classification systems depended on both photography and data – it is anthropometric data that anchored photography into an archive.[23] The photograph in both cases acted as metadata to the data of the catalogue card. In other words, the collection of data about subjects seen as aberrant was conducted in the realm of the physical – the subject him/herself was subjected to measurement. The photograph performed an important function of making data recognisable to human agents of surveillance. This system can be described as a 'sophisticated form of the archive'.[24] In the digital and further algorithmic turns, photography itself became the source of data as the measurements of one's face are now conducted by a variety of algorithms as to distil typologies, signal aberrant and further assert a more 'truthful or 'accurate' social identity.

ALGORITHMIC FACIALITY MACHINES

In contemporary algorithmic culture, measurement and evaluation of photographed faces distilled into faciality traits have been harnessed for the purpose of identifying one's race, gender, age, sexual orientation, emotional state and political preference. In the emergence of the map, both faces and identity markers/states of being must be reduced into a set of mappable elements. In the case of AI evaluating faces, in order to make inferences about one's emotional state, the face is distilled into eye traits, mouth traits, nose traits. Emotion, on the other hand, is also seen as a set of 'essential components'.[25] In this process, faciality machines produce 'face-landscape[s]' to evoke Deleuze and Guattari's terminology, where each of the two-term reterritorialises onto one other.[26] Here, both face and emotion are broken down into essential parts and then mapped onto each other. The mechanics of this coupling of faces to human emotions are detailed in a number of studies on AI and human emotion recognition. I am interested in exploring the coupling of faces to the landscape of emotion because of the elusiveness of how affect can be captured in a photograph and further evoked in the spectator of a photograph. Affect, as I will show below, might indeed be a mode of resistance of the datafication of human experience.

In reviewing the scientific literature on facial expression recognition (FER) in relation to emotion, one article stood out in particular, for it strongly reflected Deleuze and Guattari's observation that faciality machines transform faces into black and white surfaces. This particular study was conducted in 2017 by Md Zia Uddin, Mohammed Mehedi Hassan, Ahmad Almogren, Mansour Zuair, Giancarlo Fortino and Jim Torresen.[27] The authors proposed the use of a depth camera-based facial recognition system where staged facial expressions were captured and then tested. In the article, the scientists provide a succinct and useful explanation of the different ways in which faces are read as emotional data. The first method uses geometric feature vectors which consider 'geometric relationships such as angles and positions between different face parts such as eyes, ears, and nose'.[28] In this 'face-landscape correlation',[29] the face is reduced to a set of abstract topographic features that can be described geometrically and so are emotions. Indeed, facial features distilled for algorithmic use are called 'landmarks'. Emotions here are read through the relationship of geometric shapes imagined on one's face. The second method outlined in the study is 'appearance-based' where a filter is applied to the whole 'face image'.[30] Note the language here, as in the study close-up photographs of people were reduced to face images by first rendering them black and white and second applying a grey overtone so that what is visible is a grey face on a black background where the eyes and nose appear to be light grey cavities and the mouth emerges as a darker grey opening. These face images aimed to distil the face as a map showing depth through 'depth face extraction'.[31] The faces were then mapped onto six emotions 'anger, happy, sad, surprise, neutral, disgust'.[32]

I found the photographs and facial images used in this study haunting. Here, we encounter two images of a young man who has been asked to perform a 'surprised' expression.[33] The first image is labelled a 'gray pixel image' and stands for the reduction of a medium close-up to a black and white image. We encounter here a young man, his mouth half-open. He is supposed to show the motion of surprise so that the algorithm can train on what the topology of a surprised face looks like. How do we read this face? How do we connect to the human behind it? This is not the first time photography has been deployed for the purposes of a scientific understanding of affect.[34] Evoking Barthes' notion of the studium is a useful first step as it accurately describes the process of mapping signifying traits onto facial traits in the context of photography practised by both humans and machines. The studium for Barthes is 'a kind of general, enthusiastic commitment' and the decoding of the historical and political significance of 'the figures, the faces, the gestures, the settings, the actions'.[35] When I read the studium of this black and white photograph, I see a student. The expression: forced surprise. Behind the young man are a spinning fan and an office chair. The space in which he is positioned appears to be cluttered, small and hot. I can see the heat on his face reflected in the shine on his nose. His mouth is 'delimiting the field', to borrow Deleuze and Guattari's language, of surprise. It is in the right geometric shape. Looking into his eyes, however, I do not feel that the subject is 'surprised.' I see tired eyes, a bit puffy as if he did not get enough sleep or is finishing up a long day of work. I see inquisitive eyes, eyes that know that they are performing and thus know to mimic a staged emotion and not reflect a more authentic emotional state. I see tired performative eyes.

This photograph is further reduced to a 'depth image' or a seemingly three-dimensional facial map where the nose appears to be a peak while the eyes and the mouth emerge as depressions in the cranial cavity. The identity of the human behind the face is obscured and rendered irrelevant. The background is also erased and replaced with a black surface. For Deleuze and Guattari, the faciality machine 'gives its signifier its white wall and subjectivity its black hole'.[36] Here the colour scheme is inverted as if we are looking at a negative, not a positive photographic image produced by the faciality machine. We encounter a black wall and white holes of subjectivity. This face is clearly not individual, to nod back to Deleuze and Guattari's astute observation. Caught in a depth image, it appears to me as haunting, as emptied out of humanity. Through a process of erasure, it has performed 'the facialization of the entire body and all of its surroundings and objects, and the landscapifications of all worlds and milieus'.[37] Here, literally, the body and the surrounding objects are erased and subsumed by the prominence of the face. Even some faciality traits here appear to be problematic and thus require expulsion as we look for 'clean' data and 'clean' codes. Deleuze and Guattari write some 'faciality traits themselves finally elude the organization of the face – freckles dashing towards the horizon, hair carried off by the wind, eyes you traverse instead of seeing yourself in or gazing into . . .'[38] As scholars exploring the racial bias in AI have pointed out, dark skin also appears to be a faciality trait that is not compatible with the algorithmic technology. Useful facial images have and continue to be embedded in structures of whiteness. In the images of the young man I encountered, his short goatee had become such a faulty trait. In the depth image, the goatee has been marked with a black digital scribble so that it can be bypassed by the algorithms and thus not cause interference in the calculation of the facial terrain and the domain of surprise.

Artificial Intelligence 'sees' these facial images otherwise. It records the eyes, nose and mouth seen on the depth image as locations in both geometric and geographic matrixes: as a set of coordinates that are then given a geographic direction such as north, sound, west, east, north-west, north-east, south-west, south-east.[39]

These matrixes are then evaluated in terms of frequency and probability as the study reports the mean recognition rates for recognising the six emotional states listed above. A surprise was recognised at a probability of 95 per cent according to the study.[40] As such, algorithms aim to provide yet another 'common grammar' when reading a face. To evoke Deleuze and Guattari, the face here yet again functions as 'a veritable megaphone', as a 'protective screen and a computing black hole'.[41] The theoretical account of the work of the face is rendered indeed concrete in the algorithmic reterritorialisation of the face-emotion landscape. In the case study detailed here, a grey protective screen and white and black computing holes were literally visualised, measured, cartographically mapped, and then evaluated in terms of the probability of their power to deliver a veritable message consistently.

The idea of machine vision points to an important shift in the deployment of faciality machines. In the context of algorithmic culture, these machines operate or are effective not with regards to a human audience, but rather in relation to a non-human algorithm. Deleuze and Guattari ask a powerful question: 'When does the abstract machine of faciality enter into play?'[42] They point to important examples from the human context: 'maternal power operating through the face during nursing; the passional power operating through the face of a loved one, even in caresses; the political power operating through the face of the leader (streamers, icons, and photographs)'.[43] They argue that '[i]t is not the individuality of the face that counts but the efficacy of the ciphering that makes it possible, and in what cases it makes it possible' and as such '[c]ertain assemblages of power (pouvoir) require the production of a face, others do not'.[44] The face is thus embedded in economies of power where a powerful face is a face that is easily decoded, whose studium, to call on Barthes here, is easily accessible. The project of algorithms is to automate the studium and thus to shift the articulation of power as it is now framed through a technological calculation of probability.

DEEPFAKE FACES

The distillation of faces into face-landscapes through the algorithmic faciality machine has also led to a new age of making combination prints that synthesise humans out of human traits with stunning success. Here a dataset of eyes, noses, lips and chins gets recombined in order to create deepfake faces by a 'new class of algorithms, collectively known as adversarial machine learning, [which] can fashion photorealistic faces of nonexistent people'.[45] A prominent example of the power of algorithms to create uncanny human doubles is Philip Wang's 'Thispersondoesnotexist.com' (2019). Here GAN (generative adversarial network) algorithms compose 'endless fake faces' by recombining photographs and selfies that had been posted to Flickr.[46] In this case, the algorithm was fed photographs of human faces that were subsequently recombined into images of 'imaginary stranger[s]'.[47] The platform utilised in this deepfake human generation is called TensorFlow. It is an open-source machine learning platform. It has been harnessed via its StyleGAN module both by corporations and artists to create fake portraits.[48]

In unmasking the processes of the power of AI to generate fake portraits by breaking apart photographs and remixing them into seamless images, Bergstrom and West have dedicated a wonderful volume on the messiness of data titled *Calling Bullshit: The Art of Skepticism in a Data-Driven World* and have launched an elegant demonstration of the predicament of distinguishing real from fake humans as the 'WhichFaceIsReal.com' project (2019). The latter work aims to make users aware of the ease with which 'digital identities can be faked' as 'new adversarial machine learning algorithms allow people to rapidly generate synthetic "photographs" of people who have never existed'.[49] Here, users are presented with two images and are asked to identify the 'real' human, thus real photograph. There is a coupling that is signalled here between the existential realness of the human and the perceived status of the image as a photograph. One of the images is

> a real one from the [Flickr] FFHQ collection, and [the second is] a synthetic one, as generated by the StyleGAN system and posted to thispersondoesnotexist.com, a web-based demonstration of the StyleGAN system that posts a new artificial image every 2 seconds.[50]

Bergstrom and West's project demonstrated how adversarial machine learning algorithms continue a tradition of photographic manipulation that undermines the indexicality of the photograph itself and thus positions the face as a haunting technological apparition.

Algorithmic faciality machines are also the subject of Mitra Azar's 'DoppelGANger.agency' (2019). Here Azar, too, engages with the notion of algorithmically generated faces. In naming the project, Azar cleverly evokes both the idea of an apparition or a double of a human person – the doppelgänger – as well as the role that Generative Adversarial Networks or GANs play in the algorithmic synthesis of these ghostly doubles. These AI-generated faces are dubbed by Azar as algorithmic ghosts. In this project, GANs are used to generate posters of missing people by combining images into algorithmic faces and text from missing people or animal posters into an algorithmically articulated description of the missing person. The posters ask viewers to find the missing 'person'. The search for 'finding the real human' behind the missing person poster here is a futile quest. Through his work, Azar makes a powerful argument for how the photograph has transitioned in two major ways: in orientation and in constitution. First, the photograph became a selfie, redirecting the lens towards the photographer rather than towards a different subject or object:

Thus, if in the early 2000s the selfie seemed to be characterised by a certain degree of (calculated) spontaneity, an analogically constructed liveness and a form of human agency, this new form of selfie is rather defined by its trackability, its algorithmically constructed liveness, and its nonhuman agency.[51]

Second, the selfie further has transitioned into what Mark B. N. Hansen termed 'digital-facial-image'[52] and is now increasingly becoming an 'algorithmic facial image'.[53] This transition from DFI to AFI in relation to Deleuze and Guattari's notion of the faciality machine is central to Azar's work. Algorithmic facial images for him operate as hybrids where 'the user's face is simultaneously the subject and object of the interface.'[54] The user's face becomes both articulated through and further distilled into algorithmic data.

Rejecting Faciality Machines

In thinking about facility machines articulated through both the photographic camera as well as through artificial intelligence and machine 'vision', it is worth exploring ways of resisting the reduction of the face into a set of descriptive and prescriptive indicators of human traits. Here, the work of Deleuze and Guattari as well as Barthes resonates deeply with the contemporary challenges we face. Deleuze and Guattari call for a refusal of the face, while Barthes responds with an articulation of a 'punctum' in order to counter effacement. I want to outline these two strategies as they resonate with the contemporary politics of the face in algorithmic culture.

According to Deleuze and Guattari, one must reject and indeed dismantle the face. The road towards rejecting the coding of the face is through subjectivity and passion: both held by the human that beholds the face, and not by the face itself. For

> [o]nly in the black hole of the subjective consciousness and passion do you discover the transformed, heated, captured particles you must relaunch for a nonsubjective, living love in which each party connects with unknown tracts in the other without entering or conquering them, in which the lines composed are broken lines.[55]

Deleuze and Guiattari deliver a powerful appeal for living love, for not hollowing out, not entering, not calculating and coding faces but rather allowing for the unknown.

Barthes offers an alternative framework for countering the semantics of the face as an example of 'a desperate resistance to any reductive system'.[56] More specifically, he introduced the notion of the punctum in the context of photography and photographic portraiture in particular. If the studium for Barthes contains semantics and thus allows for the social and ultimately algorithmic 'reading' of identity, the punctum breaks the studium. As he argues, 'a photograph's punctum is that accident which pricks me (but also bruises me, is poignant to me)'.[57] Further, '[i]n order to perceive the punctum, no analysis would be of any use to me (but perhaps memory sometimes would, as we shall see)'.[58] These descriptions point to how the punctum is connected with human viewership. It is the observer that becomes pricked, emotionally triggered. Because the punctum is 'what I add to the photograph and what is nonetheless already there',[59] it relies on the establishment of an emotional connection between the subject of the photograph and the subject viewing the photograph. It is personal and imminent. Further, the punctum articulates power outwards, towards the audience. The spectator is not to penetrate or enter the eyes of the photographed subject. Rather, the person in the photograph becomes an emanation – '(f)rom a real body, which was there, proceed radiations which ultimately touch me, who am here'.[60] Barthes wrote about the punctum in relation to a photograph of his mother. A powerful moment in which he felt her presence emanating from the image as if she was there with him.

It is this notion of an individual punctum connected to the once presence of a real human, reflecting sun rays that then become recorded onto emulsion or camera sensor that acts as a powerful reminder of the aura or air of human beings. While the deepfake projects discussed above demonstrate the ability of AI to synthesise faces, Vincent Woo's 'Thispersonexists.net' (2020) endeavours to bring attention to the real people, whose photographs were 'used to train Nvidia's StyelGAN and serve as the raw material for thispersondoesnotexist.com'. Here, we are presented with photographs from the Flickr archive, that display the name of the photographer and a link to the original Flickr posting. The argument made here is that the photographs and people behind the AI synthesised images do exist. These are photographs of real people we posted to friends, to family, to community, as a way to document and share a real-life human experience. They hold the potential of evoking the all-so-human punctum, a notion that so far algorithms have been unable to grapple with. In this way, photography is brought back into the discourse of indexicality, of co-presence of photographer and photographed subject, of memory and experience representing a slice of life anchored in space and time. Looking at these photographs on Flickr, I encountered Ben Sutherland's 2013 portrait of a teenager at camp; a portrait for a young man in an album from 2004 titled 'Around the house'; a portrait of a young woman with bright pink hair from 2015 as part of an album titled 'Alt Summit 2015 Thursday night'; a portrait of a young child enjoying a powdery doughnut posted by David Duran in 2015 as part of an album titled 'Christmas 2014'; a portrait of Persis Bekkering at Natlab taken by Sebastiaan Ter Berg in 2018 as part of an album titled 'Literary talkshow with authors Nicci Gerard and Sean French and their editor A. J Finn at Natlab'. These descriptions are exemplary of the 'slice of life' that the faces in these photographs represent.

Framed in a medium close-up view, these images display a series of encounters with certificates of presence. The presence of a human, of a photographer, and of an 'air' held by the face. It is this notion of an 'air', 'the luminous shadow which accompanies the body'[61] that can be sensed through an engagement with the punctum rather than the studium of the photograph that resists algorithmic redefinition. For Barthes,

> the air of a face is unanalyzable (once I can decompose, I prove or I reject, in short, I deviate from the Photograph, which is by nature totally evidence: evidence is what does not want to be decomposed). The air is not a schematic, intellectual datum, the way a silhouette is. Nor is the air a simple analogy – however extended – as is 'likeness'. No, the air is that exorbitant thing which induces from the body to soul – animula, little individual soul, good in one person, bad in another . . .[62]

Barthes's 'air', 'an intractable supplement of identity'[63] and Deleuze and Guattari's 'living love'[64] speak to a rejection of practices of decomposition of the photograph and therefore of the human. It is the 'air' that holds the potential to evoke the punctum in an image and thus resist the articulation of the photograph into what Azar calls 'algorithmic facial image'.[65] In the context of an algorithmic culture in which people are reduced to images and further to a set of data that is then mapped onto new predictive frameworks, it is increasingly important to evoke discourse that rejects the 'entering', 'conquering', 'decomposing' the 'other'. In the face of the increasing datafication of everyday life, we need to remain committed to practices of connecting with 'unknown tracts', and to allow ourselves the vulnerability to be open to the possibility of being pricked by the presence of one's untamable 'air'.

NOTES

1. Nina Strochlic, 'Framed "Afghan Girl" Finally Gets a Home', *National Geographic*, 12 December 2017. Available at <https://www.nationalgeographic.com/pages/article/afghan-girl-home-afghanistan> (last accessed 22 September 2021).

2. Gilles Deleuze and Felix Guattari, *A Thousand Plateaus: Capitalism and Schizophrenia*, trans. Brian Massumi (Minneapolis: University of Minnesota Press, 1987), 168.

3. Mitra Azar, 'Algorithmic Facial Image: Regimes of Truth and Datafication', *A Peer-Reviewed Journal About APRJA* 7:1 (2018), 27–35, 28. Available at <https://aprja.net/article/view/115062> (last accessed 22 September 2021).

4. Roland Barthes, *Camera Lucida: Reflections on Photography*, trans. Richard Howard (New York: Hill and Wang, 1980), 107.

5. Kate Crawford and Trevor Paglen, 'Excavating AI: The Politics of Images in Machine Learning Training'. Available at <https://www.excavating.ai> (last accessed 22 September 2021).

6. Karen Hao, 'This Is How We Lost Control of Our Faces', *MIT Technology Review*, 5 February 2021. Available at <https://www.technologyreview.com/2021/02/05/1017388/ai-deep-learning-facial-recognition-data-history/?fbclid=IwAR3wGz2VAan9tLuph9J7vDUn0oR0FhC1zlpax7MKT5P_kstQEL8PFNPOiTE> (last accessed 22 September 2021).

7. Available at <UTKFace https://susanqq.github.io/UTKFace/> (last accessed 22 September 2021).

8. ShutterStock. Available at <https://www.shutterstock.com/image-photo/very-old-hoary-woman-face-closeup-38261362> (last accessed 22 September 2021).

9. RecruiterFlow Blog. Available at <https://recruiterflow.com/blog/recruiting-memes/> (last accessed 22 September 2021).

10. Joy Buolamwini and Timnit Gerbu, 'Gender Shades: Intersectional Accuracy Disparities in Commercial Gender Classification', *Proceedings of Machine Learning Research* 81:1 (2018), 1–15.

11. Ruha Benjamin, *Race After Technology: Abolitionist Tools for the New Jim Code* (Cambridge and Malden, MA: Polity, 2019).

12. Chad Garrison, 'Was Murder of Teen Justified? Sexagenarian Gunman Says It Was', *Riverfront Times*, 26 May 2010. Available at <https://www.riverfronttimes.com/newsblog/2010/05/26/was-murder-of-teen-justified-sexagenarian-gunman-says-it-was> (last accessed 22 September 2021).

13. Ibid.

14. Emilia Musumeci, 'Against the Rising Tide of Crime: Cesare Lombroso and Control of the "Dangerous Classes" in Italy, 1861–1940', *Crime, Histoire & Sociétés / Crime, History & Societies* 22:2 (2018), 83–106. Available at <http://www.jstor.org/stable/45215827> (last accessed 8 April 2021).

15. Carl Bergstrom and Jevin West, *Calling Bullshit: The Art of Skepticism in a Data-driven World* (New York: Random House, 2020), 45.

16. Deleuze and Guattari, *A Thousand Plateaus*, 168.

17. Crawford and Paglen, 'Excavating AI'.

18. Allan Sekula, 'The Body and the Archive', *October* 39 (Winter 1986), 3–64.

19. Sekula, 'The Body and the Archive', 16.

20. Michel Foucault, *Discipline and Punish: The Birth of the Prison* (New York: Vintage Books, 1995).

21. Mark Poster, 'Foucault and Databases', *The Mode of Information: Poststructuralism and Social Context* (Chicago: University of Chicago Press, 1990).

22. Sekula, 'The Body and the Archive', 7.

23. Ibid., 3–64.

24. Ibid., 16.

25. Luke Stark and Jesse Hoey, 'The Ethics of Emotion in Artificial Intelligence Systems', FAccT '21: Proceedings of the 2021 ACM Conference on Fairness, Accountability, and Transparency, March 2021, 782–93, 783. Available at <https://dl.acm.org/doi/10.1145/3442188.3445939> (last accessed 22 September 2021).

26. Deleuze and Guattari, *A Thousand Plateaus*, 174.
27. Md Zia Uddin et al., 'A Facial Expression Recognition System Using Robust Face Features from Depth Videos and Deep Learning', *Computers & Electrical Engineering* 63 (2017), 114–25. Available at <https://www.sciencedirect.com/science/article/abs/pii/S0045790617310613?via%3Dihub> (last accessed 22 September 2021).
28. Ibid., 115.
29. Deleuze and Guattari, *A Thousand Plateaus*, 172.
30. Uddin et al., 115.
31. Ibid., 116.
32. Ibid., 122.
33. Ibid., 117.
34. See Sander Gilman (ed.), *Face of Madness: Hugh Diamond and the Origin of Psychiatric Photography* (Battleboro, VT: Echo Point Books and Media, 2014).
35. Barthes, *Camera Lucida*, 26.
36. Deleuze and Guattari, *A Thousand Plateaus*, 168.
37. Ibid., 181.
38. Ibid., 171.
39. Uddin et al., 118.
40. Ibid., 122.
41. Deleuze and Guattari, *A Thousand Plateaus*, 179.
42. Ibid., 175.
43. Ibid.
44. Ibid.
45. Bergstron and West, *Calling Bullshit*, 35.
46. James Vincent, 'ThisPersonDoesNotExist.com Uses AI to Generate Endless Fake Faces', *The Verge*, 15 February 2019. Available at <https://www.theverge.com/tldr/2019/2/15/18226005/ai-generated-fake-people-portraits-thispersondoesnotexist-stylegan> (last accessed 22 September 2021).
47. Ibid.
48. TensorFlow. Available at <https://www.tensorflow.org> (last accessed 22 September 2021).
49. About, available at <https://www.whichfaceisreal.com/about.html> (last accessed 22 September 2021).
50. Methods, available at <https://www.whichfaceisreal.com/methods.html> (last accessed 22 September 2021).
51. Azar, 'Algorithmic Facial Image', 27, 28.
52. Mark B. N. Hansen, 'Affect as Medium, or the "Digital-Facial-Image"', *Journal of Visual Culture* 2:2 (2003), 206–28.
53. Azar, 'Algorithmic Facial Image', 28.
54. Ibid., 30.
55. Deleuze and Guattari, *A Thousand Plateaus*, 189.
56. Barthes, *Camera Lucida*, 8.
57. Ibid., 27.
58. Ibid., 42–3.
59. Ibid., 55.

60. Ibid., 80.
61. Ibid., 110.
62. Ibid., 107–9.
63. Ibid., 109.
64. Deleuze and Guattari, *A Thousand Plateaus*, 189.
65. Azar, 'Algorithmic Facial Image', 28.

PART II

REFRAMING THE CLOSE-UP

6. 'A LANDSCAPE OF FACES': *THE FAREWELL* AND ECOLOGIES OF THE FACE IN INDEPENDENT ASIAN-AMERICAN FILM

Iggy Cortez

Lulu Wang's *The Farewell* (2019) opens with the text 'Based on an Actual Lie', inviting us to read the film through conflicting registers of referential accuracy and deceptive fabulation. Adapted from an episode of the podcast *This American Life*, Wang's film has explicit ties to her lived experience, retracing her family's decision to withhold a terminal cancer diagnosis from Wang's elderly grandmother (Zhao Shu-Zhen). While Wang's fictionalised surrogate, Billi (Awkwafina) lives in New York near her parents, her paternal grandmother – whom she calls Nai Nai, the Mandarin name for grandmother – resides in Changchun, China. Nai Nai's only other son has also emigrated, to Japan, leaving her in the care of a younger sister (played by Wang's real life great-aunt Hong Lu). Given this family's complex geographic dispersal, Nai Nai's sons decide to anticipate her nephew's wedding to his Japanese wife in their native hometown. The wedding festivities merely serve as a ruse for Nai Nai's family to gather around her for what might be the last time. In their outward, and at times wavering, display of false mirth, the family's faces give phenomenological substance to the smoke-and-mirrors of their hoax in a way that resonates with the actuality of cinema's own lies – its capacity to invest diegetic fiction with the concrete physicality of the profilmic world. I want to suggest, therefore, that the face in *The Farewell* serves as a locus that links cinema's imbrication of the virtual and the real to how Asian-American subjects have been coded as unintelligible or unassimilable to the US national body. In so doing, I aim to locate how the film's aesthetic grammar interrogates and re-evaluates the imagistic dimensions of racialised being as it has been elaborated and challenged across independent Asian-American film.

The Farewell's central narrative tension arises from Billi's protests that her grandmother should be informed of her terminal condition. However, the rest of her relatives, and even her grandmother's doctor, argue that withholding a terminal diagnosis protects her from the ultimately unnecessary fear of an impending but immutable outcome, much as Nai Nai did for her own husband. Since Billi's ambivalence about her family's masquerade is initially graphed on to the cultural divergences between American and Chinese outlooks, her inner conflict signifies beyond the film's immediate narrative to reflect what David Eng and Shinhee Han call 'a process involving not just mourning and melancholia but the intergenerational negotiation between mourning and melancholia'.[1] Billi has fallen out of sync with the progress-oriented timeline of American success her relatives in China expect she will fulfil. But at the same time she feels displaced and haunted by her ancestral home which she left abruptly as a six-year-old. In Wang's film, then, the anticipatory mourning for the loss of the family matriarch resonates with and re-elaborates an unprocessed and under-acknowledged grief for a forfeited motherland that the elderly grandmother fantasmatically embodies.

Upon the film's release, its reckoning with the psychic vicissitudes of inter-generational loss and displacement were overshadowed by celebratory narratives regarding the on-screen representation of Asians in US cinema. Following its acclaimed premiere at Sundance, *The Farewell* drew widespread attention for becoming a surprise hit, drawing comparison to the domestic box-office triumph of *Crazy Rich Asians* (2018), despite their overwhelming disparities, thus framing it as a win for on-screen representation.[2] However, prompted by the sharp rise of anti-Asian violence following the COVID-19 pandemic, more recent interventions point out how repetitive and circular narratives on representation can be in their failure to address the obfuscated historical and discursive relations that determine the intelligibility of racialised social presence and participation in the first place. In February 2021, for instance, Wang was featured in a round table in *The New York Times*, entitled 'A Vision of Asian-American Cinema That Questions the Very Premise', among other notable Asian-American filmmakers. Immediately, the article casts doubts on the coherence of the very category it brings into focus, arguing that 'in recent years, as more artists and writers in the mainstream ponder Asian-American identity in their work, the unifying refrain has often been about its nebulousness'.[3] As such, the article positions Wang's film as a 'deeply specific vision' in order to counteract attempts, given *The Farewell*'s relative visibility and success, to essentialise the film into an emblematic narrative encompassing the vast hybridity of Asian-American ethnic groups.[4]

In other words, critical responses to *The Farewell* have thus taken two approaches: the first locates the film as socially indexical to 'Asian-American identity', while the other foregrounds the isolated individuality of the film's specific context, deprioritising while not exactly negating political and socio-economic correspondence with other films by Asian-American directors. But by bypassing the film's aesthetic vocabulary, or isolating it as uniquely personal and specific, both approaches risk ignoring how *The Farewell* probes and re-evaluates its own position and arrival within an existing system of racialised representation. As we will see, in fact, it is the film's self-conscious formalism that interrogates the aesthetic and symbolic conditions through which Asiatic personhood has been articulated within the field of US national culture. Drawing on these coordinates, I want to attend to how the film's reflexive excursus on cinema as a technology for racialisation – that is, its ongoing dis- and refiguration of Asiatic personhood – has been elaborated around the cinematic spectacle of Asiatic faciality. By emphasising the social and historical legacy of the Asian face's reification and abstraction into a cultural sign, Wang's film does not, as some critics might fear, stabilise Asian-American subjectivity into a homogenous category, or flatten the multifaceted disparities encompassed in the relatively recent canon of 'Asian-American cinema'. On the contrary, the film's discursive reckoning with the visual underpinnings and aesthetic legacy of Asian-American visual culture is not in contradiction with the film's narrative and aesthetic singularity but serves rather as its very precondition.

THE FACE AND NATIONAL CULTURE

From its opening credits, *The Farewell* alerts us to several key formal motifs through which it will examine diasporic familial and psychic dynamics – static shots, wide aspect ratios, and an accentuation of the face counterintuitively eschewing extreme close-ups. The film's opening credits appear against a wide static shot framing an image of a lake bordered by a mountain valley. Even though the image is slightly out of focus, we can sense it is a pictorial simulation. Artificial flowers are positioned at the very foreground of the landscape, their larger scale relative to the lake accentuating the illusion of the valley's deep spatial recession. The intended tranquility the pastoral scene aims to conjure runs counter to the errant sounds of an intercom that alert us to its presence in a hospital. It is only when Nai Nai walks into the frame to answer a phone call from Billi that the image comes more sharply into focus. The widescreen framing of the medium close-up on Nai Nai invites us to read her expression in a continuum with the visibly artificial quality of the landscape, introducing the film's aesthetic investment in the mutual articulation of face and place. For if the mountain vista's crude perspectival tricks and mass-market veneer bring into focus its failed evocation of harmonious calm, it also underscores how Nai Nai's voice and facial expression fail to conceal her anxieties. When Billi asks about her whereabouts, Nai Nai lies, claiming she is at her sister's house rather than waiting to get medical results.

The scene then cuts to Billi in a medium tracking shot walking down a New York street as she talks to her grandmother. The widescreen composition of the shot emphasises a sense of lateral spatial extension that formally echoes the preceding shot of Nai Nai in the hospital. This graphic correspondence suggests a similar symbolic continuity between Billi's facial expression and the immediate environment that surrounds her. Since their brief conversation establishes their geographic distance, we are thus also invited to read Billi's environment not only as a representative snapshot of New York but of the US landscape more broadly. Although Billi is framed in a medium tracking shot in a side-profile, rather than the emphatic frontality typically linked to cinematic spectacle of the face, we are nonetheless acutely aware of her countenance precisely because she is passing by a mural of enlarged faces composited, in turn, by other faces (Figure 6.1). The reversibility between face and place here is then hyperbolically escalated into the face *as* place, wherein facialisation embodies and telegraphs a specific location's continuity with ideals understood as central to some collective notion of the national body politic.

In a subsequent shot framing Billi at a greater distance, we can discern the overall design of the mural more clearly. The heads are spliced together from the likeness of various iconic celebrities – Janis Joplin, Jimi Hendrix, and so on – but their particularities appear occluded from the blur of the shot's somewhat shallow focus, such that they more accurately register as the inchoate synthesis of generic facial typologies. Writing on the face's paradigmatic alliance with the concept of celebrity, Michelle Cho has argued that 'face value, or the sign system of faciality, transforms a living being into a concept, in a manner that the star text exemplifies'.[5] This transposition from person to sign is only

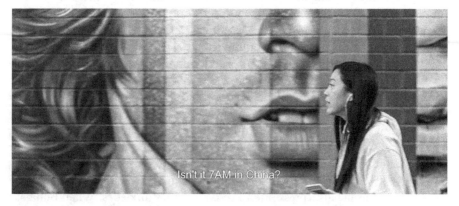

Figure 6.1 Billi (Awkwafina) walks past a mural of faces in *The Farewell* (Lulu Wang, 2019), A24.

enhanced by how each face appears drained of naturalistic skin tones in favour of a greyscale palette that mimics a black-and-white photograph. A striped row of alternating colours veils over the faces like a kaleidoscopic filter, as if to gesture towards the possibility of endless chromatic variations. The isolation and enlargement of the singers' heads, and the graphic designs' flattening of their particularities, seems to encrypt a semantic process that Cho calls 'the star text that has been condensed into dead metaphor, that is, face value'[6] such that they now appear 'depthless and unitary . . . signifying an iconic, transmissible archetype'.[7]

As the parallel editing between Billi and Nai Nai induces us to look for chiasmatic correspondences across each shot, we are thus invited to recognise how the mural also fails to denote the rhetorical message of cosmopolitan belonging it seeks to project. As the mural's different faces are recast in colours that casually dismiss the traditional semantic codes of racial legibility, the mural resonates with a narrative of abstract citizenship that Lisa Lowe has called 'the nation as a simulacrum of inclusiveness'.[8] For Lowe, the face of the abstract citizen serves as the locus through which the nation's subjects enter into a purely fantasmatic sense of cultural interrelatedness and legal and political equivalence. This interpellation into the collective social order, Lowe elaborates, hinges on 'the negation of the material conditions of work and the inequalities of the property system' as well as 'the historically sedimented particularities of race, national origin, locality, and embodiment', such that these properties are cast as extraneous or antagonistic to an underlying social order binding the body politic.[9] The mural's visual syntax of colour-blind kitsch ultimately entrenches rather than subverts the conceptual mechanisms of a normative racial regime, inducing what Lauren Berlant describes as the interpellation of racial minorities to 'identity with and desire the status of the unmarked'.[10]

Billi, however, appears visually disclocated from the mural's design, and somewhat indifferent to its address. Her side-profile slants at a contrasting angle to the uniform frontality of the mural's faces against which she appears diminished and thickly enfleshed. Her corporeality thus disrupts the uniform aesthetic of 'colour-blind', unmarked belonging its faces encode, expressing a certain social and symbolic incompatibility to its terms of inclusion. But even though she appears as a visual counterpoint to the mural's design, its subject matter cannot but enhance our awareness of her own face as that which differentiates her from the contours of abstract citizens. As Celine Parreñas Shimizu reminds us, in fact, 'the racial difference of the Asian is not so much captured in skin colour difference . . . but rather in the features of the Asian face . . . the Asian face functions like the skin, a racialised exterior supposedly indicating the threatening interior'.[11] In a different but nonetheless resonant context, Nguyen Tan Hoang's work on online sexual cruising describes a recurring pattern among gay Asian men of presenting themselves through bare-chested photos that crop out their heads. This practice of self-effacement allows them to momentarily '[pass] for a racially unmarked ideal homo body, [even though] its eventual reattachment to the Asian face undermines gay Asian cruisers' claim to sexual desirability, confirming their abject status once more'.[12] As the imagined interface between inside and outside, therefore, Asian facial phenotypes are treated as signs of an irreducible foreignness that persists even among citizens of the nation state, for 'if certain bodies *won't* change, or do so only recalcitrantly,' to quote David Palumbo-Liu, 'then it is taken as an index to their resistance or inability to assimilate.'[13]

I will return to *The Farewell*'s specific figuration of Asian faciality. But first, I want to underscore the particular affective and perceptual valences of the face's circulation as a sign in independent and narrative Asian-American cinema. Across a diverse range of Asian-American films, in fact, the face serves as the locus wherein the symbolic parameters of racial legibility are contested and renegotiated through sensory-aesthetic rather than strictly semantic or narrative terms. Through this comparison, I am not suggesting that 'Asian-American cinema', over the span of twenty years, can be reduced to a homogenising concern with facialisation. Instead, I want to underscore how formal correspondences organised around the Asiatic face in indie Asian-American film reveal shared political solidarities and strategies for disidentification between distinct diasporic lineages, while also shedding light on the shared cultural and symbolic terms that determine how racial formations are conceptualised. It is precisely this 'screen or cultural-image repertoire that inhabits us, much as language does', to quote Kaja Silverman, that is always and already implicitly under scrutiny and attempted rearticulation in the independent films I will address.[14]

MIRRORING AND GENERATIONAL RECOGNITION

While an exhaustive catalogue on the prominence of faciality in Asian-American film lies outside the scope of this essay, I will nonetheless narrow my focus on two films that share *The Farewell*'s institutional trajectory – Lee Isaac Chung's *Minari* (2020) and Michael Kang's *The Motel* (2005). Like *The Farewell*, both films premiered at Sundance and were propelled into varying degrees of critical visibility rarely conferred on API cinema in the American film industry. Chung's *Minari* focuses on a Korean-American family struggling to run a farm in rural Arkansas during the Reagan era. Released a year after *The Farewell*, Chung's film occupied a similarly central role within mainstream discourses on Asian-American representation, particularly during the yearly awards season. Like Wang, Chung was similarly featured in the same *New York Times* round table on the perceived resurgence of Asian-American cinema and the accompanying ambivalence that classification might induce among filmmakers. When asked, in fact, about the legitimacy of Asian-American identity as a category of reception and analysis, Chung argued that despite the obvious disparities across diasporic experiences, Asian-American filmmakers often share a particular affective terrain – the sense that dynamics of familial estrangement are intimately linked to the experience of national exclusion. He observes that

> it's not just an isolation that happens between us and society that tells us we're foreigners often. It's like an isolation that happens within our own families, where we don't understand our parents very well and they don't understand us.[15]

In *Minari*'s narrative climax, the spectacular display of the face probes the visceral affinity between alienated familial relations and feelings of incommensurability with the nation-state. In the film, the grandmother Soonja (Yuh-jung Youn) is a recent transplant in Arkansas, where her son-in-law Jacob (Steven Yeun) has uprooted their family. Here, he hopes to pursue his dreams of starting a farm to escape the dead-end menial jobs otherwise available to immigrants. Viewed with sometimes hostile scepticism by her grandson, David (Alan Kim), and granddaughter, Anne (Noel Kate Cho), Soonja repeatedly experiences calamities in her family's new surroundings. The gradual accretion of these misfortunes compromises her capacity for self-governance and self-containment in both the physical and psychic sense of these terms. She partially loses her ability to control her body after a stroke, peeing on herself one night, and later, in an event that will trigger the film's climax, she accidentally starts a devastating fire that will consume the family's harvested crops. As her daughter and son-in-law try to put out the fire, we witness Soonja walk away from the farm in a stunned trance. A tracking close-up shot registers her dissociated detachment from her surroundings suggesting she now views herself as an irredeemable liability and obstruction to her family's capacity to survive in the US. Her strained, listless walk away from their home seems to simply acquiesce to this landscape's apparent determination to expel her from its physical and existential boundaries. Adrift from her family and unmoored by any grounding narrative of national belonging, Soonja remains unresponsive to the acoustical surroundings, ignoring her grandchildren's cries to return home. It is only when her grandson runs to stand before her face to face that her dissociative trance is broken. If Soonja symbolically encodes the disparaged alterity of immigrant origins that perpetually locates the Asian-American 'outside the cultural and racial boundaries of the nation', to again cite Lowe, the emphatically scopic inflection of this scene suggests that any attempt to reparatively recuperate these familial-racial origins can only be psychically and culturally ratified through intersubjective recognition.[16]

Rather than frame this scene through the expected syntax of shot–counter–shot, with its implication of intersubjective reciprocity, however, this moment alternates between close-ups of Soonja's face and medium shots capturing her in the same frame as her grandchildren, David directly facing her while Anne observes them to the side. This spatial composition emphasises how the grand-mother's reattunement to her surroundings occurs not only through the affec-tive urgency and absorption she discerns in her grandson's face but also in the experience of seeing herself being seen. The film thus instantiates a process of mutual intergenerational reavowal via a familiar conceit in cinema in which 'every face-to-face is, at least potentially, also a moment of mirroring', to quote Thomas Elsaesser and Malte Hagener.[17]

Since this process of mirroring is specifically tied to forging a sense of mutual recognition across familial generations, the face-to-face motif in *Minari* evokes what psychoanalyst Christopher Bollas describes as 'the first other as mirror', a process instantiated in early childhood but never conclu-sively 'realized'.[18] Drawing on the work of D. W. Winnicott and Heinz Kohut, Bollas retreads a familiar psychoanalytic narrative in which mother–child relations initiate the subject's sense of self not only through an identifica-tion with an external image but also an external subjectivity. He writes, 'the good mother must mirror the infant, giving him back an image of himself that accurately derives from his inner experience'.[19] *Minari*, however, reverts the traditional symbolic exchange between the 'mother'-figure and her child with a grandmother–grandchild dyad, a substitution that bears upon familiar psychic territory for the Asian immigrant. In this scene, David's face encodes not only a psychic and affective validation of Soonja's presence within their family and its imagined futurity but as her (male) progeny, and an English-speaking American citizen, he also embodies what she imagines as a greater symbolic compatibility with US national culture that remains foreclosed to her as an immigrant. It is important to note that the granddaughter, Anne, does not face the grandmother, nor does the diegesis develop her subjectivity to a remotely comparable extent as her brother. It remains unclear, in fact, whether her 'expendability' to the film's core dynamics beyond her peripheral role as the 'dutiful daughter/sister' thematises and interrogates paternalistic prefer-ences for male children in Asian culture or unconsciously reinforces that very cultural script.

As the locus of his validating recognition, David's face, and the familial–national dynamics it encodes for Soonja, serves an analogous function to the mother's face as described by Bollas. Beyond the mother–child relationship, the external world is sensed by the child as hostile, unintelligible and menacing, but it is the mother's face that 're-presents the world' to the infant.[20] Similarly, for Soonja, David's face encodes a validating recognition while at the same time representing her lineage's extension and absorption into the borders of the US nation in such a way that can momentarily resymbolise the hostility of the American landscape.

The trope of mirroring in Michael Kang's *The Motel* (2003) similarly stages a sudden vertigo of intergenerational recognition between the more proximate dyad of son and mother. Rather than retread a narrative of generational conflict that casts blame on either the first- or second-generation immigrant, Kang's film explores how, for each generation, the desire for assimilation in US national culture is implicated in a reciprocal process of mutual disavowal. The film's protagonist, thirteen-year-old Ernest (Jeffrey Chyau) works in the seedy motel run by his mother Ahma (Jade Wu) when he isn't at school. Abandoned by her husband and exhausted by her thankless, unreliable work, Ahma continuously berates Ernest's new-found passion for writing, projecting a fecklessness on his ambitions that serves, as Eng and Han might put it, as a 'compensatory gesture that attaches itself to the losses, disappointments, and failures associated with immigration'.[21] Bespectacled and overweight, Ernest's physiognomy reinforces the emasculated stigma imposed on Asian men, rendering him prone to different forms of debasement and bullying. When he meets a charismatic Korean-American motel guest, Ernest's identification with him simultaneously recuperates his sense of damaged masculinity as well as his ability to project a version of himself that might be accommodated within the gendered and racial protocols of national culture. This relational development pushes him to express his hatred for his mother that is psychically bound to the cultural inheritance of racialised effeminacy she symbolises.

In the film's poignant conclusion, however, Ernest has recognised the destructive influence of the motel guest's toxic masculinity that leaves him feeling psychically and emotionally dispossessed. Ahma, in turn, has read one of her son's essays that prompts her to recognise the corrosive displacement of her anger on to him as well as their shared solitude. When the characters meet at the motel lobby, a handheld alternation between their close-ups emphasises the vertigo of an ambiguous recognition between them. Ahma intercepts her son's impassive but crying face, ignorant of his final confrontation with his forfeited ego-ideal while Ernest views his mother crying, unaware that she has read his essay. Nonetheless they hold each other's gazes, their alternating close-ups signifying the reconstitution of an intersubjective relationship that is visually reinforced by the mirror we see between them. The visual composition of this conclusion, and the formal equivalence it establishes between Ahma's and Ernest's faces, recategorises the losses of immigration and foreclosed assimilation that each character signifies, reformulating them not as oppositional dynamics but as the intimacy of an ongoing historical process, what Eng and Han describe as 'the intersubjective unfolding and outcome of the mourning process that underwrites the various psychic investments and losses connected to the immigrant experience'.[22]

Lateral Relations

In an interview on her cinematic influences, Wang establishes that she tried to 'play against . . . the expectation of what a Chinese-American family comedy would look like and feel like'.[23] *The Farewell*'s visual syntax of wide aspect ratio framings, static shots and precise blocking was motivated, she notes, by her desire to accentuate the phenomenological force of the actors' faces. Since their conflicted countenances register the lie they need to uphold, its simultaneous repression and attendant feelings of anxiety and mourning, faces possess an ecological valence in the film, materialising the affective milieu that binds the family together. At the same time, the conflicting emotional registers the faces forecast also crystallise a distinctly cinematic phenomenon tied to what Noa Steimatsky calls 'a truth of the face: its Möbius slippage of inner and outer, its equivocal visuality, its nudity bound up with its reticence'.[24] In light of Wang's attunement to the face as a key perceptual and affective property, it might appear strange that she has explicitly stated that *The Farewell* 'wasn't about close-ups', given that shot's paradigmatic alliance with the face in cinema and, as we have seen, with intergenerational dynamics in Asian-American indie film.[25] Instead, faces in Wang's film are relayed and revealed through the

> much wider aspect ratio that's traditionally used for landscapes, because we wanted to create a landscape of faces. Being able to see everybody in one frame, allows us to see the family unit as one character, because they are a character.[26]

As we have witnessed in the film's opening, in fact, *The Farewell*'s formal and conceptual syntax hinges on the symbolic reversibility of 'face' and 'place', the interarticulation between the histories of Asiatic facialisation and the repertoire of narratives and images that foster notions of national belonging. However, at the same time, the film's formal orientation towards the lateral, in its capacity to encompass a broader ensemble beyond the isolated individual, offers another visual grammar for conceptualising intergenerational relays beyond the presumed polarity the mirroring motif continues to signify in Asian-American film, even as it works to unsettle it.

Take, for instance, the first scenes in Nai Nai's apartment when we see Billi's extended family gathered together for the first time. At first, Billi's family forbids her from joining the trip since her face's transparent expressivity cannot conceal her emotional disposition. While Billi initially consents to their demands, she eventually decides to make the journey, showing up to Nai Nai's apartment unannounced while her family is gathered around the dining table. A wide frame captures their surprised reaction in a reverse shot from Billi's point of view. Some of her family turn their heads while still seated, others rise suddenly to face her, distributing their bodies across the wide frame. The recomposition of the familial ensemble into a new, more distributed configuration, creates graphic variations in height and posture that accentuates the sense of a unity that has been broken up, loosened and disseminated. This impression of dispersal, in turn, resonates with the emergence of submerged or repressed feelings the family have been keeping from Nai Nai which Billi's surprise arrival makes tacitly visible across their faces. Through the subtle yet ceaseless malleability of its internal forms, therefore, it is almost as if the family's shifting bodily relations function its collective 'face'. Recalling Wang's observation about framing the family as if they were a single character, in fact, the minor, fluctuating movements internal to their ensemble resonate with Georg Simmel's observations on how facial micromovements reconfigure the face's expressive unity, illustrating how meaning and expression are neither immanent nor static but arise out of the myriad mutable relations between different elements.[27]

Spaces and faces will continue to thematise each other's legibility. In the next scene, the wide frame accentuates its capacity to show different pockets of activity within a single spatial continuum, in this way paralleling the face's ability to capture a range of conflicting emotions on the same surface. Billi's mother, Lu Jian (Diana Lin) appears left of the shot's foreground as Billi enters the frame from the right in an adjacent room where her great-aunt is preparing meat pies her mother is frying. The rooms are connected by a sliding door left open, inviting us to repeatedly scan the width of the frame to discern the ebb and flow of the actors' paces and gestures, underscoring a kind of movement that does not occur in isolation but through the mutual transmission of bodily affect. Through these phenomenological coordinates, Wang again asks us to read the conspicuous framing and blocking of the scene alongside the equivocal expressivity of the family's faces. As Billi moves from the back room to the kitchen, she conspicuously perches her face on her mother's shoulder, aware that she is annoyed at her for reneging so impetuously on their agreement (Figure 6.2). The particular enfoldment of their bodies exemplifies how *The Farewell*'s blocking of actors exuberantly eschews the conventional, diametric opposition of face-to-face arrangements typically used to express intergenerational dynamics, whether in the same frame or via a shot–countershot convention. Instead, Wang seeks to reconfigure the conventional sensory schema through which Asian diasporic dynamics are thematised by using dramatically wide medium shots revealing characters' faces in the same frame. Within this formal device, they often appear in somewhat off-beat arrangements – Billi has a tendency to perch her head on the shoulder of both her mother and Nai Nai whenever she hugs her, for instance, and characters talk to each other whilst seated side by side rather than face to face as if to emphasise their embeddedness in a pictorial composition. In this particular scene, in order to tease and charm her annoyed mother, Billi again calls attention to her own countenance exclaiming 'look at my face, look at my face', at which point she smiles in a

Figure 6.2   Billi (Awkwafina) nuzzles her face in her mother's (Diana Lin) shoulder in *The Farewell* (Lulu Wang, 2019). A24.

broad, exaggerated manner, her arms akimbo, underscoring her capacity to manufacture positive affect in order to maintain the family's collective ruse. The static framing of the shot and its long duration emphasises how Billi continues to sustain this manic expression as she returns to her great-aunt in the adjacent room, turning her head back towards her mother as she shakes her derriere impertinently, her mother's annoyance not so much dissipated so much as casually diffused. The static, wide frames of the film are thus conducive to a kind of casual register that makes relationships appear more susceptible to a sense of mutually inflected play and movement rather than the unchanging familial solemnity close-ups tend to suggest.

Why then does this film offer a triangulation between the lateral, the facial and the intergenerational? In another context, the curator and art historian Charlotte Ickes has theorised how the time-based work of Isaac Julien and Steve McQueen visualises lateral lines of relation in the Black diaspora that supplant or displace patriarchal descent via 'their shared formal vocabularies of lateral cinematography across one or several screens'.[28] I want to extend and adapt the formal principles of Ickes's conceit to the (re)figuration of generational relations in *The Farewell*, arguing that the film's visual grammar strives to redress and resignify the Asian family's pathologisation in national culture while at the same time, and not in contradiction to this ambition, acknowledging how intergenerational familial conflict has historically served as a locus of Asiatic racialisation. The insistent lateral axis of the visual field, in fact, defamiliarises the conventional figuration of both faces and intergenerational bonds, domains through which Asiatic subjectivity has been construed as atavistic, static and totemic. Lowe observes, for example, how the governing cultural discourse's tendency to reduce and reify the psychic vicissitudes of Asian racialisation to 'first-generation/second-generation struggles displaces social differences into a privatised familial opposition' that negates how political and material forces impact experiences of racialised alienation.[29]

If this cultural script symbolises Asian familial kinship as an immutable psychic and cultural enclosure, the widescreen framings in *The Farewell* continuously emphasise the familial ensemble's continuous formal reconfiguration, instantiated by the lateral exchange and mutual correspondence of gestures and bodily affects that underscore its capacity for internal revision and transformation. By reorienting the vertical relations culturally encoded into the Asiatic face into the lateral expanse of a landscape, this formal and conceptual manoeuvre symbolises how intergenerational racial melancholia is not a static or timeless topology, nor is it an immutable psychic destiny. The film's articulation of faces through lateral arrangements conducive to movement and flux suggests that Asiatic racial formations and intergenerational kinship bonds have the capacity to be resymbolised and renegotiated through both historical and material vicissitudes as well as intersubjective alliances. By showing Billi debate her uncle in the same wide frame, *The Farewell* draws out formal correspondences between parent and child that accentuate not only their psychic and affective affinities but also their capacity to transform each other. As the film unfolds, for example, it is not only Billi's face that 'cracks up' to reveal her wavering resolve, but her family's as well, not through any kind of vertical, psychic inheritance but through a more lateral transmission of affect. Her father debates whether he should not, in fact, reveal the truth to his mother; her seemingly stoic uncle starts sobbing during the sham marriage as his wedding speech turns into a eulogy; and Lu Jian repeatedly fails to bite her tongue to express her long-suppressed irritation towards familial and cultural hypocrisies.

In an ironic reversal, in fact, Billi will eventually serve as the most reliable and resourceful family member in sustaining the lie. After the wedding ceremony, the family learn that Nai Nai has asked her housekeeper to pick up the test results of her latest medical scan. Billi rushes to the hospital, arriving just in time to intercept her grandmother's records, and together with her great-aunt she convinces a graphic designer to alter its diagnosis. The resolution of this potential catastrophe results in one of the film's most noted and enigmatic shots. Filmed in slow motion, the shot displays Billi at the centre of a wide frame flanked on either side by her parents, her uncle and her aunt, her cousin and his wife, and her great-aunt. Their decelerated gait and the release of facial strain on their countenances express a collective feeling of exhaustion and relief that appears to sync them into a psychic ensemble. The collective, open address of their faces thus produce a phenomenological experience akin to how Steimatsky describes the two-shot's ability to resituate the force of the individual face 'as part of a single greater expressive value' that '[can't] be assigned to any single face on its own'.[30] The composition of the shot and the family's binding

Figure 6.3   The ensemble cast in *The Farewell* (Lulu Wang, 2019), A24.

bodily affect de-emphasises the various lines of descent and succession within the family, resituating them in both visual and psychic terms on a lateral axis of equivalence.

The emphatically frontal disposition of their faces suggests that the family is collectively face to face with an off-screen face. In a certain reading, given the film's narrative premise, this entity would not be encompassed within a determinate presence but rather be a version of Nai Nai who exceeds her physical actuality to also include the symbolic mother/grandmother each family member has introjected and lost. This process of loss and grief occurs not only in anticipation of her literal, physical death but also through their various immigrant trajectories. In other words, Nai Nai as matriarch always and already encodes the 'mourning of mother and motherland', to again echo Eng and Han.[31] But for Wang, the aesthetic reinscription of this melancholy from something isolated and unacknowledged between generations to a lateralising conduit for mutual recognition initiates something like an alternative public collectivity that neither romanticises nor forfeits the family but resituates them as potential conspirators and companions.

Notes

1. David Eng and Shinhee Han, *Racial Melancholia, Racial Dissociation: On the Social and Psychic Lives of Asian Americans* (Durham, NC: Duke University Press, 2019), 48.
2. Halle Kiefer, 'The Farewell Says Hello to Year's Highest Per-Theater Box-Office Average, Bumping Off Endgame', *Vulture*, 14 July 2019. Available at <https://www.vulture.com/2019/07/the-farewell-makes-best-per-theater-box-office-average-2019.html> (last accessed 23 September 2021).

3. Brandon Yu, 'A Vision of Asian-American Cinema That Questions the Very Premise', *The New York Times*, 11 February 2021. Available at <https://www.nytimes.com/2021/02/11/movies/asian-american-cinema.html> (last accessed 23 September 2021).
4. Ibid.
5. Michelle Cho, 'Face Value: The Star as Genre in Bong Joon-ho's Mother', in Kyung Hyun Kim and Youngmin Choe (eds), *The Korean Popular Culture Reader* (Durham, NC: Duke University Press, 2013), 177.
6. Ibid., 178.
7. Ibid.
8. Lisa Lowe, *Immigrant Acts: On Asian American Culture Politics* (Durham, NC: Duke University Press, 2012), 5.
9. Ibid. 2.
10. Lauren Berlant, *The Queen of America Goes to Washington City: Essays on Sex and Citizenship* (Durham, NC: Duke University Press, 1997), 208.
11. Celine Parreñas Shimizu, *The Hypersexuality of Race: Performing Asian/American Women on Screen and Scene* (Durham, NC: Duke University Press, 2007), 116.
12. Nguyen Tan Hoang, *A View from the Bottom: Asian American Masculinity and Sexual Representation* (Durham, NC: Duke University Press, 2014), 198.
13. David Palumbo Liu, *Asian/American: Historical Crossings of a Racial Frontier* (Palo Alto, CA: Stanford University Press, 1999) 85.
14. Kaja Silverman, *Threshold of the Visible World* (London and New York: Routledge, 1996), 211.
15. Chung quoted in Yu, 'A Vision of Asian American Cinema'.
16. Lowe, *Immigrant Acts*, 6.
17. Thomas Elsaesser and Malte Hagener, *Film Theory: An Introduction Through the Senses* (London and New York: Routledge, 2009), 9.
18. Christopher Bollas, *Cracking Up: The Work of Unconscious Experience* (London and New York: Routledge, 1995), 241.
19. Ibid.
20. Ibid.
21. Eng and Han, *Racial Melancholia*, 50.
22. Ibid., 48.
23. Lula Wang quoted in Nick Allen, 'Lulu Wang on The Farewell, How Horror Movies Influenced Her True-life Dramedy and More', *Rogerebert.com*, 8 July 2019. Available at <https://www.rogerebert.com/interviews/lulu-wang-on-the-farewell-how-horror-movies-influenced-her-true-life-dramedy-and-more> (last accessed 23 September 2021).
24. Noa Steimatsky, *The Face on Film* (New York: Oxford University Press, 2017), 270.
25. Lulu Wang quoted in Nick Allen, 'Lulu Wang on The Farewell'.
26. Ibid.
27. I thank Alice Maurice for suggesting to put this observation in dialogue with Simmel. Georg Simmel, 'The Aesthetic Significance of the Face [1901]', in Kurt H. Wolff (ed.), *Georg Simmel, 1858–1918: A Collection of Essays* (Columbus Ohio State University Press, 1959), 276–81.

28. Charlotte Ickes, 'Radical Immersion in the Work of Melvin Van Peebles, Isaac Julien, and Steve McQueen' (PhD thesis, University of Pennsylvania, 2016), 33.
29. Lowe, *Immigrant Acts*, 63.
30. Steimatsky, *The Face on Film*, 268.
31. Eng and Han, *Racial Melancholia*, 80.

7. THE NEW TRANSACTIONAL FACE: RETHINKING POST-CINEMATIC AESTHETICS THROUGH *THE NEON DEMON*

Jenny Gunn

> Know your faces: it is the only way you will be able to dismantle them and draw your lines of flight. (Deleuze & Guattari, *A Thousand Plateaus*)

As media scholars Zara Dinnen and Sam McBean have asserted, a fascination with the face as 'a new kind of digital object' characterises much of recent mainstream narrative cinema.[1] Examining the casting of Scarlett Johansson in a trilogy of science fiction films including *Her* (Spike Jonze, 2013), *Lucy* (Luc Besson, 2014) and *Under the Skin* (Jonathan Glazer, 2013), Dinnen and McBean argue that contemporary narrative cinema's attempts to render the face as story offer a useful working through of the increasing technologisation of the face in digital culture.[2] Pointing to the rise of both digital self-mediation and facial recognition surveillance, Dinnen and McBean reference visual artist Zach Blas's concept of a 'Global Face Culture'.[3] Indeed, digital technologies of facial surveillance achieve a new level of exploitation via the achievement of the digital facial image or DFI. As Dinnen and McBean describe, citing Blas, 'Facial recognition programs work by making over the face as co-ordinates, data; such systems "substitute the meaning of faces for a mathematics of faces".'[4] As they astutely suggest, Scarlett Johansson's science fiction films seem to affectively map the anxieties surrounding this technologisation of the human face, and they are alert to the problematic use of Johansson's white femininity as a repeated and universal signifier for the 'human' in these films.[5] In their exclusive attention to the science fiction genre and to questions of the posthuman, however, Dinnen and McBean overlook the digital object of the face (and particularly the white female face as its algorithmic ideal) as a significant capital form in what I deem the post-web 2.0 era.

Coined by author and web designer Darcy DiNucci in 1999, the term web 2.0 addresses changes to the Internet around the new millennium that allowed for greater participation, user-generated content, and interoperability.[6] While all of these characteristics still exist, the continued and uncritical use of the term web 2.0, now two decades old, does not adequately address the significant changes in the experience of online media since 2010. Like post-modernism in relation to modernism, more than the 'web 3.0', which problematically suggests continual progress, the post-web 2.0 maintains continuity with the characteristics of web 2.0 but marks a noteworthy shift in user experience. With the rise of the smartphone, the increasing capacity of cloud storage, increased Internet speeds, and the rise of social media and photo-sharing sites, online experience in the twenty-teens becomes predominately image based. With the demands of social media platforms such as Facebook to use verifiable identities for account names as well as the widespread participation in practices of digital self-broadcasting via the forward-facing smartphone camera and webcam, the user experience of the post-web 2.0 is increasingly characterised by reproductive likeness and the circulation of photographic media.

Beginning with the 'selfie', contemporary practices of digital self-mediation have often been described pejoratively in the popular media as an exacerbation of cultural narcissism.[7] But both the popular psychology and psychoanalytic concepts of narcissism that inform such judgements are challenged in the philosophy of Gilles Deleuze who, writing in *Difference and Repetition* affirms narcissism as a precondition for creative invention.[8] In place of narcissism, it is through the later concept of faciality in *A Thousand Plateaus* that Deleuze and Guattari critique the ideological function of the ego and egoism.[9] As Deleuze and Guattari argue, it is through faces that the twin processes of subjectification and signification come to colonise oneself. Given the variety of new digital objects now composed of faces, it seems that we are experiencing an intensification of the facialising regime.[10] To further explore this conjunction, this chapter performs a narrative and aesthetic analysis of Nicolas Winding Refn's 2016 film, *The Neon Demon*. As I argue, via a post-cinematic iteration of the filmic close-up, *The Neon Demon* performs an immanent critique of the for-profit facialisation that characterises neo-liberal influencer culture, digital photo-sharing, and branding strategies in the post-web 2.0 of the twenty-teens.[11]

Deleuze and Guattari stress that the intensification of faciality coincides with the expansion of capitalism, associating the alienation of labour under capitalism to the already alienating processes of signification and subjectification.[12] The faciality of capitalism is suggested equally by the faces populating first coins, later paper money, and the magical thinking of commodity fetishism. In the context of advanced capitalism, the concept of faciality continues to be relevant to the analysis of contemporary digital culture and the increasingly popular practices of self-mediation, or broadcasting, that characterise social media photo-sharing practices. While Yasmin Ibrahim has importantly emphasised the exploitation of narcissism for capital growth with the rise of the smartphone, the forward-facing camera, and other wearables, the concept of narcissism fails to fully address the other predominant mode of consumption engendered by these technologies: that is, the manner in which objects of all kinds are facialised and made exchangeable within the gridded format of the newsfeed scroll in social media and photo-sharing platforms such as Facebook and Instagram.[13] Although as users we may upload the content of our choosing, it inevitably must conform to the facialising frame of these applications, which thereby render anything and everything exchangeable and monetisable as content. In such an environment, it hardly seems surprising that the human face has itself become a predominant object of exchange. Rather, I would suggest that the emergence of the selfie format in the 2010s seems metonymic of the larger operations of facialisation at work on all objects shared as images within post-web 2.0 digital technologies.

Winding Refn's *The Neon Demon* is a salient film in relation to this contemporary zeitgeist given its obsessive exploration of both a libidinal and capitalist investment in the face. Describing *The Neon Demon* as a 'film for the future' to *Cahiers du Cinéma* upon its debut at the Cannes Film Festival, Winding Refn uses tropes of both camp and horror to create a cautionary tale addressing the increasing facialisation of neo-liberal visual culture.[14] He explains its narrative premise as concerning the increasing viciousness of beauty culture and its predation on youth in contemporary digital culture.[15] As in earlier eras, today's beauty industry relies on an investment in and exploitation of the young female face. In *The Neon Demon*, 'the face' is embodied in Jesse (Elle Fanning), a sixteen-year-old ingenue recently arrived in Los Angeles to begin a modelling career.[16] The fact that the film is set in Los Angeles – the mecca for social media influencer culture – rather than the high fashion capital of New York, is an early clue as to the more salient target of *The Neon Demon*'s social and political critique.

The film begins ambiguously with an arresting medium shot of Jesse wearing a metallic blue mini-dress, splayed lifelessly across a divan with a pool of blood at her feet, dripping from a wound at her neck (Figure 7.1). From this opening shot, one may be led to believe that her throat has been slit, and she is dying (particularly given the gratuitously violent ending of Winding Refn's previous film, *Only God Forgives* (2013)). But in fact, once the camera pulls out into a long shot, revealing the presence of set lights and the flash of a camera lens, it becomes clear that Jesse is posing for a photo shoot. Although she aspires to become a fashion model, this shoot is only a favour for her friend Dean (Karl Glusman), an entry-level photographer, and precedes her later ascent to fame. The film's opening shot does, however, ominously foreshadow the film's violent end when, after having achieved fast success in the Los Angeles fashion industry, Jesse is murdered by a trio of envious competitors who murder and literally consume her body in an attempt to steal her beauty for themselves. From beginning to end then, it is clear that in the film's LA fashion world, *the look* is worth anything and everything. After the opening fashion shoot, one of Jesse's eventual assailants, the makeup artist Ruby (Jena Malone), takes Jesse under her wing, first inviting her to an industry party later that night and ultimately helping her to break into the fashion scene's tight milieu. As Ruby insists, recalling the trope of the threatening Hollywood ingenue from classical Hollywood films such as *All About Eve* (Joseph Mankiewicz, 1950), Jesse's youth and inexperience, and her 'whole deer in the headlights look', are exactly what the industry is looking for. It is thus established early on in the film that youth is a commodity that Jesse currently possesses, but one that is impossible to retain as her immediate competitors and 'it girl' predecessors in the industry, Gigi (Bella Heathcote) and Sarah (Abbey Lee), quickly realise after their displacement upon Jesse's arrival.

Winding Refn describes *The Neon Demon* as charting a journey from innocence to narcissism.[17] During the first half of the film, Jesse remains largely unaware of either her physical beauty or its power over others. This is not to say that she is blind to its potential monetary value. As she tells Dean early in the film, she was inspired to come to LA because even though she never had a talent, she was always pretty and 'you can make money off of pretty'. Yet, it is made clear in the film's narrative that both the full effect of her beauty as well as its potential exchange value surpass her naive understanding. Jesse's arrival in LA is met by all she encounters variously with astonishment, lust, envy, but

Figure 7.1   The film's spectacular first image of Jesse on a modelling shoot, from *The Neon Demon* (Nicolas Winding Refn, 2016).

always desire. As *Cahiers du Cinéma*'s Cyril Béghin rightly points out, in addition to classical Hollywood references, *The Neon Demon* knowingly recalls the narrative of David Lynch's post-modern *Mulholland Drive* (2001) and Betty's (Naomi Watts) fantasy of Hollywood discovery summed up by its famous tag line, *this is the girl*.[18] In altering the narrative context from the milieu of Hollywood film to that of the fashion industry – exchanging the actress for the model – Refn's film speaks more directly to the post-web 2.0 cultural moment: whereas the actress, Betty, still had to put in a convincing audition in order to land the part, like the aspiring social media influencer, Jesse need only show up and be seen. Her rise to success in the LA fashion scene thus recalls the notional 'famous for being famous' of well-known LA celebrity-influencers of the post-web 2.0 era such as the Kardashian-Jenners. As Winding Refn states of his character – like the social media influencer more generally – Jesse 'appears, that's all'.[19] Tellingly, in casting Elle Fanning as Jesse, he consulted only her fashion modelling work and not her previous films, concerned primarily with her ability to pose. Indeed, close-ups of Fanning as Jesse in the film, which play off her paratextual celebrity as a fashion icon and brand ambassador for fashion and makeup companies such as Tiffany and L'Oréal, unfold as a series of highly stylised poses.[20] As Naomi Fry describes of aspiring social media influencer, Dominique Druckman, a subject of Nick Bilton's recent documentary *Fake Famous* (2021), it is ironically the absence of personality that is key to the influencer's success. As fellow aspiring influencer Chris Bashir explains of Druckman, like Fanning's Jesse, her attractiveness to brands is her inherent malleability, comparing her to a 'piece of Play-Doh'.[21]

Winding Refn cites his young daughter as inspiration for the character of Jesse after having witnessed the manipulative influence of digital media beauty culture on her self-conception and sense of reality as well as its exploitation of her as a young female consumer.[22] The appetites of an increasingly predatory beauty culture characteristic of the era of YouTube makeup tutorials is personified in the film through the people surrounding Jesse, all of whom literally want a piece of her, as is made clear by Ruby, Gigi and Sarah's incorporation of Jesse in the film's graphic, cannibalistic ending. The fierce competitiveness between the models in the film is reminiscent of that between wanna-be social media influencers as examined in both *Fake Famous* and Liza Mandelup's related documentary of aspiring YouTube influencers, *Jawline* (2019). As these films explore, influencing is a 'tedious' form of labour that demands a high degree of upfront investment with little possibility of reward, and as *The Neon Demon* accurately portrays, fashion is one of its largest and most competitive genres.[23]

As her journey progresses from the new girl to fashion's hottest commodity, the primary action of *The Neon Demon* largely consists of a series of encounters between Jesse and various voracious and exploitative figures in the fashion industry – other models, fashion designers, photographers and agents. Since the film works largely within the generic patterns of horror, her eventual success as a model culminates after her infection by the titular 'neon demon', which lures her through an elaborate self-seduction sequence occurring around the one-hour mark that unfolds in a highly stylised mirrored *mise-en-scène*. Her infection by the neon demon, through which Jesse first becomes aware of her beauty's power, instigates her descent from innocence into what Winding Refn describes as a 'total' and literally monstrous narcissism.[24] Through the appearance of the neon demon, Jesse, like Ovid's Narcissus, becomes exposed to and for the first time fully aware of the intoxication and value of her own appearance through the reflection of her face. The narrative arc of this journey is sparse – little cause is established for the appearance of the neon demon or its targeting of Jesse (perhaps due to Winding Refn's budget constraints) – instead the film, and particularly this central sequence, is predominately interested in conveying mood. *The Neon Demon* draws our attention to the event of self-mediation, an overlooked commonplace in the contemporary culture of social media broadcasting, as a compelling experience of autoeroticism and self-seduction. Images from this sequence unfailingly recall modern-day uses of the forward-facing camera and their appropriation in fashion ad campaigns, which routinely sell narcissism as an aesthetic look that shorthandedly references contemporary digital culture: notable examples include a recent promo video *Vogue* magazine released on IGTV in collaboration with rapper Cardi B, or any myriad of Kardashian-Jenner promotional ads for their proprietary brands such as *Skims* or *Good American*. The titular neon colour of the demon and, moreover, the film's lighting design as a whole, likewise underscore the film's aesthetic borrowing from millennial digital culture. Popular digital photographer, Signe Pierce, who has frequently utilised neon in her work associates the colour variously with the 'hyperreality'/ futurism of Los Angeles, millennial youth culture, the escapism of the Trump era, and the neo-noir of David Lynch and Gaspar Noé.[25]

Lasting over five minutes in length, the neon demon's seduction sequence begins just after Jesse is chosen to close the runway show for fashion designer, Robert Sarno (played by an uncredited Alessandro Nivola), a coup for a new model. After the close of the show, the demon appears suddenly to Jesse in a symbolic form (an inverted triangle composed of four smaller ones). The film then cuts from the fashion show discontinuously to an unknown and darkly lit interior environment where the short mini-dress Jesse modelled for Sarno has suddenly transformed into a long gown. Here, Jesse reappears in long shot, silhouetted and emerging from the centre of a blue-lit diamond shaped doorway that redoubles the form of the neon demon. The sequence unfolds without diegetic sound, featuring only the non-diegetic soundtrack of the at-turns propulsive and scintillating score of Cliff Martinez, which as Stephane Délorme notes, itself functions as a sort of narcissistic and emotional double for Jesse throughout a film generally low on dialogue and high on affect.[26] As the composer for Harmony Korine's *Spring Breakers* (2012), Martinez's similar score here recalls Korine's earlier prescient narrative concerning a solipsistic neo-liberal youth culture as well as its similarly affective audio-visual aesthetics, reminiscent of music video.[27] Relatedly, Signe Pierce identifies cinematographer Benoit Debie's use of neon in *Spring Breakers* as the 'patient zero' for its emergence as the predominating millennial aesthetic signature of the twenty-teens. Hiring Debie after his work on Noe's *Enter the Void*, Korine requested a 'very colourful, very candy', aesthetic for *Spring Breakers* that astutely remediates the escapist, visual junk food binge characteristic of photo and video-sharing platforms such as Instagram and YouTube in the twenty-teens.[28]

Viewed in long shot at the start of the sequence, a significant distance from the blue-glowing neon demon, Jesse soon proceeds to walk towards it (as well as the camera), reiterating earlier sequences featured in the film of Sarno's runway shows. As she approaches the camera more closely, entering into a filmic close-up, the formerly symbolic demon enters the frame, transformed into a multidimensional, translucent crystal that reflects Jesse's image back to her on three of its faces. At first frightening her, these reflections together seem to possess a will of their own as they move forward towards her, no longer conforming to her own limited movements. As she watches her doppelgängers' fold into one another, the menacing blue crystal iteration of the demon disappears, replaced by a seductive neon pink one in which Jesse now becomes utterly infatuated by her reflected images, succumbing to narcissism (Figure 7.2). An autoerotic seduction proceeds to unfold as her central doppelgänger kisses and caresses the surfaces of her other reflections. Following this sequence and until her death, Jesse navigates the LA fashion world with a new and threatening awareness of her face as a commodity asset.

While this narcissistic seduction sequence is unquestionably abstract, it is also highly climactic to the film both temporally and thematically. More attentive to miming the visual excess of photo-sharing culture that to fulfilling expectations for cinematic plot, *The Neon Demon* is a film largely devoid of narrative continuity that is much more intent on cultivating mood: recalling sources as various as music video, Giallo horror and fashion advertising.[29] As an allegory of neo-liberal

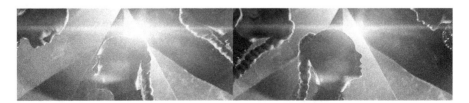

Figure 7.2   Jesse's narcissistic transformation by the titular Neon Demon, from *The Neon Demon* (Nicolas Winding Refn, 2016).

beauty culture's predations the film's narrative may be heavy-handed, but it is aesthetically astute in its reproduction of the affective investment in appearance above all else, in surface over depth, and especially in the face, all of which characterise the look of contemporary photo-sharing culture. In its emphasis on filmic affect, *The Neon Demon* employs a variety of aesthetic devices to make Jesse's beauty palpable: lighting effects such as lens flares, coloured filters, and strobe effects, manipulated frame rates, suspenseful diegetic silences, and of course its pointed reliance on Martinez's seductive score. But beyond all of this, most salient of the faciality characteristic of contemporary digital culture is the film's predominating if also paradoxical usage of the filmic close-up.[30]

Whether fashion photographers, seducers or rivals, everyone that Jesse encounters is intoxicated by her appearance, particularly her face. The most compelling example of this occurs during Jesse's first casting audition with Robert Sarno. Whereas one would anticipate a fashion designer to be most attentive to the figures of his models, in this case the audition sequence, which unfolds in a tight shot-reverse shot from low-angle shots of Sarno to high-angle shots of Jesse, leaves no ambiguity as to his singular fixation on her face. Echoing the narrative diegesis, *The Neon Demon*'s aesthetic preoccupation is itself the spectacle of Jesse's face, which the film prioritises through its tendency towards close-ups in place of fetishistic shots of her body. The film's preferred shot is by far the medium close-up. As opposed to the standard or extreme close-up, the choice of the wide-angle medium close-up renders a sort of repetitive flatness to images of Jesse that is resonant of both the fashion magazine campaign, now migrated to the contemporary context of photo-sharing platforms such as Instagram, and the monotonous action of the social media scroll through which such images are consumed (Figures 7.3 and 7.4).

Figure 7.3   Medium close-up of Jesse on a modelling audition, from *The Neon Demon* (Nicolas Winding Refn, 2016).

Figure 7.4   Medium close-up of Jesse reminiscent of fashion ad aesthetics, from *The Neon Demon* (Nicolas Winding Refn 2016).

This flattened aesthetic corresponds to the paradoxical nature of *The Neon Demon*'s close-ups, which break from the traditional function of the close-up in Hollywood cinema to reveal character emotion and interiority. Instead, the close-ups of *The Neon Demon* are properly post-cinematic. As Steven Shaviro has argued, post-cinema not only reiterates the affective experience of late capitalism but likewise of the digital technologies that fuel its acceleration.[31] Responding to the aesthetic modes and consumption practices of digital media, examples of post-cinema are most typically identified by their increasing modulations, frenetic editing patterns, and post-continuity narrative structures.[32] They may also mimic the experience of other digital media such as multiplayer games. As Shaviro explains, post-cinema breaks from the perspectival mode of passive viewing characteristic of classical cinema, instead attempting to replicate the refracted surface scanning typical of the more interactive Internet experience. In short, proponents of post-cinema argue that after the digital turn, cinema turns away from the classical narrative mode, returning to the spectacular mode characteristic of early cinema, or what Gunning deems the cinema of attractions.[33] Given the changes to the user-end experience of the web in the twenty-teens that I have emphasised through the concept of the post-web 2.0, theories of post-cinema need necessarily expand to include filmic traits such as the paradoxical close-ups of *The Neon Demon* that mimic the aesthetic look of the social media and photo-sharing practices which now dominate a great deal of contemporary user-generated content.

In *Cinema 1*, Deleuze argues that the filmic close-up allows for the unique achievement of the affection-image.[34] Whereas in the movement-image of the classical cinema, the face in close-up typically remains tethered to narrative meaning, in the affection image (more characteristic of the art cinema or what

Deleuze deems the time-image), the face is removed from its significant and subjective function and instead becomes a register of the affective encounter, synonymous with the close-up itself.[35] As Deleuze clearly states, 'There is no close-up of the face. The close-up is the face.'[36] In the close-up, the actions of the face are captured as a receptive plate whose micro-movements register an affective reaction. In the moment when the close-up accedes to the affection-image, the face becomes removed from its individuating function within the action-oriented filmic narrative. Not every close-up achieves this state, however; the affection-image is rare in the movement-image of classical Hollywood cinema where instead the normative functions of faciality preside. Deleuze argues that the affective use of close-ups is more frequently achieved in the time-image of the modern art cinema (Deleuze gives the example of Bergman's *Persona* (1966)).[37] As Greg Flaxman and Elena Oxman argue, 'If the face is caught up in or captured by a politics, the politics of the face constitutes a project to dismantle its determinations.'[38] According to Deleuze, cinema possesses this radical potentiality. Although it is not necessarily intersubjective, the affection-image always registers a relation, that is, the effects of an encounter with an external object or phenomenological other. Action-image close-ups are also equally relational even if their significance is restricted to the representational meaning of the filmic narrative.

In *The Neon Demon*, however, we experience a close-up of a third kind not yet enumerated in Deleuze's cinema books. The post-cinematic close-ups of Jesse, inspired by both the look and equally the transactional nature of the faciality of social media and digital photo-sharing sites, fail to register any external affective relations. This lack of relationality precisely captures the blank allure of Jesse and of the social media influencer more generally. As Winding Refn states, *The Neon Demon* traces Jesse on a journey from innocence to narcissism, but in fact as Freudian psychoanalysis explains, as emotional states these are not at all distant.[39] In either case, the innocent or the narcissistic face is free from the blemishes of external relation; it remains blank and therefore infinitely monetisable. These new a-relational close-ups that we witness in *The Neon Demon* are thus fully post-cinematic. Metonymic of the digital screen more generally, Jesse's face is a scannable but impenetrable surface. Returning to Deleuze and Guattari's observation that the exploitations of faciality increase in the capitalist era, the emergence of the anti-affective close-up seems a climactic development in the recent history of post-cinema worthy of further scholarly consideration.

The concept of faciality is alert to the dangers of self-alienation and the potential loss of the immanence of our affective experience to the expressive demands of the signifying subject. As the post-cinematic close-ups of *The Neon Demon* aptly convey, the face of Jesse is bereft of interiority or intentional expressivity. Its 'influencer' beauty is precisely its blankness seemingly indicative of its utter availability for external use and an inexhaustible exchange value. And yet, as in the culture of neo-liberalism more generally, the commodification of the self, traced in Jesse's narrative arc in *The Neon Demon* is inflected with an intensified ethos of competition. Whereas an early Benjaminian analysis might insist that commodification effaces aura, the issue is not so simple when considering the human as commodity. In the visual culture of social media influencing, there are faces like Jesse's that do indeed sell better, and these most often conform if not to the ideal image of a youthful white femininity then to other gendered and racialised stereotypes or what Alexander Galloway deems 'cybertypes'.[40] Indeed, in her 2019 article 'The Age of Instagram Face', Jia Tolentino describes the predominating popularity within photo-sharing sites for a vaguely ethnic white female face, the seeming algorithmic average of femininity in the age of Instagram.[41] Modelled most closely after the look of Armenian-American Kim Kardashian, the heavily filtered Instagram face – high cheek bones, narrow nose, flat chin, big lips and cat eyes – is now the most sought after goal of cosmetic procedures as reported by multiple Los Angeles plastic surgeons Tolentino interviewed.[42] Photo-sharing culture has thus exacerbated an already damaging post-feminist feedback loop in which in order to be the most monetisable online, one need already be heavily leveraged in the commodification of the self. There is, however, an additional layer of irony that Tolentino describes: in their collective attempts to 'pop' on Instagram, more and more of the faces we see look the same, a dynamic she disturbingly if astutely relates to Marc Augé's concept of post-modern architectural 'non-places'.[43] Adapting Augé's terminology, Tolentino references journalist Kyle Chayka's report on an uncanny global proliferation of an 'International Air B&B style' in the twenty-teens with the rise of social media travel tourism applications such as Four Square, whose algorithms respond to aggregate user preferences by tending to recommend similar spaces and experiences all over the world.[44] As Chayka remarks, 'aesthetic homogeneity is a product that users are coming to demand, and tech investors are catching on'.[45] He continues, intriguingly comparing this new culture of homogeneity to the psychic condition of depersonalisation.[46] In comparing her own examination of the Instagram face to Chayka's analysis of contemporary interior design, Tolentino asks us to consider further the embodied effects of digital visual culture and algorithmic aggregation, implicitly posing the question of whether we have naturally evolved from the homogeneity of the non-place to the non-face.

The entrepreneurial self of neo-liberalism is often a willing participant in this process of self-erasure as they participate in processes of self-commodification through cosmetic procedures, now seen by many as prerequisite to compete in the contemporary digital attention economy. *The Neon Demon* is importantly alert to the rigged and manipulative cruelty of this system. No matter how much entrepreneurship of the self that Jesse's rivals, models Gigi and Sarah, pursue (in the drastic form of plastic surgery and other extreme interventions), they can no longer compete with Jesse's youth, leading them ultimately to murder her by the film's end; here, competition is a zero-sum game. In addition, although Jesse is invariably desired, the stimulus of others' attraction to her is entirely transactional and self-interested. In the fashion milieu in which the film is set, Jesse is nothing more or less to others than a source of value to exploit. Whereas in an earlier film such as Max Ophuls's *Lola Montès* (1955), this process of exploitation was approached as a matter of misrecognition, reaffirming the humanity of the woman beneath her objectification, in the horror story of *The Neon Demon*, female commodification is a brutal, indisputable if also consensual reality. This is ostensibly the future that Winding-Refn's film wants to warn us against but signs of which are already visible in the contemporary context of the post-web 2.0. As Tolentino reports, the US plastic surgery market has surged in the era of injectables, and 92 per cent of such procedures are performed on women.[47]

In his final works of the early 1990s, Deleuze issues a series of warnings regarding the singular force of marketing in late capitalism. In 'Postscript on the Societies of Control', for example, he observes that 'this is no longer a capitalism for production but for the product, which is to say, for being sold or marketed'.[48] While in *What is Philosophy*, he and Guattari regret that 'the only events are exhibitions and the only concepts are products that can be sold'.[49] These observations seem particularly prescient in the context of the marketing and commodification of the self that characterises contemporary photo-sharing culture and social media influencing. Although in their late works Deleuze and Guattari may not explicitly foresee the totalising logic of the market overtaking the self, the earlier concept of faciality and their observation regarding its intensification under capitalism certainly point towards this conclusion. Like Tolentino, however, one must underscore the ironic consequences that emerge when everyone wants to stick out by looking alike. In such a context, it seems we can no longer presume to receive the promises of the cinematic close-up: neither the significant and subjectifying function of its classical form nor the opening to interiority and the traversal of affect made possible in the affection image. Abandoning the affective potential of escaping the face and of faciality, the near future represented in *The Neon Demon* is fully bought in – its post-cinematic close-ups accumulating like currency, leaving us with only more of the same.

Notes

1. Zara Dinnen and Sam McBean, 'The Face as Technology', *New Formations* 93 (Summer 2018), 123.
2. Ibid.
3. Zach Blas, 'Escaping the Face: Biometric Facial Recognition and the Facial Weaponization Suite', *Media-N* 9:2 (2013). Available at <http://median.newmediacaucus.

org/caa-conference-edition-2013/escaping-the-face-biometric-facial-recognition-and-the-facial-weaponization-suite/> (last accessed 23 September 2021); Dinnen and McBean, 'The Face as Technology', 124.

4. Dinnen and McBean, 'The Face as Technology', 125; Blas, 'Escaping the Face', n.p.
5. Dinnen and McBean, 'The Face as Technology', 133; Steven Shaviro, *Post Cinematic Affect* (Winchester and Washington: Zero Books, 2010).
6. Darcy DiNucci, 'Fragmented Future', *Print* 53 (4):32 (April 1999), 221–2.
7. See for example, Brooke Lea Foster, 'The Persistent Myth of the Narcissistic Millennial', *The Atlantic*, 19 November 2014. Available at <https://www.theatlantic.com/health/archive/2014/11/the-persistent-myth-of-the-narcissistic-millennial/382565/> (last accessed 23 September 2021); Zoe Williams, 'Me! Me! Me! Are We Living through a Narcissism Epidemic?', *The Guardian*, 2 March 2016. Available at <https://www.theguardian.com/lifeandstyle/2016/mar/02/narcissism-epidemic-self-obsession-attention-seeking-oversharing> (last accessed 23 September 2021).
8. Gilles Deleuze, 'Repetition for Itself', in *Difference and Repetition* (New York: Columbia University Press, 1995), 7–128.
9. Deleuze and Guattari, 'Year Zero: Faciality', in *A Thousand Plateaus: Capitalism and Schizophrenia*, trans. Brian Massumi (Minneapolis: University of Minnesota Press, 1987).
10. Ibid.
11. In the context of advanced capitalism, Hal Foster argues that the only possible form of critique is inherently immanent (and thus complicit) to its object of analysis, see Hal Foster, 'Post-critical', *October* (1 January 2012), 3–8.
12. Deleuze and Guattari, 'Year Zero: Faciality', 182.
13. Yasmin Ibrahim, 'Coalescing the Mirror and the Screen: Consuming the "Self" Online', *Continuum* 31:1 (2017), 104–13. In the cinema books, Deleuze explains that the concept of faces should not be restricted to human subjects, see Gilles Deleuze, *Cinema 1: The Movement-Image*, reprint edition (London and New York: Bloomsbury Academic, 2013), 63–7.
14. Cyril Béghin and Nicholas Elliott, 'Un film pour l'avenir: entretien avec Nicolas Winding Refn', *Cahiers Du Cinéma* (June 2016), 34–8.
15. Béghin and Elliott, 'Un film pour l'avenir'.
16. Ibid.
17. Ibid., 36.
18. Cyril Béghin, 'Écrin total', *Cahiers Du Cinema* (June 2016), 31–3.
19. Béghin and Elliott, 'Un film pour l'avenir', 35.
20. Ibid.
21. Naomi Fry, '"Fake Famous" and the Tedium of Influencer Culture', *The New Yorker*, 20 February 2021. Available at <https://www.newyorker.com/culture/on-television/fake-famous-and-the-tedium-of-influencer-culture> (last accessed 26 February 2021).
22. Béghin and Elliott, 'Un film pour l'avenir'.
23. Fry, '"Fake Famous"'.
24. Béghin and Elliott, 'Un film pour l'avenir'.
25. Dane Harrison and Dane Scott, 'Why We're All So Obsessed with Neon', *i-D*, 2 August 2018.Available at <https://i-d.vice.com/en_uk/article/ne54nd/why-were-all-so-obsessed-with-neon> (last accessed 26 February 2021).

26. Béghin and Elliott, 'Un film pour l'avenir'; Stèphane Delorme, 'Moment Musicaux: Narcisse, *The Neon Demon* de Nicolas Winding Refn', *Cahiers Du Cinema* (June 2016), 36–7.

27. For more on millennial narcissism and *Spring Breakers*, see Jenny Gunn, 'Deleuze, Žižek, Spring Breakers and the Question of Ethics in Late Capitalism', *Film Philosophy* 22 (Winter 2018), 95–113.

28. Harrison and Scott, 'Why We're All So Obsessed with Neon'.

29. Winding Refn has described as inspired by the segmentation of YouTube viewing practices as well as his own experience as a director of moody advertising campaigns for perfumes: see Béghin and Elliott, 'Un film pour l'avenir'.

30. Ibid.; Delorme, 'Moment Musicaux', 36–7.

31. Shaviro, *Post Cinematic Affect*.

32. On post-cinematic aesthetics, see also the edited collection available online, Shane Denson and Julia Leyda (eds), *Post-cinema: Theorizing 21st-century Film* (Falmer: Reframe Books, 2016). Available at <http://reframe.sussex.ac.uk/post-cinema/> (last accessed 11 May 2016).

33. Wanda Strauven (ed.), *The Cinema of Attractions Reloaded: Film Culture in Transition* (Amsterdam: Amsterdam University Press, 2006).

34. Deleuze, *Cinema 1*, 106–21.

35. Ibid.

36. Ibid., 111.

37. Ibid., 116–17.

38. Greg Flaxman and Elena Oxman, 'Losing Face', in Ian Buchanan and Patricia MacCormack (eds), *Deleuze and the Schizoanalysis of Cinema* (London and New York: Bloomsbury Academic, 2008), 49.

39. Béghin and Elliott, 'Un film pour l'avenir', 36.

40. Alexander R. Galloway, *The Interface Effect* (Cambridge and Malden, MA: Polity, 2012), 136–8. See also Lisa Nakamura, *Cybertypes: Race, Ethnicity, and Identity on the Internet* (New York: Routledge, 2002).

41. Jia Tolentino, 'The Age of Instagram Face', *The New Yorker*, 12 December 2019. Available at <https://www.newyorker.com/culture/decade-in-review/the-age-of-instagram-face> (last accessed 24 February 2021).

42. Ibid.

43. Marc Augé, *Non-Places: An Introduction to Supermodernity* (London and New York: Verso, 2009).

44. Kyle Chayka, 'Welcome to AirSpace', *The Verge*, n.d. Available at <https://www.theverge.com/2016/8/3/12325104/airbnb-aesthetic-global-minimalism-startup-gentrification> (last accessed 1 March 2021).

45. Ibid.

46. Chayka, 'Welcome to AirSpace'.

47. Tolentino, 'The Age of Instagram'.

48. Gilles Deleuze, 'Postscripts on the Societies of Control', *October* 59 (Winter 1992), 6.

49. Gilles Deleuze and Felix Guattari, *What Is Philosophy*, trans. Hugh Tomlinson and Graham Burchell (New York: Columbia University Press, 1996), 10.

8. BLACK FACES MATTER: CLOSE-UPS IN *SELMA, FRUITVALE STATION* AND *MOONLIGHT*

Delia Malia Konzett

Contemporary African American film directors, now more firmly in control of the medium's production apparatus, are articulating a new black film aesthetics on their own terms. This newly advanced aesthetics addresses and revises a legacy of severely biased and impaired representations in Hollywood rooted in vaudeville minstrelsy and practices of Jim Crow racial segregation. This essay will limit its analysis of this broad topic and focus in particular on the close-up of the face. A shot that traditionally mediates narrative agency, the close-up expresses empathy through the micro-physiognomy of facial reactions, and overall identification with the lead protagonist, usually defined by receiving a majority of the film's close-ups. The latter allows the spectator to experience the diegetic world directly through the hero/ine's eyes. Pascal Bonitzer posits the close-up as crucial for establishing the psychology of a character in the history of cinema, communicating a new complexity of desire and perversion: 'Once the body had been rendered immobile and attention had become focused upon the face or the gaze, the law, desire and perversion made their entrance into the cinema.'[1] Our question here is to understand how recent black film directors attempt to communicate this complexity of the gaze, the total effect of the close-up and its affiliated expressive spectrum of desire and perversion, in new ways that accommodate a black perspective, one actively depicting that black faces matter on screen and in everyday life.

My discussion will explore the innovative cinematic aesthetics of the close-up in three films: Ava DuVernay's *Selma* (2014), Ryan Coogler's *Fruitvale Station* (2013) and Barry Jenkins's *Moonlight* (2016). It will do so with a consideration of the contributions of the film's respective cinematographers Bradford Young, Rachel Morrison and James Laxton, who alongside the entire production team, helped realise the directors' unique visions on screen. All three films depart from traditional genre conventions such as the African American history melodrama (*Selma*) or the inner-city ghetto or hood genre (*Fruitvale Station*; *Moonlight*) that define audience expectations usually in terms of clichés of singular heroic action to overcome systemic oppression or pervasive milieus of criminality that entrap its inhabitants. Instead, DuVernay, Coogler and Jenkins explore in their films the mapping of narrative biographies within the symbolic framework of a diverse African American community. All three directors additionally come to their subject matter with a background in social activism and hence consider their work as a necessary correction of entrenched cultural stereotypes that have defined the African American community both from without and within.

SELMA AND THE OBSCURED CLOSE-UP OF MARTIN LUTHER KING

A filmic account of Martin Luther King's legacy runs the immediate risk of borrowing from romanticised heroic historical narratives or biopics favoured by Hollywood, as they usually provide a clearly defined male protagonist for audience identification and the celebration of his victorious individuality. Paula Massood correctly identifies in Ava DuVernay's *Selma* a subversive 'focus on the work of activism rather than individual heroics', claiming that 'while much of the film's power derives from its detailed presentation of the personalities and events leading up to the march, *Selma*'s real drama is located in the story of the nascent Voting Rights Act'.[2] This non-traditional narrative choice by DuVernay requires also a recalibration of the film's visual aesthetics, facing the double burden of making King both the centre and not the centre of the film, a strategy displayed in the film's opening scenes intercutting between King's Nobel Peace Prize speech (1964) and the prior historical event of the 16th Street Baptist Church bombing in Birmingham, Alabama.

From a narrative point of view the film frames King's appearance between two key events, namely the film's initially depicted 16th Street Baptist Church bombing in Birmingham, Alabama (15 September 1963) and the film's final sequences covering the Selma to Montgomery protests marches (7–21 March 1965). This type of narrative framing places King's interventive activism into a multilayered history of systemic racism combining white supremacy, social, economic and cultural segregation, racially profiled policing, secondary citizenship and restricted voting rights. The film gives additional focus to the female victims of the Birmingham bombing via a transitional cut to a close-up of a voting registration form filled in by Annie Lee Cooper (Oprah Winfrey) seeking to attain her voting rights. Throughout the film Martin

Luther King has to answer to his wife Coretta for both advice and his marital conduct, making the focus on women subvert the predominantly male environment of civil rights activists, their opponents and the Washington politicians. DuVernay thus revisits the historical events with a more pronounced attention given to black women as key contributors to civil rights activism.

Selma's cinematographer Bradford Young, known for his expressive lighting style supported by low-contrast filters, as well as the use of top lights and available lights rather than a fully lit set with traditional three-point lighting, introduces the audience to his enigmatic cinematography in the powerful opening scene of the film. Much has been said about the film being prohibited in its use of King's actual speeches and DuVernay rewriting them in an approximation of King's rhetorical style, thereby diminishing the historical authenticity of the film. However, critics ignore that this diminishment is used by the film strategically, not only in its sound image but also in the visual representation of King via obscured close-ups. Before coming to the crucial scene of the Birmingham bombing, the film opens on a black screen with King's (David Oyelowo) voiceover, much like the opening scene of Francis Ford Coppola's *The Godfather* (1972). The speech, rather than raising the grand rhetoric of the actual Oslo address – 'I accept this award on behalf of a civil rights movement which is moving with determination and a majestic scorn for risk and danger to establish a reign of freedom and a rule of justice' – begins with a humbler elegiac note, providing a transition to the subsequently shown bombing: 'I accept this honour for our lost ones, whose deaths pave our paths.' At this point, the camera cuts to a wide frame close-up of King centred in the image. The lighting is restricted to top lighting (no fill-in or back lighting) and makes King and his skin colour recede into the muted dark brown background of chocolate damask drapes.[3] Contrary to one's expectation in a historical drama, the first image of King appears to show no defined contours separating his face from the background and comes across as nondescript with its obscure lighting style. This presentation of King will be frequently given throughout the film, deflating his individuality while retaining his visionary presence for the civil rights movement. A notable shot of this obscure type includes even King's mugshot in prison framed as a medium close-up but treated in the same manner of assimilating him into the background (Figure 8.1). However, in this shot the lighting is harsh, frontal and unflattering with the contours more pronounced, stressing a physical awareness of being imprisoned in a systemically racist society. By comparison, his wife Coretta is usually presented with more light on her or with brighter outfits next to which King appears muted. DuVernay's film deconstructs the historical iconicity of its lead protagonist and presents him in more natural light conditions, making him instead a participant and mouthpiece in a larger collective struggle.

Figure 8.1   Martin Luther King (David Oyelowo) in prison with harsh medium close-up assimilated into the background in *Selma* (Ava DuVernay, 2014).

King's opening speech in the film eventually breaks the fourth wall with his remark, 'This isn't right.' The camera cuts back from the close-up into a wide shot of a hotel room and shows us that King's direct address to the camera was a rehearsal of his Oslo speech in front of a mirror. In the scene, he further expresses dissatisfaction with his necktie, which appears to be wearing him, and the aggrandised ceremony that stands in stark contrast to the reality in the US. After a two-shot of King and his wife facing the camera, a cut to the Oslo award ceremony flushes the Kings to the far back sitting underneath a large modern painting with the foreground being occupied by the emcee introducing King. As King steps up to the podium to deliver his speech, the film abruptly cuts away to the Birmingham church bombing with the voiceover providing a sound bridge again reminiscent of *The Godfather* and its conflicting images of sacred ritual and violence. DuVernay and Young's film, especially in its cinematography and editing style, deliberately decentres King, stressing the actual historical events that give rise to his activism with its grass-roots perspective rather than a top-down movement carried by a charismatic leader.

In close cooperation with the director DuVernay, Young recounts their intent in depicting the initial bombing scene:

> Ava DuVernay wanted to show 'the violence against the black body' that was common in the period the film takes place. 'We tried to use speed

BLACK FACES MATTER

as a way of giving us a different rendition of the moment,' Young says, explaining the use of slow motion in sequences like the bombing of the 16th Street Baptist Church that killed four young girls. 'It is violent, but at the same time, it is visual. These little girls were beautiful, but what was happening to them was not beautiful,' he says. 'And I think we had to straddle that dichotomy of making pretty pictures, but also reminding us that those moments in time were extremely, extremely violent and grotesque.'[4]

As the film cuts from Oslo to Birmingham, we find ourselves inside a church looking down a staircase. Five young girls and a boy dressed for church enter the frame from the left and proceed to go downstairs. The camera shoots the children in part-whole close-ups from the rear, the back of their heads, then showing their feet, and then their hands clasping the rail, thus fragmenting their bodies. When facing the camera, their faces are mostly out of focus and blurred. The only fully recognisable view is given to the church's colourful though muted mosaic window, connecting it back to the various works of art displayed at the festive Oslo ceremony. These art works build a graphic bridge throughout the film and King's home is later seen decorated with several paintings by Romare Bearden, the celebrated Harlem Renaissance artist. The lighting of the scene is done in a low-key style with warm sepia tones emulating Kodachrome photography and adds to the aesthetic atmosphere.[5] At mid-level, the boy leaves the group as the girls continue to proceed downward, eventually leaving the frame except for a single girl shown isolated on the steps of the staircase as a bomb burst suddenly enters the screen from the right, producing images of fragmentation and debris. This scene is shot in slow motion and also shows floating bodies suspended in mid-air in a liquid image reminiscent of the Omaha beach scene in *Saving Private Ryan* (1998) or Willa Harper (Shelley Winters) floating underwater in her submerged car in *The Night of the Hunter* (1955). Eventually, the camera cuts to an overhead shot and rotates in both directions over a now desaturated, harshly lit and hazy image of debris and bodies, articulating the violence in more realistic fashion. The violence done to the black bodies aims at their aesthetic and ceremonious appearance, producing Young's dichotomy of 'pretty pictures' and 'extremely violent grotesque' moments.

Bradford Young's reference to 'moments' and the use of slow motion shows the film mobilising a time-image rather than an action image. Philosopher and film critic Gilles Deleuze sees the emergence of the time-image connected to the disastrous violence of World War II with many films producing sleepwalking and shell-shocked protagonists deprived of agency and decisive action. The paralysis of the action image reflects a severe trauma that freezes reality into dreamlike images of pure contemplation. Deleuze describes the time-image in war films in terms similar to Young's description of the Birmingham scene:

127

'Nor is it a matter of scenes of terror, although there are sometimes corpses and blood. It is a matter of something too powerful, or too unjust, but sometimes too beautiful, and which henceforth outstrips our sensory-motor capacities.'[6] The time-image in *Selma*'s bombing scene overwhelming the senses follows this style and produces a close-up or moment of contemplation of a different kind. The entire Birmingham bombing scene can be said to become the extended time-image of King's facial close-up at the opening of the film. The close-up provides an expansion of space while the slow-motion scene offers an expansion of time. Thus, King's close-up provides via its intersection with his Oslo speech, the ceremonious aspects of award and church ceremony, the art works and the formal attire, a continued reflection on what motivates his speech, making its oratorical content visible as that of a visionary movement.

Following the Birmingham bombing, the film dissolves into the close-up of the voting registration form filled in by Annie Lee Harper, connecting the image forward to an action image as response to the violence. Unlike European postwar time-images reflecting perplexity, indecisiveness and a sense of nihilism, *Selma*'s time-images cannot indulge in this paralysis of action. Young's unorthodox time-image as a quasi-close-up of frozen history prepares the viewer for the film's final scenes depicting the protest marches moving forward on the crucial bridge crossing. The historical Edmund Pettus Bridge, named after a Southern Civil War general and Grand Dragon of the Ku Klux Klan, is introduced in a slow tracking shot capturing the bridge's name in a high angle close-up. The slow tracking speed of this close-up recalls the slow-motion bombing scene and adds a layer of sustained systemic violence preserved in the infamous name of the bridge. The shot then moves past the bridge gate facing downward and overlooks the marching crowd from an overhead perspective. These crowd scenes shot in wide format are in fact close-ups of momentous history taking place in front of our eyes and connect once again with the film's initial close-up of King and his forward-looking vision of activist change. Carolyn Giardina notes 'a Technocrane shot that drops down to the protesters on the bridge and into an eye-level view of King' and cites Young's comment: 'It's the triumphant moment when our heroes cross the bridge without state or federal interruption; it needed to feel big and intimate and iconic.'[7] By the film's end, the time-image has transformed into a utopian image that blends with the action image. King's obscured close-up and its subsequent extended time-image reaching both into the past and the future produces the contemplative gaze of the film and the unfolding of history. It combines both King's visionary activism and his spirituality – as also highlighted by his proximity to artwork – and relates it via the other important close-up of Annie Lee Cooper to the pragmatic political issue of attaining voting rights. The latter close-up is therefore sharper in its contours, whereas King's obscured close-up hovers over the entire film as a form of spirit, inspiring the daily activities of the protesters and activists.

FRUITVALE STATION, FACING FORWARD AND THE EMPATHETIC
CLOSE-UP OF OSCAR GRANT

Ryan Coogler's *Fruitvale Station* (released July 2013), based on the shooting death of Oscar Grant by a BART (Bay Area Rapid Transport) police officer in 2009, can be seen as a cinematic parallel to the Black Lives Matter movement. This movement emerged on social media in July 2013 in response to the murder of Trayvon Martin and eventually morphed into a wider activism of street protests against criminal profiling of blacks by the police and vigilante citizens. The film opens with cell phone footage of a bystander witnessing the shooting of Grant and thereby references social media as a tool that can bypass the censorship of official media, malfunctioning security cameras and police bodycams, and edited press releases by the police. As *The New York Times* film critic Lena Wilson comments on the aesthetic choices made by Rachel Morrison, the film's cinematographer: 'In the moments leading up to Oscar's shooting, Morrison portrays him as if through a cell phone: the aspect ratio becomes claustrophobically vertical, shakycam techniques mimic a handheld device, and the film is at its grainiest.'[8] This type of raw footage is also imitated throughout the film with many outdoor neighbourhood scenes shot in grainy film stock and naturalistic lighting and with the BART train periodically cutting through the shot horizontally, marking the boundary of death anticipated in the film's opening. Frequent use of handheld camera is applied to family gatherings and group gatherings, giving it a documentary quality of the unofficial and untold story behind the death of Grant.

Apart from this integration of social media footage into the film's style, the empathetic close-up takes centre stage. It is intended to humanise a lost black life, which routinely would show up as a police statistic of purported criminals meeting an untimely end during a law-and-order intervention. By the time the film was released, the court had already reached the conclusion of the wrongful killing of Grant and the film did not need to revisit the legal question involved. Rather, its main goal was to dig deeper into the dehumanising profiling to which black inner-city youths are subjected, making them a primary target for systemic violence carried out by the police and the adjoining prison industrial complex. The close-up is intended to counteract the police's othering of black lives by reinstating a face-to-face recognition with the victim and drawing attention to valuable lives lost to systemic and blind violence administered on the basis of racism. In addition, over-the-shoulder shots, stressing a forward-facing perspective, give the film a utopian horizon of hope and redemption in spite of the depicted tragedy and violence.

According to the French political theorist Jacques Rancière, the police is the antithesis of politics: 'The essence of the police lies in a partition of the sensible' and 'presupposes a distribution of what is visible and what not'.[9] As a force patrolling not only the street but also the symbolic system, the police, according to Rancière, carve up the sensorium and determine the conditions of visibility and invisibility in a society. It comes as no surprise that in the case of Oscar Grant, security cameras at the station where he was shot did not capture the fatal interaction. Additionally, a train full of passengers and potential witnesses to the incident was waved through the station rather than recorded for eyewitness accounts.[10] The police's work follows Rancière's definition by making an entire event unseen for the public, one that takes its origins by making the victim invisible and hence vulnerable to violence. A gun and a taser are confused in a moment of convenient blindness and lead to the unfortunate outcome if one were to believe the police officer. Conversely, the task of politics, according to Rancière, 'is to make the world of its subjects and its operations seen'.[11] Cinema as a technological apparatus interested in representing the full sensorium of experience in this manner closely resembles the work of politics. Hence, in *Fruitvale Station*, director Ryan Coogler and cinematographer Rachel Morrison focus on shedding light on the unseen life of Oscar Grant, one that the authorities have made systemically and symbolically invisible.

Whereas *Selma* needed to reintegrate King into the larger collective of the civil rights and voting rights movements, *Fruitvale Station*'s main goal is to isolate, humanise and individualise an otherwise anonymous victim of police violence. Rachel Morrison, known for her empathetic cinematography, makes it her task to read the face of Oscar (Michael B. Jordan) closely via intimate close-ups that betray his quick shift of and struggle between conflicting emotions. These close-ups present the psychological and interior world of Oscar's life torn between crime and the pursuit of a family life highlighted throughout the film. Oscar is no saint, as he has spent time in prison for drug dealing, cheats on his girlfriend with whom he has a daughter, loses his job for showing up late for work, and lies about it to his family. It is this drama of conflicted emotions and commitments which the camera tries to gauge and depict in his facial expressions. Significantly, many of the close-ups show not only Oscar's face for an illumination of his emotions but also capture him in over-the-shoulder shots from the rear facing forward, allowing the spectator to take in the world from his perspective.

Ryan Coogler and his production team deliberately play with the Hollywood conventions of the hood genre and the marriage melodrama, mixing these two incompatible genres. Two close-ups, namely of the street sign 'Fruitvale St' and of a bridal gown store sign (Joanna Janeth Bridal), reflect this pull between different fates as the camera tracks Oscar driving in opposite directions. On the one hand, the film revisits 'hood films', which, according to Paula Massood, 'narrate the coming-of-age of a young male protagonist and the difficulties of such an undertaking in the dystopian environment of the inner city'.[12] For example, brief neighbourhood scenes in *Fruitvale Station* evoke John Singleton's *Boyz n the Hood* (1991) with a similar focus on a volatile social environment. On the other hand, the genre of melodrama allows Coogler to insert utopian moments of sudden and unexpected change in behaviour, stressing family bonds, repentance and the pursuit of redemption that negate the hood genre's deterministic world.

Early close-ups of Oscar betray a variety of emotions, particularly during his visit to the grocery store where he attempts to get his job back. The mixture of various facial expressions ranging from communicative to hostile behaviour break up the more monotonous guarded expressions of portrayed criminals in the hood genre. This diversity of behaviour also frees up a biography for a potential remapping of its path rather than following the dead end of entrapment in one's environment. A crucial scene which anticipates Oscar's reversal is a drug run with a prior stop at a gas station. Encountering a stray dog who is subsequently fatally wounded by a passing car, Oscar is given a glimpse of his own derailed life. A tight close-up on the paralysed paws of the struck animal suggests the immobility into which Oscar has cornered himself. As he goes on to the location of the drug deal, he waits at the edge of a lake overlooking the water. The camera switches at this point to closely framed over-the-shoulder shots looking forward in Oscar's direction, when he parks his car, looks at the dashboard of a picture of him and his daughter, and walks towards the lake. Close-up profile shots then show him contemplating his life and a flashback scene sends us back to his time in prison. During a prison visit by his mother Wanda (Octavia Spencer), the camera gives us many close-ups of Oscar and his mother in a shot–reverse–shot exchange. The closely depicted conversation reflects the entire spectrum of family relations, fondness for the daughter and anger over Oscar's irresponsible lifestyle. Wanda's emotional close-ups are significant since they will contrast with the final close-ups in the hospital where she will exhibit a calm resolve and quiet mourning rather than panic, anger or despair.

Following the flashback prison scene, the film's resumes with Oscar getting rid of his drugs rather than selling them. From this point on, the film offers multiple close-up over-the-shoulder shots of Oscar when he picks up his daughter at the daycare centre or meets his extended family for his mother's birthday party, suggesting that he is now facing forward. Rather than looking closely at Oscar's face, the camera is now looking with Oscar closely at the people that matter to him most. Oscar comes clean with his girlfriend about his job situation and also confesses to leaving the drug business. His mother's birthday party and the New Year's Eve festivities melodramatically underscore the birth of a new identity. Oscar pulls a birthday card from underneath his shirt where he formerly hid his stash of drugs, and his daughter Tatiana (Ariana Neal) is shown blowing out the birthday candles on her grandmother's cake in close-up. As Oscar readies his daughter for bedtime, further close-ups depict them brushing their teeth. Both Oscar and Tatiana make funny faces not unlike pictures taken in a photobooth. The shot becomes a bittersweet snapshot of a joint future that cannot come to fruition. This shot stands in contrast to preceding close-ups of Tatiana looking apprehensive about Oscar going out late at night, anticipating the tragedy of growing up without her father. On the train to San Francisco, the film highlights a lesbian couple kissing and follows up on the motif of the couple in an encounter with a heterosexual married and pregnant couple during the New Year's festivities. This scene foreshadows a forward-looking perspective in the manner of melodramatic redemption, since Oscar indicates several times during the film that he wants to settle down with his girlfriend Sophina (Melonie Diaz), projecting a happy ending of which the film is ultimately deprived.

Close-up shots in *Fruitvale Station* are defined by their diverse emotional expressions or calmer and commemorative forward-facing perspectives. Much like Oscar's slow-motion running scene with his daughter at the daycare centre, they follow the action image to stem against entrapment and immobility, stressing the act of looking rather than a system of imposed invisibility. Tatiana and Wanda feature in significant close-ups and complete the forward-looking perspective that is cut short with Oscar. These close-ups ultimately blend with those reflecting strong emotions and exhibit more a reflective calm, pointing to a meaningful life that is taken away in violent and untimely fashion from the family. One of the most memorable close-ups of the film shows Oscar carrying Tatiana on his back at the daycare centre (Figure 8.2). These shots are inserted as flashback memories when the camera focuses on Oscar hooked up to the ventilator in the hospital in close-up. In the brief flashback sequence, shot in

Figure 8.2 Grainy and raw close-up of Oscar (Michael B. Jordan) passing his gaze onto Tatiana (Ariana Neal) facing forward in *Fruitvale Station* (Ryan Coogler, 2013).

grainy and raw style, we see him likewise in close-up turning his head towards Tatiana, meeting her eyeline, as she looks forward. This single shot dramatises the transfer of love and agency which the film communicates, as Oscar passes the legacy of his look on to his daughter, preserving his institutionally denied gaze into an uncertain future. The film subsequently cuts back to a close-up of Oscar in the hospital when his life expires.

Reconstituting Fragments of a Biography: Close-up and Vision

Like *Fruitvale Station*, Barry Jenkins's *Moonlight* (2016) invokes the hood genre but similarly deviates from its embedded nihilism into a more utopian perspective. The fragmented biography of Little/Chiron/Black is in fact reconstituted as whole through the film's use of facial close-ups that fill in the void of meaning in a life characterised by abandonment, trauma, uncertain identity and a criminal milieu. The gaze of the lead character in various stages of his life reconnects with the tropical landscape of Florida, which acts as an uplifting moral compass or utopian horizon and provides the necessary vision to sustain a biography of choice rather than contingency. Two scenes, namely Chiron's (Alex R. Hibbert) metaphorical birth to identity when learning to swim in the ocean and Black's (Trevante Rhodes) final reconnect with his first and only love Kevin (André Holland) in the Liberty City diner, will illustrate how Jenkins and his cinematographer James Laxton plot the film's existential message of finding a home and sanctuary via the use of intense close-ups.

The film's coming-of-age story ultimately brings the uprooted boy from Liberty City into a closer relationship with the landscape of Florida that surrounds him, aiding him in the learning process of self-discovery and growing maturity. A central scene in the film – a scene of instruction – is Chiron's trip to Virginia Key beach with his paternal mentor Juan (Mahershala Ali) who teaches Chiron how to float and swim, literally and metaphorically empowering him how to become secure in his surroundings. The shaky handheld camera, recalling Chiron's first anxious shot in the film, shows him now fully immersed and floating in the ocean – 'you're in the middle of the world, man', Juan says encouragingly while supporting his head and body – and then cuts back to an earlier scene with Chiron still fully dressed, testing the boundary of beach and ocean in a long shot. This scene is accompanied by Juan's voiceover that mixes with the surf of the ocean and the wind, hence giving his voice a quasi-natural authority and letting the landscape of Florida speak: 'Let me tell you something, man. There are black people everywhere. Remember that, okay? No place you can go in the world ain't got no black people. We's the first on this planet.' It is here, during this memorable voiceover, where the film makes a crucial switch from the more local world of the African American experience to the global connectedness of all black people, the black diaspora, while laying claim to the planet as its first settlers.

For the beach scene, the Ari Alexxa XT digital camera, used by Laxton throughout the film, is taken into the ocean, allowing the viewer to stay at eye level close to the characters with the waves lapping against the camera.[13] The filmmakers also chose a Hawk V-Lite anamorphic lens that stretches a small aspect ratio screen to a wide-screen format, usually featured in 35mm films focusing on panoramic landscapes such as the Western film. As Laxton explains:

> The attempt was to promote those emotions, not just to present them, but to promote them to a place where you can sense the intensity by which Chiron's character is going through these things. What it means to that character to be bullied, to have to deal with these sexual questions that he's going through in his teenaged years. Our idea was to present them visually with that same amount of intensity. Which for us meant *anamorphic lenses* that express this heightened sense of existence that I think audience members sometimes associate with bigger tent pole films but we're presenting this sort of nuanced subtle story but with that same heightened value.[14]

In *Moonlight*, with its many close-ups and domestic scenes, this widescreen format is used counterintuitively but adds to the effect of the audience's intimate proximity to the enlarged characters, blending into the landscape of Florida. The characters thereby participate in the landscape in the possible sense of dwelling in and belonging to a world. A tight two-shot of Chiron and Juan reveals swaying palm trees in shallow focus with the sound of the ocean and wind continuously pervading the scene. In this aestheticised and archetypal treatment of Florida's beach, the landscape assumes a moral dimension. Juan offers Chiron the following advice: 'At some point you gotta decide yourself who you gon' be. Can't let nobody make that decision for you.' This vision of self-determination passed onto Chiron is enlarged into the utopian vision of a global blackness not defined by hegemonic national cultural concepts.

The final diner scene in the film marks in many ways the inaugural moment of Chiron's possible escape from natal alienation and homelessness. As he passes the entrance door to the diner, he is graphically matched with a big sign that reads 'Open', indicating an opening or a way out. The scene recalls the earlier dining scene with Juan and Teresa, during which the introverted child opened up and disclosed his name. Juan is evoked in Chiron's appearance, now looking much like his mentor. The diner scene, set in a country style restaurant with cozy curtains and faux Tiffany lamps, is not without some tension as Kevin is visibly upset that Chiron is engaged in 'trappin'' (drug dealing) and asks him 'why you got them damn fronts' (teeth grills). At the same time, the scene also features significantly held close-ups when their eyes first meet at the diner counter focused intently on the mutual gaze as a form of direct communication and openness (Figure 8.3). In a second significant exchange of looks,

Figure 8.3   Reciprocating close-ups of Chiron/Black (Trevante Rhodes) and Kevin (André Holland) in *Moonlight* (Barry Jenkins, 2016).

Kevin explains his reason for cold calling Chiron in Atlanta due to 'a dude' playing a certain song, namely Barbara Lewis's 'Hello Stranger'. This sequence shows Kevin walking to the jukebox to make his point and then standing next to it gazing off frame in the direction of Chiron for considerable time, leaving an empty space for the imagination to fill in before returning to the close-up reverse shot. This shot especially indicates that there is room for reimagining and recasting Chiron's identity in the gaze of Kevin.

Visual culture theorist Nicholas Mirzoeff posits the right to look as prior to visuality, namely the established visual codes by which any national, social or economic authority proclaims and maintains its apparent legitimacy: 'The right to look is not about seeing. It begins at a personal level with the look into someone else's eyes to express friendship, solidarity, or love. That look must be mutual, each person inventing the other, or it fails.'[15] This look is certainly borne out in *Moonlight*'s close-up exchanges between Chiron and Kevin but also in *Fruitvale Station*'s empathetic camera which reinvents its lead character Oscar as more than a statistic of a fatal encounter with the police apparatus, serving as a quasi-stand-in for an intimate human gaze. Likewise, the visuality of the perception of the black gaze construed by state and law enforcement in *Selma* is radically altered in returning the close-up to the black community and its subjective and collective agency. According to Mirzoeff, 'the right to look claims autonomy, not individualism or voyeurism, but the claim to a political subjectivity and collectivity'.[16] As this essay has argued, all three directors and their respective cinematographers not only stress an activist perception but anchor this perception in the close-up wherein black faces matter in their human reciprocity, challenging the status quo of Hollywood's systemic visuality and order of things.

NOTES

1. Pascal Bonitzer, 'Hitchcockian Suspense', in Slavoj Žižek (ed.), *Everything You Wanted to Know about Lacan (But Were Afraid to Ask Hitchcock)* (London: Verso, 1992), 15–30, 17–18.
2. Paula J. Massood, 'To the Past and Beyond: African American History Films in Dialogue with the Present', *Film Quarterly* 71:2 (Winter 2017), 19–24, 21.
3. *Set Décor* on *Selma*, 21 January 2015, 1–29, 22. Available at <https://www.setdecorators.org/?name=SELMA&art=setdecor_awards_detail&SHOW=SetDecor_Film_SELMA> (last accessed 24 September 2021).
4. NPR Interview: 'A Most Vibrant Year for Cinematographer Bradford Young', 1 March 2015, 6:05 PM ET, 1–7, 2. Heard on *All Things Considered*. Available at <https://www.npr.org/2015/03/01/389481636/a-most-vibrant-year-for-cinematographer-bradford-young> (last accessed 24 September 2021).
5. Questions and Answers with Bradford Young, 'Times of Strife', *The American Society of Cinematographers* (February 2015). 'Ava said to me, "I want this film to have a Kodachrome look to it"', 1–3, 2. Available at <https://theasc.com/ac_magazine/February2015/QandAwithBradfordYoung/> (last accessed 24 September 2021).
6. Gilles Deleuze, *Cinema 2: The Time-Image*, trans. Hugh Tomlinson and Robert Galeta (Minneapolis: University of Minnesota Press, 1989), 18.
7. Carolyn Giardina, 'Cinematographer Bradford Young's Career on the Rise with *Selma, A Most Violent Year*', *Hollywood Reporter*, 9 December 2014, 1–6, 3. Available at <https://www.hollywoodreporter.com/movies/movie-news/cinematographer-bradford-youngs-career-rise-754729/> (last accessed 24 September 2021).
8. Lena Wilson, 'Rachel Morrison's deeply empathetic cinematography', *Seventh Row*, 9 May 2018, 1–17, 4. Available at<https://seventh-row.com/2018/05/09/rachel-morrison/> (last accessed 24 September 2021).
9. Jacques Rancière, *Dissensus: On Politics and Aesthetics*, ed. and trans. Steven Corcoran (London: Continuum, 2010), 36.
10. See Aisha Harris, 'How Accurate is *Fruitvale Station*?' *Slate*, 12 July 2013, 1–9, 8. Available at <https://slate.com/culture/2013/07/fruitvale-station-true-story-fact-and-fiction-in-movie-about-bart-train-shooting-of-oscar-grant.html> (last accessed 24 September 2021).

11. Rancière, *Dissensus*, 37.
12. Paula Massood, *Black City Cinema: African American Urban Experiences in Film* (Philadelphia: Temple University Press, 2003), 147.
13. 'Another strategy in accentuating the film's unique feeling is using a single Arri Alexa XT camera through the whole shoot. "The whole thing was one camera," says Laxton. "We never had two cameras actually."' Paul Moakley, 'Inside the Cinematography of *Moonlight*: The Images That Inspired James Laxton', 5/8. 'In the midst of this pivotal moment of self-discovery there's a real awareness of the camera as the water is lapping against the lens' (Ibid., 4). Available at <https://time.com/behind-the-visuals-of-moonlight/> (last accessed 24 September 2021).
14. Ibid., 5–6.
15. Nicholas Mirzoeff, *The Right to Look: A Counterhistory of Visuality* (Durham, NC: Duke University Press), 1.
16. Mirzoeff, *The Right to Look*, 1.

9. 'SHEER EPIDERMIS': 'FACE POLITICS' AND THE FILMS OF LYNNE RAMSAY

Paula Quigley

Wrapped in curtains, fishing nets, plastic bags; hidden by hair or completely cut off; faces in Lynne Ramsay's films are often absent, incomplete or inaccessible. Framed in tight close-up they can be no less remote, distanced by the preference for an opaque performance style. Similarly, motifs of facial doubling, coupled with a tendency to play with point of view, disrupt notions of the face as the guarantor of individual identity and the gateway to subjectivity. Nevertheless, Ramsay's films are regularly noted for their 'immersive' qualities, inviting 'a proximate, tactile look that produces a sense of intimacy with the image'.[1] This begs the following questions: how does the destabilisation of the face as an expressive focal point in Ramsay's films intersect with their ability to evoke 'a visceral spectatorial response'?[2] And how might this, in turn, reflect on the 'face politics' visible from portraiture to film and photography and further complicated by the eminently mutable face of the digital sphere?[3] If, as Jenny Edkins and others argue, following Deleuze, the 'face' is where discourses of individual subjectivity and sovereignty coalesce, then a politics which 'dismantles the face' and replaces a principle of separation with that of relation may be difficult to articulate within current paradigms of representation.[4] With this in mind, and focusing on Ramsay's four feature films in the context of her wider filmography, I wish to explore the ways in which Ramsay's films recalibrate our existing relationship to the face on film through a reimagining of its role in the *mise-en-scène* and, in so doing, move us towards an uncanny encounter with the 'other' on screen.

As John Welchman elucidates, as the face of Christ, the face of capitalism (on coins, currency) and the face of bourgeois individualism in humanistic portraiture, the face 'has shaped the very conditions of visuality'.[5] Implicit in this history is the metaphysical separation of the representational regime of the face, with its implications of identity, subjectivity and rationality, from the body and its associations with base, irrational and instinctual drives. In cinema, the human face is so central to our experience that, as Noa Steimatsky reminds us, it is traditionally used as a measure of shot scale: 'the face as a whole = close-up; face + upper chest = medium close-up; from the waist up = medium shot, etc. Talking about the close-up with respect to non-body objects, or parts thereof, is basically an extrapolation.'[6] While narrative cinema thinks mainly in terms of the expressive potential of the face, Tom Gunning identifies twin impulses towards science and spectacle in early cinema, which extended photography's ambition to capture and categorise the face in stasis to the face in motion.[7] Early 'facial expression' films seem to strip away notions of subjectivity; instead, the elasticity of the face is emphasised via facial contortions or the magnification of everyday actions and expressions. And if in later cinema the eyes are the 'windows to the soul', in early film the mouth and its movements could be understood as the portal to the coporeal, fascinating and repulsive in equal measure. Films such as *Fred Ott's Sneeze* and *The Big Swallow* showcase the grotesque potential of the enlarged mouth in motion or, as Gunning memorably puts it, 'partaking of the carnivalesque pleasure of the open orifice in a most unseemly manner'.[8]

As Alice Maurice argues, the mobile, mutable and unruly face that showcases its corporeal status – what Maurice calls the 'body-face' – 'threatens early cinema's vulnerable status as art by recalling vaudeville and other "low" popular forms – in particular, blackface minstrelsy'.[9] The transition from the 'body-face' to the 'screen face' (that is, the face endowed with subtle expressivity as opposed to engaged in displays of vulgar physicality), depends on 'a kind of decapitation'; that is, the literal and figurative separation of the face from the body.[10] Literal in that the head, or more specifically the face, is cut off from the body in close up; figurative, insofar as the successful integration of these close-ups into narrative cinema depends on the face acquiring an elevated status, untroubled by connotations of mindless carnality. Indeed, Gilberto Perez suggests that D. W. Griffith's relative restraint in introducing close-ups of the face into his Biograph films having integrated close-ups of objects almost from the outset was because he considered it 'a lover's privilege' to intrude on so intimate an area.[11]

The erotics of Griffith's close-ups of Lillian Gish aside, what Maurice calls 'body-centered forms of spectacle and performance'[12] give way to a focus on the face and this, in turn, is supported by a movement from the mouth to eyes. If the face is that part of the body most linked with ideas of individual identity then, as Anne Nesbet suggests, 'the eyes may be said to be the "face" of the face', insofar as the eyes are the part of the body that we most wish to dissociate from the fact of their fleshiness.[13] The disavowal of the fleshy composition of the face, especially the eyes, in favour of notions of expressivity and interiority is supported by the shift from the close-up being 'read in terms of scale (giganticism)' to the close-up being perceived in terms of 'distance (closeness or intimacy)'.[14] This sense of an incremental proximity underpins the conventional editing pattern of cutting from long shot to medium shot to medium close-up, culminating in a close-up of the face. As Ellen Gamerman outlines, in classical cinema, the impact of this is managed by being employed sparingly relative to today's standards. In the current context however, close-ups of faces are deployed much more frequently, often throughout the entire film. In short, we have arrived at what Gamerman calls 'the age of the enormous head'.[15]

Since the 1960s, the 'intensified continuity' style of American mainstream cinema has been defined by increasingly close shots, especially of the face.[16] Less expensive than long shots, easier to edit and more suited to streaming on small screens, close-ups have become the mainstay of mass-market cinema, and a reliance on close-ups of the face for emotional affect has become the calling card of many contemporary filmmakers, such as Barry Jenkins. 'There's always a moment', says Jenkins, 'where the audience has to look directly into the eyes of the character in order to really feel what they're feeling.'[17] For Ramsay, too, the face can figure prominently (*Morvern Callar*, for instance, focuses on Samantha Morton's face in almost every shot), but its role as revelatory is refused. Eyes, also, can be less important for what they reveal than for what they reflect. Elsewhere, Ramsay leaves the face out of the picture entirely, in favour of close-ups of hands, feet and bodies. For Raymond De Luca, in so doing, 'Ramsay practices . . . a cinematic form of decapitation. Ramsay's camera maims her protagonists.'[18] From my perspective, this move is best understood as a reframing of the traditional hierarchy of face and body, which, in turn, facilitates an uncanny encounter with the face *as* body.

If Ramsay's films do not encourage the conventional investments offered by mainstream cinema in 'the age of the enormous head', they cannot easily be identified with modernism's 'moments of head-lopping iconoclasm' either, which, as Welchman reminds us, force us to reflect on the face as the figure par excellence of pre-modern humanism by way of its absence or reconfiguration.[19] Michael Haneke's first feature, *The Seventh Continent*, denies access to its protagonists' faces for several minutes at the outset. Instead, the film begins with shots of hands and feet performing banal, everyday tasks; the emphasis is on the repetition rather than the richness of everyday life. Their disengagement from the middle-class world they inhabit provides the immediate context for the family's decision to commit suicide. Within this, 'facelessness' speaks to the alienation and disaffection of the late capitalist condition. Ramsay, on the other hand, could not be accused of 'anthropological detachment'.[20] Less an intellectual reflection on the 'death of affect' in the modernist mode (as we might consider Haneke's film to be in the best possible sense),[21] Ramsay's protagonists make intimate, invested contact with their lived environment and the material fact of the face comes into play as a terrain where questions of identity and alterity are envisaged and explored.

Ramsay frequently cites Robert Bresson as an important influence on her own aesthetic.[22] While clearly there are significant differences between the two in terms of tone and style – Ramsay's *mise-en-scène* can veer from 'mesmeric to hard reality',[23] whereas Bresson rejected the use of professional actors, special effects and non-diegetic music[24] – we could argue that Ramsay shares two crucial things with Bresson: an abiding sense of the extraordinary potential of sound in cinema and a deep regard for 'the way things are'.[25] Bresson's early reputation for ascetic spiritualism has been replaced with an appreciation of his attention to the 'sensual details' of the quotidian world.[26] As James Quandt puts it, 'The elliptical, sometimes clipped rhythm of Bresson's editing, the physicality of his sound world . . . and his fragmentation of bodies through truncated framing – the focus on torsos, legs, and hands, in particular – amplify this sense of materiality.'[27] Famously, Bresson insisted that his 'models' (the non-actors he favoured), empty their features of expression. In the words of André Bazin, 'We have the countenance of the actor denuded of all symbolic expression, sheer epidermis.'[28] In Ramsay's case, the idea of the face as 'sheer epidermis' can stretch both ways: that is, the face as opaque, 'just skin', blocking our attempts to 'read into' facial expression and assign subjectivity, and the face as sheer, transparent, revealing the void, the corpse, that is always already there. In both cases, the effect could be said to create a kind of 'uncanny valley', a gap between the familiar and unfamiliar that provokes uncertainty and reflects on the privileged role of the face in cinema and beyond in determining notions of individuality, identity and interiority.[29]

Ramsay's short film, *Gasman*, opens with a shot of a man's hands polishing a shoe, while a pair of small, bare feet run past in the blurred background. The dense texture of a patterned carpet typical of countless homes in the 1970s comes into focus and the soft, rythmic sound of the shoe brush blends with the surrounding sounds: a woman's voice, a child singing, white noise. More hands, those of another child, pour sugar over a toy car; we hear the heightened sound of its swoosh and crunch as the car brakes and swerves and a Christmas song blares from the radio. A drag on a cigarette, a quick kiss, the painful tug of a party dress over a head and finally, a face. In just under two and a half minutes these opening shots capture a sense of the domestic, glimpsed also in Ramsay's first short film, *Small Deaths*, where family interaction is less about face-to-face exchanges and more about bodies coexisting and coming into contact with each other and their surroundings in small, shared spaces. Pale, bony knees, sharply delineated vertebrae and hands that reach and fail to grasp speak to a presence in the world that is profoundly corporeal and relationships that are fundamentally physical as much as abstract or emotional. One of the film's few lingering close-ups shows Lynne (played by Ramsay's niece, also Lynne Ramsay), the young girl whose face is the first we see, confronted by her own likeness in a way that suggests there are not only two versions of herself but also two versions of her father. Broadly speaking, in that shift from bodies to faces Lynne's initial familial intimacy is replaced by a sense of loss: of her sense of her father and her sense of herself.

The uncanny encounter with a face that is 'strangely familiar' threatens the foundation of identity. In the Freudian context, an uncanny experience is where feelings of familiarity and unfamiliarity coexist. It is a subject of aesthetics and, in this, the figure of the double is of particular thematic concern: 'originally an insurance against destruction to the ego', once this childlike or 'primitive' belief is abandoned, 'the "double" reverses its aspect. From having been an assurance of immortality, it becomes the uncanny harbinger of death.'[30] The double presents the paradox of encountering oneself as 'other': 'the logically impossible notion that the 'I' and the 'not-I' are somehow identical'.[31] A sense of the destabilisation of categories also subtends Kristeva's notion of the abject. The abject is 'what disturbs identity, system, order. What does not respect borders, positions, rules. The in-between, the ambiguous, the composite.'[32] The distinction between the two resides in their relationship to the (un)familiar: 'Essentially different from "uncanniness", more violent, too, abjection is elaborated through a failure to recognize its kin; nothing is familiar, not even the shadow of a memory.'[33] If the uncanny is something that is strange but feels familiar, the abject is that which is familiar but feels foreign. In *Gasman*, the uncanny, as 'something which ought to have remained hidden but has come to light',[34] is literalised in Lynne's realisation of her father's 'double life', a betrayal she was barely beginning to intuit in 'Ma and Da'.[35] In a broader sense, the doubled face gives up its secret: that the skin that separates the 'I' and 'not-I' is 'sheer' at best.

The sight/site of the (un)familiar face ('She looks like you!') threatens to erode the boundary between the self and other, the response to which is abjection ('No she doesn't, she's ugly!'). The abject can be uncanny when we recognise something familiar within it, before it was 'cast out', such as the corpse. For Kristeva, 'The corpse . . . is the utmost of abjection. It is death infecting life. Abject.'[36] In Ramsay's films, uncanny encounters with images of lifeless faces, either dead or drained of affect, recur throughout. During the title sequence of *Ratcatcher*, set in the midst of the binmen's strike in Glasgow in the 1970s, the diaphanous layers of a lace curtain twist in slow motion, beneath which the blurred features of a child's face begin to emerge; with eyes closed and mouth open, it has the aspect of a corpse. In Ramsay's words, this image, 'slightly like a shroud', 'points to the fact that the wee boy's going to die in some kind of subconscious way'.[37] The curtain as 'sheer epidermis' covers a face that already speaks of its own death.[38] This is echoed in a later shot of another child with a fishing net over his face, who escapes the same fate of death by drowning (he is 'fished out' of the canal by the protagonist's father (Tommy Flanagan)).[39] This motif is returned to and reworked in *You Were Never Really Here*. Joe (Joaquin Phoenix), a traumatised hitman who was abused by his father as a child, repeatedly attempts suicide. In the opening sequence, a plastic bag, animated by Joe's desperate breaths, is the 'sheer epidermis' that covers his face and offers the promise of asphyxiation.[40]

In *Ratcatcher*, close-ups of the boys' faces operate according to a logic of repetition that blurs the boundaries between self and other, the living and the dead. Edkins quotes artist Suzanne Opton describing how her portraits of soldiers' heads laid sideways on a flat surface, 'as if they were dead', capture the idea of death as an integral part of the soldiers' identity.[41] Ramsay's propensity to film her protagonists' expressionless faces in the same position similarly blurs the distinction between the living person and the dead body. As has been noted, in *Ratcatcher*, the close-up of James (William Eadie) as 'a picture of serene contentment', with his head laid sideways as his mother combs lice from his hair, is eerily reminiscent of the close-up of Ryan (Thomas McTaggart) after he drowns.[42] In *We Need to Talk About Kevin*, repeated shots of Eva's (Tilda Swinton) evacuated face from this angle demonstrate her own 'life sentence' following Kevin's massacre of his father, sister and peers.

In *Kevin*, the face as 'sheer epidermis' figures as a permeable membrane where identities merge in ways that are intimately connected with the politics of motherhood. The film de-emphasises dialogue in favour of a highly expressive *mise-en-scène* that layers shards of the past and present, infused with Eva's recollection. Within this, the enmeshed maternal relationship is crystallised in an image of facial doubling. Eva's face transforms into Kevin's (Ezra Miller) when plunged into water, an element that features in Ramsay's *oeuvre* as a fluid reminder of death and rebirth. For Kristeva, the inherently violent yet essential separation from the mother's body is the primary process of abjection: 'Matricide is our vital necessity, the *sine qua non* condition of our individuation.'[43] While the abject can become attached to other objects and experiences – blood, excrement, even the skin on the surface of milk – all abjections are repetitions of this primary repudiation. In *Kevin*, as Sue Thornham argues, Eva's desire to be self-contained is shattered by the uncontrollable embodiment of pregnancy and motherhood.[44] Kevin extrudes faeces, snot, saliva; his 'behaviour insists on the messiness of the body, on the fleshy, the organic, the abject – and insists that Eva recognise this, together with her own rage and fear at her entrapment'.[45]

In this, the corporeal materiality of the face, and especially the eyes, is reasserted in ways that render the (un)familiar face abject. De Luca draws our attention to the moment in *Ratcatcher* when James's mother (Mandy Matthews) sees Ryan's dead body lying face down by the canal. The dirty window through which she anxiously views the scene is reflected on her iris. De Luca notes that 'a similar shot recurs in *We Need to Talk About Kevin* when an archery target is shown seared onto Kevin's pupil as he plots his bloodbath'.[46] The eye does not just reflect the target, however; in Ramsay's films, the eye is a target. In *You Were Never Really Here*, a bullet through the eye turns the beloved mother (Judith Roberts) into the abject maternal corpse imagined by the film's allusions to Hitchcock's *Psycho*.[47] In *We Need to Talk About Kevin*, Kevin's sister, Celia (Ashley Gerasimovich), loses an eye while in Kevin's care. For Freud, the fear of 'being robbed of one's eyes' can be read as a substitute for the fear of castration, itself the root cause of the uncanny.[48] In this scenario, Celia is cast in the role of eyewitness, both to the unsuccessful process of subject positioning within the narrative and to the horror of our own exposure to the eyes – 'the "face" of the face' – as 'sheer epidermis'; the empty eye socket is a visceral reminder of the void where the 'subject' should be. The symbolic enucleation of the cinematic face is underlined by a visual pun: an extreme close-up of Kevin's mouth as 'open orifice' sucking obscenely on a lychee, whose resemblance to an eyeball is unmistakeable.

In *Kevin*, the 'countenance as flesh' reasserts the fact of its corporeal existence to uncanny effect.[49] Within this, the female face, in particular, defies gendered expectations of emotional expressivity. In terms borrowed from Lauren Berlant, Jackie Stacey describes Tilda Swinton as 'the mistress of flat affect'.[50] Swinton's 'capacity for flatness', she writes, 'unmakes and remakes more conventionalised femininities, especially as articulated through popular genres in which the woman's interiority is so frequently the register of legible affective intensity'.[51] For Sarah Louise Smyth, this provides a framework within which to read Swinton's 'muted' performance in *Kevin*, 'as a performance of sociopolitical maternal ambivalence'.[52] In a grotesque corroboration of this thesis, film critic Alexander Walker claimed to be so enraged by Samantha Morton's 'barren face of affectless catatonia' in *Morvern Callar* that he 'ached to smack some life into it'.[53] Walker's language is revealing; the 'barren' female face, unwilling to perform the conventional female labour of expressing emotion on screen, is not permissible within a paradigm that conflates female performance with 'feminine' expressivity.

In *Morvern Callar*, the intense concentration on Morvern's face is not rewarded with revelation. The politics of resistance inherent in placing her impassive face at the centre of the film, unmoored from conventions of eyeline matching or a consistent point of view, reflects on questions of identity and interiority that are posed from the outset. The film begins with Morvern embracing the corpse of her dead lover. Elliptical close-ups of her face laid sideways – recalling her fellow protagonists in Ramsay's filmography who are similarly situated on the cusp of life and death – shift to extreme close-ups of her hands as, eyes closed, she gently traces the slashes on his skin, her fingers coming so close they blur as they stretch to intertwine with his. The intimacy of this exploration is abruptly shattered; Morvern's separation from the traumatic reminder of her own materiality is echoed by our sudden estrangement from the scene as a result of a more distanced perspective, our eye drawn to the bright red blood in the centre of the frame. While this 'makes sense' of the preceding shots, it does so at the expense of our proximal attachment to their tactile properties.

Ramsay's fascination with the irruption of the abject – the scab on Margaret Anne's (Leanne Mullen) knee that captivates James in *Ratcatcher*, or the bloodied tooth that Joe examines closely having strenuously extracted it from his own swollen mouth in *You Were Never Really Here* – allows for an acknowledgement of the corporeal as irreducible to a regime of representation. Following her boyfriend's suicide, Morvern touches blood, bodies, water, worms, earth, insects. Morvern's attention does not discriminate – the urbane publishers think she is joking when she responds to their question about her stay in Spain by saying 'It's really beautiful . . ., I like the ants' – and this creates a space for the viewer to adopt a similar perspective in relation to the physiological fact of her 'affectless' face. At the end of the film, Morvern's face flashes up, surrounded by music and moving bodies and once more illuminated by pulsing light. Briefly, she looks back at us, but in the final shot she turns away, eyes closed, immersed in her own environment. As 'sheer epidermis', her face refuses to fix any of the identities (Morvern Callar? Jackie? Olga?) she has slipped in and out of along the way, and the irony of her being identified as the 'distinctive, female voice' of her (faceless) boyfriend's dead body is not lost.

Relieving the female face of the burden of expressivity allows for a critical reappraisal of the role of the female body as abject/object on screen. In *You Were Never Really Here*, the female face attests to a history of cinematic, social and sexual violence, either inscribed on the skin (as on the bruised face of the unidentified woman who stares back from the subway station) or as 'cinematic' spectacle. Young girls' faces, smiling in photographs, scream when seen through a camera lens, and presage the rictus grins frozen on the faces of victims of sex trafficking glimpsed in the splinters of Joe's recollection. The uncanny doubling of the mother's face articulates cinema's history of casting (off) the ageing female body as abject. Joe's mother sits in a rocking chair, eyes closed, mouth open, a photograph of her as a young woman placed prominently beneath a picture of a bird; her face is 'strangely familiar' to us from film history. Her later emergence from the bathroom in a satin slip, her white hair around her shoulders, reveals Marion Crane and Mrs Bates to be one and the same, and doubles back to Nina (Ekaterina Samsonov) – now 'the [Hitchcock] blonde is a trafficked kid' – whose 'affectless' face bears witness to women's abjection within popular genres of mainstream cinema.[54]

Ramsay's treatment of the face as doubled and/or emptied of affect opens onto an uncanny encounter with the 'other' on film. If the face has a privileged position in the formation and circulation of enlightenment ideals of person-hood, the uncanny, as scholars have argued, can be read as the 'the obverse side of the modern subject and its scientific, secular rationality'.[55] Or, as Julie Park puts it, 'the uncanny represents the dread return of excess and indeterminacy.'[56] In Ramsay's films, the face as 'uncanny' both exceeds and resists its role in determining individual identity. As engorged mouth and eyes that are 'only pits of blackness'[57] we come up against the face as both corporeal materiality and structuring absence. The doubled face casts doubt on notions of individuality based on a differential system of identification, and the face as opaque reflects back on systems of social and sexual signification. And yet, Ramsay's films are oddly optimistic, ending with glimpses, whether real or imagined, of alternative futures for her traumatised protagonists. Edkins traces how 'a fear of closeness of contact with or merging into other people' is embedded in the idea of the person as a separate individual: 'The face then is the primary means of separa-tion.'[58] Perhaps, in 'undoing' the face, Ramsay allows us to reimagine – however briefly – the relationship between 'I' and 'not-I'.

Notes

1. Tina Kendall, '"The in-between of things": intermediality and *Ratcatcher*', *New Review of Film and Television Studies* 8:2 (2010), 183.
2. Raymond De Luca, 'Dermatology as Screenology: The Films of Lynne Ramsay', *Film Criticism* 43:1 (March 2019). Available at <http://dx.doi.org/10.3998/fc.13761232.0043.102> (last accessed 24 September 2021).
3. Jenny Edkins, *Face Politics* (Abingdon and New York: Routledge, 2015).
4. Ibid., 167.
5. John Welchman, 'Face(t)s: Notes on Faciality', *Artforum International* 27 (1998), 131.
6. Noa Steimatsky, *The Face on Film* (Oxford: Oxford University Press, 2017), 3, n. 2.
7. Tom Gunning, 'In Your Face: Physiognomy, Photography, and the Gnostic Mission of Early Film', *Modernism/modernity* 4:1 (January 1997): 1–29.
8. Ibid., 23.
9. Alice Maurice, *The Cinema and Its Shadow: Race and Technology in Early Cinema* (Minneapolis: University of Minnesota Press, 2013), 90.
10. Ibid., 70.
11. Gilberto Perez, *The Material Ghost: Films and their Medium* (Baltimore: The Johns Hopkins University Press, 1998), 349–50.
12. Maurice, *Cinema and Its Shadow*, 88.
13. Anne Nesbet, *Savage Junctures: Sergei Eisenstein and the Shape of Thinking* (London: I. B. Tauris, 2007), 28.

14. Mary Ann Doane, 'Scale and the Negotiation of Real and Unreal Space in the Cinema', in Lúcia Nagib and Cecília Mello (eds), *Realism and the Audiovisual Media* (London: MacMillan, 2009), 66.

15. Ellen Gamerman, 'Hollywood's Extreme Close-up', *The Wall Street Journal*, 21 January 2017. Available at <https://www.wsj.com/articles/the-close-up-close-up-1485000003> (last accessed 24 September 2021).

16. David Bordwell, 'Intensified Continuity', *Film Quarterly* 55:3 (Spring 2002), 16–28.

17. Barry Jenkins quoted in Zack Sharf, 'Paul Thomas Anderson, Master of the Close-up, Is Jealous of Barry Jenkins' Shots', *Indiewire*, 23 November 2018. Available at <https://www.indiewire.com/2018/11/paul-thomas-anderson-jealous-barry-jenkins-close-ups-1202022891/2018> (last accessed 24 September 2021).

18. De Luca, 'Dermatology'.

19. Welchman, 'Face(t)s', 131.

20. Peter Bradshaw, 'Haneke's House of Horrors', *The Guardian*, 30 April 2008. Available at <https://www.theguardian.com/film/filmblog/2008/apr/30/hanekeshouseofhorrors> (last accessed 24 September 2021).

21. Christopher Sharrett, '*The Seventh Continent*', *Senses of Cinema* 34 (February 2005). Available at <https://www.sensesofcinema.com/2005/cteq/seventh_continent/> (last accessed 24 September 2021).

22. See for instance Lynne Ramsay quoted in Annette Kuhn, *Ratcatcher* (London: BFI, 2008), 82.

23. Ramsay quoted in Kuhn, *Ratcatcher*, 85.

24. Richard Hell, 'Consuming Passion: Bresson and *The Devil, Probably*', in Bert Cardullo (ed.), *The Films of Robert Bresson: A Casebook* (London and New York: Anthem Press, 2009), 169.

25. Ibid., 171.

26. Kent Jones, *L'Argent* (London: BFI, 1999), 91.

27. James Quandt, 'On *Au hasard, Balthasar*', in Bert Cardullo (ed.), *The Films of Robert Bresson: A Casebook* (London and New York: Anthem Press, 2009), 83.

28. André Bazin, '*Le Journal d'un curé de campagne* and the Stylistics of Robert Bresson', in André Bazin, *What Is Cinema?* Vol. 1, trans. Hugh Gray (California and London: University of California Press, 1967), 136.

29. The phrase 'uncanny valley' was coined by Masahiro Mori to describe the dip between attraction and repulsion that lifelike robots can inspire.

30. Sigmund Freud, 'The "Uncanny"', in Sigmund Freud, *The Standard Edition of the Complete Psychological Works of Sigmund Freud*, Vol. XVII, trans. James Strachey (London: The Hogarth Press, 1919), 235.

31. Gry Faurholt, 'Self as Other: The Doppelgänger', *Double Dialogues* 10 (Summer 2009). Available at <https://www.doubledialogues.com/article/self-as-other-the-doppelganger/> (last accessed 24 September 2021).

32. Julia Kristeva, *Powers of Horror: An Essay on Abjection*, trans. Leon S. Roudiez (New York: Columbia, 1982), 4.

33. Ibid., 5.

34. Freud, 'The "Uncanny"', 241.

35. 'Ma and Da' is the first of three vignettes that comprise Ramsay's short film, *Small Deaths*.

36. Kristeva, *Powers of Horror*, 4.

37. Ramsay quoted in Eileen Elsey, 'Her Stories: Lynne Ramsay Talks about Narrative Structure and the Gender of Storytelling', *Vertigo* 2:4 (Spring 2003). Available at <https://www.closeupfilmcentre.com/vertigo_magazine/volume-2-issue-4-spring-2003/her-stories/> (last accessed 24 September 2021).

38. With thanks to Alice Maurice for drawing my attention to Deleuze's work on Ingmar Bergman in this context. See Gilles Deleuze, 'The affect as entity', in Deleuze, *Cinema 1*, trans. Hugh Tomlinson and Barbara Haberjam (London: Continuum, 1986), 97–104.

39. Annette Kuhn makes this observation also. Kuhn, *Ratcatcher*, 57.

40. Several critics have highlighted the repetition of this motif across *Ratcatcher* and *You Were Really Here*. De Luca, for instance, notes: 'In the opening sequences of *Ratcatcher* and *You Were Never Really Here*, physical materials (lace, plastic) intermediate characters' corporeal experiences of life and death.' De Luca, 'Dermatology'. Similar images recur across Ramsay's films; for instance, the billowing curtain at the beginning of *Kevin* that acts as a thin 'skin' between Eva's current life and the realisation of death, or the towel that drapes like a death mask over Joe's face in *You Were Never Really Here*.

41. Suzanne Opton quoted in Edkins, *Face Politics*, 16.

42. Kuhn, *Ratcatcher*, 33.

43. Julia Kristeva, *Black Sun: Depression and Melancholia*, trans. Leon S. Roudiez (New York: Columbia University Press, 1989), 38.

44. Sue Thornham, '"A Hatred So Intense . . .": *We Need to Talk about Kevin*, Post-feminism and Women's Cinema', *Sequence* 2:1 (2013), 1–38.

45. Ibid., 17.

46. De Luca, 'Dermatology'.

47. De Luca also notes the striking resemblance between Joe's mother's corpse and Mrs Bates in *Psycho*. He writes: 'Indeed, what shocks us most after Hitchcock unveils Mrs Bates at the end of *Psycho* is her hollowed-out eye sockets and, in *You Were Never Really Here*, Joe's mother is killed by a shot to the face, which gouges out one of her eyes. The image of Joe's dead mother with her mouth agape directly recalls Mrs Bates's toothy leer.' De Luca, 'Dermatology'.

48. Freud, 'The "Uncanny"', 230.

49. Bazin, 'Bresson', 133.

50 Jackie Stacey, 'Crossing Over with Tilda Swinton – the Mistress of "Flat Affect"', *International Journal of Politics, Culture and Society* 28 (2015), 243–71.

51. Ibid., 252.

52. Sarah Louise Smyth, 'Postfeminism, Ambivalence and the Mother in Lynne Ramsay's *We Need to Talk about Kevin* (2011)', *Film Criticism* 44:1 (2020). Available at <http://dx.doi.org/10.3998/fc.13761232.0044.106> (last accessed 24 September 2021).

53. Alexander Walker, 'Morvern Callar', *Mail Online*, n.d. Available at <https://www.dailymail.co.uk/tvshowbiz/article-145422/Morvern-Callar-Cert-15.html> (last accessed 24 September 2021).

54. Several critics have noted the film's revision of *Psycho*. J. M. Tyree, 'Anti-*Psycho*-Logical: Notes on Lynne Ramsay's *You Were Never Really Here*', *Bennington Review* 6 (2018). Available at <https://www.benningtonreview.org/jm-tyree-anti-psycho-logical> (last accessed 24 September 2021).

55. Ewa Ziarek, 'The Uncanny Style of Kristeva's Critique of Nationalism', *Postmodern Culture* 5:2 (January 1995). Available at <http://pmc.iath.virginia.edu/text-only/issue.195/ziarek.195> (last accessed 24 September 2021).

56. Julie Park, 'Unheimlich Maneuvers: Enlightenment Dolls and Repetitions in Freud', *The Eighteenth Century* 44:1 (2003), 46.

57. E. T. A. Hoffmann quoted in Park, 'Unheimlich', 59.

58. Edkins, *Face Politics*, 166.

10. FACING LIFE IN THE OPEN: THE (POST)HUMANIST WORLDMAKING OF *MY OCTOPUS TEACHER*

Angelica Fenner

Cinema has always posed a form of worldmaking, one predicated upon instrumentalising an inhuman mode of perception, that of the camera, to capture, preserve and variously come to terms with material reality, but thereby, unwittingly or by design, also conjuring another world altogether. From the interventions of montage, cinematography and sound emerges an anthropocentric viewpoint limited solely by the scale and scope of what the human can conceive. Simultaneously, lens-based media bear the potential to interrogate that self-same anthropocentricism, fulfilling what James Cahill coins 'cinema's Copernican vocation'. Cahill's pronouncement is directed at the early work (1924–49) of French filmmaker Jean Painlevé, whose scientific training in comparative anatomy was shaped by childhood visits to the Normandy coast and is evidenced in documentaries with such titles as *La pieuvre* (*The Octopus*, 1928), *Le Bernard – l'hermite* (*The Hermit Crab*, 1929) and *L'hippocampe* (*The Seahorse*, 1934). These enact what Cahill describes as 'the twinned capacities for potentially revolutionary scientific discovery and anthropocentric displacement' and entail a 'shift in attention – from self-regard to nonhuman other, and the ripples or impact that such a perceptual pivot may have on one's self-image'.1

The sustained lure of 'self-regard' is confirmed in cinema's preoccupation with the human face throughout the medium's history, such that spectators seek in screen characters infused via close-up with moral, psychological or affectives qualities some form of narcissistic confirmation of their own respective experience. The human face also boasts a more extensive and variegated historical tradition of social coding than does the facialisation of non-human animals, with the latter seldom accorded the status of individual persona in visual media. When they are, this attribution is generally and perhaps unavoidably accompanied in both production and reception by varying degrees of anthropocentric bias and/or anthropomorphic indulgence. The cinema herein participates in 'the anthropological machine', the prevailing system of ideas that have generated the dichotomy between animals and 'human' via a mode of philosophical and ethical thinking that sorts everything into either bare life or the human.[2] For early film theorists treating the face on screen as an aesthetic object imbued with moral potential, the assumed reference point was similarly the human, even as Béla Balázs also displayed enthusiasm for 'the face of things' and for non-human animals.[3] Of the latter, he remarked, 'How fascinating are the physiognomy and the expressions of animals! And how mysterious it is that we understand them!' although 'only by analogy, of course'.[4] Moreover, in contrast to actors performing to achieve the impression of authenticity, he maintained 'For animals there is no question of illusion; it is all the most genuine reality.'[5]

My ambition is to continue the work of complicating film theory's facile distinction, including Balázs's reluctance to concede the capacity for non-human life forms to alternately dissimulate or to 'perform authenticity'. The recent Netflix production, *The Octopus Teacher* (Craig Foster and Pippa Ehrlich, 2020), which secured Best Documentary Feature at the 93rd Academy Awards, offers a fruitful vehicle for unpacking the stakes of such an endeavour. Nature documentary filmmaker Craig Foster, previously known for his ground-breaking film *The Great Dance* (2000) about the San bush-hunters of the Kalahari Desert, veritably travels in the wake of Painlevé's earlier study and interpretation of radical morphological alterity among marine fauna. But Foster also ventures further by surrendering to a phenomenological and tactile ethology, one in which he becomes participant observer, a protagonist autobiographically inscribed into the interspecies encounters shot along the southern tip of South Africa's Cape Peninsula. The insights gleaned help visualise for film audiences important ground also recently covered in Peter Godfrey-Smith's philosophical treatise on octopuses.[6] Yet when Foster confesses, 'I hadn't been a person overly sensitive towards animals before', a lingering blind spot in the film's posthuman pedagogy emerges, one residing in omitting the qualifier 'other' before his reference to animals. He thereby unwittingly focalises the overall difficulties of extricating oneself from anthropocentric legacies that continue to inhere in speech and discourse, and that also find their dis/articulation in the production of visual media.

Too long understood in referencing 'the animal' was its opposition to the human, an act of repression whose originary violence resides in belying that the human is also animal, and that those deemed 'the non-human' cannot simply be lumped into one ontological category. That quandary inspired Derrida's neologism, *animot*, which draws attention to the aforementioned inadequate signifier while also phonetically encompassing the plural *animaux*.[7] The presumption of an ontological and ethical divide between humans and non-humans has been the Cartesian linchpin of much continental and analytical philosophy, which arrogates for the human species the claim to a unique capacity for rational, and by extension, moral and ethical thought. More recently scholars across disciplinary frameworks have taken up the 'question of the animal' (Derrida, Wolfe, Haraway, Agamben) as deeply implicated in pushing us to rethink assumptions about Being, both our own and that of others. While this 'turn' has made room to include non-humans in its deliberations, a truly post-humanist posthumanism, one in which other beings achieve a kind of personhood at the same time that we acknowledge our animality, remains elusive, even as Critical Animal Studies moves as along an asymptote towards that goal.

The autobiographical narrative that frames *The Octopus Teacher* facilitates a degree of self-reflexivity about the technological affordances that both enable and constrain its emergent posthumanist perspective. Like so many stories of personal transformation, this one grew out of an existential crisis. Seated in his home, facing the camera and addressing an unseen interlocutor, Foster recounts how he found himself burnt out by the stress of his freelance job, alienated from his family and losing inspiration. What lodged in his memory following the shooting of his previous film in the Kalahari Desert, however, was the steadfast attention cultivated by the indigenous animal trackers towards the minutest details within the broader web of life. Corroborating footage from that earlier film, he recalls, 'The trackers were inside the natural world and I was outside of it. And that was fine, for a while, but I had this deep longing to be inside as well.' Indeed, for a time, he wanted nothing more to do with a film camera and editing suite ever again. Rather than travel to undertake new projects, he resolved in 2010 to stay put and cultivate an analogous form of connection with the local underwater flora and fauna of the rock pools in False Bay, where he had enjoyed free diving as a young boy.

Several years into this endeavour, which entailed using an underwater camera to document his daily forays into a roughly 200-square metre intertidal zone, he caught sight of a small, speckled octopus. She captured and sustained his attention during daily dives across the span of a year, during which he tracked the brief life cycle of a highly intelligent invertebrate species that must learn to fend for itself in the absence of any social parenting. This specimen represented one of the minute number that survive to adulthood from among, on average, half a million eggs a female octopus will release once in its lifetime before succumbing to senescence and slow death by starvation biochemically induced by the reproduction process. From observing the ingenuity of this one cephalopod in eluding predators, her surprising moments of creativity and play, her recovery from the loss of a limb, her reproductive cycle and swift decline into death, he not only learned to respect the intelligence of what is essentially a larger snail without a shell but also entered into what he experienced as a relationship mutually predicated upon precarious trust, curiosity, and certainly, from his side, a deep affection, which he felt and many a spectator might also surmise to have been reciprocal.

The manner in which the apparatus is wielded bears the potential to alternately subjectify or objectify that which it depicts, be it sentient life, object, element or mineral. Part and parcel of subjectivisation is what we could call facialisation, the means by which an entity or thing comes to assume a face, understood in the basic sense of a form (from the Latin verb *facere* 'to make', and thereby assume a form or *facies*). Yet the face is not just any form but one that bears a forward orientation, a look towards something that anticipates and responds to the world before it, as implied in Indo-European words for 'face' that are based on the verb root 'to see': for example, in Old English *wlitan*, 'to see, look', becomes *andwlita*, 'face, countenance', or in German, *Antlitz*. A façade, in turn, can be attributed to any outward-oriented surface that also bears character, be that a monumental landscape, a built structure such as a house with windows and a door that presuppose the possibility of visual exchange between its inhabitants and those beyond its walls, and to everyday objects that become a site of potential projection and referral in relation to (implicitly) human agents. As such, the face is a territory, at once abstract and concrete, with faciality negotiating between the specificity of a particular face and its status as abstract 'machine'.[8] If film theory has primarily taken up the cause of human protagonists, I argue that filmic faciality can renegotiate the 'animal question' and that a film like *The Octopus Teacher* pursues in cinematic terms the philosophical exploration others have undertaken to 'humanise' the animal and probe the animal in the human.

I am taking the footage at 'face value', drawing conclusions from the effects cinematographic techniques enable and the shot-to-shot relations that emerge via visual montage, including the *ekphrasis* generated by cross-cutting Foster's voiceover and filmed testimonial recollections of that memorable year with corroborating underwater footage. If facialisation can be said to be what brings to the fore personhood, the sense of an individual persona, then this is already evidenced in the spectator's first striking encounter with the octopus via footage Foster explains also constituted his own unwitting first glimpse of her, where personification assumed astonishing form. While swimming, he became aware in his left peripheral vision of an anomalous object resting on the sea floor, which a corresponding close-up reveals to be an artfully assembled sculpture of seashells (Figure 10.1). Even the surrounding fish seem confused by its appearance, flitting curiously around it. A second later, the assemblage flies

Figure 10.1   The molluskan mistress of disguise and dissimulation, from *My Octopus Teacher* (Craig Foster and Pippa Ehrlich, 2020).

into disarray, the flailing arms of an octopus fleetingly glimpsed as it rockets away via jet propulsion. Foster learned, in retrospect, that this species can, in seconds, collect up to 100 shells with the suctions under its arms and thereby drape and camouflage itself to appear like coral or other inanimate flora or fauna. Such an act of dissimulation demonstrates a capacity to anticipate the gaze of others and to deflect the possibility of meeting that gaze by instead hiding its own countenance, lest this betray its status as living prey. Intrigued, Foster followed her further, and witnessed her wrap an unwieldy flat strand of kelp around herself like a cloak, permitting one eye to peer forth from its recesses to observe the new species of sea animal that had entered her habitat. When he explains wryly, 'I didn't know that I had come in at the end of this longer drama', he assumes she was previously pursued by a predator, while overlooking the possibility that his own entry into these waters initiated her recourse to the 'seashell disguise'.

What ensued over the next month was a game of hide and seek in which she evaded the newcomer through refuge in her den, camouflage or pushing her boneless body into the nearest crevice. Yet on day twenty-six of Foster's diary entry, he was able to establish 'first contact' when he laid his own body close to a crevice with arms held close to his torso to convey 'disarmament', and his face in close proximity to hers as she clung tenaciously to the safety of a rock while peering back at him. A close-up in two-shot and the camera's lighting – intrusive, when we consider how sensitive octopodes are to light – make visible an extraordinary, almost impossible encounter. Positioned slightly behind the octopus, the camera orients the viewer to identify with her bodily vulnerability: palpable are both her innate, heightened fear and the quivering curiosity that compels her nonetheless to unfurl one limb enough to cautiously touch his face, including his mouth, and thereby 'study' his contours with her taste and smell sensors.

Of course, Foster's countenance poses an equally estranged sight even for human spectators, on account of his swim cap, face goggles and incongruous prone position on the sea floor, intended to minimise his imposing bodily size. The encounter only emerges out of a mutual willingness to risk vulnerability: he, by presenting her his face, a site where vital sensory organs are concentrated, and she, through tolerating unusual proximity to a body part most sea creatures direct at her when approaching as predators, with mouth poised to attack and devour. It may thus be significant that she reaches out to probe specifically his mouth, as if investigating why it's not opening wide to consume its prey and determining what other function it might serve, even as she'll never come to know its communicative role as purveyor of human speech on dry land.

To contemplate faciality with the octopus thus invites us to think anew about what constitutes a face. In the spherical human skull: two frontal-facing eyes, a centred nose bone and nostrils, and a mouth, all bookended by laterally facing ears. The cephalopod, by contrast, consists, as its name implies, of a combined torso-head directly attached to limbs. Yet there is still a frontal orientation; indeed, the flesh sac that contains the brain, the digestive tract and three hearts variously floats underneath or in front of its fleshy 'head' or mantle, the two slit-like eyes located not exactly frontally but protruding from either side of the mantle. Siphons are located just below the eyes for oxygen exchange, propulsion and excretion, while its mouth is located underneath the torso-head, concealed at the centre of the radius formed by eight limbs. This invertebrate physiognomy necessarily reterritorialises our understanding of how facialisation maps onto sensory organs and their signifying and communicative potential. For what is a face in our conventional understanding, if not the central site of exchange between a bounded interior, that is, the body and the world beyond – a boundary or threshold enabling uptake of organic material, gas, liquid and sensorial input (sights, sounds, smells, tastes). As such, it is necessarily a zone of heightened sensitivity, with survival dependent on swift autonomic processing of incoming sensory data. At the same time, the resulting affective responses also become zones of expressivity, whether direct or disingenuous. This appears true for both the octopus and the human.

Yet if the face is understood as a concentration of sensory organs, one has to rethink entirely the relationship between brain, body and 'face' when accounting for the fact that, as Foster also explains, *octopus vulgaris* actually possesses nine brains, of which eight are located in its limbs. It has about 500 million neurons (as many as a dog), of which two-thirds are distributed along those limbs, whose extensive network of suctions (10,000 neurons per sucker) serve as sensors possessing both a sense of touch but also the capacity to sense chemicals, that is, the functions of smell and taste. Although we might hazard to organise faciality around the eyes as the prevailing sensory organ governing our own orientation towards the world, a possibly less anthropomorphic view could also incorporate these eight limbs, whose skin surface moreover contains photoreceptors that enable a form of vision. An extreme close-up of the tip of one limb connecting with Foster's arm at a later stage in the narrative makes visible the effort entailed for each individual suction to wilfully adhere to his skin surface and gather data.

There is, moreover, a literal sense in which the octopus species is well versed in the language of moving images. It grasps the concept of figure and ground, its own and that of others, constantly assessing its environment – both scanning optically and probing through its suction sensors for colour, shape and texture – and in response, morphing its own protean anatomy to variously blend in with that ground by rendering itself an image, one disingenuously posing as effigy of other existing life forms, whether fish, shell or plant. This invertebrate does so in a manner that signals its understanding of the selective significance of figuration for eluding specific predators, banking on the likelihood that the latter will assign these effigies the status of ground, not prey. In the service of those aims, its body can pass through a space as small as the size of its own eye, can acrobatically twist and compress limbs and head to conform to specific shapes and structures, and can modulate its skin pigmentation via colour-changing cells (chromatophores) filled with sacs of pigment that expand and contract to produce an array of alternately colourful or muted hues. Even the texture of its skin can be adjusted by controlling the size of projections (papillae) to generate small bumps, tall spikes, or horns that may appear smooth, variegated spotted or speckled.

In this mutability, the octopus arguably functions analogously to a *dispositif*, formally distributing relations between spaces and sights, between living entities and objects, while also arranging itself accordingly. Both the film theoretical invocation of the *dispositif* and its political genealogy have a bearing here. French film theorist Jean-Louis Baudry loosely distinguishes between, on the one hand, the basic apparatus of cinema, for example, the equipment and operations necessary to the (re)production of film, and, on the other, the *dispositif* as the conceptual, immaterial arrangement that positions, indeed, produces, the subject as a point of view, one that is the effect of a particular form of address.[9] I would venture so far as to suggest that the cephalopod sensory-motor-schema operates analogously to the cinematic apparatus. This creature visually and haptically registers (that is, records) impressions of its immediate environment and then, through transformations in its own body, projects for other animals an image that corresponds with those surroundings, even if the image produced appears to lack [or does it?] the indexical relationship, that is, photochemical imprinting of light, otherwise associated with photography. Simultaneously, the octopus is invested in eliding the operations of its own apparatus, of generating an impression of reality that, in its ideal, relies on a certain 'persistence of vision' among other animals glancing at the megapixel screen the cephalopod's body may transform into at any moment; in the process, the 'seams' of the illusion will be glossed over by roving predators focused more on shape than on the finer details. Certainly, the octopus could be said to have a 'disposition' towards these strategies, meaning its body is equipped with certain properties, 'and properties play causal roles in a thing's interaction with the world about it'.[10] That does not mean the octopus is limited to these, and although they are neither entirely necessary (although certainly highly utile towards survival) nor entirely normative, they are potential forces that can be and are actualised.

While these autonomic forces are innate to the octopus, survival is predicated upon the skill and strategy with which these properties are implemented, which also requires practice. And when they are actualised, that *dispositif* also produces a viewing position for other marine fauna predicated upon a degree of disavowal by both parties, the one wilful, the other potentially duped. Because the octopus's very survival relies on wielding these representational powers over predators, it would be tempting to further frame this in pseudo-Foucauldian terms, had the French philosopher lived long enough to think power beyond the context of human society. Yet the body of the octopus is not an instrument of domination per se, it's simply a site for distribution of powers and intensities made visible, however discontinuously, through particular arrangements of bodies, its own and others, which can and do sometimes converge to form a provisional *tableau vivant* on the marine floor.

Foster and Ehrlich's documentary is a cinematic tour de force, capturing in vivid colour and texture a striking array of sculptural forms this molluskan mistress of disguise assumes, each exemplar achieving a remarkably convincing illusion of veracity. The resulting tableaux are not necessarily always motivated by the impetus to survive, as Foster was able to deduce through sustained daily observation. As she grew accustomed to his presence, she gradually let down her guard and displayed moments of extraordinary lyricism captured on film. He recounts on one occasion observing her dart to and fro in the water amid schools of fish whose direction altered in dramatic synchrony, an aqueous mass ornament impelled, perhaps, by changes in the water current or other stimuli. Struck by her unusual swaying movements and initially pondering whether she might be stalking the fish as prey, he finally concluded that she was in fact inspired – perhaps by something akin to idle boredom – to swish her arms back and forth in whimsical imitation of the fishes' movements. The behaviour captured on film appears strikingly reminiscent of how idle children sometimes indulge a protean urge to mimic non-human morphologies and movements observed in their surroundings.

This glimpse into non-human 'play' uncannily recalls Foster's own inclination towards bodily mimicry, his self-professed desire 'to become partially amphibian'. Accoutrements attending that zoomorphic ambition include long rubber fins to propel him forward more powerfully, a face mask enhancing underwater vision, and the breathing nozzle enabling his sustained gaze upon the seafloor while swimming along the water's surf. He rejected use of a scuba tank and wetsuit, intuiting that he needed to remove every barrier possible between himself and his environment. 'Putting some skin in the game' amid frigid water temperatures as low as 8°C veritably intensified his empathy for and identification with the cephalopod's haptic apprehension of her surroundings via every pore of her vulnerable flesh. Otherworldly two-shots of the undulating limbs of both octopus and amphibious human hovering beside one another in the water signal attunement each to the other's movements, despite the dramatic disparity in corporeal size (Figure 10.2). Neither species was habituated to inhabiting space in proximity to the other and thus, some of the most compelling footage to emerge from that singular year captures this emergence of new bodily orientations predicated upon trust in the 'face' of radical alterity. As spectators of this film, we, too, relinquish customary reliance on the notion of a face as focal point, acculturating to the expanse of the

Figure 10.2   New bodily orientations in the 'face' of radical alterity, from *My Octopus Teacher* (Craig Foster and Pippa Ehrlich, 2020).

entire body as an analogous orientation, a site receptive to and communicative with surrounding objects.

Sara Ahmed's queer phenomenology elucidates how internalised societal norms and actions selectively orient our bodies towards particular objects, creating a perceptual field where certain objects are pulled closer while others become non-perceivable. Although Ahmed is referencing the operations of heterosexuality, which she describes as 'a force on the surface of the skin' functioning as a straightening device that curbs any desires that might otherwise veer off course, her model can also be brought to bear on our orientation towards other animal species, and they towards us.[11] For their non-normative bodies (relative to our own) confront us with difference and thereby open up new ways for inhabiting space in relation to others. Recall, after all, that Foster's orientation towards the octopus was the indirect result of a swerve, when something – the unusual 'shell sculpture' – in his left peripheral vision derailed the fixed path of his gaze upon the sea floor.

One of the (literally) most 'gripping' moments comes close to the story's midpoint, following months of mutual observation and shared moments of tentative touch, when the octopus spontaneously leaps onto Craig's chest, clinging to him and allowing him to stroke her torso/head. It is an astonishing moment of bodily interface, which some film reviewers have framed, only half ironically, as queer interspecies romance (Figure 10.3). Although I don't share this anthropomorphic interpretation, I would concur that the relationship forged

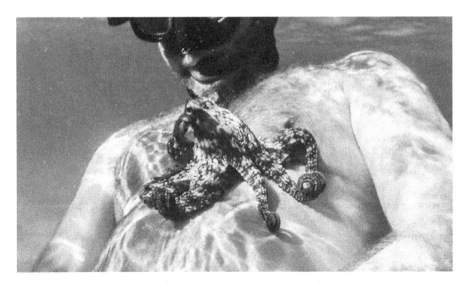

Figure 10.3   An interspecies tête-à-tête, from *My Octopus Teacher* (Craig Foster and Pippa Ehrlich, 2020).

is indeed queer in that it is oblique to the way either species is accustomed to orienting itself towards other sea creatures. Lacking any precedence, the octopus nonetheless displays a clear cognisance of the territorial 'layout' of Foster's anatomy: his torso poses an ideal 'landing field', big and flat enough for her suctions to adhere, and her choice of a frontal orientation also ensures she is able to hold his gaze and 'read' his face, which would not be the case were she to land on, say, his thigh or shoulder. What renders her bold move so striking is that it appears initiated solely for the pleasure of contact in the absence of any ulterior motive.

The interactions between these two disparate species produce a contact zone between dramatically different, even mutually incompatible worlds: that of terrestrial life governed by gravity and drawing oxygen from the gaseous layer surrounding the earth, and subaquatic life that floats while filtering oxygen through gills or siphons. As Foster points out early on, 'There's a line that can't be crossed.' Technology plays a significant role in mediating between these realms and is complicit in the worldmaking that enables a provisional posthuman intimacy, one simultaneously also inhuman. Ehrlich and Foster's camerawork and editing bring forth this contradictory reality, in which Foster and the octopus as living protagonists become existentially bound to the apparatus, their kinship only gaining an (after)life through the latter's operations. In one of the most suspenseful scenes, image and sound editing conspire to offer a heart-wrenching glimpse of the impossibility for either human or cephalopod to venture long beyond their respective ecologies to inhabit the shared world of the film story. The octopus has been stalked by a shark for hours but has managed to elude him; she suddenly jets rapidly upwards towards the blue sky visible beyond the water's surface in a final bid for safe harbour. In a seamless edit, she slithers awkwardly onto the rocks, the camera popping out of the water almost simultaneously to continue tracking her.

When the camera lens abruptly breaks the water's surface, this also breaks the spell of enchantment upon spectators of this subaquatic dream world. The diver's gasps for air after having remained underwater longer than ideal are a disorienting signal that we've returned to the gaseous world of the terrestrials. Yet so fully sutured are we to the plight of the octopus in this chase scene that we lose our orientation as to the sound's origins: is it our gasping, the diver's, or attributable to the octopus herself, whose three hearts must be panting with exhaustion and her siphons struggling to respire outside water? The threat on her life is real, forcing her to resort to unfamiliar territory in the effort to rest, regroup and then return to her habitat. Her disorientation in this environment mirrors ours in the apparatus, being at once existential and spatial, as two worlds collide and their status as refuge or peril becomes ambiguous, revealing the story to occupy an interworld, a utopian zone that is literally nowhere.

Other scenes similarly inspire the Western imagination shaped by literary and art history, whether fairy tales or high art. Foster's very first moment of physical contact with the octopus was captured on film in close-up as he carefully extended his arm to the octopus and she reciprocated by unfurling one arm to tentatively lay it upon his hand, like some interspecies handshake. Moments later she wrapped the very end of one limb around his fingertip, while her suctions carefully adhered and 'read' for further clues. The gesture invites a *detournement* of Michelangelo's mural, *The Creation of Adam* (1512) (Figure 10.4), often reduced in pop culture to the synecdoche of God's hand extending the spark of life from his finger to that of Adam, who mirrors in bodily repose his creator. Subjected to this archetypal overlay, the contact between Foster and the octopus similarly sparks anew the animal question, probing at the division between human and non-human animal by refiguring the tenuous link between heaven and earth, divine and mortal, creator and creation as that between the human's capacity to think beyond the limitations of their known being and the non-human animal's imputed state of captivation (that is, Heideggerian *Benommenheit*, lacking self-awareness).

It would be all too tempting to extrapolate further to read this as a documentary about a human animal extending kinship to the non-human, widening the latter's horizons and expanding its already formidable intelligence. This metaphor of uplift even gains spatialisation when the octopus on another occasion ventures to settle on his hand as he floats in the water, and to his surprise,

Figure 10.4   A posthuman(ist) detournement of Michelangelo's *The Creation of Adam*, from *My Octopus Teacher* (Craig Foster and Pippa Ehrlich, 2020).

chooses to remain there as he ascends to the water's surface to draw air. Yet the broader film narrative actually overturns this fantasy of humankind made in God's image to 'have dominion over the fish of the sea . . . and over all the wild animals of the earth'.[12] Instead, it is Foster who comes to recognise his self-incurred alienation from the saline medium that originates all life. The female octopus represents this fecundity, reproducing her species and then completing the cycle by succumbing to consumption by other prey. Her pedagogy resides in the fact that, by voluntarily acknowledging him – metaphorised in the tiny limb reaching to touch his finger – 'she helped me to see that I am part of this place and not separate from it.' What Foster must (re)learn is how to reconnect with his place within a broader zoontological framework while surrendering some of his investment in an autonomous self.

As both the film's co-director and its first-person narrator, Foster may appear to have the last word in this vitalist and phenomenological ethology of inter-species encounter. Framed frontally as he sits at a table in his home, which faces onto the Cape shoreline below, he submits to the confessional mode elicited by the silently running camera as 'psychoanalytical stimulant'. When his voice catches or he falls silent at the memory of the octopus's death, his face is also shown in close-up, re-humanising the amphibian cyborg we otherwise watch floating in murky waters. Intercutting his retroactive auto-analyses with onei-ric subaquatic footage corroborates Derrida's claim that, as autobiographical animals, we gain subjectivity by distinguishing ourselves from others, includ-ing other animals, whom we have subjected in order to stake our own singular claim to subjectivity.[13] And yet, the film title's playful allusion to tutelage also posits a relational subjectivity: Foster has also learned from and been irrevers-ibly transformed by the encounters with the octopus, as presumably has she by him (having proven herself a quick study). As Derrida observes, we underesti-mate how much the Other resides in the self, whose heteronomy is by no means founded solely in the human.

What octopus and human share, also with other species, is a habit of fol-lowing signs, scents, and clues, not necessarily always knowing where they will lead or what they will reveal, nor how they will come to be part of us, whether through consumption, through memorable encounter, or knowledge and insight gained. The pun in the French title to Derrida's volume, *L'Animal que donc je suis* (2008) similarly plays off the double meaning of the verb *suis*, both 'I am' and 'I follow'. All animals are trackers, and this quality binds the zoontologies of both Foster and the octopus. Foster's ethology entailed veritably stalking this octopus, learning to recognise traces of her presence on the ocean floor in the debris she left behind, voyeuristically inserting a camera into rocky crevices to intrude into locations the octopus sought out precisely in order not to be seen, and moreover shining camera lighting onto a creature that shies from glare. Yet, to his great surprise, even flattery, he too found himself being surreptitiously followed by the octopus, who presumably sought to understand his strange ways as much out of curiosity as for her own survival.

In turn, there is no discounting the pleasure global spectators have derived in 'following' this viral documentary, most especially in the pandemic year of 2020. Streaming platforms like Netflix have benefited as never before from captive audiences seeking to escape imposed quarantine by following alluring online portals either into a comforting past or brave new worlds of the present and the future. There's a serendipity to how Foster's search for escape and healing within the stand of kelp forest near his home has fed a new public hunger. While implementing the camera as a practice-based tool of (self-)exploration, he found himself inhabiting that (meta)physical space and time Agamben (2004) coins 'the Open': an ontological vacuum, an interval located somewhere between the destructive binaries differentiating human from animal. Frigid water temperatures approaching a threshold that would ordinarily swiftly eradicate warm-blooded life instead, in Foster's words, 'upgrades the brain, your whole body comes alive', while also stretching its capacity to ration oxygen to the 'interval' of six minutes. He thereby entered a zone of pure receptivity to what he calls 'the forest mind', cancelling a civilisational cacophony whose arbitrary onto-political grammar Agamben retraces to Ancient Greece and Aristotles' *Politics*. When the category of human life gets assimilated into that of the citizen in the polis, Agamben infers life is only regarded as human when a political status attaches to it predicated upon 'rights'. Outside that adscription, sovereign power governs over life as raw matter, deemed dispensable outside its potential commodity value. Fosters project takes a political turn towards dismantling that 'anthropological machinery' from within by bringing the agency and singularity of diverse ontologies into focus and thereby putting a face, even a name and a claim to rights, to all that has otherwise been relegated to the catch-basin of 'nature'. As early as 2012 he cofounded The Sea Change Project 'to get this great African Sea forest recognised as a global icon, like the Serengeti or the Great Barrier Reef'. The making of *My Octopus Teacher* helped to further 'brand' the kelp forest in popular awareness. Says Foster, 'You have to name a place in order for people to care about and protect it.'[14] If this ambition appears to echo those of earlier land pioneers staking territorial claims, his preservationist ethos actually strives to remedy and reverse those colonialist incursions.

In negotiating species alterity through faciality, *My Octopus Teacher* also taps into our pandemic-induced sensitivity to the latter's articulation. Foster's face goggles recall the headgear that began to mediate our every public encounter, as we compensated through heightened eye contact and intensified affect for what got lost in muffled exchanges delivered from behind cloth or paper masks. The subaquatic world he explores gains further canny resonance among those who have navigated the virtual aquarium of videoconferencing, encountering one another across the distortions of another liquid medium, this one comprised of digital ones and zeros that occasionally glitch. We've learned to endure the indignities of speech cut off mid-sentence or distorted beyond comprehension, and of faces that spontaneously freeze in unflattering or comical grimaces, not to mention odd apparitions (children and non-human animal companions) paddling by in the background. Reduced to two-dimensional faces struggling to achieve co-presence across the frame, we've gained some pointers from Foster's encounter with a singular member of the species *octopus vulgaris*. Her legacy remains not only the baby octopuses spawned in her final weeks of living but also the profound lessons in mutual enchantment across perceptual planes, requiring provisional trust, respect and resilience in uncertain times.

Notes

1. James Leo Cahill, *Zoological Surrealism: The Nonhuman Cinema of Jean Painlevé* (Minneapolis: University of Minnesota Press, 2019), 3.
2. Georgio Agamben, *The Open: Man and Animal*, trans. K. Attell (Standford: Stanford University Press, 2004).
3. Béla Balázs, *Early Film Theory: Visible Man and The Spirit of Man*, ed. Erica Carter, trans. Rodney Livingston (New York: Berghahn Books, 2011), 46.
4. Ibid., 60.
5. Ibid., 60.
6. Peter Godfrey-Smith, *Other Minds: The Octopus, the Sea and the Deep Origins of Consciousness* (New York: Strauss, and Giroux Farrar, 2016).
7. Jacques Derrida, *The Animal That Therefore I Am*, ed. Marie-Louise Mallet, trans. David Wills (New York: Fordham University Press, 2008), 35.
8. Gilles Deleuze and Félix Guattari, *A Thousand Plateaus: Capitalism and Schizophrenia*, trans. Brian Massumi (Minneapolis: University of Minnesota Press, 1987), 180–1.
9. Jean-Louis Baudry, 'Ideological Effects of the Basic Cinematographic Apparatus', and 'The Apparatus: Metapsychological Approaches to the Impression of Reality in the Cinema,' in Philip Rosen (ed.), *Narrative, Apparatus, Ideology: A Film Theory Reader* (New York: Columbia University Press, 1986), 286–99, 299–318.
10. Stephen Mumford, *Dispositions* (Oxford University Press, 2003), 118.
11. Sara Ahmed, *Queer Phenomenology: Orientations, Objects, Others* (Durham, NC: Duke University Press, 2006), 107.
12. Genesis 1: 26–8, New International Version.
13. Derrida, *The Animal That Therefore I Am*.
14. Aryn Baker, '*My Octopus Teacher* Became a Viral Sensation on Netflix. Its Human Star Craig Foster Wants the Film to Inspire Change', *Time*, 10 November 2020 Available at <https://time.com/5909291/my-octopus-teacher-craig-foster-interview/> (last accessed 24 September 2021).

11. *BÊTE NOIR(E)*: ANIMALITY, GENRE AND THE FACE IN *BORDER*

Alice Maurice

Ali Abbasi's *Border/Gräns* (Sweden, 2018) tells the story of Tina (Eva Melander), a border agent with a difference. She can literally sniff out those with something to hide; she can smell 'shame, guilt, rage', and 'other things' as Tina sheepishly puts it when pushed to explain her special powers. She is a recognition device – and yet she remains a mystery, mostly to herself. Tina's face marks her difference: heavy-lidded, low-browed and with mottled skin, her face disorients the viewer, making Tina hard to recognise or reconcile and activating the viewer's urge to *detect* her identity. Even though the film ultimately identifies her as a troll, for most of the film she is represented as a mysterious human defined by her affinity with animals and by her super-sensory powers. Combined, her 'animal' traits and the morphology of her face define her as a kind of stranger and watchdog over the human race. Meanwhile, though she presents and is identified as female, that, too, is thrown into question as the film progresses. As such, Tina occupies the border in more ways than one, as boundaries proliferate and attenuate in the film: between human and non-human, male and female, legal and criminal, moral and immoral. All of these boundaries are located, reoriented or challenged, in one way or another, at the site of the face – which is itself a kind of limit or boundary: between self and other, between interiority and exteriority, between, as Deleuze puts it, 'individuation' and 'social role'.[1] I want to think about the face here in a dual way – both in terms of its function in the film and in terms of the actor's makeup and performance – to explore how this film both does and does not provide access to Tina via her face, and how we might think about the possibilities of the face as mutable object and body part. In this sense, I want to suggest that this film – and the reliance on prosthetic makeup for the main character – can get us 'beyond the close-up' (and its role in defining the face as icon, fetish or access point to a spiritual essence) to the face's fleshy materiality, highlighting the tensions between the over-coding of identity in the face and its transformational powers. I suggest that in *Border*, the face connects the contested sites of gender, genre and animality.

THE FACE AT THE BORDER

The camera, too, has been understood as a detection device, and this revealing function of the camera was particularly activated and associated with theories of the close-up and the face. Whether in Béla Balázs's theory of the 'micro-physiognomies' revealed in close-up, or in Jean Epstein's theorisations of *pho-togénie*, the idea that the close scrutiny of the face by the camera would yield something the naked eye could not – that it would 'tear away the mask' – was common. At the same time, the wonders of the face in close-up have typically been associated with the beauty, harmony and unity of the face as an aesthetic unit. Georg Simmel, the early twentieth-century sociologist and cultural theorist who influenced Balázs and others, accounted for the face's 'unique importance to the fine arts' by referencing its 'inner unity' – the fact that a change to any part of the face 'immediately modifies its entire character and expression'.[2] Too much deviation outside the face's 'narrow limits' of motion (such as stretching, drooping, gaping), anything that would pull apart this balance and unity, would not only be ugly or 'unaesthetic', it would threaten to destroy precisely what signified the 'properly human' for Simmel: 'the absolute encompassment of each detail by the power of the central ego'.[3] As such, the face is unlike the body; its balance reflects the mind. With its morphological difference and its relative 'closed-offness', Tina's face challenges the limits (*gräns*) of the face in close-up: we often don't get what we've come to expect from it.

Sometimes, we don't get the face at all. We are introduced to Tina from behind: in a wide shot, Tina stands at the edge of the water, her back to the camera, a big cargo ship dominating the left side of the frame. The first 'close-up' we get is of her hand, picking up a bug. The camera drifts up to Tina's face in profile, looking down as she gently places the bug on a twig. From this quiet scene, we cut to a very different context, with Tina at her job as a border agent. The next shot is a more standard medium close-up – we see Tina's full face for the first time, now indoors, at the border security checkpoint. A glowing red light on the wall colours the left side of her face (Figure 11.1).[4] This shift from nature, and natural light, to artificial environment is stark. Here, Tina is placed before us for inspection – even as she is in in the act of inspecting or detecting: a detector that detects what the standard metal detectors and x-ray

Figure 11.1 Tina's face, the red light at the border, from *Border* (Ali Abbasi, 2018).

machines cannot. So, we watch her watching, scrutinise her as she scrutinises those crossing the border. Her activity as an agent of the state doubles back on our own urge to identify what we see. Once we've seen her do her job – catching a young man with booze in his luggage, sensing it before seeing it – we cut to Tina driving home. Again, we see her from behind, this time the back of her head, her hair blowing in the wind as she drives down the road towards gradually greener spaces, as we see the woods and the sunlight glinting through the trees. It's as if she is freest when no one – not even the film audience – is looking at her face. We never get the reverse shot of her driving; we only see her again once she's home.

That dynamic – the back and forth between nature and culture, freedom and restriction – punctuates the movie, ultimately dividing its narrative in two as well, as the film toggles between its bleak, noir-ish crime story, with its cold colours and institutional settings, and the budding romance and story of self-discovery that takes place in the woods, with idyllic scenes of communion with nature, animals and, ultimately, with a stranger named Vore (Eero Milonoff), who will bring those two worlds together in the end. But I want to linger for a moment on that first full shot of Tina's face, reddened by the light at the security checkpoint. We get the connection here, between the red light denoting a stopping point, and Tina's face as a kind of stop sign. She is the one who stops people – in her function at the border, stopping people so their bags can be searched, stopping people because they trigger her senses – but her face also stops people in other contexts: at a supermarket, and in other everyday contexts, Tina's face (and later, Vore's) stops people in their tracks. People stop to stare or turn away. Even those she stops at the border refer to her person, not just to her function. The first victim of her super-sensory detection powers mutters off-screen, 'Ugly bitch. I can't stand that kind' – neatly yoking her gender, her face and her apparent 'kind' or 'race'. The irony of Tina, an apparent outsider/stranger guarding the border will be compounded (or perhaps undone) later, when she is identified as a troll – troll lore including, among other things, Scandinavian folk tales in which the creatures live under bridges, requiring humans to trick them in order to cross.[5]

But the redness on Tina's face in this scene stops me in another way – it makes me think of the prosthetic makeup that the actor, Eva Melander, is wearing, and of the way it absorbs or reflects the light. Is her skin behaving like skin or like silicone and paint? Much of the discussion of Melander's performance was focused, not surprisingly, on the effects makeup. In general, the commentary around extreme makeup effects tends to focus on how the actor performs or communicates emotion through or despite the heavy makeup – the idea that the makeup will function as a mask and will limit the actor's ability to emote in a legible way. And that was certainly the case with discussions of the makeup in *Border*. But in a number of interviews, when Ali Abbasi is asked how he came to choose Melander for the part, he talks about being initially too obsessed with finding a type and notes that he needed to pull away from an obsession with physical appearance. He describes Melander's audition and how he was amazed by her because, when playing out a scene in which she meets Vore, the love interest, for the first time, she blushed: 'She was red all over her face,' says Abbasi in an interview with *Film Comment*, 'and I started blushing, too.' He goes on to note,

> A lot of actors can change their physicality, their way of talking, but the most difficult thing is when you can create a signal or an emotion or an impulse that's so strong that it takes over your body and you don't really know what it's going to do with you.[6]

The thing is, with all that prosthetic makeup, it would be hard for a blush, on the part of the actor, to read. So, it's interesting to me that we get this artificial reddening of the face, heightened by the artificiality of the makeup, which does not communicate an emotion or a bodily response coming from within Tina, but something coming from without. Like the use of shadows in classic film noir, the red light bifurcates the face, suggesting a split identity – this would often be a kind of moral/immoral split in film noir, while here we might take it to signal the troll identity 'underneath' the human. But, unlike shadow, the red here accentuates skin tone and surface, highlighting the relation (or lack thereof) between inside and outside. It accentuates the disconnect – this sense of closed-offness, or even suppression, not just of emotion (on the part of her character), but of the body.

Blushing has played an important role in the history of the discourse on facial expressions, emotions, and the distinction between humans and animals.

As he made clear in *The Expression of Emotions in Man and Animals* and else-where, Darwin found blushing particularly fascinating. As Lucy Hartley puts it in her study of nineteenth-century face culture, 'Of all expressions, blushing was, to Darwin, the most peculiar to humans', and he found the phenom-enon 'a fundamental and imponderable subject'.[7] Darwin linked blushing to the 'moral sense' and to self-consciousness – qualities he identified as particular to humans – and with 'an acute sense of being observed'.[8] If we think about this in the context of this shot, the reddening of Tina's face – a kind of 'arti-ficial blush' – signals the fact that while Tina scrutinises those crossing the border, she is also an object of their scrutiny (and ours). At the same time, it questions whether she possesses this definitively human self-consciousness, this social shame – since the reddening is coming from the light, not from a blush. Nonetheless, it will become clear as the film progresses that the 'moral sense' is in fact the keenest of Tina's super-sensory (and, perhaps, extra-human) pow-ers, and the red light holds out the possibility that she recognises shame not just because she can smell it, but because she feels it in herself. The red-faced Tina might redound upon us as well, as we are aware – and possibly ashamed of – our need to stare at and ponder her unusual appearance. The 'blush' here thus references the multiple ways in which the body and emotion are used both *as* and *at* borders – the way they are 'bound up', as Sara Ahmed reminds us, 'with the securing of social hierarchy: emotions become attributes of bodies as a way of transforming what is "lower" or "higher" into bodily traits'.[9] It is also worth noting that this light reddens but does not beautify – unlike the blush, which has also long been associated with specifically feminine beauty, with many theorists of beauty, facial features and expression noting the flush of a woman's face and bosom as enhancing physical and sexual attractiveness (this of course inspiring the cosmetics that mimic the suffusion of blood to the face).[10] Tina seems to fail the blush test on both fronts ('blushing is human'; 'blushing is pretty/feminine'). With her canine qualities and a face that diverges from conventional feminine beauty norms, she commits a kind of double sin. She is, as the irritated male traveller puts it, an 'ugly bitch'. The offhand com-ment, like the off-kilter blush, mixes the literal and the figurative, the animal and the human.

For all of Abbasi's insistence on looking for something apart from physi-cality in performance, the design of the makeup effects – the construction of Tina's face – came down to features and flesh, and Abbasi tended towards the oversignifying and overdetermination of physical traits. The makeup artist on the film, Goran Lindstrom, recounts in interviews that, in the process of figur-ing out the makeup, he kept asking Abbasi what he was looking for, but notes that the director 'didn't really have a clear idea of what he wanted' for Tina's look. At first, Abbasi offered a 'famous painting of a Neanderthal' as a model, but Lindstrom rejected that straight away as 'too much'.[11] Most of Abbasi's suggestions were, in fact, deemed 'too much' – in particular he seemed obsessed with the idea of a 'monobrow' which the makeup artist rejected again as 'too much' or 'too cliché'. Lindstrom describes his goal with Tina as 'trying to stay away from making her too anything, really'.[12] But the overall theme of the look was 'animalistic' and 'ugly' and 'less feminine' (with 'ugly' and 'less feminine' seeming to be synonymous in the makeup plan).

While there was no particular animal in terms of the goal of the look, that particularity becomes important in performance, as Melander studied dogs for the way she would use the nose and teeth as Tina. Tina's most prominent expression involves the nose twitching along with the upper lip, as she picks up scents. The discovery that sets the plot in motion involves Tina sniffing a cell phone. We get a close-up of Tina with the phone to her nose – remarkably, what she has found is a memory card full of child pornography, which involves her in the larger investigation of a child exploitation ring. The anatomy of scent becomes even more the focus a bit later, when Vore enters the picture. Tina picks up Vore's scent before he enters the frame. The primacy of smell over vision is made clear: framed in medium close-up, Tina stands at the border checkpoint, alert, as her nose and lips begin to quiver. We cut to an extreme close-up of her mouth, the upper lip twitching, baring her teeth. Only then do we cut to a shot of her eye. Finally, we get the reverse shot of a traveller (Vore) in the distance, approaching the border. In her official capacity as border guard (and later, as investigator of the child pornography ring), her sense of smell is most typically associated with disgust. Here, however, Vore sets off something else, and her sense of smell becomes associated with sexual attraction – though the line between attraction and disgust will become less clear as the story unfolds. Tina knows by smell; she is led by her nose.

In general, it is Tina's sense of smell that most denotes her 'animalistic' nature in the film, though she also shares scenes of quiet communion and reflection with animals, especially with a recurring fox (Figure 11.2). Tracing the history of smell in Western philosophy, Akira Lippit reminds us of the role of smell in defining the boundary between animal and human – with the sense of smell associated with animals and 'lower forms of existence', recalling an evolutionary past of being close to the earth, stooped over in posture rather than upright.[13] At the same time, smell opens us up to the other; citing Horkheimer and Adorno, Lippitt notes the connection between the sense of smell and the desire 'to be taken over by otherness'.[14] Unlike sight, which accentuates that boundary between self and other – which objectifies – smell permeates and pervades. As soon as Tina smells Vore, the possibility of devouring – and being devoured by – the other opens up; her sense of herself both opens up and breaks down, as Tina's curiosity about Vore (whose name suggests voraciousness) will turn into curiosity and confusion about herself and who, or what, she is.

Figure 11.2   Tina connects with a fox, her face reflected in the window, from *Border* (Ali Abbasi, 2018).

TROLLING GENDER/TROLLING GENRE

So, on the one hand Tina is imagined to be 'like an animal', and the filmmakers did not want her to look too much like 'anything' but, on the other hand, she was also meant to be a troll. Not 'like a troll', but actually a troll. She begins to question her identity when she meets Vore, likely the first person she has met who resembles her, who appears to be her 'kind'. Early on, she explains to him, 'As a child I thought I was special . . . but then I grew up and realised I was just a human being. An ugly, strange human with a chromosome flaw.' Later, she asks Vore directly, 'Who am I?' and he answers unambiguously, 'You're a troll, like me.' (Interestingly, earlier, when she first asks, 'Who are you?', Vore answers ambiguously, 'I travel.'). This is then translated in a specific way in the makeup plan: As Lindstrom puts it, 'We didn't want them to look like fairy tale trolls; we wanted them to look like some kind of race that functions in our society.'[15] This combination of a vague animality/difference ('not too much like anything, really') with a definitive identity (troll) marries the mythical with the racial and socially situated group. Further, the film charts a transformation that expresses outwardly Tina's process of increasing self-awareness – she knows she's a troll and so she starts to look different. The director 'wanted the character to become more animalistic, as she becomes more familiar with her own instincts and her troll self', Lindstrom reports, which translated, in terms of the makeup, into making her 'less feminine', and with Abbasi returning, again, to 'that monobrow idea' (the makeup department offered a 'slight monobrow' as a compromise). Tina's look does become 'more masculine' over the course of the film, with facial hair, eyebrows, costuming and hairstyle shifting, along with the lighting and framing of Tina's face (Figure 11.3). Tina also becomes

Figure 11.3   The makeup artists aimed for a more 'feminine' look early in the film (top), and a more 'masculine' look towards the end (bottom), from *Border* (Ali Abbasi, 2018).

increasingly assertive and even aggressive: she confronts her father about her true identity and his role in taking her away from her biological (troll) parents; she dominates her boyfriend's dogs, who used to bark ferociously when they saw her; and she also evicts the boyfriend, Roland (Jörgen Thorsson), a freeloader who has clearly been using her for her house. After first throwing Roland's TV out the door, she tells him to leave; when he asks if she's serious, her answer clarifies while also offering a nod to her changed appearance and bearing: 'Do I look like I'm joking?'

Gender fluidity is about more than makeup effects in the film. The status of Tina's (and Vore's) genitals is wrapped up with the status of the story, not only triggering twists of plot, but provoking shifts in genre and character conventions as well. In its bleak crime procedural plot, *Border* conforms to what is popularly called 'Scandinavian noir', but the troll love story adds a strong dose of the fable or fairy tale. *Border* is quite clear and often literal in its exploration and celebration of transgressing limits and pushing boundaries. This proliferation of boundaries and borderline figures means that Tina and Vore – the supposed trolls – end up standing in for many kinds of marginalised others. Given the focus on border security, their 'outsider' status points strongly to the experience of immigrants and migrants in the contemporary climate of xenophobia and the rise of right-wing political parties in Sweden and in Europe more generally. Abbasi, an immigrant himself (the filmmaker grew up in Iran and emigrated to Stockholm in 2002), has noted that he identifies to some extent with the position of the outsider who sees European society through a particular lens.[16] But the way the characters reference transgender identity – and the overall play with gender identity and biological sex – seems most clearly linked to the play with genre. Tina and Vore are not transgender humans (because they are not human), and yet they are creatures who challenge stable gender identity and who transform over the course of the film. And questions of gender identity traverse the genre boundary between the 'realism' of the crime film and the 'fantasy/fable' elements of the film. Early on, in Tina's second encounter with Vore at the border, she subjects him to a strip search, conducted by the male border guard, only to find that Vore has been (seemingly) misgendered. The guard gruffly informs Tina that he shouldn't have done the search and that the traveller in question 'has a vagina'. Importantly, in this same moment Tina learns that Vore has a scar on his tailbone matching her own (which turns out to be where their tails were surgically removed, a marker of their trollness). Later, in the budding love story, when Tina first tries to explain her 'difference' to Vore, she notes, first, her genital difference. After saying that she is an 'ugly human with a chromosome flaw', she points to her genital area and says it has to do with 'down here' and that she 'can't have children'. Finally, when Tina and Vore have sex for the first time, Tina discovers new functionality to her genitals, and the film offers a close-up of a phallic organ that emerges from Tina's genitals, and which allows her to penetrate Vore. While the mix of realism and fantasy may make for uncomfortable and potentially exploitative references to real-world marginalised communities, the film's insistence on the non-human status of its central characters is part of an effort (successful or not) to question the validity of these categories of 'humanness'. Certainly, playing with gender allows the film to further disrupt genre and genre expectations, especially in its reliance on noir tropes. If Vore begins the film as the noir archetype of the mysterious (male) drifter who comes to town ('I travel'), he ends, perhaps, as the film's femme fatale.

Genre identity and genre labels seem to be a sticking point for Abbasi. In an interview during the European Film Awards (EFA), the director bristles at the mention of genre, noting that 'people have this fetish for genre – what genre is this, what genre is that'. Rejecting the notion of being a 'genre director', Abbasi goes on to say that a 'random YouTube clip is more representative of the kind of reality that [he's] interested in'.[17] But what kind of reality is that? It seems clear that this 'reality' is tied to randomness, contingency and uncertainty – to the wildness associated with animals/nature and with the roving camera that captures them. This freedom and the kind of feeling it offers – what James Cahill has called the 'potential animal sensibility and creature feeling triggered by moving image media'[18] – seems to guide the film's style in the love story/ fairy tale portions of the film, the scenes featuring Tina and Vore communing with animals, eating worms, and generally frolicking in lakes and forest. To be sure, these pastoral scenes are Edenic, and run the risk of rehearsing standard clichés about primitive 'natural Man' – and certainly the film relies on the logic of fables or mythology in using animals or non-human creatures in order to teach humans a moral lesson. But these parts of the film are also marked by floaty, hovering camera work, drifting focus, and a kind of uncertainty in the image which mitigates and complicates a symbolic landscape or romanticised aesthetic. The film aims for immersion – whether in the quiet scene between Tina and a grasshopper that opens the film, or in the literal immersion of Tina and Vore in the water and in the rain, where the fluids from their bodies and the fluids on their bodies merge. These scenes tend to focus more on heads than faces – the characters are often shot in profile, heads poking out of the water or looking up at the sky, decentred or at the edge of the frame (Figure 11.4). In addition to conjuring images from mythology, these headshots retain their connection to bodies and physical experience, unlike classical close-ups of the face, which tend to stand in for psychology and subjectivity, tethered more to the logic of narrative than to the body.

As Tina gains knowledge about herself and those around her, the division between the two halves of the film (crimes story/fairy tale) begins to erode. As noted earlier, Tina discovers that Vore is involved in the child pornography ring, and as the plotlines begin to overlap, the boundary between the wild

Figure 11.4 Tina is often shot in profile, looking up, especially in natural settings, from *Border* (Ali Abbasi, 2018).

reality, romanticism and ecstatic sexual discovery of the scenes in the woods and the buttoned down, clinical realism of the crime procedural breaks down. And thus by the end of the film, I would argue, the burden of that wildness, of that 'kind of reality' that Abbasi is looking for, is borne by Tina's body, and especially by her face.

THE FACE ERUPTS

When Tina realises that she is a troll and that she was taken from her birth parents – that her entire identity has been a lie told to her by her father – she has a kind of traumatic break. She runs to the woods, the place where she usually finds peace, but she is disoriented, grasping at the earth and gasping for air. Though she is 'in her element', she also seems uprooted. We watch as she slides down a muddy slope; we get a close-up of her hand grabbing a clump of grass and earth, followed by a quit cut, mid-motion, to a shot that quickly traverses the side of her face, landing first on an extreme close-up of her eye, then drifting over to another extremely close framing of her mouth, and finally cutting back to the shot of one eye and sliding over to the other – both eyes staring, dead-fish-like, past the camera. The image goes in and out of focus, and Tina makes guttural sounds, as if she's choking. Her face is streaked with tears, rain and dirt. She is a kind of wounded animal. The idyllic 'back to nature' quality that the film has set up gives way here to abjection.

After this episode, she seems angry but also empowered to take up space in a new way: it's at this point that she throws out the boyfriend who has been taking advantage of her, and she also confronts Vore about his role in the child pornography ring. He steals babies from humans and sells them for exploitation, he confesses. Here, Vore seems to take perverse pleasure in acting out troll lore – the idea, in some Scandinavian folklore, that trolls steal babies and replace them with 'changelings' – and translating it into a real-world dimension and motivation. He does it, he explains, for revenge on the human race, for what they have done to their kind (including taking them away from their parents): 'You've heard of changelings . . . They took us, I take their children.' He concludes, 'They must suffer as we've suffered.' When Tina calls him 'sick', he replies, untroubled: 'I would be if I were human, but I'm not, thankfully.' His actions, and his logic, disgust Tina, triggering all of her senses, and the confrontation between Tina and Vore plays out as a 'face off': we see each of their faces in close-up as they growl at each other, baring their teeth in an aggressive contest for moral and physical dominance. As they face each other, the sound of their growls merges with a music track that sounds like wind, and the sound becomes distorted, with breath sounds, growls, vocalisation/sobs mixing until it crescendos into Tina's powerful roar (Figure 11.5). At this point, we are focused solely on Tina's face, and it's clear that a storm is raging; she has

Figure 11.5   Tina's face erupts, from *Border* (Ali Abbasi, 2018).

reached a level of power that scares Vore, and he backs down, looking at her with a mixture of fear and confusion. Tina's face has won the day. In the silence after the storm, Tina's face is wet with tears, mucus, spittle. The image blurs for a moment, and she walks away from Vore and out of frame.

This is not just an expression of emotion, of anger or disgust – it is an eruption. This eruption reminds me of Jean Epstein, French filmmaker and theorist and perhaps the most well-known proponent of *photogénie*, and his discussion of the close-up in his 1921 essay, 'Magnification'. Or, more accurately, it makes me rethink that essay. Describing the face in close-up breaking into a smile, he writes:

> Now the tragedy is anatomical. The décor of the fifth act is this corner of a cheek torn by a smile . . . Muscular preambles ripple beneath the skin. Shadows shift, tremble, hesitate. Something is being decided. A breeze of emotion underlines the mouth with clouds. The orography of the face vacillates. Seismic shocks begin. Capillary wrinkles try to split the fault. A wave carries them away. Crescendo. A muscle bridles. The lip is laced with tics like a theatre curtain. Everything is movement, imbalance, crisis. Crack. The mouth gives way like a ripe fruit splitting open. As if split by a scalpel a keyboard-like smile cuts into the corner of the lips.[19]

Now, it's important to note that this passage from Epstein is about small movements, the consistent shifting of a face about to smile, magnified in close-up, such that it becomes an anatomical drama – but even though Epstein dramatises the micromovements of expression here, he combines theatrical, anatomical and natural metaphors to suggest a seismic event. Tina's face does not behave like a traditional face in the 'American close-ups' that Epstein claimed to 'love' and about which he waxes poetic here;[20] this is not how human emotion is usually played – rather, it is as if she is about to burst through her mask, as if she is about to turn inside out. Although the overriding metaphor in the Epstein passage is theatrical, the underneath is nature: faults, breezes, clouds, waves, fruit. It seems to me that Tina is indeed about to 'split open' here. What is 'being decided' here is whether Tina can reconcile her moral sense with her kindred feeling for Vore. In the history of movie makeup, there has always been a fear of immobility – the stiffness of makeup that would stifle movement and expression; the history of both glamour and effects makeup has been to move towards more flexible material.[21] And yet here, the mask-like nature of Tina's features – the prosthetic mask the actor wears and the resulting *reduction* of the possibility of micro-movements – helps to create the war within that Melander's performance enacts. The mask activates the thinginess of the face while also animating and animalising. And while Epstein's 'crescendos' were silent, metaphoric and coenaesthetic/synaesthetic (vision suggesting sound), the sound comes to a literal crescendo in the scene between Tina and Vore.[22] With Tina's face, we get the sense that it isn't about entering another spiritual dimension through a glowing film face, but rather about cracking the surface, unleashing the connection between face, flesh and fluids. If 'the face is a horror story',[23] as Deleuze and Guattari tell us, it is a horror of subjectivity and signification, but also of category, identity, and genre. It is a boundary that must be crossed, transgressed, escaped. Ultimately, it cannot contain all that it is asked to contain. Here, 'Tina' can no longer contain herself.

CONCLUSION

'Tina' it turns out, is not even her real name – thus it is a container that functions like a mask, in the sense of concealing or adding a second skin to the troll baby who would be raised as human. In Tina's final scene with her father (who is wheelchair-bound and suffering from dementia), she asks if her birth parents had named her. He tells her she was originally called 'Reva'. And while she finds the name Reva 'beautiful' (and it might suggest revelation, an *unmasking*), the name recalls the trauma of her past – 'reva' is Swedish for 'tear' or 'wound'. Given the film's release in 2018, the name also resonates in another way, suggesting the identification and surveillance apparatus of the state, particularly the practice of profiling in the name of 'border security'. REVA is the acronym for 'Rättssäkert och Effektivt Verkställighetsarbete', meaning 'Legally Secure and Efficient Enforcement'. REVA was 'a government initiated project lasting between 2008 and 2014, which sought to increase the number of executed deportations of illegal immigrants from Sweden'.[24] This policy, the subject of fierce debate in Sweden, aimed at the 'internal control of foreigners' (ICF) and manifested most notably in practices such as the profiling of people in the Stockholm underground.[25] And so the misnaming of Tina/Reva recalls the euphemistic naming that masks the state violence done to individuals and groups in the name of border security, which brings us back to Tina's position as border security guard and her 'positioning' – the multiple ways in which she occupies the border and challenges the very boundaries she polices. Meta Mazaj identifies the 'border aesthetics' of the film with catachresis (drawing on a sense of catachresis as the 'improper use of a word that points to meaning's underlying instability').[26] Mazaj notes that, in its generic instability and its insistence on a reciprocal relation between literal and figurative meaning, *Border*

> unravels conventional approaches to the border as a topographical category with self-evident social consequences . . . [and] reframes the fraught, value-coded space of the border, generating an uncanny imaginary that serves, in turn, as a catachrestic topos that forges new sensory cognition of the world.[27]

The border as 'topography' is related – historically and discursively, literally and figuratively – to the 'topography' of the face, and to the physiognomic urge: the will to read and measure the social world through the face, from physiognomy to facial recognition and racial profiling. Tina, the borderline figure who stands at the border, the stranger who scans strangers, will eventually explode boundaries and categories to arrive at a morality that is neither divorced from embodiment nor tied to an ideal category of the human. As Tina asks Vore in the end, 'I don't want to hurt anyone. Is it human to think that way?' The face at the border – the face that is read but also the face that is 'red' (with societally induced shame) – this face will finally be a face that owns its own profile. And this is why it's important that the film returns the face to the body – ironically through the mask – not as substitute or fetish, but as a prosthetic body part and a fissured, faulted and transformative terrain unavailable to those who would map it.

Notes

1. Gilles Deleuze, *Cinema 1: The Movement-Image*, trans. Hugh Tomlinson and Barbara Habberjam (Minneapolis: University of Minnesota Press, 1986), 99.
2. Georg Simmel, 'The Aesthetic Significance of the Face,' in Kurt Wolff (ed.), *Georg Simmel: 1858–1918: A Collection of Essays* (Columbus: Ohio State University Press, 1959), 276.
3. Simmel, 'The Aesthetic Significance', 277.
4. Interestingly, in the story from which the film is adapted, the 'ugliness' of Tina's face is partly due to a burn she suffered from a lightning strike as a child, leaving it red on one side: 'The part of her face that had been turned to the trunk had been

burned so badly that the skin never healed properly and retained a permanent dark red tinge.' See John Ajvide Lindqvist, 'Grans', in *Let the Old Dreams Die*, trans. Ebba Segerberg (New York: Thomas Dunne Books, 2013), 14.

5. I'm thinking, for example, of the Norwegian folk tale 'Three Billy Goats Gruff'.
6. Nicolas Rapold, 'NYFF Interview: Ali Abbasi', *Film Comment*, 21 September 2018. Available at <https://www.filmcomment.com/blog/nyff-interview-ali-abbasi/> (last accessed 6 February 2021).
7. Lucy Hartley, *Physiognomy and the Meaning of Expression in Nineteenth-century Culture*, Cambridge Studies in Nineteenth-century Culture 29 (Cambridge: Cambridge University Press, 2001), 167.
8. Hartley, *Physiognomy*, 177. On shame, being observed, and the animal/human divide, see also Jacques Derrida, *The Animal That Therefore I Am*, ed. Marie Louise Mallet, trans. David Willis (New York: Fordham University Press, 2008).
9. Sara Ahmed, *The Cultural Politics of Emotion* (Edinburgh: Edinburgh University Press, 2014), 4.
10. Hartley, *Physiognomy*, 76–7.
11. Matt Grober, 'With Little Money and Even Less Time, "Border" Makeup Designers Turn European Talents into Trolls', *Deadline*, 4 December 2018. Available at https://deadline.com/2018/12/border-goran-lundstrom-makeup-prosthetics-neon-oscars-interview-1202512832/> (last accessed 26 September 2021).
12. Ibid.
13. Akira Lippitt, *Electric Animal* (Minneapolis: University of Minnesota Press, 2000), 123–5.
14. Max Horkheimer and Theodor Adorno, *Dialectics of Enlightenment*, cited in Lippitt, *Electric Animal*, 124.
15. Grober, 'With Little Money'.
16. Wendy Mitchell, 'Director Ali Abbasi on how Cannes title "Border" channels "the experience of being a minority"', *ScreenDaily*, 10 May 2018. Available at <https://www.screendaily.com/features/director-ali-abbasi-on-how-cannes-title-border-channels-the-experience-of-being-a-minority/5129033> (last accessed 3 March 2021).
17. 'EFA 2018 – Interview with Ali Abbasi', YouTube video, 4:52, 22 July 2019. Available at <https://www.youtube.com/watch?v=IqwG7h9ISHE> (last accessed 26 September 2021).
18. James Cahill, 'A YouTube Bestiary', in Paul Flaig and Katherine Groo (eds), *New Silent Cinema* (New York: Routledge, 2016), 281.
19. Epstein, Jean, 'Magnification and Other Writings', trans. Stuart Liebman, *October* 3 (Spring, 1977), 9.
20. Ibid.
21. I discuss the very early history of movie makeup and expression in 'Making Faces: Character and Makeup in Early Cinema', in Marina Dahlquist et al. (eds), *Corporeality in Early Cinema* (Bloomington: Indiana University Press, 2018). See also Drake Stutsman, 'The Silent Screen, 1895–1927', in Adrienne McLean (ed.), *Costume, Makeup and Hair* (New Brunswick, NJ: Rutgers University Press, 2016), 21–46.

22. For a discussion of corporeality, coenaesthesia, and *photogénie*, see Christophe Wall-Romana, 'Epstein's Photogénie as Corporeal Vision: Inner Sensation, Queer Embodiment, and Ethics', in Sarah Keller and Jason N. Paul (eds), *Jean Epstein: Critical Essays and New Translations* (Amsterdam: Amsterdam University Press, 2012), 51–73.

23. Gilles Deleuze and Felix Guattari, *A Thousand Plateaus: Capitalism and Schizophrenia*, trans. Brian Massumi (Minneapolis: University of Minnesota Press, 1987; 2002), 168.

24. Stina Fredrika Wassen, 'Where Does Securitisation Begin? The Institutionalised Securitisation of Illegal Immigration in Sweden: REVA and the ICFs', *Contemporary Voices: St Andrews Journal of International Relations* 1:1 (2018), 78.

25. Ibid.

26. Meta Mazaj, 'Border aesthetics and catachresis in Ali Abbasi's *Grans/Border* (2018)', *Transnational Screens* 11:1 (2020), 35. DOI: 10.1080/25785273.2019.1682229.

27. Ibid.

12. *HEJAB* AS FRAME IN *TEN* AND BEYOND

Sara Saljoughi

In the penultimate scene of Abbas Kiarostami's *Ten* (*Dah*, 2003, Iran), we are witness to an utterly unexpected event: an unveiling. A young woman passenger in the car of Mania, the film's protagonist, takes off her *hejab* in front of the camera. At the beginning of the scene, we see the young woman with a white *hejab* wrapped tightly around her head and tied severely at the chin. The excess material of the veil, beyond where it has been tied, is dramatically billowed on her chest. The whiteness of the veil has a cold, blue tone and is stark against the young woman's black clothing and the black seats and frame of the car. In the window to her left, we see a vivid reflection of the veil from the side. The reflection mostly shows the material of the white veil, with only a sliver of the woman's profile. Unlike the reflection, the shot centres the young woman's face and frames it with the white veil. This character was introduced in an earlier scene, where she appeared in a loose-fitting black shawl whose spacious relation to her face intimated her carefree and casual attitude. Her new, austere garb conveys a different mood and prompts Mania to say, 'You've become so modest. Why have you tied it like that? It doesn't suit you.'

The young woman has been telling Mania about a break-up precipitated by the discovery that her boyfriend doesn't want to marry her and is in love with someone else. When Mania asks after the tightness of her *hejab*, the shot returns to the young woman and the image loses focus and blurs slightly due to the car driving over large bumps in the road. She begins to undo her *hejab*, at first loosening the tie and holding the material away from her face. A facial roundness that was composed by the structure of the tight veil gives way to an

Figures 12.1 and 12.2   Left, first appearance of young woman passenger in *Ten* (Abbas Kiarostami, 2003), who appears later in a more pious form of *hejab* (right).

elongated visage. As she holds the veil away from her chin, it stretches against the sides of her face, once again containing the face, which has the effect of emphasising the roundness of her cheeks. In a series of rapid, tidy movements, she pulls the *hejab* around her face and then away from it, moving towards the back of her head, all while looking at herself in the mirror. This process reveals to us and to Mania that she has fully shaved her head. 'What happened?' and 'it suits you,' offers Mania, to the woman as she cries, her gaze turned down. Here the fabric puffs around her face, appearing more voluminous, seeming substantial enough to hold her in this moment of vulnerability. In stops and starts, prompted by Mania, the young woman completely removes her *hejab*, without which her face seems to have shrunk, the proportions of the image uncannily altered. With the veil removed, her face loses any soft roundness, revealing instead an oval shape made more pronounced by her shaved head.

The removal of the young woman's *hejab* illuminates how the veil affects and transforms the face. Where the term 'unveiling' suggests that the removal of the veil reveals something previously concealed, observing the face in this process turns our attention to another matter entirely. What is 'unveiled' here is not something that the veil concealed, but rather something about the veil itself. By paying attention to the face in this moment in *Ten*, we can untangle its dynamic relation to the veil. In doing so, we can begin to try to answer a key question about this relation: how can we conceptualise the (cinematic) aesthetics of the veil as an aesthetics of the face?

Considerations of the face in cinema have largely overlooked the presence of the *hejab*. Nowhere is the *hejab*, or veil, a more ubiquitous presence than in contemporary Iranian cinema, which is mandated to follow Islamic guidelines of representation that require women to be veiled on screen. Yet the scholarship on Iranian cinema has not considered the veil in its relation to the face, or vice versa. Instead, scholars have emphasised the relation between mandatory on-screen veiling and theories of the gaze. Furthermore, scholars have commented on the political mobilisation of the veil to serve competing ideologies of nationalism. In Iran, this includes forced unveiling during the first Pahlavi period and forced veiling with the establishment of the Islamic Republic of Iran (IRI), while in France and elsewhere it emerges in the debates on *laïcité*. All of these discussions focus on the attachment of the veil to women's bodies and accordingly, the terms of the debates have to do with questioning the role of the *hejab* in women's agency. This essay considers the veil in terms of an aesthetics of the face, and therefore quite apart from the troubling binary that it is either a guarantor of Islam's oppression of women or an autonomously chosen sartorial practice that variously signifies piety and/or politics.

Hejab is an Islamic term referring to practices of modesty, which vary in terms of their style and degree. With the addition of a definite article, the *hejab* refers to the object known in English as the veil. This translation of *hejab* bares the ideological emphasis on concealment and exposure that figure Western understandings of this object. Veil, which in English refers to something that covers and obscures,[1] hints at an array of opinions and judgements that turn on Orientalist anxieties of knowledge and interpretation. A veil begs to be lifted, such as in the Christian ceremony of marriage, and this desire for revelation is an integral part of the political debates on *hejab* in the West, though it is often an unconscious desire. When thinking *hejab* through the figurative use of the word veil, it becomes impossible to conceive of it as anything other than a system of concealment and obscuration. Taken together, however, 'veil' and '*hejab*' help to conceptualise how this object and practice affect the aesthetics of the face in cinema.

As both practice and object, *hejab* is central to contemporary Iranian cinema. After the 1979 Iranian Revolution, which established the IRI in place of the ousted monarchy, cinema in Iran changed in significant ways. Initially film production and exhibition were put on pause for several years, only to be later revived when the new regime recognised the nation-building potential of cinema. The desire for an Islamic cinema was perhaps most visibly conveyed through the government's creation of new Islamic guidelines on representation. Issued by what was then called the Ministry of Culture and Islamic Guidance, the rules pertaining to representation focused on women and heterosexual interaction. The biggest change required women to be veiled on screen, regardless of the fictional scenario within the film. Further guidelines restricted the display of lust, desire and sexuality on screen, even between married characters. These guidelines were 'commandments for looking' (*akham-i nigah kardan*) stemming from a general 'rule of modesty' that extended the new laws of the IRI onto screen space.[2] According to these laws, all women and girls over the age of nine were to be veiled in public and in the presence of men outside their families.

By extending Islamic laws of modesty to the screen, the Islamic Republic aimed to create a cinema that was not extensive with the perception of film as a corrupting technology responsible for importing foreign cultural values. The representation of women in Hollywood and in Iran's dominant commercial cinema (*film farsi*) was one of the primary reasons for the attack on cinema during the 1970s revolutionary fervour, as well as in its wake. The religious objection to cinema stemmed from its staging of a space of desirous looking, one that was particularly irresistible due to *film farsi*'s tendency to portray looking relations in scenes featuring women as scantily clad dancers and singers in nightclub and cabaret scenes, where they are watched by male customers. The staging of such spaces in popular cinema defiantly challenged cultural norms that bore the influence of Islamic morality even before the change in regime.

The requirement that women be veiled on screen created new looking relations, albeit ones that continue to be determined by the desire of a heterosexual male spectator. In her field-changing book, *Displaced Allegories: Post-revolutionary Iranian Cinema*, Negar Mottahedeh demonstrates how the veil's disruption of the desirous gaze nevertheless points reflexively to the heterosexual male viewer in the movie theatre. If women must be veiled on screen, the assumption is that they are always being looked at by men. For this reason, Mottahedeh refers to post-revolutionary Iranian cinema as 'the apotheosis of 1970s feminist film theory'.[3]

In addition to its configuration of new looking relations, many scholars have commented on the veil's further interference with realist film strategies, noting that its presence in diegetic private spaces creates an illogical mode of representation that tethers the diegesis to the spectators watching the film.[4] For example, the appearance of the veil in homosocial spaces where women convene, or in a scene depicting a mother at home with her children, breaks any notion of screen space as a discrete and contained story world. Whereas in lived reality women would not be wearing the *hejab* in such circumstances, the object's appearance in the filmed version of these spaces creates an opening between the film world and the time and space of spectatorship. The actresses are veiled because men unfamiliar to them are or will be watching them. No longer is the diegesis a world upon which we gaze as voyeurs, as Mottahedeh deftly demonstrates, but one in which spectators are always already present. Mottahedeh's argument about the veil does not address the aesthetics that emerge in the *hejab*/face relation. The emphasis she places is on the reflexive nature of the veil, which points to the presence of the male spectators watching the film.

HEJAB AS FRAME

A conceptualisation of the aesthetics of the veil/face takes the question of reflexivity in a different direction. Where Mottahedeh discusses the veil as a reflection of the constructed (male) gaze, I connect the veil to the film frame, which is a different aspect of the language of cinema. With this shift, we can begin to fill the absence of an aesthetics of the veil/face that comes with a focus on the gaze.

While the *hejab*'s function is conceptualised with regard to the figure of a female body, its appearance on screen is always in relation to a distinct unit of that body – the face. In its particular relation to the face, the *hejab* does not conceal. Most practices of wearing *hejab*, ranging from the loose shawl worn by Mania in *Ten* or the traditional full body *chador* worn by religious women in Iran, keep the face exposed.[5] Wrapped around the face, the *hejab* functions as an immediate frame, one that is within the larger film frame. If the *hejab* is always the frame of any given face, it is necessary to examine how it functions as frame.

The *hejab*'s framing function privileges the face as the focus of our attention, which also dismisses the inclusion of the face within a system of modesty. In its relation to the *hejab*, then, the face becomes both more and less significant. This is important for the grammar of post-revolutionary Iranian cinema, for it removes the face as part of the equation of the female body that necessitates on-screen veiling. Seen from the point-of-view of an Islamic cinema, the face itself is but another object in the *mise-en-scène*.

Yet, the very quality of a frame is its function in directing our look at a given object or sets of objects. As a frame within the frame of the film image, the *hejab* can be understood as prompting us to look at the face in isolation. The face appears almost as relief contra what is around, behind and beyond its frame, the *hejab*. It is necessary to return here to the question of artificiality and realism in post-revolutionary Iranian cinema. By pointing to the constructedness of the object(s) framed, the frame (in general terms) also confers composition and artificiality to that which it contains. When understood as a frame within a frame, the *hejab* points specifically to the face as the site of acting, as a constructed element of the *mise-en-scène*, rather than an element of an unmediated profilmic reality. Therefore, while the concept of the *hejab* as frame affirms Iranian cinema as always already in reflexive acknowledgement of the spectator, it directs that spectator's look to the face as the most destabilising element of the image. Much hinges on the role of the face within *hejab* as a representation system, for if *hejab*, following Mottahedeh, disrupts realism, then the face is called upon to guarantee some degree of realism. Though framed by the *hejab*, the face remains visible, as it would without a *hejab*. The female face in this context is a stable connetion to 'reality' and also something that destabilises the promise of modesty offered by the *hejab*. Seeing the face thus framed, the spectator must put together and imagine a realist scene that is not being offered on screen, thereby engaging in the desirous imagining that the Iranian state's modesty guidelines aim to foreclose. Much like the close-up, the face framed by the *hejab* emphasises both what is shown and what is not shown.

One of the most iconic images of post-revolutionary Iranian cinema is a close-up of actress Soosan Taslimi's face as she is caught in the process of wrapping her scarf around her face. The shot comes from Bahram Beyzai's 1986 film *Bashu Gharibe Kuchak* (*Bashu the Little Stranger*), in which Taslimi plays one of the two central roles. The shot is our (and the protagonist Bashu's) first glimpse of Taslimi's character. In her discussion of the film, Mottahedeh alludes to the manner in which this shot tests the boundaries of the then recently established modesty guidelines.[6] We do not see Taslimi's hair; the image is not technically violating the representation laws. But to see the face framed in the process of becoming properly covered points to the *hejab*'s potential function as a material element of the *mise-en-scène*. In this understanding, the veil's primary role is to frame the face. This close-up of Taslimi emphasises the framing function of the veil. She holds each end of the scarf on either side of her face. She pauses, rather dramatically, in the middle of this motion. Rather than hurrying to put on her veil (as would conventionally be done with the announcement of a male voice), she pauses in the act. This pause, captured by the duration of the close-up, draws our attention to the way the veil frames the profilmic reality as shifting from a private to public context. While Taslimi's character has been alone in her farm fields with her children, she now rises to fix her veil as the male stranger Bashu (albeit a child) enters the scene. His arrival and our presence as spectators, require her to be in modest dress. What's interesting, however, is that the framing of her face in this manner draws attention to the ways in which Taslimi the actresss and N'ai, the character she plays, are both embroiled throughout the film in the act of acting. N'ai is played by Taslimi in a very physical manner. Her facial gestures are exaggerated, her vocal utterances (not just language but the sounds of various animals, such as the *caw* of crows) are pronounced and playful. All of these elements of the *mise-en-scène* point to a certain artificiality, one that appears in the modesty system's disruption of realism in private space, but more pointedly one that is signalled by the way Taslimi holds the scarf around her face in this introductory moment. This returns us to Mottahedeh's argument: that the presence of the veil in post-revolutionary Iranian cinema is a marker of the technology of cinema. In other words, it functions much like the appearance of the camera in modernist cinema. It reminds us of the very constructedness of the diegesis and betrays any desire of that space being wholly self-contained. It is for this reason that Mottahedeh argues the classical voyeurism of cinema is disrupted by the rules on representation in post-revolutionary Iranian cinema. Simply put, the presence of the veil is an immediate acknowledgement of the spectator. Understanding the veil as a frame deepens our understanding of how this cinema mediates the face.

Figure 12.3   Soosan Taslimi in *Bashu, the Little Stranger* (Bahram Beyzai, 1986).

HEJAB AS FRAME IN KIAROSTAMI'S FILMS

Kiarostami's cinema has often been discussed as a cinema of frames. In an interview, Kiarostami remarks, 'I've often noticed that we are not able to look at what we have in front of us, unless it's inside a frame.'[7] This statement reflects what has been described as Kiarostami's realist cinema that 'declares its artifice'.[8] Even before his final and posthumously completed film, *24 Frames* (2007), the director frequently spoke on the importance of frames in his broader body of work as a poet, photographer and filmmaker. Kiarostami's penchant for shooting in cars – which extends beyond *Ten* to include nearly all of his post-revolutionary works, as well as his first feature *Gozaresh* (*The Report*, 1977), made before the Revolution – is illustrative of his approach to framing. In his car films, the treatment of the windshield is emblematic of his continued exploration of the window/frame tension that has long preoccupied filmmakers and film theorists. Kiarostami rejects the pure window notion of reflection, emphasising the windshield as a particular view of the world. The frame of the windshield, or of the car, is often featured in the film frame. Kiarostami's *mise-en-scène* emphasises the reflection of the driver and passenger, prominently framing these aspects of the image. In *Ten*, he uses a stationary camera to enact a mode of framing that teases out the dynamic between the open and closed frame. The closed feeling of the film's framing mimics the feeling of sitting in a moving vehicle. When Mania and her young son Amin argue about Mania's divorce from Amin's father, they are both intensely upset. With the camera's fixed position and how it frames the face in each shot, we are forced to look at faces and to feel locked in the emotions of the characters. This intense fixity of the framing guides the spectator to the face. Despite being a medium close-up, each shot feels like it extends an invitation similar to that offered by a close-up. The stationary camera, however, also employs depth-of-field to provide a view into events taking place beyond the car, most of which are male passersby observing the women in the car who are speaking in front of two cameras.

Ten is Kiarostami's first film to feature a woman in the leading role. The film is divided into ten conversations that take place inside the car of Mania (director and actress Mania Akbari). She is the driver, and we are witness to conversations she has with various passengers, most notably her son Amin, and five women, ranging from family to strangers to whom she offers a ride in Iran's informal and hospitable economy of ride sharing. For the first seventeen minutes of the film, we see Amin and we only hear Mania's voice. When he reached the height of his fame in the mid-1990s with the Koker trilogy, Kiarostami faced criticism for the occlusion of women from his body of work. Iranian critics, in particular, grappled with Kiarostami's international success. While audiences around the world celebrated the filmmaker's simple plots and exquisite landscapes, the domestic response to his success included some discomfort around the claims of 'realism' in his films.[9] The rural setting of most of his internationally acclaimed post-revolutionary films, and their featuring of poor or working-class people, did not reflect a full picture of Iran. These criticisms are familiar as they were also voiced in the pre-revolutionary period when films like *The Cow* (*Gav*, Dariush Mehrjui, 1968) were censored for portraying rural images that challenged the country's attempts to present itself as modern.

The more significant criticism of Kiarostami, however, had to do with what many perceived as a short-sighted response to the post-revolutionary representational guidelines. Most of his films featured either children or male protagonists, which allowed him to avoid the false realism of the new representational regime. For example, in her reading of women in Kiarostami's cinema, Mottahedeh describes them as an 'absent presence'. This status is a reminder of the association of women with the apparatus of cinema, the very technology that produces Kiarostami's work.[10] In 1993's *The Wind Will Carry Us* (*Bad ma ra khahad bord*), this absence is remarked upon in a complex scene that is almost entirely dark and gives voice to the male protagonist's unfulfilled desire to watch a young woman milk a cow. Unsurprisingly, this film's nod to the absence of women in Kiarostami's work has been widely discussed in studies of Iranian cinema.[11]

In *Ten*, however, not only does the director feature a woman protagonist, but all of the conversations pertain to issues central to women's lives. These range from marriage and divorce, motherhood, and the search for autonomy. Most of the conversations are between women and reveal the constraints of living and working in a patriarchal society. One conversation is between Mania and a sex worker who mistakenly got into Mania's car, thinking her a potential client. The two women discuss sex work, sexual pleasure and achieving orgasm, adultery, marriage, unwanted pregnancies and abortion. Kiarostami's sudden employment of a female lead seems to have come with a bold step directly into social issues that the state censors out of Iranian cinema. The film's thematic focus on women's issues, in other words, is inextricable from its infamous 'unveiling scene' and from its status as Kiarostami's first woman-centred film.

In his 2008 film *Shirin*, Kiarostami's focus on women takes a full turn towards the aesthetic. The film features 114 women (113 well-known Iranian actresses and Juliette Binoche) watching a film in the cinema. The film is entirely comprised of medium close-ups and close-ups of the women. We never see the film that they are watching. Elsewhere, I discuss Kiarostami's treatment of the face in *Shirin* by emphasising its mobilisation towards a critique of the modesty laws and what they have foreclosed in Iranian cinema's imagination of spectators.[12] In *Shirin*, the *hejab* can be understood as functioning in a number of ways. This film, even more so than *Ten*, focuses on the relationship between the *hejab* and the face. In the case of a series of shots featuring Golshifteh Farahani, the intense pink hue of her *hejab* served to blur the (male) spectators behind her and bring into focus her tear-filled face (Figure 12.4). The *hejab*, therefore, is a part of the *mise-en-scène* that mediates focus on her face. Rather than simply affording her modesty, the *hejab*, by virtue of its function in the *mise-en-scène*, invites spectators into the intimate moment of her spectatorship. The interaction between the *hejab* as object and *hejab* as modesty in these shots points to the tension that always exists when the *hejab* appears on screen. The medium demands a requisite intimacy, particularly through devices such as the close-up. Yet that intimacy is also what is promised to be controlled through the system of modesty. By focusing instead on framing, it is possible to disrupt the binary of intimacy/modesty, which is a repetitive form of the revelation/concealment discourse of the veil in the West. In *Shirin*, the *hejab*'s role in visually articulating depth-of-field (through colour), becomes the primary mechanism by which it assumes its framing function. The close-up and the *hejab*-as-frame work together to draw our attention to the *hejab* as having a much more ambiguous presence in the image. When read as a frame, the *hejab* can take on a wide array of functions within a film, mirroring the broader potential of framing in general. It allows an aesthetic analysis of the *hejab* in film to move in new, unanticipated directions.

Figure 12.4   Golshifteh Farahani in *Shirin* (Abbas Kiarostami, 2008).

The aesthetics of the *hejab*/face provide generative ways to rethink the image in Iranian film studies beyond the question of the male gaze. Conceptualising the face as a distinct unit within the system of *hejab* on screen can enrich our understanding of film language in an Islamic context. At the same time, precisely because of its overdetermined status, the *hejab* as an object of the *mise-en-scène* is due for inquiries that emphasise its aesthetic dimensions and how they function within the broader film text. It is, of course, undeniable that an aesthetics of the *hejab*/face requires accounting for a politics of the *hejab*/face. Can we imagine the politics of this aesthetics as something that goes beyond the politics of self-reflexivity? Furthermore, would this allow us to conceptualise the politics of the veil more generally in a way that goes beyond the (liberal democracy) framework of individual freedom and choice?

Notes

1. 'veil, n. 1', *OED Online*, March 2021. Available at <https://www-oed-com.myaccess. library.utoronto.ca/view/Entry/221919?rskey=r4tUB4&result=1&isAdvanced=false> (last accessed 2 April 2021).
2. Negar Mottahedeh, *Displaced Allegories: Post-revolutionary Iranian Cinema* (Durham, NC: Duke University Press, 2008), 9.
3. Mottahedeh, *Displaced Allegories*, 34.
4. See Hamid Dabashi, *Close-up: Iranian Cinema, Past, Present, Future* (London: Verso, 2000); and Michelle Langford, *Allegory in Iranian Cinema: The Aesthetics of Poetry and Resistance* (London: Bloomsbury, 2019). Joan Copjec calls these 'virtual

exterior spaces'. See Copjec, 'The Object-Gaze: Shame, *Hejab*, Cinema', *Gramma* 14 (2006), 163–82.

5. The notable exceptions to this are the *niqab* and *burqa*, practices of *hejab* that fully cover the face and that are not commonly used in Iran.

6. Mottahedeh, *Displaced Allegories*, 21–2.

7. Imogen Sara Smith, 'In Our Time: Abbas Kiarostami's *24 Frames*', *Film Comment*, February 2018, n.p. Available at <https://www.filmcomment.com/blog/24-frames/> (last accessed 29 September 2021).

8. Gilberto Perez, 'Where is the Director?' *Sight and Sound* 15:5 (2005), 18–22.

9. See Azadeh Farahmand, 'Perspectives on Recent (International Acclaim for) Iranian Cinema', in Richard Tapper (ed.), *The New Iranian Cinema: Politics, Representation and Identity* (London: I. B. Tauris, 2002), 86–108.

10. Mottahedeh, *Displaced Allegories*, 100.

11. See Dabashi, Mottahedeh, Copjec, among others.

12. Sara Saljoughi, 'Seeing Iranian Style: Women and Collective Vision in Abbas Kiarostami's *Shirin*', *Iranian Studies* 45:4 (2012), 519–35.

PART III

MAKING FACES: CELEBRITY, PERFORMANCE, SELF

13. THE FACES OF GINGER: BEAUTY MAKEUP, FACIAL ACTING AND HOLLYWOOD STARDOM

Adrienne L. McLean

In 1936, the magazine *Stage* published an article by Leonard Hall called 'The Glamor Factories of Hollywood' ('In goes a Cinderella. Out comes a princess of plastic pulchritude'). The primary example Hall gives of how the studios manufactured glamour 'just as certainly as the quack of Donald Duck' is Greta Garbo. Hall claims, in fact, that 'the Somnolent Scandinavian was the first baby doll to be glamorised in the modern Hollywood sense, and she remains to this day the outstanding product of the art'. He recounts in detail the early efforts of the 'glamor mechanics' to improve the woman with 'lank blonde hair and heavy-lidded eyes', which, besides dieting and exercise, included the affixing of 'spurious eyelashes so long that they dipped in her consommé in the commissary'. The only unusual element Hall can point to in his chronicle is that, in contrast to other Hollywood 'Cinderellas', Garbo adopts glamour as 'strictly a studio proposition', and that off the screen she and her star image look like 'badly matched twins. There is a faint family resemblance, and no more.'[1]

Given my essay's title, naturally I want to contrast Hall's assessment with that at the centre of Roland Barthes's famous 1957 piece 'The Face of Garbo', in which he focuses on Garbo's 'admirable face-object', her 'at once perfect and ephemeral' visage, in the final long close-up at the end of *Queen Christina* (1933). It is not exactly a 'mask', nor a 'painted face', he writes, but 'a kind of voluntary and therefore human relation between the curve of the nostrils and the arch of the eyebrows' which together produce a 'thematic harmony' of 'extreme beauty' to which the appellation 'divine' could reasonably be applied.[2]

Despite his references to the 'human', then, Barthes envisions the 'classical star face', in Noa Steimatsky's words, as 'removed from any pretense of natural expressivity, the pretense of sharing in the reality of ordinary mortals – the spectators'.[3] Leaving aside the fact that in the pursuit of stardom Garbo's face was altered as much or more than those of many of her colleagues,[4] the 'pretense' of which Steimatsky speaks is a relationship as well, not only between the star and her 'ordinary' fans but between the face as the stable denominator of stardom and/as authenticity and Hollywood's belief from at least the 1920s that it was always also a canvas of a sort, even for the 'straight' (non-character) roles in which most film actors became stars in Hollywood. The intersections and paradoxes of this relationship are embodied, figuratively and at times literally, in the star image of Ginger Rogers.

Rogers was Garbo's contemporary – she was born in 1911, Garbo in 1905 – but I have little doubt that Barthes would have relegated Rogers, who had been in show business since winning a Charleston contest in Texas in 1925, to the category in which he places the young Audrey Hepburn, the 'infinite complexity' of whose countenance even in the early years of her film career gave Hepburn 'charm' rather than the 'essence' that Garbo possessed. For better or for worse, Rogers is now known primarily as the dancing partner of Fred Astaire in nine black and white musicals the team made at RKO from 1933 to 1939. But while the success of those films contributed mightily to the growth of her clout in Hollywood (as they did to his), they have tended to block out the rest of her extensive career, during which, as this essay will explore, she actively embraced mutability in her face and hair as a value rather than a stage that many, if not most, film players passed through on their way to stardom.[5]

As early as 1934, after some twenty-seven Hollywood features (two with Astaire), Rogers was already being pointed to as 'another player who has run the gamut from brunette to red-head to blonde'.[6] But as the use of 'another' here indicates, this did not necessarily brand her as unusual. Fan magazines are full of material devoted to stardom's rites of passage, such as a 1935 *Modern Screen* article that lauds rather than mocks 'the metamorphosis of Ginger Rogers' to 'sophistication and chic' through 'three stages of [her] haircombs'. Although the photos are of Rogers in film roles, the text works to make her the agent of her own appearance so that readers 'tired of looking at the same face' could change theirs using the advertised products that the magazines depended upon for revenue.[7] It was only later in her career, especially in retrospective evaluations following the demise of the studio system altogether, that Rogers became the object of something like scorn for the instabilities of her face and hair. Dance critic Arlene Croce, in her canonical study of the Astaire–Rogers films, refers caustically to Rogers's desire always to be 'something more' rather than remaining the 'goddess' that, or whom, she believes Astaire 'made' out of the twelve-years-younger actor, writing that, after the team broke up in 1939,

Figure 13.1   Reading from left to right and top to bottom, frame enlargements of Ginger Rogers in *Queen High* (1930), *42nd Street* (1933), *Gold Diggers of 1933* (1933), *Swing Time* (1936), *Primrose Path* (1940), *Lucky Partners* (1940), *The Major and the Minor* (1942), and *Week-End at the Waldorf* (1945).

'you hardly knew what hair or eyebrows she would turn up in next, playing what kind of role', and claiming that '[p]robably no other major star has so severely tried the loyalty of her public by constantly changing her appearance and her style'.[8] To Croce, as perhaps to Barthes, 'constantly changing' implies a fundamental lack of taste or class (the latter determining the former), thereby precluding the 'essence' of which Barthes speaks and that the 'ageless' Astaire presumably possessed as well. This in spite of the fact that Astaire was a deeply uneducated brewer's son from Omaha whose national stardom depended mightily on the development in 1931, two years before the balding middle-aged man made his first film after a career in vaudeville and on Broadway since childhood, of invisible hair lace for the toupées that made him and so many of his colleagues more attractive on the screen than they were in real life.[9]

Indeed, it is striking how reluctant Barthes is to face (so to speak) the dependence of Garbo's beauty on cosmetics and hairdressing. Especially since in the close-up to which he devotes his attention it is easy to see that, in addition to the augmentation of her lips, her eyelids are lined and shadowed not only above the lashes but in the orbital crease, and the lashes themselves have been thickened with mascara. Even the 'arch of the eyebrows' that he so admires was largely created through precise plucking and pencilling, and the velvet surface of her face would not have been possible without greasepaint and powder. Although the medium-length hair bob that Garbo wore in virtually all of her modern roles was of a shade that Michaela Krützen, in her book about the star's fabrication, calls 'astonishingly inconspicuous', it, too, was always perfectly styled.[10] Instead, Barthes simply asserts that Garbo remains 'always herself', carrying 'without pretence . . . the same snowy solitary face'. He does not mention her final appearance on the screen in the comedy *Two-Faced Woman* in 1941, when MGM tried to counter Garbo's diminishing box-office returns (she had been one of the stars – as was Fred Astaire after a couple of films without Ginger Rogers – named box-office poison by US exhibitors in 1938) partly by changing the fashions of her makeup and hair, after which she retired from the screen forever.

In other words, the 'classical' Hollywood star face to my mind can never be completely separated from the 'beauty makeup', as the industry called it (the term comprised hairdressing as well, though the crafts also had separate public identities), that is so crucial to its construction. Yet Rogers also introduces interesting complications here as well, because throughout her career she was taken to be one of the most 'natural' and 'unspoiled' of Hollywood's stars – as 'American as apple pie', in the words of one of her four *Life* magazine cover stories (this one in 1942, the cover photo showing her without obvious cosmetic blandishment), 'because Americans can identify themselves with her . . . She is not uncomfortably beautiful. She is just beautiful enough. She is not an affront to other women. She gives them hope that they can be like her.'[11] And while she played a number of show-business professionals in several films (and in most of the Astaire–Rogers vehicles, as did he), she also embraced working-class roles from the 1930s through to the 1950s, winning an Oscar as the white-collar protagonist of *Kitty Foyle* in 1940 ('I think you'll agree that Ginger Rogers and Kitty Foyle are the same,' said director Sam Wood in her third *Life* cover story).[12] And several times she appeared on the screen without benefit of the usual cosmetic enhancement, something that Garbo did not risk.

The calibrating of glamour and naturalness in Rogers's image therefore goes beyond Richard Dyer's famous aphorism that the star is always both ordinary and extraordinary, or even Edgar Morin's assertion that 'Beauty is the actress in the movies. The star can be entirely inexpressive'.[13] Joan Crawford – to whom Rogers was frequently compared since both began their careers by winning Charleston contests, were hard workers, and made films in a range of different genres – also claimed to go without makeup in certain of her film roles, but nevertheless Crawford's face became almost as iconic as that of Garbo.[14] I believe that the basis of this sort of discrepancy – that, regardless of how big a fan of Ginger Rogers one might be, she does not come immediately to mind as a 'movie star' of the Garbo or Crawford vein – is due to the fact that cosmetics and coiffures were not the only elements that introduced mutability into her star image, even if the object of analysis is restricted to the face.

James Naremore has written about the 'gestureless acting' of the film face, pointing out that, in contrast to Pudovkin's notion that 'gesture is completely dispensed with' in the close-up, 'the muscular arrangement of the eyes and mouth are themselves a form of gesture'. Naremore also claims that movie actors had to 'learn to control and modulate behavior to fit a variety of situations' because a 'small mannerism or emotional reaction that would be automatic in real life can utterly destroy a scene'.[15] While Barthes is at pains not to call Garbo's face a mask, there is little doubt that what he finds so 'classic' there is tied to an absence of expression. Paul Coates, in his book *Screening the Face*, refers to Garbo's 'divine' visage as 'near-unchanging': it moves 'so little, [and is] subject to so little distorting variation', that it does 'acquire some of the qualities of the mask', a mask that then had 'more opportunity to impress itself on memory and become icon-like: "Divine" indeed', he concludes.[16] Krützen, too, writes about Garbo's close-ups in terms of their stillness: 'It is not richly varied facial expressions that she uses in the close-up; rather, her trademark . . . is her stillness, her rigidity.'[17] In contrast, Rogers sported an unusually mobile countenance, routinely exhibiting, even in tight close-ups, certain tics and mannerisms that accompany or are produced by sometimes exaggerated facial gestures. But she clearly did not 'destroy' anything, for these are all there in her films for us to notice. That said, a number of them disappear or are minimised over time, and while we will never know who or what prompted the alterations, my point is that she intentionally modified not only what was applied to or arranged around her face but also managed the substrate, the literal 'foundation', under the blandishment as well, in ways that seem unconnected to acting or characterisation as such.

For good reason, Rogers's career will always be tied to her stint in what Garson Kanin once called 'Astairerogersland', but she was an enormously durable and prolific star across nearly three decades. I believe that the 'infinite complexity' of her face and hair – even while a goddess in Astairerogersland – was one of the primary sources both of her appeal and her usefulness to the 'ordinary mortals' who followed her on the screen and in promotional and publicity material until the studio system was no more. Not only was her ability to persist as a leading lady – in ways that Garbo perhaps recognised that she could not – substantially tied to the mutability of her appearance, that mutability continued, though on a diminished continuum and in different facial registers, even after some of Rogers's roles became 'remote and grand', in Croce's words, in the mid-1940s.[18] Ginger Rogers is less anomalous than hyperbolic, then, in how she enacts procedures and ideals that were taken to be normative for Hollywood's stars and would-be stars and whose meaning devolved to their images rather than the fictional characters they played. She is unusual not in the fact of but the degree to which she attempts to use cosmetics and coiffures expressively in her films while maintaining the star glamour that they were designed to produce, and the same is true of the disappearance of some of the 'distorting variations' of her facial gestures over time. Before turning to Rogers's own engagement with beauty makeup in a selection of her film texts, I first offer a brief discussion of it and its function as a major constituent of virtually all Hollywood women's stardom (and men's too, though neither they nor the studios liked to admit it).

There is No Excuse for a Mistake

Beauty makeup, an obviously gendered term that was in use at the studios by the mid-1930s, is the result of the confluence of many interrelated technical, aesthetic, ideological, industrial and commercial circumstances. The most salient of these here are the conflicts between Hollywood's fluctuating interest in visual realism and its desire to give everything – cars, sets, props, animals and people – what Mary Astor later referred to as that 'just from a beauty parlor' look.[19] Although it is often confused with glamour, even stars who were not considered glamorous still wore beauty makeup on the screen and for publicity photos, and it would not be too much to say that, throughout the studio era, it was the basic or underlying mode of appearance for most stars regardless of genre or narrative implausibility – sleeping, bathing, illness and the like, along with any number of period anachronisms. Concomitantly, the appearance of women stars and featured players was perpetually tied to the desire of cosmetics manufacturers and makeup men – by 1937, when the crafts were unionised, makeup artists and department heads were always men and hairdressers women[20] – to corner the vast consumer marketplace to enhance their own fame and fortune, both through proprietary products and the touting of themselves as unique 'experts' who could 'correct' any face to the illusion of perfection.

Figure 13.2   Ginger Rogers in Max Factor cosmetics ads from 1936, 1942, and 1944.
Collection of the author.

After only a few features, then, Ginger Rogers was already part of an end-
lessly self-referential loop by which men designed the looks of stars and then
employed them to advertise beauty products that women could buy to make
themselves look like stars (Rogers was a Max Factor model in the 1930s and
1940s, the ads tracing the changes in her appearance and hair colour across
time). Given that she made nothing but black and white films as what would
appear to be a blonde during most of the 1930s (her first Technicolor film was
Lady in the Dark in 1944, in which she is also blonde), I do wonder what spectators made of the fact that dialogue, and some fan magazine articles, described
the same hair as blonde in some contexts and red in others (or her eyes as blue
or green), particularly since Max Factor's principle of 'color harmony' in his
consumer cosmetics line was based on eye and hair colour.[21]

The fact that such perfection had to be achieved efficiently and for many
stars and productions at once led to another important element in the standardisation of beauty and handsomeness, namely the makeup chart. These
charts were schematic line renderings of a human face on which makeup artists
indicated with coloured pencils what cosmetics went where, and how and to
what ends, on particular actors. I see these charts, which theoretically enabled
the production of the same face from film to film and even on loan-out, as in
some ways the literal basis of what fashion historian Alicia Annas calls classical
Hollywood's 'photogenic formula', by which she means the 'modern' makeup
that was applied to non-character stars, or would-be stars, if they were to be
seen in close-up for any length of time.[22] But at base, like beauty makeup itself,
charts were somewhat paradoxical entities – designed to create individual characters in fiction films, but also reliably to reproduce the recursive signs of the

star as a star. Hollywood's most famous cosmetics 'experts', such as the West-more dynasty of makeup artists and Factor and his corporation, swore publicly that the standardisation of beauty was not their intention, rather that such makeup was only 'a medium through which one may express one's individual-ism, personality and charm, and improve on nature', as Perc Westmore wrote in 1937: 'There can be no error – there is no excuse for a mistake. A miracle is expected and a miracle it must be.'[23]

But the most efficient way to produce the 'individualism' of a new player was often a matter of imitation, and in general all of the 'attractive' women in any given film are made up similarly to one another. Rogers claims in her 1991 autobiography never to have imitated anyone – oddly, Croce criticises Rogers for looking like 'her imitator [italics mine], Priscilla Lane', in 1939[24] – but certainly her formula makeup was similar to that of other young women within any of her films or compared to those of her colleagues, and corresponds to fashions of the time (how it does so is one of those chicken–egg problems that historical study always instantiates). For example, when by the end of the 1930s the lip lines of Bette Davis, Joan Crawford or Katharine Hepburn (or Greta Garbo) began to be drawn outside their natural contours rather than in the smaller, starkly outlined 'rosebud' or 'cupid' style of earlier years; or their eyebrows were no longer graphically thin lines but more or less 'natural'; or their eyelashes grew more articulated rather than heavier – all of this perhaps a response to the austerity of the times – so were those of Rogers. Unfortunately, information about stars' agency in the material application of their formula beauty is, with a few exceptions, lacking or contradictory, though given the omnipresence of cosmetics use by women across the US well before the 1930s I have no doubt that a notoriously ambitious star like Rogers – with a stage mother, Lela Rogers, to match – made her opinions known. In her autobiogra-phy, Rogers maintains that, but for her 'blonding' in 1931 from the 'deep chest-nut with a touch of henna' that she had worn in her early film career (a 'touch of Egyptian Red' had been added at Lela's suggestion when Rogers starred in *Girl Crazy* on Broadway in 1930), every choice and change in her hair colour was her decision, 'based on my understanding of the role' (the one 'mistake' she owns up to was dying it black for *Lucky Partners* in 1940).[25]

Rogers does mention Mel Berns, the makeup executive at RKO during most of her time there, but primarily in conjunction with her attempt to prove that she could play Queen Elizabeth opposite Katharine Hepburn in *Mary of Scotland* in 1936. RKO was even ready to hire the fictional English actress whom Rogers and Berns created with cosmetics and wigs (Rogers's 'bratty imitative clever-ness', in Croce's words, provided the accent), though upon discovering the truth the studio denied her the role because they believed her star image could not accommodate it.[26] That said, generally Berns seems to have taken, or suggested, a lighter hand to Rogers's eyes, especially, such that while she invariably sports artificial eyelashes (they are ubiquitous on most female stars by the end of the 1920s), compared to her earlier looks in films made for Paramount's East Coast studios, Fox and Warner Bros, her eyes are bright and open, the thick dark liner, shadow and mascara replaced by more subtle treatments concentrated on the upper lids. And as I turn to now, regardless of who applied it, much of the mutability of Rogers's star image in the 1940s came from how she employed formula beauty as signifiers of acting and characterisation, partly through creating it as a structuring absence on some features but not others. Indeed, as she branched out from the musicals and comedies that had made her so popular, she seemed to substitute alterations in beauty makeup for some of her 'natural' facial expressions as she attempted – not always persuasively – to reconcile the actor with the glamorous star.[27]

Put on One Mask, Take it Off, Put on Another

The primary reason that *42nd Street* (1933), in which Rogers is a featured player, remains one of my favourite of her films is the wide variety of facial gestures she makes in her scenes. As the sardonic Ann Lowell – more famously 'Anytime Annie' (*42nd Street* is a pre-Code film) – she cocks and furrows her brow, rolls her eyes, twists her smile, wrinkles her nose, sneers and makes moues of disgust that even today earn howls of delight from audiences. They also render her character's sacrifice of her own chance at stardom to the stiff but charming mannequin played by Ruby Keeler – on the grounds that Keeler is more talented – a flaw of narrative plausibility, to say the least. The surreal choker close-ups of Rogers's face as she sings 'We're in the Money' in *Gold Diggers of 1933* reveal more quirks of expression, such as tightened lips that dimple her chin. While many of these can be found in the first three Astaire–Rogers vehicles too, they become more infrequent once she begins to play characters who are upper class rather than disguised as such (Anytime Annie is introduced to us in a monocle affecting a British accent).

In Rogers's early roles, in other words, her expressions mobilise many parts of her face, and the metamorphosis to 'sophistication' and, paradoxically, to 'serious actress' therefore also involved learning to modulate and suppress this activity, particularly in relation to her eyes and mouth. In September 1936, *Photoplay* wrote that 'Ginger Rogers is going to a school of experience to achieve, of all things, glamour. And she's achieving it. She gives more thought to poise and diction,' which itself makes glamour the result of a muting, a restraining, of the normative or human in the service of becoming a goddess.[28] Moreover, while an expressive visage might be assumed to be of greater value for any actor, Rogers won her Oscar only after she had learned to subdue certain *kinds* of expressiveness in her face (this is in addition to not blinking or swallowing during non-comic close-ups, which had become Hollywood conventions during the silent era). Even if Rogers's formula beauty as created by cosmetics had remained static, then, she would still have looked quite different by the end of the 1930s.

Croce is correct that it was primarily after 1939 that Rogers began the most violent recalibration of her formula beauty, but it was often in the interests of what Rogers herself calls 'realism'; as she states in her autobiography, she was 'willing to appear less than perfect if it suited my character'. In *Primrose Path* (1940), in which, in her words, she plays a 'poor teenager', she 'chose not to wear any makeup' and dyed her hair brown, because she thought it was 'more appropriate' for the role. In *Heartbeat* (1946) – Rogers was then in her mid-thirties but cast as a 'simple street girl' – she also 'decided not to wear too much makeup'.[29] But in both films, and in *Kitty Foyle*, Rogers is wearing carefully applied cosmetics in literally every scene – dressed artificial eyelashes regardless of context (including lying in a hospital bed after giving birth to a baby who dies), lipstick that enlarges and reshapes her mouth, sculpted eyebrows and, always, clean and more or less fashionably styled hair. Exceptions to the latter do occur for various reasons, such as when she is playing children as she does in flashback in *Kitty Foyle* or for a farcical reason in the comedy *The Major and the Minor* (1942) (in which she also plays her own mother through a streak in her hair but with no adjustments to her face other than spectacles; Lela appears in the film as her 'real' mother). Yet when Rogers's character is introduced to us wearing a sweatshirt and pigtails early in *Primrose Path*, above the braids is a perfect marcel wave that remains there throughout the vicissitudes of her life in a rundown slum. (In *Heartbeat* Rogers's hair is far more obviously 'just from a beauty parlour' in even more implausible circumstances; she plays a Paris pickpocket.)

What Rogers means by 'less than perfect' comes primarily from one of the most loaded elements of formula beauty, namely the treatment of her skin. In all of these films her face does indeed, in her words about *Heartbeat*, 'shine like a polished apple' in some scenes.[30] To her, or to Mel Berns, the apparent absence of powder – some spectators thought she actually had 'shiny stuff' on her face, which may well have been the case;[31] the mole on her left chin that she will emphasise in the 1950s is still visible only as a slight bump – is enough to signify metonymically as a rejection, at least temporarily, of star glamour. This is not to say that her lip shades are not adjusted too; as was the case at all studios, her lips appear closer to her skin tone when she is supposedly twelve, ill or playing an old lady. But 'perfect' white skin, and its racialised and racist (and classist) history in US culture as in Hollywood's modes of representation more broadly, was so primary a feature that merely adjusting its degree of shine could function to flip the framework of interpretation into a different register (Joan Crawford claimed to go without makeup in *Strange Cargo*, also in 1940, her shiny and in a few shots freckled skin meant to indicate that she was near death from dehydration and exposure – and at her direst point she even briefly doffs artificial eyelashes).[32] There is little difference in Rogers's facial acting or cosmetics when she is *being* a young adolescent in *Kitty Foyle* and *impersonating* one in *The Major and the Minor*, which produces the vertiginous sense that the fake adolescent in the latter film should head to Hollywood and become Ginger Rogers – indeed, her beauty makeup as a working-class girl at the film's opening and as a glamorous young woman transformed by love at the end are identical. And while set design and costuming are as usual doing significant supportive work here, it should be noted that these shiny but otherwise perfect faces were, almost invariably, shot with soft focus and glamour lighting in the close-ups.

No studio-era Hollywood film really approaches the levels of clinically observed realism that we expect in films today (many tenets of the Production Code actively precluded it). Yet the curiously large number of lines and scenes in Rogers's films that refer to or represent masks and masquerades also indicate, or at least gesture towards, the distance between realism and glamour as well. While narrative tropes of disguise are not rare (Garbo masquerades as a man in *Queen Christina*), it would appear that many writers and art directors associated disguise as such with Rogers's image and wrote it into the plots and *mise-en-scène* of her films even away from the singing show-dancers she often plays in her musicals (including the bulk of the Astaire–Rogers vehicles). Besides her several 'roles' in *Kitty Foyle* and *The Major and the Minor* and her dual disguise as Anytime Annie, she plays a radio star whose virginal public image is contrasted to her private sexualised desires in *Professional Sweetheart* (1933); a Midwest farm girl masquerading in Paris as a fake Polish countess turned nightclub performer in *Roberta* (1934); a television host who becomes, in flashback, a silent film star in *Dreamboat* (1952); and a Broadway stage actress tired of 'pretending' in *Forever Female* (1953). In *In Person* (1936), she even plays a star of film musicals who dons buck teeth and a black wig – photos of which RKO refused to circulate publicly, so drastically, if briefly, did they alter her formula beauty – to get away from the adoring public who has driven her to a nervous breakdown. Even literal masks are featured in several of her films – lifelike copies of her face adorn chorus dancers in *Shall We Dance* (1937), placed there by Astaire's character in lieu of his ability to romance the 'real thing' because of a farcical misunderstanding. And in *Week-End at the Waldorf* (1945), ironically a remake of *Grand Hotel* with Rogers playing a jaded movie star in a variation of the ballerina role that Garbo herself had played in 1932 (the plot of *Grand Hotel*, but not its stars, are discussed in dialogue), she holds up the masks of comedy and tragedy to her face: 'From a fan,' she says, 'Most appropriate present I ever got – history of my life. Put on one mask, take it off, put on another.'

I find *Week-End at the Waldorf* one of the most poignant of Rogers's films, because she is so boring in it but clearly believes that she is demonstrating 'fine acting' in the confident control she radiates over the now fairly small range of expressions to which she limits herself – a raised eyebrow or slightly cocked head here, a rueful smile there, intense steady gazes in love scenes (her beauty makeup is without flaw throughout). To be sure, there are brief flashes of the more human or comic sensibilities that made her so appealing in the 1930s and early 1940s. This is also the case with her performance in *Monkey Business* (1953), in which she plays an attractive but middle-aged professor's wife who temporarily becomes an annoying child, a teenager, and a terrified young woman on her wedding night, invoking each transformation through not much more than changes in hairstyles, exaggerated frowns and grimaces, and tone of voice (Rogers is a life master at crying convincingly without benefit of either real or glycerin tears). Moreover, one of the perks of becoming a big star was having named 'experts' design your looks, such that Rogers reports being thrilled that Sydney Guilaroff – one of the few male hairdressers to the stars in studio-era history – designed her hair for MGM's *Week-End at the Waldorf* and *The Barkleys of Broadway* (1949), the latter her tenth and only Technicolor film with Astaire.[33] But Guilaroff's sculptural and outré – and huge – coiffures, like her costumes, are usually designed to produce glamour rather than a convincing characterisation, and the result is that, in combination with the increased rigidity of her face in many scenes (and her affected vocal tones), Rogers has ironically now become a 'movie star' rather than the actress that she wanted to be and that she took her Oscar to endorse.

I WENT TO A MASQUERADE

As she entered her forties, Rogers's face devolved more and more into an unchanging mask that aimed to recall her youthful image but instead accentuated how far removed she was from it (I use 'mask' here as Hans Belting does in his book *Face and Mask*, as an 'operative concept' that stands for 'the indistinct boundary between face and mask').[34] Despite her overdetermined embrace of mutability and metamorphosis from the 1930s through to the 1940s, in the end Rogers's stardom followed much the same trajectory as that of others whose stories were based on a 'rise' and whose end goal, even reward, was increased sophistication and glamour. But this rise also had built into it the obsolescence of most women stars, because Hollywood had little interest in providing models for female stardom other than that of the 'young modern'. When a star reached her mid-thirties, she could be maligned if she attempted to be *au courant* but also if she refused to change or tried to retain what was 'becoming' to her if it was no longer fashionable. If Garbo represents the 'fragile moment' when the cinema became fascinated with 'mortal faces' and 'the clarity of the flesh', in Barthes's words, and the change from the 1930s to the 1950s represents the 'passage from awe to charm' in relation to the human visage, then in

Figure 13.3   One of the latter-day glamour images of Ginger Rogers, this one from *Movieland* (March 1948), when she was no longer being featured on US fan-magazine covers. While her hair is a bit long, this image approximates the photogenic formula that she would retain, with small variations, through the rest of her public life. Media History Digital Library.

some sense the deified female face is the sign of both the achievement of stardom as well as its inevitable end.

To conclude, if I prefer the many faces of Ginger, or those of other less 'totem-like' stars, to that of Garbo, it is precisely because of their 'pretense of natural expressivity', the ways that they mediated between the ordinary and the perfect. I agree with Croce that some of Rogers's later performances are cringe-inducing (reciting the 'Marseillaise' in French in *The Barkleys of Broadway* while playing an actress who is playing the young Sarah Bernhardt is a sequence I have only watched once in my many viewings of the film). Or that, while Rogers herself was a 'decently accomplished serious actress', what Croce calls 'La Rogers' can 'almost make you forget it'.[35] But arguably more than any other star – even Crawford – Rogers understood that her value lay in balancing recognisability and processes of becoming, and it was perhaps inevitable that, over time, that canny awareness would begin to manifest itself as more and more desperate, even grotesque, attempts to remain at once stable and always new. When Rogers's character tells her [real] mother at the end of *The Major and the Minor* that she had just been to a masquerade, she could have been speaking of her star image, the only difference between Rogers and most other 'straight' actors lying in how much farther she pushed the analogy. We know how the story ended, but in her most interesting roles, and often in her star image, Rogers deploys metamorphosis strategically, as a means to some desired end for her as well as her characters. In this sense her popularity during her heyday surely stemmed less from her fans' 'loyalty' than from showing them, too, how to use beauty makeup and facial acting to become 'something more'.

Notes

1. Leonard Hall, 'The Glamor Factories of Hollywood', *Stage* (July 1936), 18–20.
2. Roland Barthes, 'The Face of Garbo', *Mythologies*, trans. Annette Lavers (New York: Hill and Wang, 1972), 56–7. All Barthes quotations in this essay are from these two pages.
3. Noa Steimatsky, *The Face on Film* (New York: Oxford University Press, 2017), 105.
4. See Michaela Krützen, *The Most Beautiful Woman on the Screen: The Fabrication of the Star Greta Garbo* (Bern: Peter Lang, 1992).
5. For more on Rogers see her autobiography *Ginger: My Story* (New York: Harper-Collins, 1991); Homer Dickens, *The Films of Ginger Rogers* (New York: Citadel, 1975); Jocelyn Faris, *Ginger Rogers: A Bio-Bibliography* (Westport, CT: Greenwood, 1994).
6. Fay Lemmon, 'Makeup Box Is First Ordeal of the Film Aspirant in Hollywood', *Dallas Morning News* (c. March–April 1934), n.p. (clipping in author's collection).
7. Mary Biddle, 'Beauty Advice [Tired of looking at the same face? Then change your coiffure as Hollywood does!]', *Modern Screen* (November 1935), 16–17, 94–5.

8. Arlene Croce, *The Fred Astaire and Ginger Rogers Book* (New York: Galahad Books, 1972), 172.

9. Hair lace toupées or wigs have edges made out of fine thread or human hair that can be pasted down with spirit gum and covered with cosmetics, making the 'joins' invisible even in close-up. For more on the history of 'straight' as well as beauty makeup from the silent era through the 1960s, or on any references to or claims made about these topics in this essay, see Adrienne L. McLean, *All for Beauty: Makeup and Hairdressing in Hollywood's Studio Era* (Chicago: Rutgers University Press, 2022).

10. Krützen, *The Most Beautiful Woman*, 79.

11. 'Ginger Rogers: She Adds New Chapter to Her Success Story', *Life* (2 March 1942), 61.

12. 'Kitty Foyle', *Life* (9 December 1940), 88.

13. Richard Dyer, *Stars* (London: BFI, 1979); Edgar Morin, *The Stars* [*Les Stars*, 1957], trans. Richard Howard (Minneapolis: University of Minnesota Press, 2005), 131.

14. Larry Carr's photo book *Four Fabulous Faces* (New York: Arlington House, 1970) includes both Garbo and Crawford, as well as Gloria Swanson and Marlene Dietrich.

15. James Naremore, *Acting in the Cinema* (Berkeley: University of California Press, 1988), 40.

16. Paul Coates, *Screening the Face* (New York: Palgrave Macmillan, 2012), 88.

17. Krützen, *The Most Beautiful Woman*, 19.

18. Croce, *The Fred Astaire and Ginger Rogers Book*, 178. The World War II context for Rogers's most extreme style changes deserves more attention as well.

19. Mary Astor, *A Life on Film* (New York: Delacorte Press, 1971), 185.

20. Any exceptions to this gender division, like Dorothy Ponedel in makeup or Sydney Guilaroff or Larry Germain in hairstyling, only prove the rule. For more on the labour history of the crafts, see McLean, *All for Beauty*, especially Chs 2 and 3.

21. Following *Lady in the Dark*, Rogers remained some version of blonde until her death in 1995.

22. Alicia Annas, 'The Photogenic Formula: Hairstyles and Makeup in Historical Films,' in Edward Maeder (ed.), *Hollywood and History: Costume Design in Film* (London: Thames and Hudson, and Los Angeles: Los Angeles County Museum of Art, 1987), 52–77.

23. Perc Westmore, 'Corrective Make-Up', in John Paddy Carstairs (ed.), *Movie Merry-Go-Round* (London: Newnes, 1937), 116.

24. Rogers, *My Story*; Croce, *The Fred Astaire and Ginger Rogers Book*, 172.

25. Rogers, *My Story*, 97, 240.

26. Ibid., 170–5; Croce, *The Fred Astaire and Ginger Rogers Book*, 176.

27. It should be noted that Rogers's voice also deepens in tone with every lost facial gesture.

28. Sara Hamilton, 'Freedom Is Glorifying Ginger', *Photoplay* (September 1936), 78.

29. All from Rogers, *My Story*, 215, 275.

30. Ibid., 275.

31. Preview cards for *Primrose Path*, Paul Becker collection, Margaret Herrick Library, Academy of Motion Picture Arts and Sciences, Beverly Hills, California.

32. Joan Crawford, with Jane Kesner Ardmore, *A Portrait of Joan* (New York: Doubleday, 1962), 125. For more the representation of skin on the screen see

Richard Dyer, *White: Essays on Race and Culture* (Abindgon and New York: Routledge, 1997); Alice Maurice, *Cinema and Its Shadow: Race and Technology in Early Cinema* (Minneapolis: University of Minnesota Press, 2013); McLean, *All for Beauty*.

33. Rogers, *My Story*, 283.
34. Hans Belting, *Face and Mask: A Double History* [2013], trans. Thomas S. Hansen and Abby J. Hansen (Princeton: Princeton University Press, 2017), 18.
35. Croce, *The Fred Astaire and Ginger Rogers Book*, 172.

14. AT FACE VALUE: CONSUMING THE STAR IMAGE

Koel Banerjee

An advertisement for a package tour of Europe masquerades as an invitation from Yash Raj Films, wooing potential consumers to travel in a manner only seen in the movies.[1] The iconic picture of Shah Rukh Khan and Kajol, as the characters Raj and Simran from the superhit film *Dilwale Dulhania Le Jayenge* (Aditya Chopra, 1995), invites the consumer to embark on 'an enchanted journey to Switzerland'. *Dilwale Dulhania Le Jayenge*, with its box-office success premised on a depiction of an image of the desired 'good life' of global mobility, consumerist aesthetics, and a reified notion of a timeless India tradition personified by the Non-Resident Indian, is no accidental choice for such promotional material. With its strategic deployment of the star image, the advertisement encourages us to 'feel like a star when you get photographed as Abhishek Bachchan and Rani Mukherjee', and even to 'experience the magic of the same location where Shah Rukh Khan fell in love with Kajol'. The carefully curated stills, from films that depict Indians at home in the world, provide the template for the ones at home to aspire to. This advertisement, with its fusion of the travel brochure and the film-still, shows that in neoliberal India, it is no longer enough to just watch cinema, one *has* to live it as well.

Following in the film stars' footsteps, the consumer can live a life just like the movies. Yash Raj Film's (YRF) Enchanted Journey advertisement sheds light on the ways in which the image of the film star, displayed prominently in the advertisement, becomes the locus of the spectator's cinematic desires as well as the consumer's extra-cinematic aspirations. This alignment of cinema's pleasures and consumerist cravings is made possible by the advertisement's careful positioning of the star image, bringing together actor and character. In his reading of the sociological implications of the film star, John Ellis notes that the star image, an amalgam of the film text, the persona and the extra-cinematic texts, functions both as an 'invitation to cinema', and an 'impossible paradox'.[2] The star image invites fans to the cinema with the promise of synthesising its various, often contradictory, aspects. The star image, Ellis explains, hinges on the star's being, at once, both ordinary and extraordinary. While Ellis's reading focuses on the ways that the star image invites fans to the cinema, the YRF Enchanted Journey advertisement also points to the ways in which in contemporary Bollywood, the star image is not just an invitation to cinema. Rather, it is an invitation for the spectator to explore a brave new world – a world of consumerist aspirations ushered by the restructuring of the Indian economy in the 1990s.

In this emerging neoliberal consensus, the star's face, a shorthand for the star image, becomes endowed with an investable economic surplus. In his study of the contemporary political economy of the film star and other celebrities, Barry King notes that in the era of the free market and with the proliferation of sites of consumption of the star image, we have entered 'a new stage in the commodification of personality and the formation of exchange value out of what appear to be the natural values of the person'.[3] Extending Marx's theorisation of commodity fetishism, King argues that we are now witnessing the rise of celebrity fetishism, an advanced expression of commodity fetishism in the mode of personification:

> The ostensive character-signifying attributes of the actor are his or her *use value* to audiences and fans who negotiate and adapt the framework of social types to construct a narrative of the self. The actor's persona is the market driven selection of his or her professionally conditioned attributes to construct a self as *exchange value*.[4]

This exchange value is not only realised in films and star-endorsed products; every aspect and attribute of the star's personality has to appear useful to others in order to be saleable. Thus, stars become the emblem of the consumerist tendencies potentiated by the neoliberal era. They provide an ideal of what to buy and how to live, to which the fans aspire. The star's face, their most recognisable and marketable attribute, now comes to signify the promises of the consumerist good life. It signals at once the fan's desire for the success that the star exemplifies and the fan's aspiration for commodities and lifestyles endorsed by the star. The face also provides a way for the fan to approximate the star image, that is, refashion their self-image in the image of the film star. The star's fetishised face becomes emblematic of both the ideal of life and the impossibility of attaining it.

This essay focuses on *Fan* (Maneesh Sharma, 2016), a film in which a fan's all-consuming desire to remake himself in his favourite star's likeness has tragic consequences.[5] While the film highlights the cinematic and extra-cinematic ways in which the star image is desired and consumed by the fans, it ultimately presents a cautionary tale about the limits of such consumption, and more importantly, of such desire. The desire to consume star images and star-endorsed commodities (including films) is fuelled by the distance between the star and fan. This distance is one that the fan seeks to undo through unending consumption of the star image. However, as Ellis notes in his sociological account of stardom, one of the several contradictions of the star image is that the chasm between the star and his fan can never be bridged. *Fan* tests and transgresses this distance, one that is not only essential to the star–fan relationship, but also to the consumerist aspirations that the star image has now come to represent. In so doing, this essay argues, *Fan* points to the limits of neoliberal consumerism. It serves as a cautionary tale for unchecked desire.

In *Fan*, Shah Rukh Khan plays two characters: the Bollywood film star, Aryan Khanna and Gaurav Chandna, Aryan's biggest fan. The film also draws on Shah Rukh Khan's real star image, which serves as parallel text to its narrative. In fact, *Fan* opens with footage from Shah Rukh Khan's 1992 film, *Deewana*. It cuts to a shot of a young Gaurav looking at Aryan Khanna's image on a billboard endorsing a haircare product. This pattern, of alternating between excerpts from Shah Rukh Khan's films to a stargazing young Gaurav, is repeated throughout the sequence. This underscores the ways the star image – through films, product endorsements and interviews – becomes the fan's ego ideal. A fan, like the star, is made. Significantly, though, we do not see Gaurav's face at first: his back faces us as he faces the billboards, staring at the star's face as one would stare at a mirror. The fan's face, here, in its being a replica (albeit an imperfect one) of the star's face is the big reveal of this sequence. And the film's narrative, as we realise later, is driven by the interplay of sameness and difference between the star's recognisable face and that of the fan.

This opening scene blurs distinctions between the reel and the real. Using footage from Shah Rukh Khan's early films, interviews and awards shows, it charts both the rise of Aryan Khanna and the evolution of the young Gaurav into his devout fan. Indeed, Gaurav not only identifies with his favourite star, but has also physically fashioned himself in the star's likeness. Gaurav's voiceover, which anchors the visual collage of the opening sequence, highlights the ways the fan 'cut–copy–pastes' everything the star does. Yet, it also acknowledges the symbiotic relationship between the star and the fan. That is, the fans, who make and remake themselves in the star's image, also make the star. As Gaurav reminds Aryan later in the film: 'main hoon toh tu hai' ('You are because I am').

Gaurav's monologue highlights another paradox of the star–fan relationship. Although worlds apart, the star and the fan are (in the fan's mind) one.

The opening sequence, then, functions as a *bildung* of the fan as we witness Gaurav grow from a child to an adult, his obsession with Aryan increasing over time. In his seminal study of stardom, Richard Dyer notes the various 'congealed labour' that goes into making the star image.[6] *Fan* presents us with its corollary as it shows the labour that the fan puts into remaking himself in the image of the star. While we see Aryan's face throughout the sequence, we only see Gaurav's face at the end of his monologue when he introduces himself, not as Gaurav, but as Aryan Junior. We then realise that the fan is made in the likeness of the star – his face is a facsimile of the star's face.

The film's opening does not only map Aryan Khanna's rise to superstardom and Gaurav's increasing obsession with Aryan, but also charts the rise of consumer society in India and the role that Bollywood and its film stars played in bringing about this transition. Recall here that Gaurav is introduced as a child staring at a billboard – an advertisement for a haircare product endorsed by Aryan Khanna. In a later scene, a slightly older Gaurav looks at another Aryan Khanna billboard – this time for computers that will, via the World Wide Web, bring the world into the Indian middle-class household. More advertisements follow as Aryan becomes the face of various consumer goods, ranging from chocolates and cookies to Swiss watches and Korean cars. Aryan's face, like the brands and goods he endorses, becomes yet another commodity in circulation. It is his face that sells posters, film magazines and, most importantly, the promise of class mobility.

The impact of the transition from a protectionist economic regime to a neoliberal one was not limited to the market. Rather, the economic policies implemented by the Rajiv Gandhi-led government had far reaching consequences for Indian national identity, particularly for its urban middle class. The new urban middle class, as sociologist Leela Fernandes notes, now came to view itself as the 'hegemonic sociocultural embodiment of India's transition to a committed liberalizing nation'.[7] Fernandes argues that it is primarily on the basis of its claims on a canny consumerism that the new Indian middle class distinguished itself from its older traditional counterpart that had embraced 'Nehruvian state socialism and Gandhian ideals of austerity' during the period of postcolonial emergence.[8] In a similar vein, Maitreyee Chaudhury points out that the market reforms led to a complete overhaul of middle-class values and virtues, now favouring consumption over thrift.[9] Chaudhury also notes that the urban middle class's turn towards consumerism also led to a refashioning of the public discourse, recalibrating the ideals of masculinity and femininity. Based on a study of English-language print media advertisements, she points out that the 'upmarket' male now emerges as the ideal Indian man:

> The new mantra for the Indian male is power and success. He has to be rich and glamorous. He has to be at the top of his job early in life. But along

with this consolidation of a Western male model, we also have an affirmation of gentler qualities in men. He is no brute, a point evident in a whole array of adverts sponsored to create an image of the complete man.[10]

Thus, liberalisation also led to the rise of the metrosexual man – an image that Shah Rukh Khan's star persona, with its emphasis on good looks, chiselled body, designer outfits and success, embodies.[11]

Although India's turn towards neo-liberalism and the concomitant rise of a consumer society took place only in the early 1990s, the refashioning of the urban middle class as the consuming class was some time in the making. The urban middle class's desire for consumption of luxury goods was one important reason behind the financial reforms. In their study of India's neoliberal turn, economists Jayati Ghosh and C. P. Chandrasekhar point out that the urban middle class, a politically privileged class, was able to influence the state's economic policies for their own material gains.[12] Desiring to remake itself in the image of its counterparts in other developed countries, the Indian urban middle class leaned towards a consumption-oriented globalisation. In addition, this desire for luxury goods, both domestic and imported, soon came to be a crucial aspect of its class identity, global visibility and political power.

The Hindi film industry played an important role in catalysing the transition from a society of producers who emphasised thrift and pecuniary restraint to a society of aspiring consumers. The Mumbai-based film industry, now refashioned as 'Bollywood', emerged as a 'culture industry' with all its ideological underpinnings.[13] Bollywood, officially recognised by the Indian state as an industry in 1998, helped the state's mandate of restructuring of the public sphere in the wake of liberalisation. Bollywood films increasingly turned towards spectacle as its new narratives rendered neoliberal consumerist excesses into the norm. Bollywood, then, is more than cinema; rather, it designates a whole way of life. As a culture industry, it instructs new consumers on canny and savvy ways to navigate not just the world of newly available goods, but also the world itself as newly minted cosmopolitans.

During this transition from a middle-class ethic of thrift to one that leaned towards conspicuous consumption, Bollywood film stars, with their public visibility, success, and consumerist lifestyles, came to provide the template of a desired good life for their fans. The popularity of stars as mascots of the desirable good life is unsurprising.[14] Shah Rukh Khan, Sudhanva Deshpande points out, emerged as the 'consumable hero' of neoliberal India, a by-product of the liberalised market. According to him, Shah Rukh Khan, the market-friendly hero, a 'yuppie' with no history or anti-establishment feelings, is also able to commodify a reified image of eternal Indianness.[15] In so doing, the consumable hero of neoliberal India comes to represent its very ideal by synthesising upper caste values (including an emphasis on good looks) with consumerist desires (embodied in the star's lifestyle). Shah Rukh Khan's career, his journey from middle-class origins in Delhi to the Bollywood superstardom, is referenced by *Fan* – as the character, Aryan Khanna, is largely based on Shah Rukh Khan himself.[16] The reference to Shah Rukh Khan's origin story further reinforces the myth of his stardom, which, for his middle-class fans, becomes emblematic of all the possibilities that the neoliberal consumerism has to offer and their realisation through labour.

Fan accounts for the various modes of formal and informal circulation of the star image as the use-value promise of a nascent consumer society.[17] It deploys the narrative device of the film song to comment on the intermedial ways in which the fans consume the star image. For example, the song *Jabra Fan* (Big Fan) narrates the discourse of stardom from the point of view of the fan. The song begins with a medium shot of the titular fan, once again with his back turned towards the camera, looking at the countless pictures of the star that cover the walls of his room. In the dimly lit room, the excess of Aryan's photographs and cutouts seems overwhelming and obsessive. Gaurav's voiceover accompanies this visual: 'Gharwale bhi na mere, samajhte nahin hai kabhi kabhi. Woh sirf star nahin hai, duniya hai meri' ('My family often does not understand. He is not just a star: he is my whole world'). As this suggests, the fan is always misunderstood – by his family, and even by the star.

The song does not only celebrate the fan (who in turn is celebrating the star), but also the various ways in which the star image is consumed. It lists the ways in which the star image circulates and is consumed in the digital era, where Twitter and Facebook allow the fan to have a semblance of an unmediated relationship with the star. As the star rises in fame and stature, so does the fan's obsession. *Jabra Fan*, presented from Gaurav's perspective, notes the new sites of the consumption of the star image – digital platforms like Google, Twitter and Facebook. And even as these sites become the new avenues through which the fan feels closer to the star, these platforms, including Google, cannot compete with what the fan knows about the star. *Jabra Fan* declares that the fan sees the star in his dreams, and even when he looks into the mirror. In short, in his magnificent obsession, the fan fancies himself as the star's copy.

Further, *Jabra Fan*, an anthem for fandom, makes the case that the star image, with all its attendant excesses, has become a part of our every day. For instance, even as it depicts the huge hoardings of the star endorsing different products dot the skyline, it also draws our attention to the informal economy that equally partakes in the attractions of the star image. The circulation of the star's face guarantees the value of a wide range of goods and services. Consider that the roadside homemade popsicle seller uses the same image of the star's face as the manufacturers of an international brand of instant noodles. The star's face, through these iterations, functions not only as an invitation to the shopping mall with their

Figure 14.1   *Fan* (Maneesh Sharma, 2016).

imported merchandise; it also invites fans into an auto-rickshaw, adorned with posters of film stars, with its charisma. It is no surprise then that the excesses of the star image, through these exchanges across various media, have become the norm for a consumer society.

Fan also hints at another aspect of the star–fan relationship: the dynamic between the real and the fake. Gaurav, who calls himself Aryan Junior, competes at various star lookalike contests where he enacts scenes from Aryan's films.[18] He wins a trophy at one such event and sets off for Mumbai in order to present the prize to Aryan on his birthday. However, even as his greatest achievement is in being acknowledged as the best Aryan Khanna lookalike, he remains not only a 'fake' but a lesser fake at that. Compared to Aryan's ageing, yet well-groomed, muscular looks, the younger Gaurav is shorter, bucktoothed, with a wider jawline and (as the film often draws our attention to) a significantly less-chiselled nose. One of the film's marketing highlights was the expensive prosthetics used to ensure that Aryan and Gaurav look different.[19] Neepa Majumdar notes that the film's narrative derives its motivation from the dynamic between the real (star) and the fake (fan) which plays out at three fundamental levels:

> The first dynamic is the relation between 'fake' and 'real' star/fan, with a greater interest in the fake or the copy or the duplicate in its many manifestations, both material and conceptual, and at many levels, including lines of dialogue . . . The second, closely related dynamic is between interchangeability and singularity. Here, real and fake are strategically rendered indistinguishable in specific moments in the film that are required by the narrative but also point to larger arguments regarding fan and star relations . . . The third dynamic is between liveness and mediation or presence and absence, worked out in the film as an acknowledgement of

the changing sites of star presence in contemporary entertainment, with a stronger emphasis and capital investment in stage shows than in the cinema.[20]

While the relationship between the star and the fan often has an aspect of mimicry, Gaurav is not content at being a mere replica of the star. He *needs* Aryan to acknowledge his devotion. He travels to Mumbai to give Aryan the trophy he had won as a birthday gift. When he reaches the star's mansion, he realises that he is but one in a sea of fans. He catches a glimpse of Aryan when he steps out to wave to his fans. In his pathological obsession, Gaurav seeks ways to prove to his idol that his devotion exceeds that of any ordinary fan. He attacks a younger star, who wants to replace the ageing Aryan as the new superstar, in the hope that this will get Aryan to acknowledge their connection. However, to Gaurav's dismay, Aryan is not impressed by Gaurav's actions. And to make matters worse, when they meet face to face for the first time, Aryan dismisses Gaurav's conviction that the fan is entitled to the star's time. A disillusioned Gaurav finally realises the one-sidedness of the star–fan relationship. He plans to exact revenge on Aryan. He is back in his room – the walls are still covered in pictures of Aryan – but this time, he does not face them as he did in the opening sequence. Instead, he has his back to the wall. The scene uses key light to blur the difference between the star and fan's faces. He takes all the pictures of Aryan off his wall and sets fire to them. Ironically, the matchbox that he uses also has Aryan's face on it. With this act, Gaurav vows to reverse the star–fan dynamic: now the star will have to chase his fan.

It is only when the star refuses to acknowledge how alike he and the fan are that the pathologically obsessed fan decides to 'become' the star. *Fan* repeatedly emphasises how Aryan and Gaurav look the same but not quite. While the film uses prosthetics to ensure that Gaurav and Aryan are distinguishable from one another, it also highlights their similarities when Gaurav pretends to be Aryan in order to destroy his reputation. Gaurav follows Aryan to London where he impersonates the star at Madame Tussauds wax museum. The copy, Gaurav, passes for the original, Aryan, as he poses with yet another copy, the wax statue. And when a crowd gathers to take pictures of 'Aryan' with his replica, Gaurav (as Aryan) lists the ways that the statue is nothing like him. Drawing attention to his face, Gaurav insists that the wax replica is a poor imitation. He points out that their noses are nothing alike and that no one smiles the way Aryan's wax statue does. The facial structures that distinguish Gaurav and Aryan, that is the nose and the mouth, are highlighted as Gaurav dismisses the statue. When the manager of the museum protests at the way 'Aryan' handles the wax statue, 'Aryan' declares that here is yet another white man who claims to own his face. The face becomes the contested site where this dynamic between the fake and the original plays out. He kidnaps a woman at gunpoint to escape being arrested by the security guards. And once outside, Gaurav, with a quick change of outfit, changes back into his own self as he makes his way out of the museum. The malleability of the star/fan's face is crucial in this scene. Madam Tussaud's is a significant spot for Gaurav to begin his mission to destroy Aryan, primarily because one of the markers of Bollywood's increasing global visibility is the rising number of Bollywood stars on display. It is significant that the destruction of the star image takes place at the wax museum with the desecration of the statue. The first step of Gaurav's revenge takes place at the site where people go to see lifelike replicas of stars.

While Aryan is arrested for Gaurav's actions at the wax museum, Gaurav makes his way to Dubronvik where Aryan is supposed to perform at the wedding of an industrialist's daughter. There, posing as Aryan, Gaurav molests a woman. The real Aryan is, once again, blamed for the act as the copy now passes off as the original. Gaurav also destroys the public–private divide that stars uphold when he impersonates Aryan and breaks into his residence. Threatening Aryan's wife with a gun, Gaurav proceeds to destroy Aryan's photographs and awards. And on the dismantled shelf, Gaurav places his prize from the lookalike contest. The prize that he wanted to present to Aryan as a sign of his devotion finally finds its place in his house.

The film's denouement takes place at the very lookalike contest in which Gaurav had participated as Aryan. However, this time, the star imitates his fan. Gaurav watches as Aryan impersonates him on stage and even flirts with his girlfriend. Angry, Gaurav tries to shoot Aryan. What follows is a protracted battle between the star and the fan – life here imitates art as this sequence bears strong resemblance to similar scenes in the movies. After their final face/off, Gaurav jumps off a building to his death. His last words are addressed to Aryan who attempts to save him: 'Rehne de, tu nahin samjhega' ('Leave it, you won't understand'). Even with his last words, the fan pays a homage to the star. At one level the dialogue reminds Aryan that the fan's love for the star is not only unrequited but is also misunderstood (as obsession). And on the other, it refers to another popular dialogue from a Shah Rukh Khan hit, *Kuch Kuch Hota Hain* (Karan Johar, 1998): 'Kuch kuch hota hai Rahul, tum nahin samjhoge' ('Something happens, Rahul. You wouldn't understand'). The use of the informal pronoun *tu* instead of the more formal *tum* (which is used in the original dialogue from which it takes its cue) suggests an intimacy that the fan feels with the star.

The film's closing sequence inverts the opening one. *Fan*, which opened with a collage of Aryan's rise to stardom, ends with a photo montage of Gaurav. Gaurav, whose face was hidden throughout the opening sequence, here faces us in a series of selfies. We see him in front of the wall of Aryan's photos, with his trophy, with a security guard at Aryan's residence, in the hotel where Aryan had stayed when he first came to Mumbai, and finally celebrating Aryan's birthday with a cake. Even in his selfies, as he puts his best face forward, he positions himself as the star's (lesser) double. In his study of consumer culture, Zygmunt Bauman cautions: 'The saints of the stardom cult are, like all saints, to be admired and held as an example, but not emulated.'[21] Bauman argues that fans do not make the same sacrifices as the star whose success is based on both dedication and self-denial. Though the star's success is unachievable for the fans, consuming like the star provides a way for the fans to be closer to the star. In this light, *Fan* is a cautionary tale about the making of a consumer gone wrong. The star image not only teaches us to desire, but also how to desire. The fan can desire the star, and even desire to be more like the star, but to desire to be the star violates the star–fan relationship. Gaurav, in his obsession, desires the star in ways that transgress the unwritten laws that govern the relationship between the star and the fan. In his attempt to undo the distance on which the star–fan relationship is premised, Gaurav not only proves to be a wanting fan, but also a flawed consumer.

NOTES

1. 'YRF Enchanted Journey', was a tie-up between the Indian film production house, Yash Raj Films, the Kuoni Travel Group venture SOTC and Brandinvest AG, to promote Swiss tourism. Although the advertisement serves as a direct invitation to its readers to travel to Switzerland, the obsession of Bombay cinema with the Swiss countryside long predates this. The first Hindi film to be shot in Switzerland was *Sangam* (*Convergence*, Raj Kapoor, 1964). It was followed by countless others, including: *An Evening in Paris* (Shakti Samanta, 1967) and *Prem Pujari* (*Worshipper of Love*, Dev Anand, 1970). Yash Chopra, Aditya Chopra's father, shot many of his films in Switzerland. The Swiss tourism industry recognised his contribution in making Switzerland a popular holiday destination for Indians by naming a train after him.
2. John Ellis, 'Stars as a Cinematic Phenomenon', in Leo Braudy and Marshall Cohen (eds), *Film Theory and Criticism* (Oxford: Oxford University Press, 2004), 601.
3. Barry King, 'Stardom, Celebrity, and the Money Form', *The Velvet Light Trap* 65 (2010), 10.
4. Ibid., 12.
5. An earlier version of this research appears in my doctoral dissertation where I discuss *Fan* as an instance of Bollywood's self-reflexive turn and the rise of consumer citizenship in India. Koel Banerjee, 'Commodity, Citizen, Copy: Bollywood and the Aesthetics of Consumption' (PhD thesis, University of Minnesota, 2018).
6. Dyer points out: 'The star image is then a given, like machinery, an example of what Karl Marx calls "congealed labor", something that is used with further labor (scripting, acting, directing, managing, filming, editing) to produce another commodity, a film.' Richard Dyer, *Heavenly Bodies: Film Stars and Society* (London: Routledge, 2011), 5.
7. Leela Fernandes, *India's New Middle Class: Democratic Politics in an Era of Economic Reform* (Minneapolis: University of Minnesota Press, 2010), 30.

8. Ibid.
9. Maitreyee Chaudhury, *Refashioning India: Gender, Media, and a Transformed Public Discourse* (Hyderabad: Orient BlackSwan, 2017), 88.
10. Ibid., 97.
11. In a related transition, the image of the new Indian woman underwent a similar refashioning. After liberalisation, questions of feminist choice, empowerment and freedom became irrevocably tied to consumption, individualism and monetary success.
12. C. P. Chandrasekhar and Jayati Ghosh, *The Market That Failed: Neoliberal Economic Reforms in India* (New Delhi: Left Word, 2009).
13. For an overview of the ways that Bombay cinema was transformed into what is now known as Bollywood, see Ashish Rajadhyaksha, 'The "Bollywoodization" of the Indian Cinema: Cultural Nationalism in a Global Arena', *Inter-Asia Cultural Studies* 4:1 (2003), 25–39.
14. The popularity of stars as mascots of the desirable good life is unsurprising. As Dyer observes, 'Stars are examples of the way people live their relation to production in capitalist society. Stars articulate what it is to be a human being in contemporary society; that is, they express the particular notion we hold of the person, of the "individual".' Moreover, in a consumer society, stars do not merely articulate what it is to be human, they embody its very ideal. Stars are the greatest adverts of the neo-liberal good life. In the persona of the star, their lifestyles, their patterns of consumption, is the greatest endorsement of consumerism. See Dyer, *Heavenly Bodies*, 5.
15. Sudhanva Deshpande, 'The Consumable Hero of Globalised India', in R. Kaur and A. Sinha (eds), *Bollyworld: Popular Indian Cinema through a Transnational Lens* (London: Sage, 2005), 202.
16. Every biography and almost every documentary on Shah Rukh Khan emphasise that he came to the Bombay film industry without any prior family connection to someone in the industry. His ambition to succeed in a nepotistic industry is referenced in a BBC documentary, where he tells the interviewer that when he came to Bombay (now Mumbai), he wanted to own the city. Tales about Khan, then a fledging star, standing in front of Ville Vienna, a sea-facing bungalow, vowing that he will own it someday are now part of the Bollywood folklore. That he did buy it a few years later and renamed it *Mannat* (Prayer) serves as a reminder to his fans that in capitalism wishes do come true.
17. I borrow the term 'use value promise' from W. F. Haug, who extends the scope of what Marx called use value by emphasising the independence of the promise of use value in the realm of exchange. The use value promise of the commodities in a consumer society integrates the consumer into the structure of the commodity when the consumer begins to conceive her own worth in economic terms. See Wolfgang Fritz Haug, *Commodity Aesthetics, Ideology and Culture* (Amsterdam: International General, 1987), 52.
18. Neepa Majumdar draws our attention to such fan practices, including copy-stardom, which she approaches as mimetic fandom: 'Mimetic fandom (a term I borrow from Matt Hills but use differently from him) is central to the film in the sense that Gaurav, the fan, is not only a look-alike but also copies and performs the star's dialogue,

dance steps, and gestures, and eventually even mirrors and equals the star's own moves in action sequences. This kind of mimetic fandom exists not only in the film's diegesis but also in fan practices, the most common of which is the copied haircut, but also takes on other forms of mimicry.' Neepa Majumdar, 'Embodiment and Stardom in Shahrukh Khan's Fan', *Framework* 58:1–2 (2017), 147.

19. The prosthetics used in the film garnered attention and media coverage. For instance, see Don Groves, 'Video Reveals How Shah Rukh Khan Was Transformed In "Fan"', *Forbes*, 19 April 2016. Available at <https://www.forbes.com/sites/dongroves/2016/04/19/video-reveals-how-shah-rukh-fan-was-transformed-in-fan/?sh=731e2fe73809> (last accessed 1 October 2021).

20. Majumdar, 'Embodiment and Stardom', 14.

21. Zygmunt Bauman, *Work, Consumerism and the New Poor* (Maidenhead: McGraw-Hill Education, 2007), 36.

15. THE FACE IS THE LIE THAT TELLS THE TRUTH: RENÉE ZELLWEGER AND THE MEDIATED POLITICS OF AGE, SELF AND CELEBRITY

Brenda R. Weber

On Monday, 20 October 2014, Renée Zellweger, the actor largely known for playing the 'wanton sex goddess'[1] and famously flawed Bridget Jones, shocked the world with an entirely new appearance that many argued made her unrecognisable.[2] Appearing at *Elle* magazine's annual Women in Hollywood awards, Zellweger's face evoked 'audible gasps' from the audience and paparazzi.[3] *The New York Daily News* quoted an anonymous source, 'When people got up close to her, they were taken back by what she had done to her face. Everyone was whispering about how different she looked.'[4] Seemingly, the rest of the press was in full agreement. 'Renée Zellweger looks unrecognisable,' noted the *Huffington Post, UK*.[5] While still conventionally attractive with long blonde hair and luminously white wrinkle-free skin, press accounts agreed that she didn't look like 'herself'. Indeed, later in the day *Huff Post UK* published a list of five stars who looked more like Renée Zellweger than Renée Zellweger: Juliette Lewis, Christina Applegate, Cameron Diaz, Sarah Jessica Parker and Rosie Huntington Whitely. Using journalist Amanda Hess's turn of phrase, Zellweger had become reduced to an imitation of herself.[6] The consensus among all reports was that Zellweger had not only made use of but that she had over-indulged in age-defying technologies (specifically plastic surgery), turning herself into a sign board for excess and a cautionary tale about female vanity and celebrity culture.[7] As I will note further in this essay, Zellweger resolutely denied that her appearance was the result of plastic surgery, arguing instead that she was simply happier, an emotional state that had written itself 'naturally' on her face. 'Did she or didn't she?' became the rallying cry around Renée Zellweger, a question intent on getting at the truth represented by her face.

The title of my essay is a turn on Pablo Picasso's famous musing about art:

> We all know that Art is not truth. Art is a lie that makes us realise truth, at least the truth that is given us to understand. The artist must know how to convince others of the truthfulness of his lies.[8]

In Picasso's rumination, art is a signifier whose meaning, or signification, is greater than itself. It can gesture toward truth, illuminate truth, and most significantly, create a convincing approximation of truth, a power that entirely dismantles the possibility that an absolute truth is understandable on its own terms. I use the semiotic power of the face to perform a similar work. There is, of course, no absolute truth in the appearance of the face. As a sign it is notoriously unreliable, shifting and sagging over the lifespan, changing through exposure to sun or darkness, growing puffy or gaunt, scarred or sallow. Mediation of the face complicates these factors all the more. The face can be painted to accentuate some qualities and to de-accentuate others, retouched to smooth imperfections, lit to appear as if a thousand tiny candles glow from within. None of this is natural, but all of it has been naturalised through advertising, film and television techniques, social media filters and print journalism fascinated by the celebrity face. Of chief importance to my discussion in this essay about Renée Zellweger's face, then, is how the 'did she or didn't she' debate naturalises certain terms, like the 'self' and even 'natural' itself, making those terms seem stable when they are quite fluid. In this case, the face is the lie that concocts a new truth, a truth that fantasises about a natural constancy of the self and body against the backdrop of its maddening mobility.

To quote from a handful of cosmetics ads that sum it up nicely, the aim is to: 'Stop wrinkles in their tracks', 'arrest the signs of ageing' and appear 'naturally flawless'. Doing so will fix the face in time, which will (the logic goes) make a person always recognisable, always themselves. As such, the fantasy suggests that identity is consistent and inviable because the *sine qua non* of recognisability, the face, is believed to emit the signs of identity with consistency and inviability. Whether the face does this through anti-ageing assistance or biology (to reference another cosmetics ad, through 'DNA or Olay'), the governing logic indicates that any intervention done on the face in the service of identity is warranted. Unless, as we see in the case of Zellweger, plastic surgery (or any number of non-surgical interventions like lasers, Botox and peels) 'go too far' by revealing their own presence, in effect 'outing' the star's inability to look 'natural' and giving the lie to a notion that natural ageing doesn't also change one's appearance and perhaps sense of selfhood. The morality tale offered by

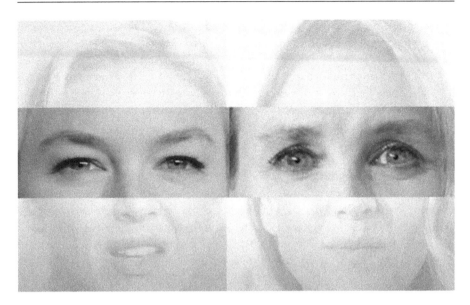

Figure 15.1   Under the diagnostic gaze ('Top Cosmetic Surgeon Discusses Renée Zellweger Plastic Surgery Rumors', YouTube video: https://www.youtube.com/watch?v=eI-iEVtg7RI).

Renée Zellweger's appearance thus speaks to a cultural desire to immobilise the plasticity of the face as a referent for the identity that the face seems to anchor, all while appearing as if you have done nothing.

SURVEILLANCE AND THE DIAGNOSTIC GAZE

Journalists Nate Jones and E. Alex Jung argue that 'more than any other actress of her generation', Zellweger's appearance offers a 'shorthand for her career'.[9] They also note, rightfully, that it is not just her face but her body that has been the target of scrutiny for many decades, 'ever since she gained weight for *Bridget Jones's Diary* (and lost it for *Chicago*), Zellweger's been too fat, too thin, too Botoxed, too *something*'.[10] In this, Zellweger has long served as a cultural mirror, held up so that we might see her imperfections and our own desires more clearly. The 2014 Women in Hollywood moment that opens this essay is thus not different in kind in the spectatorial critique it directs at Zellweger, but it is different in degree in that contemporary press accounts insisted on teaching readers to look at the star through a powerful and misogynistic cultural lens that reduced her to a series of 'bad' choices, made legible on her face. British papers piled on in their scrutiny of the actor and their determination for readers to develop a diagnostic gaze that could appreciate the harm her face represented. 'Stop what you are doing,' cried Britain's *Metro*. 'Renée Zellweger has a whole new face.'[11] Katie Baillie, writing for *Metro*, breathlessly reported,

> The actress attended a premiere of a different kind this week – the one of her new face. We kid you not. That really is Renée Zellweger. You know, the one who made Mark Darcy fall crazy in love with her, and who made it acceptable to be a normal, curvy girl.

Apparently, Baillie said this without irony, since it was actually the zaftig *character* Bridget Jones who made Mark Darcy fall in love with her and made normal-girl curves acceptable, not the sinewy *actor* Renée Zellweger, who caused these outcomes. The actor famously worked like hell to lose Bridget's pounds from her otherwise lithe body as soon as filming was complete.

Mediation around Zellweger's 'new look' continued in a manner that put her under the diagnostic gaze. Baillie noted, for example, 'Well apparently her own face wasn't acceptable, so she's completely changed it with some new puffy cheeks, a wrinkle-free forehead and an entirely new set of eyes.'[12] The *Daily Mail* was equally astounded: 'What Has Renée Zellweger done to her face?' reporter Rebecca Davison gushed, engaging in a variation of what Carole Spitzack insightfully identifies as the masculinised, power-rich evaluative gaze of surgeon over the feminised docile body of the patient.[13]

As it concerns the 'did she or didn't she' of Zellweger's face, the epistemological challenge led to a mediated double-down on expert testimony that could 'prove' which procedures would have accounted for the change in Zellweger's appearance. Wrote MailOnline:

> Dr Alex Karidis of London's Karaidis Clinic, who has never treated Renée, told the publication he believes Renée may have had an upper eye lift. He reasons: 'The distance between the brow and her eye is much smaller than before.' According to Dr Karidis, the 45-year-old's brows don't appear to be higher than before, suggesting she hasn't had a brow lift. Karidis says her flawless forehead could be down to the use of Botox.

Here the surgical gaze is taught with exacting precision.

Offering not only a pedagogy on what might be done but an advertisement for cosmetic procedures, the MailOnline continued with another doctor's expert opinion:

> Dr Yannis Alexandrides, MD at 111 Harley Street who has also never treated Renée, states that some of the actress's change in appearance could be primarily down to non-surgical procedures. 'At 44, Renée should have some signs of wrinkles and loss of elasticity, however her

face is line free and smooth, which suggests to me that she may have had a Thermage treatment. The procedure uses radio frequency to tighten elastin fibres and stimulate collagen and gradually improves the quality of the skin and tissue over a period of six months – it's a popular option for patients who are interested in a face lift but aren't ready for surgery.'[14]

On the US daytime show, *The Doctors*, resident plastic surgeon Dr Andrew 'Drew' Ordon, took the hypothetical out of the question 'Did She or Didn't She?', restabilising epistemological certainty by literally writing arrows on Zellweger's face in felt-tipped marker, thus re-establishing the semiotic roadmap for surgical change.[15] Other news sources also used the conventions of marking the body in preparation for plastic surgery to write a truth on Zellweger's body that she, herself, denied, superimposing arrows and explanations on Zellweger's image and fixing the certainty of her private choices. The logic behind these on-screen displays were clearly meant to undo Zellweger's denials, providing ontological clarity in the midst of epistemological uncertainty.

These rhetorical flourishes worked through a diagnostic gaze that put pundits and readers in the authoritative, agentive and masculinised role of doctor and reinscribed Zellweger into the passive, objective and feminised role of body, completely undoing the possibility of agency for her as a putative cosmetic surgery consumer. Wrote a reporter for the *Daily Mail* in its own form of spectatorial scrutiny: 'The *Jerry Maguire* actress looked almost unrecognisable with her super line-free forehead, altered brow and suspiciously puffy face, although she has never admitted to getting surgery.'[16] Many British pundits worried about the fate of their iconic loveable Bridget: 'Her new look leaves us with one huge question: How on earth will they explain this at the upcoming *Bridget Jones* movie?'[17] Speculation was equally intense in the US. Writing for *The New York Times*, Alex Kucynski reported that Zellweger had 'flooded news outlets', and ABC news spoke of Zellweger 'burning up the Internet'.[18]

A Feminist Call to Arms

The discursive energy wasn't entirely focused on Renée's new face; it was also absorbed with the nature of that change. Did she get plastic surgery, or didn't she? Not only had Zellweger never admitted to getting plastic surgery, she flatout denied it. Zellweger dismissed the allegations of plastic surgery as 'silly'. The change in her appearance, she said, could be attributed to the natural processes of ageing and living a 'happy, more fulfilling life'. 'I'm glad folks think I look different!' Zellweger told *People*.[19] 'My friends say that I look peaceful. I am healthy. I'm thrilled that perhaps it shows.' If this is the case, then it was her former younger appearance that was the imposter-self, the puffy cheeks and slightly hooded eyes that had so marked her star brand a false signifier of her true selfhood.

Zellweger's denials created both an epistemological problem and a feminist crisis. Media discussions began to centre on how it was possible for her to look the way she did without plastic surgery's intervention, while counter-discourses mobilised feminism to bolster opposite ends: either to claim that Zellweger was duped by a beauty culture that demanded eternal youthfulness from women or to counter reactions that condemned these critiques as robbing Zellweger of her choice to do whatever she wanted with her body. All of these discourses worked on and through the striated, cross-platform media that is sustained by professional and amateur production – from major outlets like CNN and *The New York Times* to gossip sites like Just Jared and TMZ, from blog posters to the 'real people', as opposed to the paid journalists, of various online periodicals (including, as I will soon discuss, Renée Zellweger herself). As media scholar Tonya Horek observed about the hyper-scrutiny of Zellweger's appearance, 'the speed and intimacy of this kind of counter-response . . . has galvanized the ways we as "users" now engage and interact with stars (and indeed they with us)'.[20] Omni-media provided a whole different version of truth about Renée.

Indeed, Zellweger became a rallying clarion call for third-wave feminism, which embraces beauty culture as legitimate acts of self and desire. 'Yes, she looks drastically different, but you can't blame her for trying to fight time, trying to fight age. It would be great to grow old gracefully,' wrote Erika Soutier, editor of *The Stir*. 'If you can have a little help, then why not utilize it.'[21] Yet, just as suddenly, the issue turned to refrains of second-wave feminism, which often denounces beauty culture as objectifying to women: how could Zellweger have capitulated to the body/beauty pressures that women face, her transformation to a blander, prettier, younger version of a woman not only distancing herself from the star brand and individual uniqueness of Renée Zellweger but also serving as a poor role model to women in the culture? 'Has the quest for perfection gone too far?' asked ABC's *Nightline*, using Renée Zellweger as Exhibit Number One in its indictment of plastic surgery culture (former supermodel Janice Dickinson, who is represented as a surgery junky, sealed the deal for the prosecution). In the *Nightline* piece, the reporter Neal Carlinsk intones Zellweger 'didn't seem to be herself' because 'she looks physically different', all in a voice of mocking amusement that suggests this is all just so much ridiculous fluff.[22] Thus speaks the voice of patriarchy about the follies of beauty culture for women.

As a lead-up to the premiere of *Bridget Jones's Baby* in 2016, the controversy raged on. Writing for *Variety* and in advance of the 16 September 2016 release, film critic Owen Gleiberman asked, 'If she no longer looks like herself, has she become a different actress?'[23] Gleiberman contended that Zellweger went the way of most Hollywood starlettes, who use plastic surgery as 'a ritual of our vanity-fueled image culture'. Yet, this (and its implications for women in beauty culture) bothered him less than a niggling feeling that Zellweger had done harm to her character, Bridget Jones. He writes,

> The movie's star, Renée Zellweger, already had her 'Did she or didn't she?' moment back in 2014, and I had followed the round-the-world scrutinizing of her image that went along with it, but this was different. Watching the trailer, I didn't stare at the actress and think: She doesn't look like Renée Zellweger. I thought: She doesn't look like Bridget Jones! Oddly, that made it matter more. Celebrities, like anyone else, have the right to look however they want, but the characters they play become part of us. I suddenly felt like something had been taken away.

If Zellweger cannot be blamed for her forays into aesthetic enhancement, he claimed, she can be faulted for grievous injury to her character, Bridget Jones. What he, or most any other media critic failed to mention was not only had Zellweger's face altered Bridget's countenance, but her body was different too – largely because Zellweger refused to gain the weight she had put on to play Bridget in *Bridget Jones's Diary* and *Bridget Jones: The Edge of Reason*. The famously pudgy Bridget became the famously skinny Renée.

Failing in Effortless Naturalness

But Gleiberman didn't stop there. He used his piece to launch a diatribe against the artificiality of Hollywood actors and their precarious hold on confident selfhood. He wrote:

> Today, more than ever, movie stars look like models, and there's a pressure on them to conform to certain 'standards'. The amount of cosmetic surgery that goes on in Hollywood would shock almost anyone who learned about it, because the truth is that a great many stars who *don't* look nipped and tucked, and who publicly decry plastic surgery, have had the work done. But that, by definition, is to keep them looking younger, to keep them looking like 'themselves'. (That's why you can't tell.) The syndrome we're talking about is far more insidious, because when you see someone who no longer looks like who they are, it's not necessarily the result of bad cosmetic surgery. It's the result of a decision, an ideology, a rejection of the self.

These are fighting words. And Gleiberman got plenty of blowback. In the interest of brevity, I won't detail the full tsunami he inspired, but I do want to point to a few highlights. Writing a guest column for *The Hollywood Reporter*, actor Rose McGowan called the critique 'vile, damaging, stupid and cruel'.[24] She equated Gleiberman to an online bully and indicted all of Hollywood as being complicit in his cruelty by not coming to Zellweger's defence. 'You are an active endorser of what is tantamount to harassment and abuse of actresses and women,' she retorted. 'It also reeks of status quo white-male privilege.' McGowan wasn't wrong.

Zellweger herself published a response called 'We Can Do Better' in the *Huffington Post*, three weeks after the *Variety* column hit. She called the concerns about her face inconsequential,

> [J]ust one more story in the massive smut pile generated every day by the tabloid press and fueled by exploitative headlines and folks who practice cowardly cruelty from their anonymous internet pulpits. Not that it's anyone's business, but I did not make a decision to alter my face and have surgery on my eyes . . . This fact is of no true import to anyone at all, but that the possibility alone was discussed among respected journalists and became a public conversation is a disconcerting illustration of news/entertainment confusion and society's fixation on physicality.[25]

Zellweger's post slamming tabloid news culture and *The New York Times*'s interest in it came a month after actor Jennifer Aniston wrote a similar *Huffington Post* blog saying she was sick of being harassed by photographers and tabloid reporters.[26] Aniston declared, 'I am not pregnant . . . I'm fed up with the sport-like scrutiny and body shaming that occurs daily under the guise of "journalism", the "First Amendment" and "celebrity news".'[27] Like Aniston, Zellweger said the speculation and criticism of her physical appearance left a 'problematic' message for younger generations, and 'triggers myriad subsequent issues' including image, equality and health. 'It's no secret a woman's worth has historically been measured by her appearance,' Zellweger said.

> Too skinny, too fat, showing age, better as a brunette, cellulite thighs, facelift scandal, going bald, fat belly or bump? Ugly shoes, ugly feet, ugly smile, ugly hands, ugly dress, ugly laugh; headline material which emphasizes the implied variables meant to determine a person's worth.[28]

But here, the public taunting of Jennifer and Renée provided a bigger pay-off than they perhaps realised. It got under the celebrity persona and through to the persons inside, the women inside. It inspired both stars to engage in direct address with a public, to write a piece in first person, to reveal their own opinions, hurt feelings and calls for change. The vulnerable and furious self-arising in and through media.

As we can see from the waves of these debates, for some Zellweger's 'crime' was not that she engaged in plastic surgery (if she did) but that she would lie about it. For others, the issue is that Zellweger's altered appearance provided startling evidence of an oppressive beauty culture that demands eternal and pretty youthfulness from mature women. For others still (and if the *Huff Post* article is to be believed, this is particularly the case for Zellweger) the heart of the problem is media itself and a seeming collapse between entertainment and news.

GASLIGHTING AND THE SEMIOTICS OF AGE

The debate about Zellweger's face is unlikely to end soon, largely because it is fuelled by an intermedial and ever-growing archive of old and new media that thrives on these moments of controversy hinged to investments in both the beautiful and 'the natural' that are often tied to the appearance of youthfulness. That it incorporates both calls for feminist empowerment and rights to privacy makes the topic all the more enduring. And that these cultural narratives are inscribed on the body and faces of celebrities, who must often monetise both privacy and appearance in the service of their star brand, makes these matters all the more tenuous. But scandal aside, these sorts of mediated discussions tell us a good deal about age, beauty and investments in selfhood.

Indeed, yet another flash point has emerged from the controversy surrounding Zellweger's face: the disingenuous relation between what we see and what we are allowed to talk about. Writes journalist Elizabeth Bromstein about Zellweger's altered appearance: 'What's with this weird argument that it's somehow anti-woman or anti-feminist to do anything other than pretend you don't notice anything?'[29] Or as Rosie O'Donnell said on *The View* in her inimitable style,

> If somebody who is a public figure drastically changes their appearance so that they're unrecognisable, are we as a society supposed to pretend we don't see it? I agree we shouldn't be mean about it but to actually observe the fact that she looks drastically different than she used to, if it's not done in a mean, judgemental tone, I think it's OK. Otherwise it's the elephant in the room.[30]

Elephant in the room it may be, but it is also a more serious denial of history and experience that could well be equated with gaslighting, in this case by pretending that the appearance of eternal youthfulness is a 'natural' by-product of clean living and lots of sleep. Said actor Ali Wentworth on *The Wendy Williams Show*,

> I had my eyes done a few years ago, and I went online, I couldn't find anything about it. I went to celebrity friends and asked, 'Who did your eyes?' And they all said, 'I haven't anything done.' . . . And this is my point . . . when I look at magazines or I see these celebrities and they say, 'I just drink a lot of water and hike.' I say, don't do that to me. Because I look at these magazines and feel so disgusted, fat, and inadequate. Just tell the truth.[31]

As *Flavorwire* commentator Sarah Seltzer opined about the furore related to Zellweger's debated use of plastic surgery, the real issue is that Zellweger's appearance had

> broken the invisible pact that women are supposed to make: be beauty ducks, who look tranquil and eat hamburgers above the surface but are paddling beneath: working out, dieting, plucking, nipping, tucking and buffing all the time just out sight so we can appear this perfect.[32]

Amanda Hess reinforced this idea in *Slate* noting,

> In Hollywood, 'aging gracefully' is a euphemism for 'good plastic surgery', the kind that successfully skirts an unarticulated line between sagging and frozen. (See Sandra Bullock). Character actresses like Melissa Leo can grow into great careers later in life, playing hard, complicated broads, but our baby-faced ingénues are specifically prized for their youth; it's nearly impossible for them to 'get better' with age.[33]

Notions of ageing, gaslighting, truth and identity take us back to where we started – a desire for epistemological and ontological certainty, articulated in stable selfhood revealed through the gaze and made legible through the fantasy of a face that does not change. According to all outward appearances, this face doesn't age and so thus, the logic goes, will never sacrifice its 'rightful' link to selfhood. These debates about women, appearance and ageing evidence the way that media discourses serve as pedagogical tools on the meaning of selfhood and how aesthetic surgery (and its correlatives like Botox or microdermabrasion) operate along a slippery hermeneutic that both affirm and deny the 'authentic' expression of one's self through the body. These issues also reinforce Wendy Chapkis's prescient observation:

> However much the particulars of the beauty package may change from decade to decade – curves in or out, skin delicate or ruddy, figures fragile

or fit – the basic principles remain the same. The body beautiful is woman's responsibility and authority. She will be valued and rewarded on the basis of how close she comes to embodying the ideal.[34]

VINDICATION OR VICTIMISATION?

In this consideration of Zellweger's face, plastic surgery stands as a powerful, and potentially frightening, tool in the alienation of body (and brand) from self, while age and how it encodes itself on the body complicates what it means to look like oneself.[35] While other representations of aesthetic plasticity, specifically the reality television makeover, resolutely reinforce the claim that selfhood is more successfully secured through aesthetic interventions like plastic surgery – allowing subjects to declared with delight, 'I'm me now!' – the world was seemingly aghast by Zellweger because she no longer looked like herself.[36] 'I'm not me anymore!' just didn't have the same celebratory ring to it. Zellweger's new face was also alarming according to press accounts because it distanced her from the appearance of, arguably, her most famous character, Bridget Jones, who has become iconic with Zellweger's brand.

While this cautionary tale about a star's purported use of plastic surgery might seem to undo the reality TV ethos for transformation in the service of revealing the 'real' self inside, Zellweger's new face actually reinforces the point of the stable self from two different sides since selfhood remains the fulcrum on which these arguments for and against plastic surgery balance. In this, media

Figure 15.2   Renee-as-Judy, from *Judy* (Rupert Goold, 2019).

and celebrity provide a concentrated pedagogy attesting to the absolute necessity to locate the self, love the self and beautify the self as gestures of modern
belonging. Ironically, within the complicated logic of aesthetic alteration, plastic surgery can also serve as a tool of redemption. For if plastic surgery can
push a star outside of the circumference of her own brand and lead her fans
to ask, 'Who is that person?' to NOT engage in plastic surgery exposes all
women-identified bodies to a different charge – as Anne Balsamo reminds us –
that 'they failed to deploy all possible resources for a "better life"'.[37] In effect,
she is damned if she does, and more damned if she won't.

It is perhaps an exquisite irony that the 'did she or didn't she' scandal re-
emerged in 2019 in the lead-up to the premiere of *Judy*, a feature-film biopic
about the classic Hollywood actor and gay icon Judy Garland, starring Renée
Zellweger. In advance interviews, the controversy over Zellweger's appearance
was continually cited as a real-life experience that qualified her to play the
famously troubled and drug-addicted Judy Garland with sympathy and a kind
of honest grit.[38] *Judy*'s director Rupert Goold noted to *Vanity Fair*, 'I wanted
somebody who could make something intimate and emotionally available and
fragile of a sort of hardened icon.' The fact that Zellweger had endured the
tabloids 'being catty about the fact that she doesn't look like she did when she
did *Jerry Maguire*', resonated with the director.[39]

As media scholar Thomas J. West noted, Zellweger was critically praised
for her 'uncanny ability to embody Garland . . . she literally seems to *become*
her . . .'[40] Media journalist Jonathan Van Meter similarly observed, 'Zellweger
is riveting as Garland,' praising, in particular, Zellweger's physical portrayal of
Garland, both her pretzel-like contortions and her 'arms akimbo'.[41] This loss of
the appearance of Renée in the service of Judy no doubt led to Zellweger winning
the 2020 Academy Award for best actress; here 'Renée Zellweger doesn't look
like Renée Zellweger' serving as evidence of her acting cunning rather than as
indictment of a precarious selfhood and the slippery unrecognisability of her face.
But continuing with its pedagogy on the diagnostic gaze, press accounts reminded
readers that the fifty-year-old Zellweger wore heavy makeup, false teeth and prosthetics to portray the forty-seven-year-old Garland, a form of 'age face' so obvious
that it could be appreciated as artistry.[42] Renée-as-Judy was a face that transparently told a lie, all while putting a stark spotlight on the 'real' face of Renée, a face
that could not be deciphered as either true or false, as either natural or augmented.

If the controversy over Zellweger's face reveals deep cultural anxieties about
gender, age, celebrity and the fluidity of appearance over time, we might argue
that Zellweger might still have the last laugh. The transition from celebrated
to suffering to ascendant has in many respects transformed her into what some
consider to be iconic status. While according to the rubric for gay icons established by Georges-Claude Guilbert she isn't quite there yet because she does
not 'tick enough boxes' qualifying her for iconic status,[43] Van Meter believes

Zellweger already possesses both the fragility and the steeliness, the level of suffering and the 'need to put on a bit show for everyone' that fully qualifies her for iconic status. If this is the case, Zellweger might eclipse her own recognisability, serving as both sign and signpost for a version of imagined womanhood that is bigger than itself.

NOTES

1. *Bridget Jones's Diary*, directed by Sharon Maguire (2001).
2. Ann Oldenburg, 'Renee Zellweger Doesn't Look Like Renee Zellweger', *USA Today*, syndicated, 24 October 2013. Available at <http://www.indystar.com/story/life/people/2013/11/05/renee-zellweger-doesnt-look-like-renee-zellweger/3441827/> (last accessed 6 October 2021).
3. Matt Bagwell, 'Renee Zellweger Looks Unrecognisable', *Huff Post*, 21 October 2014. Available at <http://www.huffingtonpost.co.uk/2014/10/21/renee-zellweger-face-surgery-pictures_n_6019670.html> (last accessed 12 March 2015).
4. Beth Stebner, 'Renee Zellweger's New Face: Plastic Surgeons Tell Us What the Actress May Have Had Done', *New York Daily News*, 24 October 2014. Available at <http://www.nydailynews.com/life-style/renee-zellweger-new-face-surgeons-article-1.1982221> (last accessed 6 October 2021).
5. Bagwell, 'Unrecognisable'.
6. Amanda Hess, 'It's Horrible to Be an Old Woman in Hollywood', *Slate*, 3 March 2014. Available at <https://slate.com/human-interest/2014/03/kim-novak-liza-minnelli-and-june-squibb-at-the-oscars-how-hollywood-treats-aging-actresses.html> (last accessed 6 October 2021). For an excellent analysis of playing the self as a trope that extends across cultures, see Wendy Doniger, *The Woman Who Pretended to Be Who She Was: Myths of Self-Imitation* (Oxford: Oxford University Press, 2006).
7. Victoria Pitts-Taylor, *Surgery Junkies: Wellness and Pathology in Cosmetic Culture* (New Brunswick, NJ: Rutgers University Press, 2007).
8. Pablo Picasso, Letter to Marius de Zayas, 1923. Available at <http://projects.mcah.columbia.edu/arthumanities/websites/picmon/pdf/art_hum_reading_49.pdf> (last accessed 6 October 2021). Philip Core suggests an earlier derivation of the phrase, when Jean Cocteau in 1922 declared, 'I am a lie that tells the truth.' See Camp: *The Lie that Tells the Truth* (London: Plexus, 1984).
9. Nate Jones and E. Alex Jung, 'A History of Everyone Freaking Out About Renée Zellweger's Face', *New York Magazine*, 1 July 2016. Available at <https://www.vulture.com/2014/10/history-of-freakouts-over-renee-zellwegers-face.html> (last accessed 6 October 2021).
10. Ibid. Michelle Smith offers a persuasive reading of both Zellweger and fellow actor and reported plastic surgery recipient, Meg Ryan. Both actors, she argues, received criticism for having allowed cosmetic surgery to 'destroy the unique features and charm that were key to their popularity' (p. 2). Smith rightly notes that with the passage of time, neither actor looks like the career-defining character from decades early due to their own ageing processes. Michelle Smith, 'Meg Ryan's Face and the Historical Battleground of Ageing', *The Conversation*, 16 June 2016. Available at

<http://dro.deakin.edu.au/eserv/DU:30090186/smith-megryansface-2016.pdf> (last accessed 6 October 2021).

11. Katie Baillie, 'Stop What You Are Doing: Renée Zellweger Has a Whole New Face', *Metro*, 21 October 2014. Available at <http://metro.co.uk/2014/10/21/stop-what-you-are-doing-renee-zellweger-has-a-whole-new-face-4914561/> (last accessed 6 October 2021).

12. Ibid.

13. Carole Spitzack, 'The Confession Mirror: Plastic Images for Surgery', *Canadian Journal for Political and Social Theory* 12:1–2 (1988), 38–50.

14. Cassie Carpenter, 'I'm Glad Folks Think I Look Different!' *MailOnline*, 22 October 2014. Available at <https://www.dailymail.co.uk/tvshowbiz/article-2802651/renee-zellweger-calls-plastic-surgery-rumours-silly-attributes-new-face-healthier-happier-lifestyle.html> (last accessed 6 October 2021).

15. *The Doctors*. 2008 – present. CBS Television Distribution.

16. Rebecca Davison, 'What Has Renee Zellweger Done to Her Face?' *MailOnline*, 21 October 2014. Available at <http://www.dailymail.co.uk/tvshowbiz/article-2801157/renee-zellweger-looks-drastically-different-elle-event.html#ixzz4bQJYJ0Yg> (last accessed 6 October 2021).

17. Bagwell, 'Unrecognisable'.

18. Alex Kucynski, 'Why the Strong Reaction to Renee Zellweger's Face?' *The New York Times*, 24 October 2014. Available at <https://www.nytimes.com/2014/10/26/fashion/why-the-strong-reaction-to-renee-zellweger-face.html> (last accessed 6 October 2021).

19. J. D. Heyman, 'Renee Zellweger to People: "I'm Glad Folks Think I Look Different"', *People*, 22 October 2014. Available at <http://people.com/celebrity/renee-zellweger-opens-up-about-different-look/> (last accessed 6 October 2021).

20. Tanya Horek, '#ReneeZellweger's Face', *Celebrity Studies* 6:2 (2015), 261.

21. *The Wendy Williams Show*, season 6, episode 30, 'Hot Talk/Chef Fabio Viviani', directed by Debbie Miller, featuring Wendy Williams, aired 24 October 2014, Debmar-Mercury.

22. 'Renee Zellweger "Happy" People Think She Looks Different', *ABC News*, n.d. Available at <http://abcnews.go.com/Nightline/video/nightline-renee-zellweger-glad-people-26392638> (last accessed 6 October 2021).

23. Owen Gleiberman, 'Renee Zellweger: If She No Longer Looks Like Herself, Has She Become a Different Actress?' *Variety*, 30 June 2016. Available at <http://variety.com/2016/film/columns/renee-zellweger-bridget-joness-baby-1201806603/> (last accessed 6 October 2021).

24. Rose McGowan, 'Rose McGowan Pens Response to Critics of Renee Zellweger's Face', *The Hollywood Reporter*, 26 July 2016. Available at <http://www.hollywood-reporter.com/news/rose-mcgowan-blasts-varietys-renee-908489> (last accessed 6 October 2021).

25. Renée Zellweger, 'We Can Do Better', *HuffPost*, 6 August 2016. Available at <http://www.huffingtonpost.com/renee-zellweger/we-can-do-better_b_11355000.html> (last accessed 6 October 2021).

26. For a fascinating analysis of Aniston's career and her centrality to discursive concerns about gender, age, motherhood (or lack thereof) and 'temporal failure', see Susan Berridge, 'From the Woman Who "Had It All" to the Tragic, Ageing Spinster: The Shifting Star Persona of Jennifer Aniston', in Deborah Jermyn and Su Murray (eds), *Women, Celebrity, and Cultures of Ageing: Freeze Frame* (London: Palgrave Macmillan, 2015), 112–26.

27. Jennifer Aniston, 'For the Record', *HuffPost*, 12 July 2016. Available at <https://www.huffpost.com/entry/for-the-record_b_57855586e4b03fc3ee4e626f> (last accessed 6 October 2021).

28. 'Renee Zellweger Slams Media Speculation About Plastic Surgery', *Reuters*, 15 August 2016. Available at <http://www.reuters.com/article/us-people-reneezellweger-idUSKCN10G2EL> (last accessed 6 October 2021).

29. Elizabeth Bromstein, 'I Am Not an Awful Person for Wondering About Renee Zelleger's Face', *HuffPost*, 9 August 2016. Available at <http://www.huffingtonpost.ca/elizabeth-bromstein/renee-zellwegers-face_b_11407390.html> (last accessed 6 October 2021).

30. *The View*, season 18, episode 28, 'Ty Burrell/Fred Savage & Danica McKellar', directed by Ashley S. Gorman, featuring Whoopie Goldberg, Rosie O'Donnell, Nicolle Wallace and Rosie Perez, aired 22 October 2014, ABC.

31. *The Wendy Williams Show*, 'Hot Talk'.

32. Sarah Seltzer, 'Yes, Those Pictures of Renée Zellweger Are Disturbing. But Why?' *Flavorwire*, 21 October 2014. Available at <https://www.flavorwire.com/483856/yes-those-pictures-of-renee-zellweger-are-disturbing-but-why> (last accessed 6 October 2021).

33. Amanda Hess, 'Renee Zellweger's New Face is Too Real', *Slate*, 21 October 2014. Available at <https://slate.com/human-interest/2014/10/renee-zellweger-plastic-surgery-in-hollywood-women-over-40-get-a-new-face-or-disappear.html> (last accessed 6 October 2021).

34. Wendy Chapkis, *Beauty Secrets: Women and the Politics of Appearance* (London: South End Press, 1999), 14.

35. This essay expands on my earlier considerations of age, beauty and identity, published as 'The Incredible Invisible Woman: Age, Beauty, and the Specter of Identity', in Maxine Craig (ed.), *The Routledge Companion to Beauty Politics* (New York: Routledge, 2021).

36. Brenda R. Weber, *Makeover TV: Selfhood, Citizenship, and Celebrity* (Durham, NC: Duke University Press, 2009).

37. Anne Balsamo, *Technologies of the Gendered Body: Reading Cyborg Women* (Durham, NC: Duke University Press, 1995), 66.

38. For a few examples, see Rod McPhee, '"I Wasn't Healthy" Renee Zellweger Reveals She Struggled with Life and the Pressures of Fame Just Like Judy Garland', *The Sun*, 1 October 2019. Available at <https://www.thesun.co.uk/tvandshowbiz/10046652/renee-zellweger-judy-garland-similar-lives/> (last accessed 6 October 2021).

39. Laura Regensdorf, 'Inside Renée Zellweger's Transformation for Judy, from Button Nose to Custom Wig', *Vanity Fair*, 2 January 2020. Available at <https://www.

vanityfair.com/hollywood/2020/01/renee-zellweger-judy-garland-transformation-hair-makeup> (last accessed 6 October 2021).

40. Thomas J. West III, 'A Star is Reborn: Embodiment, Empathy, and *Judy* (2019)', *Medium*, 17 February 2021. Available at <https://medium.com/screenology/a-star-is-reborn-embodiment-empathy-and-judy-2018-54f8a0510f67> (last accessed 6 October 2021).

41. Jonathan Van Meter, 'Renee Zellweger's Lost Decade', *New York Magazine*, 3 September 2019. Available at <https://www.vulture.com/2019/09/renee-zellweger-judy-garland.html> (last accessed 6 October 2021).

42. Media scholar Deborah Jermyn has contributed greatly to a nuanced analysis of gender, age and mediation. Jermyn reminds readers that 'one of the important interventions to be made by ageing studies into the cultural presumptions surrounding ageing is to question the very process of how we define age itself, and the inadequacy of merely ascribing a numerical figure to it' (p. 10). Surely, Zellweger's prosthetic wrinkles to play a younger woman gives evidence to Jermyn's claim. Deborah Jermyn, 'Introduction: "Get a Life Ladies. Your Old One is Not Coming Back": Ageing, Ageism and the Lifespan of Female Celebrity', in Deborah Jermyn (ed.), *Female Celebrity and Ageing: Back in the Spotlight* (London: Routledge, 2013), 1–14.

43. Private correspondence with the author, 12 February 2021. Guilbert identifies the gay icon as a complex paradigm influenced by biography, career and appeal. For more on Guilbert's fascinating accounting of just what creates the gay icon and the cultural work she performs, see Georges-Claude Guilbert *Gay Icons: The (Mostly) Female Entertainers Gay Men Love* (Jefferson, NC: McFarland & Company, 2018).

16. MEDIATING THE HUMAN IN FACIAL PERFORMANCE CAPTURE

Tanine Allison

Constructing a photorealistic digital human has long been considered the 'holy grail' of digital visual effects. While there are many components to constructing a digital human, the face is among the most important. The face serves as the body's most direct marker of identity and the place where the self is communicated to others. But the face is also one of the most difficult parts of the human body to adequately simulate in computer-generated imagery. Humans evolved to recognise faces and spot the most minute facial expressions, as well as the ways that they might be unnatural. The face is made up of many moving parts, including forty-three specific muscles connecting to fourteen different bones. These muscles and bones – along with skin, lips and eyes – move differently in every person, thus creating the particular facial tics, quirks and expressions that become recognisable as part of a person's identity. Recreating all of these elements in a computer program, with sufficient detail and subtlety to fool the human eye, is a daunting challenge.

Efforts to create a photorealistic digital human have been aided by performance capture, a set of techniques that record the facial and bodily movements of a human performer and apply them to a digital character. By involving an actor – often a well-known actor in a highly publicised role – performance capture places the efforts of a human performer at the centre of digital character construction, rather than the work of programmers and digital effects artists. However, performance capture is a compromise between an ideal process that would seamlessly transfer a human performance to a digital character and a technological solution that crafts a performance solely out of the ones and zeroes of a computer. Despite promotional rhetoric to the contrary, performance capture does not record every nuance of a performance and transfer it magically to a digital being. While the process does record elements of an actor's performance, it typically combines that fragmentary and incomplete data with software programs, digital facial models, and animation to create the final computer-generated (CG) performance. Thus, performance capture participates in a representational binary. On the one hand, cinematic technologies aim to directly record a facial performance; on the other hand, digital technologies allow for the complete fabrication of a face. Performance capture attempts to mediate between these two poles of digital representation, showcasing the human performer at the heart of the digital character, while at the same time using advanced animation tools to simulate a performance as a computer-generated, programmed product.

This essay explores the outcomes of this representational binary in performance capture-based digital characters of the last two decades. In examples ranging from *Pirates of the Caribbean: Dead Man's Chest* (Gore Verbinski, 2006) to *Gemini Man* (Ang Lee, 2019), I examine how the contradiction between capture and simulation played out in the specific production processes of visual effects-heavy films. With a special focus on digital de-ageing, I demonstrate how, over time, filmmakers acknowledged the importance of human facial performance and developed more advanced technologies to capture it. But filmmakers also learned that they could never fully capture these ephemeral moments and miniscule movements. Instead, they relied on the other end of the spectrum – the simulation programs at their disposal – to fabricate the appearance of human-like idiosyncrasies purely in their digital programs. Ultimately, I explore how this dual process reflects competing visions of human interiority and the role of the face in expressing it.

PERFORMANCE CAPTURE AND THE DIGITAL FACE

Because of the human face's foundational place in the expression of self, digital faces are put under intense scrutiny. If the face is the most obvious outward presentation of identity, then the believability of a computer-generated character will likely turn on the construction of the face. In his book *Face and Mask: A Double History*, scholar Hans Belting questions whether digitally constructed faces without a specific human referent, like those of the computer-generated cast members of the ground-breaking *Final Fantasy: The Spirits Within* (Hironobu Sakaguchi, 2001), still retain the cinematic and empathetic power of conventionally recorded human faces on screen. Looking at other digital faces constructed by technologies like biometrics and automatic facial recognition, he argues that these techniques transform faces into abstract data, a compendium of 'exterior details with no expressive value'.[1] Therefore, the previously communicative human face becomes an opaque mask.

Belting explores the argument that what he calls 'cyberfaces' – that is, digitally created faces – are not faces at all but rather masks. In fact, the cyberface, he suggests, is a 'total mask' that is 'basically no longer a mask, because nothing and no one is there anymore whom it represents or conceals'.[2] While he acknowledges that the cyberface follows a long history of creating fictional faces, he also recognises the revolutionary nature of digital tools that 'have power over the simulation of life without the need for a living bearer of a mask or the existence of an original from the world of the living'.[3] In other words, advanced visual techniques can now create photorealistic human faces that are not depictions of or stand-ins for actual people; there is no referent – no person to whom the face refers or belongs.

Performance capture assuages this existential angst by recentring the human performer within the construction of a digital character. Early techniques, dubbed 'motion capture', focused solely on the gross movements of the body, placing tracking markers on the major joints in order to record basic motions, abstract those movements into data points moving in three-dimensional space and apply those data points to corresponding positions on the digital character's body. In this way, the movements of a performer – often wearing a tight-fitting unitard and covered in glowing dots – can be transferred to a digital model. While this digital model is often a human representation, the proportions of the dots can be altered to apply the movements to apes, aliens, robots and other computer-generated creatures. The term 'performance capture' specifically refers to a more sophisticated form of motion capture that tracks and records movements of the face as well as the body. More recently, though, performance capture describes any number of techniques – including cyberscanning, videogrammetry and lidar – that collect data about human bodily and facial performance and apply that data to a computer-generated figure. I use performance capture here in the broader sense of any technique that aims to record elements of an actor's performance and apply them to a digital character.

Publicity materials about performance capture tend to exaggerate the transparency of the process, making it seem like human performance goes in one end of the machine and seamlessly attaches to a digital character on the other. In 2009, for instance, director James Cameron claimed that the performance-capture system designed for *Avatar* could 'get 100 percent of what the actor does. Not 98, not 95, but 100 percent. Every nuance [of] their creation on the set is preserved.'[4] As the examples below will show us, performance capture is thought to preserve the 'essence' of a human performance and almost magically transfer it to a virtual character. However, these promotional discourses tend to ignore the crucial role that programmers and animators play in the construction and performance of a digital character. In her analysis of the labour politics of motion capture, Misha Mihailova has pointed out that the rhetoric of the transparency and immediacy in motion capture ignores the labour of animators and visual effects artists; this neglect stems from their differing positions of power within the film industry.[5] Actors are highly visible and represented by the powerful Screen Actors Guild, which has lobbied for better pay and contractual benefits for motion-capture performers. In fact, the Guild advocated for a shift from the term 'motion capture' to the more actor-centric term 'performance capture' in order to emphasise the actor's contribution and push for better pay and benefits for motion-capture performers.[6] Conversely, animators and visual effects artists are not in the public eye, lack union representation and typically lack profit participation.

In the examples I explore below, we will see how filmmakers mediate between two poles of representation: capture and simulation. Capture refers to recording processes that aim to document or preserve a performance. While traditional film cameras record the external appearance of actors, performance capture records other aspects of a performance – such as movements – but does not necessarily record external appearance. It provides a document of abstract motion disconnected from the visual. Yet, like traditional film cameras, performance capture still attempts to record and preserve a performance. On the other end of the spectrum, simulation provides a manufactured construction of a performance using animation or software tools. Instead of providing a record of an external event or appearance, a simulation creates a fabrication of that event or appearance. I chose the term 'simulation' over others like 'construction' or 'manufacture' specifically because simulation involves the replication of behaviours rather than just the exterior form.[7] While a simulation may be computer-driven or animated by an artist, it reconstructs an object and puts in in motion by replicating its exterior and/or actions. Capture documents, while simulation fabricates.[8]

A photorealistic digital human or computer-generated character may be the result of either capturing processes or simulation. Filmmakers may directly apply performance-captured movements and expressions ('capture') or design and animate a CG character completely from scratch ('simulation'). Because of the sophisticated nature of digital visual effects, a viewer cannot necessarily detect the origin of the performance when watching a digital character. As we will see below, performance capture is hyped as more naturalistic, providing more emotional and compelling digital performances, but digital animation is also incredibly sophisticated, drawing on more than a century of animation research to construct incredibly lifelike digital models and performances. In the examples I explore below, the filmmakers mediate between the capture pole and the simulation pole of digital character generation in their attempt to bring something authentically human and real to the screen.

'THE MAN OF A THOUSAND FACES': EARLY EXPERIMENTS WITH
PERFORMANCE CAPTURE

In the early 2000s, filmmakers found ways to capture and apply the facial performances of actors to increase the naturalism of digitally animated faces. The character of Gollum in the *Lord of the Rings* films served as an early exemplar for the use of performance capture (then still called 'motion capture') in Hollywood cinema. Cast as the computer-generated devolved hobbit, Andy Serkis gained attention for his role and thrust performance capture into the spotlight. Publicity materials that highlighted the similarities between Serkis's facial expressions and those of Gollum suggested a transparent transferal of interiority from the performer to the digital creation (Figure 16.1). Referencing promotional photos like these, Lisa Purse writes that performance capture

> allows the technological process to be conceptually minimised in favour of a visible form of performance creation in which the human contribution is highly legible, via the paratextual footage of actors emoting and gesturing expressively in special suits and camera head rigs.[9]

By bringing the human performer to the fore, these images also demonstrate the advantages to having a human model for a digitally animated character. Although facial capture was too rudimentary at the time to allow for facial

Figure 16.1   The behind-the-scenes featurette 'Bringing Gollum to Life' illustrated the similarities between actor Andy Serkis and the computer-generated character modelled after him in *The Lord of the Rings: The Two Towers*. ©*The Lord of the Rings: The Two Towers*, DVD, directed by Peter Jackson (Los Angeles: New Line Home Entertainment, 2002).

expressions to be truly 'captured' from Serkis's performance, the character model was adapted to better match Serkis's facial proportions and allow for the replication of some of his characteristic expressions.[10] The filmmakers learned that nuanced facial movements, unique to the performer, add a naturalistic variety to a digital character's emotive possibilities.

Shortly after Gollum and Andy Serkis made the public aware of performance capture, the producers of *Pirates of the Caribbean: Dead Man's Chest* discovered first-hand the benefits of modelling a digital character after a human performer when they cast Bill Nighy as the film's villain Davy Jones. In the film, Davy Jones is a fierce pirate captain who, like Gollum, became monstrous over time, merging with various sea fauna to develop a cephalopodic face with a beard of tentacles and a crab claw for a hand, among other changes. While they had planned for Davy Jones to be completely computer-generated, they worried that the digitally animated face would look insufficiently realistic. Bill Nighy, hired to provide vocal performance and motion capture for Jones, wore grey makeup around his eyes and mouth in case the digital eyes and mouth created for the character were inadequately naturalistic and expressive. (Eyes that look 'dead' and mouth movements that do not match the words spoken were common complaints about early CG characters, such as those in *Final Fantasy: The Spirits Within*.) Ultimately, Davy Jones's entire face, including eyes and mouth, was computer-generated, but Nighy still had an important effect on how the face was developed. ILM animation supervisor Hal Hickel explained:

> We started work on Davy Jones quite a while before they cast the part. To be honest, the way I imagined the character was initially a bit limited. I saw him as a terrific, mean villain, with a lot of gravitas, but I assumed he'd be very stoic and stone-faced. Bill Nighy brought so much to the character – weird humor, tons of odd eccentricities – more, I think, than any of us had imagined. I figured we'd get through the first couple of sequences with him, and by then would have built up a library of facial animation controls to handle most of the scenes that came our way. But Bill was the man of a thousand faces. In every shot he would make some odd facial expression we hadn't seen before, and we'd stop, and think, 'What's he doing *now*?'[11]

Hickel's explanation demonstrates the significance of capturing the human idiosyncrasies that actors bring to a role, particularly in how they move their faces. Whereas Hickel imagined that he would be able to quickly construct a library of Bill Nighy facial movements to draw from in the animation, instead he found that Nighy continued to surprise them with unique expressions and 'odd eccentricities'. This led them to redesign the character's face to incorporate more of Nighy's own facial structure, including his prominent cheekbones and

Figure 16.2   The face of the cephalopodic villain Davy Jones in *Pirates of the Caribbean: Dead Man's Chest* (Gore Verbinksi, 2006) was completely computer generated.

distinct upper lip. In the end, Davy Jones is recognisable as Nighy, even though Jones's face ends in fleshy, moving tentacles and he has no nose (Figure 16.2).

In the first decade of the twenty-first century, performance capture received public attention, with actors like Andy Serkis and directors like James Cameron (*Avatar*) and Peter Jackson (*The Lord of the Rings, King Kong*) making claims in the press about the superiority of this new visual effects process. However, these actors and filmmakers were reluctant to admit publicly that, despite the remarkable visual similarities between performers like Nighy and Serkis and the digital characters based on them, those shared facial expressions were more likely to be simulated after the fact than actually captured during a performance. In the early 2000s, a less publicised development in facial animation made as much – or more – of an impact on the creation of digital faces during this time. Instead of relying on facial capture from Andy Serkis, the *Lord of the Rings* effects team spent two years developing a new facial animation system for Gollum based on sculpted expressions that could then be modified using sixty-four sliders. The controls modified individual elements that allow for subtle actions like nose wrinkling or a slight eyebrow raise. Bay Raitt, the facial lead animator for Gollum, sculpted 875 combination shapes that were used like keyframes to mark the possible expressions for his face. These expressions were combinations of 10,000 different muscle shapes.[12] This system went on to be called 'blend-shape' animation, and it has been incredibly influential on how faces are designed. While working with individual actors taught filmmakers the value of having actors' performances serve as the basis for digital characters – particularly in their unique facial expressions – these projects ultimately spent more time and effort on developing blend-shape and other animation tools. Instead of directly capturing the little nuances of facial performance like Bill Nighy's 'odd eccentricities' with performance capture, these films actually ended up simulating these details with animation software programs. Performance capture gained the public's attention, but blend-shape animation more deeply impacted production pipelines for the future.

CAPTURING THE ACTOR'S 'ESSENCE' IN DIGITAL DE-AGEING

After nearly a decade in which performance capture and blend-shape animation served as competing visions for how to create a digital face, some filmmakers sought a more direct pathway between a performer's facial expressions and those appearing on a digital character. This desire became more pronounced as a number of films were produced that called for digital humans, not just digital characters. In projects like *The Curious Case of Benjamin Button* (David Fincher, 2008), *Rogue One: A Star Wars Story* (Gareth Edwards, 2016) and *The Irishman* (Martin Scorsese, 2019), filmmakers wanted to retain the visuals of an actor's performance as well as the emotional essence thought to be provided by performance capture. Yet, because these films imagined human characters at different ages than the desired actors, they wanted to go beyond conventional recording techniques and use digital tools to alter the appearance of the actors on the screen.

In many of these films, producers have sought explicitly to directly copy an actor's facial performance onto a digital character. These projects have attempted to reduce the amount of animation needed and to devise processes that reduce the friction between the original performance and its 'capture' and application. For example, the production team for *The Irishman* claimed that animation was not used in a single shot of the film. Visual effects supervisor Pablo Helman stated,

> When you start messing around with [animation], it changes the performance a bit – and how much it changes may depend on how much coffee the animator had that morning! So we decided not to go that route. There was a conscious effort to do this without going into animation.[13]

In this instance, the animators (with those potentially jittery hands) were replaced by an automated system named Flux, or Face Lux, that automatically matches the actors' expressions on display in the recorded footage with corresponding expressions built into the digital models (Figure 16.3). To my mind, this still counts as animation (an artificial bringing to life) of the digital model, but through a highly automated system that further removes the process from the agency of animators and visual effects personnel. It certainly does not conform to a true elimination of animation from the process, which would imply a frictionless process in which Martin Scorsese 'captures' the emotions and expressions of his performers on film and then the magical Flux process spits out a younger double instantaneously. While statements like Helman's evidence

Figure 16.3   *The Irishman* (Martin Scorsese, 2019) used new software to produce de-aged versions of its stars, including Robert De Niro.

a desire for the 'capture' side of the binary, visual effects techniques have not managed to truly exclude the 'simulation' side.

The attempt to reduce or eliminate animation altogether aligns with the goal of digitally producing younger versions of the starring actors. Instead of creating wholly imagined human characters (as in *Final Fantasy: The Spirits Within*) or non-human characters (like Gollum or Davy Jones), these films depict recognisable actors at various ages. Earlier films might have achieved this with heavy makeup or prosthetics; they may have even cast different actors to play different parts of a character's life. Instead, these more recent projects try to produce the visual illusion of a single actor playing a character throughout his or her life. The goal is to maintain all of the actor's trademark facial expressions – the squints, half-smiles, smirks and nose crinkles – while altering the outward appearance of the face to remove (or occasionally add) the traces of age. The common term for this in both the press and the industry is 'de-ageing'.

The combination of aged actor and de-aged character has led to some bizarre philosophical musings about the nature of experience and age in the construction of characters. For instance, in relation to *The Irishman*, which featured de-aged (and aged) versions of septuagenarian actors Robert De Niro, Al Pacino and Joe Pesci at ages ranging anywhere from their thirties to their eighties, the digital model supervisor Paul Giacoppo explained,

> We were trying to retain the essence of each actor, basically – their *current* essence, not their previous essence when they were younger ... [Y]ou're seeing a 36-year-old De Niro playing a role, but with all the life and acting

experience of the De Niro who is in his 70s. It is almost a metaphysical thing, and we talked about it all the time.[14]

Similarly, in promotional material for *Gemini Man*, in which Will Smith plays an assassin battling a younger clone of himself (a de-aged and fully computer-generated character), Smith stated, 'I couldn't have played [the younger clone] Junior at twenty-three years old, but now I'm able to understand and capture both characters because of the amount of experience that I've had as an actor.'[15] These productions want to have younger versions of star actors, thus extending their acting range substantially, but also want to be able to draw from the considerable experience and maturity of older actors. The 'essence' that filmmakers want to capture is that of the mature and seasoned actor – but with a youthful appearance. The actors put on their younger selves like digital masks, suggesting that they are even more capable of playing their younger selves now than they were then. De-ageing techniques allow for these strange amalgamations of past and present personas.

Although performance capture allowed for the *Gemini Man* team to recreate Will Smith's bodily movements, the crux of the computer-generated character, a younger version of Smith, was found in the facial performance (Figures 16.4 and 16.5). The producers went to great lengths to record Smith's skin texture, pore structure and facial proportions. The key to getting a realistic version of him, though, lay in the movement, or animation, of the face. Visual effects supervisor Guy Williams explained:

> At the beginning of this, I thought the hardest thing would be to make a compelling digital human being; but we got there pretty readily. The greater challenge involved performance. The animation is where this lived or died. If any shape in the animation was off, if any transition of shapes was even slightly off, the entire thing fell apart. He only had to look to his right one pixel off or smirk one pixel off, and it stopped being Will Smith. It looked fantastic and it totally looked like a human being – but it looked like Will Smith's cousin, not Will Smith.[16]

As we saw in the case of Bill Nighy playing Davy Jones, it was the nuances of the facial expressions that made the computer-generated version of a young Will Smith believable – in this case, not only as a human being, but also as a specific personality that we have come to know well over a career of more than three decades. In this instance, while the filmmakers sought to 'capture' specific facial expressions from Will Smith, they acknowledged that the recreation of those fine movements had to be created or modified by animation. This is a far cry from the 'no animation' claims of the producers of *The Irishman*. Nevertheless, both projects used advanced digital tools to try to produce accurate 'copies' of actors' faces and those faces' trademark expressions and quirks.

Figures 16.4 and 16.5   *Gemini Man* (Ang Lee, 2019) utilised performance capture to construct a fully computer-generated de-aged version of Will Smith. ©Paramount Pictures, *Gemini Man – Behind-the-Scenes Featurette (2019)*: https://www.youtube.com/watch?v=wcXOigIgGvw.

PROBLEMS WITH THE 'XEROX': LIMIT CASES IN THE PRODUCTION OF DIGITAL FACES

The focus on an individual actor's specific 'eccentricities' can lead to problems when these minute details cannot be captured directly or when the performance-capture process fails to provide enough of those tiny distinctions. In these instances, animation software takes an even broader role to simulate the

Figure 16.6   The performance of a young Carrie Fisher as Princess Leia in *Rogue One: A Star Wars Story* (Gareth Edwards, 2016) was computer-generated and animated.

miniscule idiosyncrasies that eluded the capture process. To take one example, *Rogue One: A Star Wars Story* digitally recreated Carrie Fisher's performance as a young Princess Leia (Figure 16.6). While they originally planned to apply a digital facial model of young Leia to the body double, Ingvild Deila, they ultimately replaced Deila's entire on-set performance with a computer-generated character – except for Deila's hand, a particularly difficult part of the body to recreate. The digital performance was based on keyframe animation, digital scans of the actor, and some motion-capture data – not from Carrie Fisher herself, but from Deila, who was ultimately airbrushed out of the frame, as it were.[17] While the goal of the filmmakers was originally to 'capture' as many elements from Carrie Fisher and Ingvild Deila as possible, they ultimately had to use animation software to simulate nearly the entire performance.

Similarly, *Blade Runner 2049* (Denis Villeneuve, 2017) constructed a digital model of a young Rachael, Harrison Ford's android love interest in the original film who was played by Sean Young. The digital model was meant to be based on combined performances by Young and an age-appropriate body double, Loren Peta. The production went to great lengths to capture Young's performance of Rachael, even though the character's entire screen time in *Blade Runner 2049* is only a few minutes. The production flew Young out to Budapest, where the production was filming, for a 'secret' facial capture session where the production team utilised Dimensional Imaging's 4D videogrammetry rig and various scanning processes to capture her performance of the short scene.[18] On set, Loren Peta was filmed in costume; later they replaced her head with that of the digital model they had created based on Young's youthful appearance and her recent performance capture. However, the filmmakers found that the head replacement did not effectively create the character they were looking for, and ultimately, the visual effects team ended up hand-animating the entire performance – choosing to simulate the actress instead of using the captured material.[19]

In both *Rogue One* and *Blade Runner 2049*, the performance capture and digital scans of the actors were not considered sufficient; the 'essence' of the actor somehow failed to come through. Instead of further capturing the performances of the original actresses – or even their stand-ins – animators took over to try to create the minute details of the original performances through animation software. One wonders whether these women were deemed 'too old' to adequately portray their younger selves – a barrier not faced by the various male actors who have performed as younger versions of themselves, such as the septuagenarian stars of *The Irishman*. Gus Cook has noted that male stars like Andy Serkis and Tom Hanks (in *The Polar Express*) have been able to 'explore performance capture as a liberating, expressive medium, a new frontier for classical acting', while female stars have received more limited performance-capture roles, typically as 'monstrous, hypersexualised bodies', like Zoe Saldana as the Na'vi princess Neytiri in *Avatar* or Angelina Jolie as Grendel's mother in *Beowulf* (Robert Zemeckis, 2007).[20] The performances in *Rogue One* and *Blade Runner 2049* were similarly limited, to the point that the women's performances were effectively erased and replaced with animation.

The difficulty of capturing the unique details of a performance is even starker when films attempt to recreate posthumous performances.[21] David Fincher's experience in 2007 making an Orville Redenbacher commercial with a digitally generated version of the late popcorn mogul defined how he subsequently approached *The Curious Case of Benjamin Button*, a landmark film for digital ageing and de-ageing. As they would with *Benjamin Button*, the production created a digitally animated head of Redenbacher and composited it with the recorded body of an appropriately aged stand-in actor. After the commercial spurred negative reactions – some called it 'Orville Deadenbacher'[22] – Fincher and his team desired an approach that would create a more direct copy of the actor. Fincher explained:

> On the Orville Redenbacher spot, we learned everything *not* to do on *Benjamin Button*. We learned that we needed to minimise the amount of keyframe animation that had to be done, because there are all these weird little behavioral clues that an actor is constantly using in his performance, and those things are like a behavioral fingerprint. Rather than try to copy that with animation, what I wanted was a process by which you could literally xerox an actor's performance onto a CG character. I wanted something that wouldn't have to rely on the interpretation of an animator.[23]

As had earlier production teams, Fincher learned that 'weird little behavioural clues' are at the heart of a realistic facial performance. And like the producers of *The Irishman*, Fincher sought to eliminate animation in favour of a direct copy, or 'xerox'. In the case of Orville Redenbacher, now deceased, it was very difficult for them to reconstruct those idiosyncrasies using a replacement actor, even one who could do a good impression of the original performer. Subtle and perhaps even imperceptible facial cues signal an individual's identity; a digital character without those little tics cannot be adequately identified as the original actor. Animation was needed to try to simulate those idiosyncrasies after the fact.

For *Rogue One*, the team that recreated a de-aged version of Princess Leia was also tasked with constructing a digital version of Grand Moff Tarkin, played in *Star Wars: Episode IV* (George Lucas, 1977) by the now-deceased Peter Cushing. Like *Benjamin Button* and the Orville Redenbacher spot, *Rogue One* used head replacements to bring the actor back to life as the character he played in the original film of 1977. The producers of *Rogue One* cast an actor, Guy Henry, of about the same build as Cushing. Henry performed on set and provided performance-capture data that drove the animation of a digital head replacement model that was designed to match Cushing in *Episode IV*. They also did facial scans of Henry with Disney Research's new performance-capture software that reconstructs facial movements without using dots or markers. In an appropriate allusion to the female monsters referenced above, this system is named Medusa.

However, the *Rogue One* team ran into trouble when they applied Henry's facial-capture performance to the model of Tarkin. The 'essence' of Tarkin was missing. Animation supervisor Hal Hickel explained:

> Guy Henry seemed a lot like Peter Cushing on set, but the first time we mapped his facial performance onto Tarkin, it suddenly didn't look like Tarkin anymore. That was because of the way Guy was using his mouth, and how he expressed himself. So we had to pursue the spirit of Guy's acting choices, re-interpreting them as Peter Cushing's expressions and phonemes.[24]

Instead of using Henry's facial performance-capture data, the visual effects team used the software program Flux – also used in *The Irishman* – to analyse the extant footage of Peter Cushing himself in *Episode IV* and add Cushing's specific facial movements into their face-shape library for the digital Tarkin head. When performance capture let the filmmakers down, blend-shape animation stepped in to simulate the performance, combining the 'spirit' of the replacement performer with the specific face shapes and 'phonemes' of the deceased actor.

In all of these de-ageing examples, filmmakers made an effort to get past animation to directly and transparently capture a performance, particularly of a face. The desired 'xerox' process would not only convey external appearance, but also transfer the 'weird little behavioural clues' that seem to convey the essence or identity of a performer. However, time and time again, the teams ran up against difficulties in the process, whether it be a lack of data, an inability to 'scan' those expressions directly into a computer or even the lack of a living performer to recreate the performance. Despite the rhetoric surrounding the ability of performance capture to seamlessly convey a performance from human to digital model – Cameron's '100 per cent' claim, for instance – the technology is far more limited in its actual application. While directors say they want to reduce animation and 'xerox' the face automatically, the best way for them to retain the little nuances of a facial performance is often to recreate those facial tics with digital animation.

CONCLUSION

The urge to 'xerox' a human face directly onto a digital character expresses a more extreme form of the desire to 'capture' a human performance and seamlessly transfer it to a virtual body. When filmmakers say they want to retain the 'essence' of a performer, often what they mean is that they want to retain the actor's face and its trademark movements and expressions. In other words, they see the actor's identity as being synonymous with the face, or at the very least, its distinctive facial movements. Hans Belting's concern with what he calls the 'cyberface' is its status as a compendium of data rather than a living, breathing interface with a real consciousness. In these instances of performance-captured digital faces, the data points reference real actors and their unique 'essence', as displayed by their faces. This mitigates against the existential uncertainty that completely imaginary digital creatures might provoke when they do not refer to any actual human, living or dead. Digital faces driven by performance capture therefore serve as masks for actual human beings, not the 'total mask' without human referent that Belting warns against.

These digital masks, though, are constructed in a unique way – combining the methods of 'capture' and 'simulation' into one. The capture model, because it often ignores external appearance, aims for some deeper kernel of a person or performance that comes from within. Because performance capture tracks ephemeral and immaterial elements, it can be aligned with an inside-out model of being. A performance comes from the inside – the interiority of the self – and is transferred into the digital model's exterior, providing the 'ghost' or soul in the 'shell' of the digital body. On the other hand, simulation techniques construct the outward-facing elements of a performance or person – the specific details of a person's skin, facial shapes, and micro-expressions. These technologies can be aligned with an outside-in model in which getting the external details right creates the impression of a corresponding interior. One paradigm finds the emotion on the inside and brings it out, while the other constructs the emotion externally and then it is recognised as an internal experience.

Because we have seen how these two models often work together in the examples above, we should see the digital human as a mixture of both – internal and external cues that work together to create the impression of human life and authentic emotion. This dual movement reminds us that the face functions both as an expression of interiority and as a set of exterior signs mediated through social and cultural meanings. De-ageing technicians seek to retain the external details of a face in order to express an interior 'essence' or performative quality. This gives us an insight into the original performance. At the same time, though, simulated details provide a mask – an impression of Robert De Niro-ness, Orville Redenbacher-ness or Princess Leia-ness that may not be based on an actual performance at all. This raises the possibility of authentic performances being made without actual performances of living people. De-aged performances could be used in future projects, even after the performer has died. In order to be successful – both in the industry and in the press – performance-capture techniques have drawn on both inside-out and outside-in strategies of representation, allowing for the magic that brings digital creatures to life and extends the careers of performers into their old age.

Notes

1. Hans Belting, *Face and Mask: A Double History* (Princeton: Princeton University Press, 2017), 199.
2. Ibid., 240.
3. Ibid., 241.
4. Quoted in Lisa Bode, *Making Believe: Screen Performance and Special Effects in Popular Cinema*, Techniques of the Moving Image (New Brunswick, NJ: Rutgers University Press, 2017), 19.
5. Mihaela Mihailova, 'Collaboration without Representation: Labor Issues in Motion and Performance Capture', *Animation: An Interdisciplinary Journal* 11:1 (2016), 40–58. Available at <https://doi.org/10.1177/1746847715623691> (last accessed 6 October 2021).
6. Ibid., 43–4.
7. See, for instance, the way simulation is discussed in video games studies: Gonzalo Frasca, 'Simulation versus Narrative: Introduction to Ludology', in *The Video Game Theory Reader* (London: Routledge, 2003), 221–36.
8. The distinction I draw between 'capture' and 'simulation' mirrors discussions of indexicality and iconicity in creating the realism effect of cinema. This debate is beyond the scope of this essay, but I argue in an earlier piece relating to Andy Serkis's work in *King Kong* (Peter Jackson, 2005) that motion capture can fruitfully be considered as a form

of 'digital indexicality'. See Tanine Allison, 'More than a Man in a Monkey Suit: Andy Serkis, Motion Capture, and Digital Realism', *Quarterly Review of Film and Video* 28:4 (1 July 2011), 325–41. Available at <https://doi.org/10.1080/10509208.2010.50 0947> (last accessed 6 October 2021).

9. Lisa Purse, *Digital Imaging in Popular Cinema* (Edinburgh: Edinburgh University Press, 2013), 55.

10. Joe Fordham, 'Middle-Earth Strikes Back', *Cinefex* 92 (January 2003), 78.

11. Quoted in Joe Fordham, 'Beneath the Barnacles', *Cinefex* 107 (October 2006), 78.

12. Gregory Singer, 'The Two Towers: Face to Face with Gollum', *ANIMATIONWorld* (blog), 17 March 2003. Available at <https://www.awn.com/animationworld/two-towers-face-face-gollum> (last accessed 6 October 2021).

13. Quoted in Jody Duncan, 'Nothing Short of Witchcraft', *Cinefex* 168 (December 2019), 100.

14. Quoted in Duncan, 'Nothing Short of Witchcraft', 100–3.

15. Paramount Pictures, *Gemini Man Behind-The-Scenes Featurette*, 2019. Available at <https://www.youtube.com/watch?v=wcXOigIgGvw> (last accessed 6 October 2021).

16. Quoted in Jody Duncan, 'Uncanny', *Cinefex* 167 (October 2019), 70.

17. Joe Fordham, 'Sacred Ground', *Cinefex* 151 (February 2017), 78.

18. Joe Fordham, '2049 Foresight', *Cinefex*, 155 (October 2017), 76.

19. Ibid., 77.

20. Gus Cook, '*Beyond: Two Souls*, Performance Capture, and the Negotiatory Nature of Control', *The Velvet Light Trap* 81 (March 2018), 18–28. Available at <https://doi.org/10.7560/VLT8103> (last accessed 6 October 2021).

21. For more on posthumous performance, see Lisa Bode, 'No Longer Themselves? Framing Digitally Enabled Posthumous "Performance"', *Cinema Journal* 49:4 (2010), 46–70.

22. Tom Feran, '"Orville Deadenbacher" Ads Called Cutting Edge, Creepy', *Houston Chronicle*, 14 February 2007, sec. Technology. Available at <https://www.chron.com/business/technology/article/Orville-Deadenbacher-ads-called-cutting-edge-1539207.php> (last accessed 6 October 2021).

23. Quoted in Jody Duncan, 'The Unusual Birth of Benjamin Button', *Cinefex* 116 (January 2009), 75.

24. Quoted in Fordham, 'Sacred Ground', 64.

17. *BECOMING* A WOMAN: THE MANY FACES OF CANDICE BREITZ

Hannah Parlett

To become a woman is a purposive and appropriative set of acts, the acquisition of a skill, a 'project', to use Sartrian terms, to assume a certain corporeal style and significance. (Judith Butler, 'Sex and Gender in Simone de Beauvoir's *Second Sex*')

In 2003, Candice Breitz invited visitors to the KOW gallery in Berlin-Mitte to witness a series of re-enactments. Breitz (born in Johannesburg in 1972) is a Berlin-based artist whose multichannel moving image installations have been shown internationally since 1994. She works within the found footage tradition, restaging and editing objects of popular culture and mass media. This rich archive includes news reels, music videos and crucially, Hollywood films. The new installation, *Becoming*, saw the artist occupy the roles of seven actresses (Cameron Diaz, Julia Roberts, Jennifer Lopez, Meg Ryan, Neve Campbell, Reese Witherspoon and Drew Barrymore). Breitz carefully selects a short sequence from each actress's performance in a popular romantic comedy, a genre reaching the apex of its commercial success in the early 2000s. Each excerpt chosen by Breitz is a moment shot in close-up, placing the Hollywood star's face centre stage. Extracting and isolating each scene from the rest of the film's diegesis, this 'cut and paste' of sorts strips the moment of its original narrative sense. In each work, 'two televisions are set back-to-back inside a wooden structure: the first monitor displays the "original" footage (for example, Julia Roberts excerpted from *Pretty Woman*), while the second monitor plays back Breitz's re-performance.'[1]

Paying meticulous attention to the micro-movements of facial muscles in these Hollywood scenes, the artist labours to reproduce the same gestural expression as the actress. Taking note from Cameron Diaz in *The Sweetest Thing* (2002), she purses her lips. Following Jenifer Lopez in *Angel Eyes* (2001), Breitz squints her eyes, and so on. The film's original soundtrack accompanies Breitz's copy as the voice of each actress comes to ventriloquise the artist's own body, which is screened here in black and white against the lush, vibrant tones of the 'rom-com' clips. Played on loop in the white cube, both sets of performances are trapped in a potentially endless recirculation of the affect they stage.

In her close interrogation of corporeal performance in *Becoming*, Breitz provokes a reflection on the role of the human face on screen and its complex encounter with the film spectator. More particularly, Breitz's work proffers a critique of predominantly white femininity, with the exception of Jennifer Lopez, and the way it is inscribed by the mechanics of Hollywood cinema.[2] Her work poses questions about how viewers respond to facial gesture as a vehicle of emotion, affect and subjectivity and the pedagogical function the face on screen might play. Her practice thus contributes to critical discourses on faciality and expression within the cinema, a theoretical concern as old as the moving image itself.

The following essay places Breitz in dialogue with the work of the early film theorist, Béla Balázs. Born in Hungary in 1884, Balázs was a film critic and scriptwriter who would go on to produce, as Noël Carrol writes, 'one of the

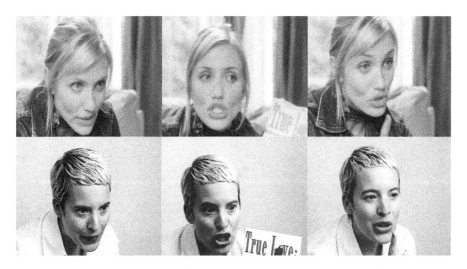

Figure 17.1 *Becoming Cameron* (Candice Breitz, 2003). Consisting of 7 dual-channel video installations: front view. Courtesy: KOW, Berlin.

earliest systematic attempts' at film theory.[3] An acquaintance of Max Weber, Walter Benjamin and Sergei Eisenstein, Balázs led 'the sort of life about which contemporary intellectuals might fantasize'.[4] For Gertrude Koch, he was 'like Siegfried Kracauer, a rather typical representative of the European intelligentsia of the first third of this century – an allround educated personality without steady income'.[5] In his first treatise *Visible Man* (1924) and later in *The Spirit of Film* (1930), Balázs argued that the advent of cinema would liberate bodily expressiveness and restore the audience's sensitivity to it, which had been obfuscated and abstracted by the dominance of print. The face, as exhibited by the burgeoning art of the cinematic close-up, is central to Balázs's film philosophy, which, as Koch has illustrated, relied upon a model of 'anthropomorphic poetics. Crucial to Balázs's thought is the notion that film gives visual shape to a physiognomic quality in human beings, in animate and inanimate nature, and that film is the first medium in history capable of expressing this quality.'[6] He proposed that cinema's visual economy will 'retrain viewers in learning to look closely at the expressiveness of faces and bodily gestures, thus extending our perceptual resources'.[7]

Though their contributions to the study of film are separated by almost a century, Breitz and Balázs are nonetheless united in the central place they assign to the role of corporeal expression in their respective accounts of the moving image. The following essay starts by putting *Becoming* in conversation with this early film critic as a way of tracing the evolution and shifting meaning of facial gesture on screen, from the era of Charlie Chaplin and Asta Nielsen,

Figure 17.2 *Becoming Jennifer* (Candice Breitz, 2003). Consisting of 7 dual-channel video installations: back view. Courtesy: KOW, Berlin.

through to Meg Ryan and Neve Campbell. Across such a historical trajectory, Breitz's practice implies, cinematic facial performance abandons its function as a deferent and authentic window into human interiority and consciousnesses and has instead morphed into an affective model controlled by the mechanics of an image-saturated mass culture. The essay will pay particular attention to the suggestion posited by Breitz's work that there is something particularly imitative about the constitution of the female subject in late capitalism, in so far as it depends upon a citable bank of feminine tropes as expressed through facial gesture. Operating in the service of a patriarchal hegemony, this set of gestures denote and prescribe the normative corporeal expression of 'feminine' emotion and in so doing, invites spectators to efface their own subjectivities and give themselves up to the face on screen. Turning to contemporary queer-feminist theory (especially the work of Lauren Berlant and Jackie Stacey), the essay will meditate on the affective exhaustion of the face on screen as staged by Breitz.

Balázs to Breitz: Cinema's First and Second Century

The questions posed by early film philosophy remain pertinent to contemporary reflections on the image. In her study of the face on film, Noa Steimatsky argues that these questions, which initially emerged in 1920s Europe,

> have not expired, as some moments of academic film studies seemed to imagine; they persist and beg for reconsideration in light of new technologies and shifting media practices, and in view of historical situations that have thrown that earlier cinematic modernity itself into crisis.[8]

Returning to this theoretical history enriches our reading of Breitz's critical engagement with on-screen affect in the post-millennial gallery.

As one of the first critics to reflect on the potential of the new medium, Béla Balázs was tasked with demonstrating film's status as a unique art form, ontologically different from both literature and theatre. As Carroll writes, Balázs's theory had to respond to objections from contemporary sceptics who denied that film (and photography) could be art 'on the grounds that they merely reproduced or recorded reality'.[9] He countered such a claim by locating the medium specificity of film in its expressive quality, demonstrated most aptly by the face shot in close-up. The birth of cinema was a welcome antidote to the conceptual and linguistic nature of print culture which, for Balázs, had alienated the human subject. In *Visible Man* (1924), he comments on the utopian possibilities of this invention with great enthusiasm:

> In a culture dominated by words, however, now that the soul has become audible, it has grown almost invisible. This is what the printing press

has done. Well, the situation now is that once again our culture is being given a radically new direction – this time by film. Every evening many millions of people sit and experience human destinies, characters, feelings and moods of every kind with their eyes, and without the need for words. For the intertitles that films still have are insignificant; they are partly the special meaning that does not set out to assist the visual expression. The whole of mankind is now busy relearning the long-forgotten language of gestures and facial expressions. This language is not the substitute for words characteristic of the sign language of the deaf and dumb, but the visual corollary of human souls immediately made flesh. Man will become visible once again.[10]

Balázs employs the vocabulary of 'legibility' to suggest that cinematic gesture is like a syntax to be rehearsed and practised, and significantly, the face on screen is to be read, decoded or interpreted. Here, subjective interiority is accessible to the human eye via corporeal exteriorisation. According to this logic, the individual self and the 'soul' will become intelligible to the recently emancipated viewer as she gains fluency in this newly restored visual landscape. The camera thus acquires a pedagogical role in this passage, immersing and equipping the cinematic spectator with a new set of emotive abilities. Koch has illustrated how Balázs's meditations on film were inspired by contemporary Expressionist traditions and the heritage of German Romanticism, including most notably the work of his teacher Georg Simmel. For example, Simmel's essay on the sculptures of Auguste Rodin shares similar reflections on '(e)motion, the dominance of facial expression, nature as *état d'âme*, as physiognomic landscape'.[11] Balázs extended this expressionist impulse to the film screen, maintaining this notion that 'the psychic and the visual intersect, paradigmatically, in the arena of the face'.[12] In case of any doubt from sceptics, he revealed that the camera's ability to communicate with a subject purely through the optics of physical expression, and without recourse to narrative or language, gave cinema its own unique, radical and potentially revolutionary specificity. He wrote with genuine optimism about the progressive opportunities this new artform could offer, providing a global and universal means of address.

In *Visible Man*, Balázs narrated an important historical shift in the culture of European industrial modernity. The arrival of film at the turn of twentieth century ushered in the transition from print to the cinema as the dominant technology of mass communication. In Balázs's neat teleology, the birth of one artistic medium coincided with the death of its predecessor. The work of Candice Breitz appears during a similar moment of technological flux, as cinema's dominance gives way to a new media landscape some critics have described as 'post-cinematic'.[13] This era bears witness to new modes of cinematic production and distribution as the classical institution is threatened with obsolescence. In fact, Breitz's appropriative and reflexive methodology, rupturing the ideological, spatial and temporal mechanisms of conventional narrative film, is an index to this historical juncture. The sacred space of the movie theatre from Balázs's era is refused by Breitz's practice as she dismembers the Hollywood text and screens its fragments in the gallery.[14] She belongs to an important tradition explored by Erika Balsom in her major study of the explosion of the moving image in contemporary art which, she writes, coincides with cinema's growing self-consciousness about its own decline: 'Cinema becomes a preoccupation of contemporary art precisely at a time when it is perceived to be in crisis due to the increasingly consolidated hegemony of new, electronic media.'[15] If Balázs's film theory serenaded the birth of cinema, might we say that Breitz's practice constitutes an elegy?

For Balsom, the contemporary art installation 'is a primary site at which notions of cinema have been renegotiated and redefined in recent decades'.[16] Video artists such as Breitz 'exhibit cinema' not only in their literal display of film texts in gallery spaces but crucially, in the sense in which they hold cinema out to view and subject it to scrutiny: 'They offer numerous answers to the question of what cinema might be and, in so doing, may be understood as engaging in film theory through practice.' Following Balsom's seminal thesis, I argue that Breitz is responding to questions about cinema originally posed by early film philosophy, as in the work of Balázs. Both film theorists, one working in cinema's first century and the other in its second, locate the medium's crucial intervention (for better or worse) in the realm of emotional expression, gesture and corporeal performance. Balázs and Breitz both reflect on what cinema might be by asking what the face on screen might do.

JACKIE, NOT MARILYN: 'BECOMING' A WOMAN AS GENRE

Through subversive strategies of recycling and bricolage, Breitz's video installations dismantle typical modes of cultural consumption in order to uncover the latent messages lodged within familiar objects of mass culture. Prior to *Becoming*, Breitz employed this disruptive praxis in the *Babel Series* (1999), which cuts and slices snippets from popular songs. Extracting soundbites such as 'Ma' (appropriated from Queen's 'Bohemian Rhapsody') and 'Da' (Madonna's 'Papa Don't Preach'), the installation estranges lyrical fragments from their host melody and generates a cacophony of noises which resemble an infant's first experimentation with language, typically beginning with an address to 'Ma' or 'Da'. Reflecting on this pre-linguistic and pre-verbal stage of character development, Breitz's skilful manipulation of popular soundtrack proposes that the formation of the post-modern subject occurs in an environment saturated with instructions from pop idols. The installation also intimates that we come to foster a child-like dependence on these figures. In *Becoming*, Breitz will transfer her interest from these sonic cues to the visual and gestural training offered by Hollywood performers. By robbing audiences of the rhythmic pleasures of melody and lyrical coherence, the artist suspends the visitor to *Babel Series* in unfamiliar territory. The mass object becomes untethered from its usual associations with enjoyment, participation and legibility.

Becoming launches a similar attack on spectatorial comfort. Breitz selects close-ups from scenes where the lead female protagonist is engaged in the corporeal art of seduction as she tries to secure heterosexual romance. The installation exposes the most damning moments of the romantic comedy text and problematises each film's ability to provide leisurely immersion and catharsis. In the clip taken from *Pretty Woman* (entitled *Becoming Julia*), Roberts's Vivian playfully leans backwards over a hotel balcony: 'It's making you nervous? What if I just lean back a little bit like this? Would you – would you rescue me, if I fell? It's really high. Look – no hands, no hands.' As Sonja Longolius writes, Breitz isolates this short scene as a way of unveiling the broader ideological impulse of *Pretty Woman*: '"Would you rescue me" is, of course, the crucial question that condenses the whole storyline of the romance movie. Will the wealthy yet lonely corporate raider Edward rescue the fun-loving prostitute Vivian from her precarious environment?'[17] The thirty-nine-second clip 'further distils Vivian's role to that of a bold yet totally dependent woman whose only hope, through seduction, is to be rescued by a man'.[18] Breitz alienates these incriminating moments from the longer narratives which might conventionally grant them contextual legitimacy, or at least allow them to unfold quietly and

Figure 17.3 'Would you rescue me if I fell?' from *Becoming Julia* (Candice Breitz, 2003). Duration: 39 seconds, 3 frames. Courtesy: KOW, Berlin.

insidiously back into the text. In Garry Marshall's original edit, Julia Roberts's dialogue is addressed directly to Richard Gere's off-screen character who we see respond in a reverse shot. Breitz, however, does away with this continuity and leaves Roberts alone on loop in a silent void, asking if someone will rescue her. These revised fragments uncover the genre's characteristic structural form, where the entire physical, social and psychic life of the female subject is organised around her relation to the male love interest.

In divesting these Hollywood clips of their potential for pleasurable absorption, *Becoming* responds to a call-to-arms issued almost thirty years earlier by the feminist film critic Laura Mulvey. Inspired by Freudian and Lacanian psychoanalysis, 'Visual Pleasure and Narrative Cinema' described the voyeuristic and anonymous scopophilia promised by the spectacle of femininity on screen. Mulvey argued that the only remedy to this situation was the destruction of visual pleasure as a radical weapon and a fundamental shift from filmic absorption to critical distance. In the final lines of the famous essay, she writes:

> The first blow against the monolithic accumulation of traditional film convention (already undertaken by radical filmmakers) is to free the look of the camera into its materiality in time and space and the look of the audience into dialectics, passionate detachment. There is no doubt that this destroys the satisfaction, pleasure and privilege of the 'invisible guest'.[19]

Mulvey pursued the creation of a new radical film language and a feminist counter-cinema, which sought to alert her audience 'to the status of the camera as object and as instrument, rather than transparent aid to voyeurism'.[20] *Becoming* extends this avant-garde tradition and pushes it to new heights in the contemporary gallery space as these submerged contents rise to the surface. The installation refuses absorption and makes the spectator forcefully conscious of her own status as viewer, Breitz's status as editor and Hollywood's status as a seductive but phallocentric image regime.

In *Star Gazing*, the feminist film theorist Jackie Stacey asks: 'If the images of women we see on screen are produced for the "male gaze", how do female spectators relate to such expectations?'[21] Stacey alludes to just one of the numerous points of contention embedded in Mulvey's influential thesis, which has suitably invited criticism from scholars (not least bell hooks) who highlight the essay's exclusionary failure to account for non-white, queer and trans subjectivities.[22] Breitz's 2003 exhibition proffers one possible response to Stacey's question. As the title of the installation and the artist's meticulous copycat labour suggests, Breitz's reply is unequivocal: female spectators attempt to *become* these on-screen figures. It is possible for Breitz to 'become' Julia or Cameron, because normative femininity emerges as an intelligible corporeal style and generic category, replete with a bank of affective conventions and gestures to be mimicked and reinscribed on the spectator's body. These mimetic endeavours are actively endorsed and encouraged by Hollywood's 'dream factory' and they map onto the broader development of the gendered subject in everyday social life. The modest television sets used to play each set of clips seem to recall the intimate and domestic environment of childhood or adolescence, as if to suggest that these tropes stage a home invasion and flood the private interior lives of female subjects. The installation's spatial arrangement thus anticipates our increased access and proximity to celebrity faces via new technologies and networks of communication. The title of the exhibition also references the MTV reality television show of the early 2000s where participants were given the chance to re-enact one of their idol's music videos and 'become' Britney Spears, for example, through makeover and intense choreography.

Breitz shows that to 'become' a woman in the contemporary post-modern visual landscape is to accumulate and enact a pre-packaged set of gestures that these seven Hollywood actresses have made quotable. Breitz's edits, however, are not identical reflections of the original performances. She strips each clip of its vibrant colour, disrobes the body of the feminine attire worn by each actress (replacing it with stark androgynous garments) and relieves the face of cosmetic modifications. This aesthetic blankness performs a kind of flattening, emptying out each scene of its expressive texture. The mechanical reproduction of each gesture, to borrow from Walter Benjamin's famous description of the camera's technological operations, dooms each expression to a potentially eternal fate of automatic reiteration and renewal.[23] Breitz exhausts the cinematic body of authentic affect and each corporeal display takes on a robotic impulse. The face on screen is drained of its expressive properties, no longer the corporeal organ by which human souls are 'immediately made flesh' as Balázs noted with such enthusiasm. In dialogical opposition to Balázs's impassioned 'anthropomorphism', the face in Breitz's practice is situated at the very outer limits of the human. As the figure carefully moulds the flesh of the face to match each Hollywood display, we might wonder if Breitz's uncanny double is a clone, an alien or even a machine trying to 'become' a human female by learning the generic codes of normative femininity as modelled so conspicuously by these stars.

This reading of 'flattened affect' and 'heterosexual femininity *as* genre' draws on the ground-breaking work of queer theorist Lauren Berlant and its subsequent application to cinematic performance by Stacey. Both critics are concerned with 'how we might theorize the changing significance of those affects traditionally assigned to femininity within the emergence of an intimate public sphere'.[24] In *The Female Complaint*, Berlant tracks the origins of 'women's culture' in the

US, which coincides with the proliferation of cultural commodities marketed towards female subjects. These objects work to generate a sense of commonality among women through shared consumption and engagement with 'sentimentality'. Though they chronicle the beginning of this affective sphere almost two centuries before the commercial success of the rom-com genre, Berlant's description of this intimate public feels remarkably apt for interrogating the fantasies and psychic tenets of the films in Breitz's installation:

> Everyone knows what the female complaint is: women live for love, and love is the gift that keeps on taking . . . From the nineteenth century on, we witness in women's culture's stories the many kinds of bargaining women do to stay in proximity to the work of love at the heart of normative femininity, the utopian and pathetic impulses behind this bargaining, and its costs and pleasures, including the tragicomic pleasures of the love plot's incompleteness up to and often beyond death.[25]

The characters featured in *Becoming* engage in these labours of love, pondering the intricacies and complexities of heterosexual romance. For Berlant, this shared affliction of surviving love and its various painful disappointments fosters an imagined connection to other female subjects, an illuminating insight which might help make sense of the familiar attempt to market new cinematic releases around gender, from the mid-century melodrama to the millennial 'chick flick' of Breitz's era. Femininity thus emerges *as* genre, accompanied by temporal and historical fluctuations. Berlant writes:

> To call an identity like a sexual identity a genre is to think about it as something repeated, detailed, and stretched while retaining its intelligibility, its capacity to remain readable or audible across the field of all its variations. For femininity to be a genre like an aesthetic one means that it is a structure of conventional expectation that people rely on to provide certain kinds of affective intensities and assurances.[26]

For Breitz, the romantic comedy film contributes to this predictable construction of sentimental femininity as legible 'genre' to be read and reprinted. Returning to Balázs's early formulation, 'the long-forgotten language of gestures and facial expressions' is mobilised here as a vehicle of mimicry and effacement. Rather than facilitating the historical recuperation of singularity and inner subjectivity, this recovered language of facial expression (and its traversal into 'genre') enacts another form of synchronisation and abstraction.

Stacey draws on Berlant's theory of 'flat affect' to illustrate how the performances of British actress Tilda Swinton work in dialogue with Hollywood genres of feminine affect. Swinton's modes of 'underperformance' contradict 'the conventional expectations of feminine emotional expressiveness and legibility in popular cinema' and reverse the generic expectations imposed on cinematic femininity as a site of intense affect, depth and romantic intensity. Stacey anchors her argument in an analysis of Swinton's appearance as three artificial clones and their inventor in Lynn Hershman Leeson's *Teknolust* (2002), released a year before Breitz's installation in Berlin. One of the clones, Ruby, is tasked with sperm retrieval and therefore must learn the art of heterosexual seduction as a means of securing her own biological reproduction. To do this, Ruby takes instruction from 1950s starlets, including Elizabeth Taylor and Kim Novak, and mechanically delivers de-contextualised one-liners from famous noirs in an attempt to seduce, just as Breitz will re-enact the gestural expressions of 1990s sweethearts, such as Meg Ryan and Neve Campbell. The director plots the inscription of these codes on the artificial clone subject by screening stills of these classical Hollywood texts (such as *The Man with the Golden Arm*, 1955) on Ruby's body as she sleeps. Stacey writes: 'The artifice of femininity (of having to make it up or copy an idea of it) becomes a technical accomplishment in the bodily absorption of the props of seductive masquerade.' As with Breitz's mimetic efforts,

> mimicry becomes a form of emptying out of emotional depth as inauthenticity circulates across different templates and generates new copies of itself . . . In contrast to her Hollywood predecessors, Swinton is the conductor of affect, not its originator or its essential embodiment.[27]

Figure 17.4 'Becoming Legally Blonde' from *Becoming Reese* (Candice Breitz, 2003). Duration: 39 seconds, 3 frames. Courtesy: KOW, Berlin.

In *Becoming*, Breitz's double similarly disposes of any relation to organic or authentic human affect. The facial expressions she imitates are severed from their interior origin and land on her face through artificial transference. Reese Witherspoon's melancholic sobs are drained of their lived context (Elle Woods's boyfriend breaking up with her) and reappear on Breitz's body without anchor. These 'feminine' affects are thus exposed as historically contingent generic codes with the potential to be appropriated by the filmic spectator. As Berlant and Stacey warn, these conventions come to infiltrate the interior worlds of consumers and provide the affective language we rely on to make sense of everyday sociality and relationality. By challenging the Hollywood star face's claim to emotional transparency, Breitz simultaneously reasserts the opacity of flesh and the unintelligibility of the face on screen. The performer rebuffs the desire to know what is going on behind the eyes and 'under the skin' as her corporeal display of romantic intensity is revealed as sheer artifice.

The installation solicits a value judgement on the success of these re-enactments, as spectators (consciously or not) are compelled to compare Breitz's copy against the original clip. *Becoming* publicly suspends this immaterial labour between the twin poles of success versus failure, recalling the screen test and the unstable promise of landing a 'role'. Femininity's status as a slippery performative mode to be learnt and perfected, with varying degrees of success, is also legible in the diegetic universes of the romantic comedies Breitz references. In *Pretty Woman*, Julia Roberts famously strolls down Beverly Hills' Rodeo Drive in search of the expensive and refined wardrobe necessary to inhabit the genteel femininity required by her male love interest. Borrowing heavily from generic tropes of feminine respectability (originating in texts such as George Bernard Shaw's *Pygmalion*), other scenes in the film see Vivian tutored in proper etiquette and behaviour. Her legitimacy as an appropriate romantic partner is in a continual state of reiteration and renewal, a metamorphosis maintained in service to Edward. In the clip extracted by Breitz from 2001's *Legally Blonde*, Reese Witherspoon's beaming expression mutates into tears of disbelief: 'You're breaking up with me?' Although the success-driven plot of *Legally Blonde*, which sees Elle Woods go to Harvard Law School, is available to a feminist reading, Breitz excavates this early scene to remind us that the character's journey is motivated around the male love interest, after he tells Elle he needs to marry 'a Jackie, not a Marilyn' if he is to become a senator. Elle must learn to embody an alternative 'genre' of femininity and traverse the imagined boundaries separating the hypersexualised, coquettish blonde and the polite, preppy brunette. The female subject's cultivation of academic knowledge is pursued as a route to 'becoming Jackie' and leaving behind Marilyn.

The cultural legacy of these two women, rumoured to have been in a battle for John Kennedy's affections, have become commodified and ossified into static categories of feminine style and affect: 'Are you a Jackie or Marilyn?' In an episode of *Mad Men*, advertising executive Don Draper taps into the selling power of this tight dichotomy, which encapsulates the era's appropriation of 'Jackie' and 'Marilyn' as emblems that could be recycled and quite literally sold: 'Jacqueline Kennedy. Marilyn Monroe . . . Because we want both, they (women) want to be both.'[28] In the scene from *Legally Blonde* that *Becoming* revisits, Elle is reminded of the imperative to cite this historical bank of feminine types if she is to succeed in overcoming the 'female complaint'. Breitz restages Witherspoon's romantic melancholy and proffers an extra-diegetic interrogation of Hollywood femininity as genre.

FACTORY GIRL

Breitz's inclination towards various modes of repeating, recycling and copying might be attributable to her interest in the work of pop artist Andy Warhol, the subject of her doctoral dissertation at Columbia University. Like Warhol before her, Breitz is interested in laying bare the mechanics of mass (re)production and the affective implications of mass consumption on the subject. Jonathan Flatley has recently written of the former's libidinal desire to 'like' everything. For Flatley's Warhol, this word holds a dual resonance, referring both to positive affective attachments to objects (from Coke and Campbells soup to celebrities) and his corpus's aesthetic orientation towards similarity, repetition and imitation. For Warhol, this 'likeness' is an inevitable consequence of our existence in a mass-mediated society and an extricable feature of our emotional and psychic lives: 'We are, each of us, going back to the Marilyn or Elvis or James Dean model.'[29] One should note how the institution of cinema and the iconicity of its stars is central to these patterns of mimesis. Flatley continues:

> What makes us all 'look and act alike', then, is a shared relation to and reliance on consumption . . . which banks on and repeats the same basic (melancholic) structure of human relationality, ever and again offering the promise of being like the object you did not get and cannot be.[30]

In Breitz's work, Meg Ryan and Julia Roberts have succeeded James Dean and Marilyn Monroe as the ideal models and faces consumers can refer to and as such, she illustrates the mimicry that will inevitably follow suit.

Breitz's copies exhaust and flatten the affective life of the face of both performer and spectator. This process of emptying the human face of its singularity is legible in Warhol's praxis, most notably in the various silkscreens and films he is known for. He was instrumental in the aforementioned commodification of 'Jackie' and 'Marilyn' as consumable feminine objects through abstraction. He appropriated and mechanically reproduced existing photographs of both women, flattening the original portrait into a vivid cartoonish print. Josh Cohen has argued that this aesthetic penchant for vacancy and indifference was

Warhol's defensive response to the trauma of both corporeal and psychic pain, an affect that was all too human and too real. In an interview with *Art News* in 1963, Warhol stated, 'I think everyone should be a machine'.[31] Taking refuge in the fantasy of a neutral body, Cohen writes that the artist 'was forever seeking to cultivate his own machinic neutrality only to find himself wrenched out of it by the alien eruption of desire . . . Warhol was taking vengeance on the very fact of feeling'.[32] Breitz is similarly interested in the potentialities of technology and the non-human as a means of wearing out the respective pains and pleasures of human affective life. In *Becoming*, human affect faces the same fate as Warhol's mass-produced soup cans. Vulnerable to surveillance and capture by the mechanics of the non-human camera, these corporeal performances lose their specificity in space and time.

Becoming belongs to an important genealogy of feminist cinematic practice which critically challenges and contradicts 'the centrality of feminine emotional legibility to the place of the woman in the history of cinema'.[33] Most obviously, Breitz's project recalls the work of feminist visual artists such as Cindy Sherman, whose 1977 *Untitled Film Stills* series reflect on popular fictionalised femininity and questions the authenticity of the self against the backdrop of 'superficial guises' and 'cultural cliches'.[34] (The inclusion of *Becoming* in 'The Cindy Sherman Effect', a 2020 exhibition charting the influence of Sherman's *oeuvre* upon contemporary artists, attests to this lineage.) However, Breitz's work also speaks to a number of recent narrative feature films, such as Lynn Hershman Leeson's *Teknolust* and more recently, Jonathan Glazer's *Under the Skin* (2013), that meditate on affect and stylised femininity through the experiences of a non-human figure. In the latter, set in contemporary Glasgow, an alien acquires the epidermal shell of a human woman and is tasked with harvesting the meat of human male bodies. She learns the codes of heterosexual flirtation and Glazer draws our attention to the artifice of the endeavour. Her non-human status separates her from the affective worlds of the human universe she comes to inhabit, and the flat performance of Scarlett Johansson as the alien generates meta-textual dialogue with the generic codes of Hollywood femininity as genre. As Ara Oserweil writes, in documenting the alien's journey to perform as or perhaps even 'become' a human woman, the film flags up conventional affective femininity's exposure to violence and manipulation: 'When she begins to relinquish her emotional detachment and empathize with others, she renders herself vulnerable to the injuries of the world.'[35] Entitled 'The Perils of Becoming Female', her review suggests that the film issues the following warning: 'If you are sexed female, beware of becoming human.'[36] In these three works, each performer must absorb generic feminine affects to master the art of seduction, indexing the expansive labour required to satisfy patriarchal desire in contemporary neoliberal universes. On *Becoming*, Artforum critic Jennifer Allen writes: 'Breitz' copies, seen together, present the female body as a vast archive that holds but one message. Get the guy.'[37]

Following Warhol, Breitz intimates that there might be a kind of unexpected pleasure or relief in draining the body and face of genuine human affect. At the very least, this vacancy might alleviate the multiple pressures heaped on the female subject to be decoded. She stitches together a new extra-diegetic universe from the scraps of the romantic comedy genre, a meta-textual orbit which puts Hollywood's latent instructions centre stage. If, as Simone De Beauvoir famously stated, 'one is not born but rather becomes a woman', Breitz lays bare the mechanics and equipment required for such a project. The artist's assembly line is composed of facial expressions, gestures and affects, the various 'parts' essential to the satisfactory production of what Judith Butler describes (reflecting on de Beauvoir) as a 'certain corporeal style and significance' necessary to enact this process of becoming woman.[38] To the extent that *Becoming* serves to queer Hollywood femininity, it is through dissection and reproduction, as if Breitz were offering a form of facial drag, where the main punchline is the predictability of gendered tropes and their machinic repetitions. This 'factory' of sorts negates the romanticism and humanism of earlier theorisations of the face on screen as a site of stable identification, recognition and emotional expression. Undergoing continuous modification and refashioning, the face re-emerges under Breitz's eye in a state of transformation that matches the temporality of the cinematic as an animated mode of representation.[39] If Balázs celebrated the restoration of the 'visible man' through gestures, Breitz instead suggests that both the gendered subject and face on screen are in constant states of flux and imitation. Unsettling any claim to possession or essence, her installation compels us to remain attentive to the face on screen as it is enmeshed in its very own process of 'becoming'.

Notes

1. 'Becoming, 2003', KOW Gallery Berlin. Available at <https://kow-berlin.com/artists/candice-breitz/becoming-2003> (last accessed 20 February 2021).
2. Breitz's later work *Love Story* (2017) enacts a more critical and explicit interrogation of whiteness in the contemporary attention economy. Breitz comments on the way the spectatorship demanded by Alec Baldwin and Julianne Moore's performance of a generic sentimentality subjugates the real-life stories of refugees in the contemporary migrant crisis in Europe.
3. Noel Carroll, 'Béla Balázs: The Face of Cinema', *October* 148 (2014), 53–62.
4. Ibid., 62.
5. Gertrud Koch, 'Béla Balázs: The Physiognomy of Things', trans. Miriam Hansen, *New German Critique* 40 (1987), 167.
6. Ibid., 168.
7. Carroll, 'Béla Balázs: The Face of Cinema', 56.

8. Noa Steimatsky, *The Face on Film* (New York: Oxford University Press, 2017), 22.

9. Carroll, 'Béla Balázs: The Face of Cinema', 56.

10. Béla Balázs, 'Visible Man', in *Early Film Theory: Visible Man and The Spirit of Film*, trans. Rodney Livingstone, ed. Erica Carter (New York: Berghahn Books, 2010), 10.

11. Koch, 'Béla Balázs: The Physiognomy of Things', 170.

12. Steimatsky, *The Face on Film*, 29.

13. Steven Shaviro, *Post Cinematic Affect* (Winchester: Zero Books, 2010).

14. Although *Becoming* does not engage explicitly with online culture, this 2003 work nonetheless anticipates the dismemberment and remixing that is today *de rigueur* in contemporary online meme culture, and on time-based media platforms such as Tik Tok, where videos are often comprised of nothing more than snapshots of affect and gesture that are borrowed from film, television and pop culture more generally.

15. Erika Balsom, *Exhibiting Cinema in Contemporary Art* (Amsterdam: Amsterdam University Press, 2013), 11.

16. Balsom, *Exhibiting Cinema*, 13.

17. Sonja Longolius, *Performing Authorship: Strategies of 'Becoming an Author' in the Works of Paul Auster, Candice Breitz, Sophie Calle, and Jonathan Safran Foer* (Bielefeld: transcript-Verlag, 2016), 31.

18. Ibid., 31.

19. Laura Mulvey, 'Visual Pleasure and Narrative Cinema', *Screen* 16:3 (1975), 18.

20. Alice Blackhurst, '"The Camera Glides but Never Settles" between Chantal Akerman's La chambre and Laura Mulvey's Riddles of the Sphinx', *A Nos Amours*, 25 September 2015. Available at <https://anosamoursblog.weebly.com/blog/the-camera-glides-but-never-settles-between-chantal-akermans-la-chambre-and-laura-mulveys-riddles-of-the-sphinx-by-alice-blackhurst> (last accessed 7 October 2021).

21. Jackie Stacey, *Star Gazing: Hollywood Cinema and Female Spectatorship* (London: Routledge, 1994), 9.

22. See bell hooks, 'The Oppositional Gaze: Black Female Spectators', in *Black Looks: Race and Representation* (Boston: South End Press, 1992), 115–31.

23. Walter Benjamin, 'The Work of Art in the Age of Mechanical Reproduction', in Jessica Evans, Stuart Hall (eds), *Visual Culture: The Reader* (London: Thousand Oaks; New Delhi: SAGE Publications, 1999), 72–80.

24. Jackie Stacey, 'Crossing Over with Tilda Swinton: The Mistress of Flat Affect', *International Journal of Politics, Culture and Society* 28 (2015), 243.

25. Lauren Berlant, *The Female Complaint: The Unfinished Business of Sentimentality in American Culture* (Durham, NC: Duke University Press, 2008), 16.

26. Ibid., 4.

27. Stacey, 'Crossing over with Tilda Swinton', 248.

28. *Mad Men*, 'Maidenform', ABC, August 2008.

29. Jonathan Flatley, *Like Andy Warhol* (Chicago: University of Chicago Press, 2017), 12.

30. Ibid., 12.

31. Quoted in Flatley, *Like Andy Warhol*, 1.

32. Josh Cohen, *Not Working: Why We Have to Stop* (London: Granta, 2018), 35–47.

33. Stacey, Crossing over with Tilda Swinton', 249.

34. Bettina M. Busse, 'The Cindy Sherman Effect: Identity and Transformation in Contemporary Art', in *The Cindy Sherman Effect: Identity and Transformation in Contemporary Art* (Munich: Schirmer/Mosel, 2020), 17.
35. Ara Osterweil 'Under the Skin: The Perils of Becoming Female', *Film Quarterly* 67:4 (June 2014), 47.
36. Ibid., 50.
37. Jennifer Allen, 'Critics' Picks: Candice Breitz, Galerie Max Hetzler', *Artforum*, 6 September–18 October 2003. Available at <https://www.artforum.com/picks/candice-breitz-5448> (last accessed 20 February 2021).
38. Judith Butler, 'Sex and Gender in Simone De Beauvoir's Second Sex', *Yale French Studies* 72 (1986), 38.
39. Vivian Sobchack, 'The Scene of the Screen: Envisioning Photographic, Cinematic, and Electronic Presence', in Shane Denson & Julia Leyda (eds), *Post-Cinema: Theorizing 21st-Century Film* (Falmer: REFRAME Books, 2016), 100.

18. THE FACE AS TECHNOLOGY[1]

Zara Dinnen and Sam McBean

We often think of digital media as substitutions for face-to-face interaction. To discuss new media inter-facial encounters is to interrogate the binary supposition that the face as new media image is in opposition to the embodied, biological face. Yet, as feminist and critical posthumanism has taught us, there are no autonomous humans and machines. Ambient technological systems are busy constructing our faces all the time; humans, in Barad's words, are entangled, lacking an 'independent self-contained existence'.[2] Whether on Facebook and Snapchat, at airports or traffic stops, biometric facial recognition is an indelible part of software in everyday life. As Sarah Kember notes, ambient facial recognition technologies implicate new media modes of surveillance in vernacular new media culture; such 'systems normalize and naturalize a culture in which the joint operation of marketing and surveillance is becoming dominant'.[3] The artist Zach Blas has called this contemporary vernacular our 'Global Face Culture'.[4] Global face culture is exemplified by 'biometrics and facial detection technologies', as well as popular modes of facial expression, such as selfies. The personalised new media face culture of social media is an effect of 'ever obsessive and paranoid impulses to know, capture, calculate, categorize, and standardize human faces'. As Blas suggests, global face culture is 'explosive and emergent', and so 'the very meaning of a face – what it is, does, and communicates – is continuously redefined'.[5]

In this article, we contribute to thinking about the emergence of the face in digital culture. Building on work in the fields of art history, cinema studies, media studies and surveillance studies, which have long established a technological interest in the human face, we move this critical discourse on by locating in contemporary popular culture, and Hollywood narrative cinema in particular, anxieties about, and play with, the face as a new kind of digital object. Much film studies and cinema theory has been invested in the significance of the face as seen on screen, and in particular on the close-up – on the tension between the narrative and abstract signification of a cut-up, blown up face-image. While the close-up is not always of a face, as Mary Ann Doane argues, 'the face is indissociably linked with the process of *effacement*, a move beyond codification' – a function of the close-up.[6] For Doane 'the close-up' is 'simultaneously posing as microcosm and macrocosm, detail and whole'. Doane suggests the attachment to the close-up in film theory is an attachment to a 'simulacra' of wholeness in the face of 'accelerating rationalization, specialization'.[7] These paradoxical connotations of cinema are historically constituted with facial recognition technologies. Recognising this history, we want to frame contemporary digital cinema within the conditions of global face culture. Although surveillance is a heightened mode of existence under global face culture, cinematic modes of looking have always been complexly related to surveillance. Writing on these intersections in terms of 'surveillance cinema', Catherine Zimmer notes that 'from the simplest narratives of early cinema to the most complex psychological, aesthetic, philosophical and political explorations of contemporary film, narrativity and surveillance have continued to intersect in dynamic and structurally significant ways'.[8] Cinema is a means by which the 'production of visible bodies' can be recognised in terms of 'mediated visibilities and surveillance'.[9]

The project of making visible bodies has always also meant the production of raced and gendered bodies. Early surveillance technologies were used to monitor and capture people who had escaped slavery, producing, as Zimmer puts it, 'identity along racial lines, while at the same time disavowing identity in order to maintain the racialized subject as object'.[10] Early cinematic narratives 'were engaged in a similar project, producing the black figure as an identity that is without identity: a signifier upon which the narrative can turn'.[11] The production of race, of bodies, through regimes of surveillance and the mediated visibilities of cinema is also the production of a technological subject. In the words of Wendy Hui Kyong Chun, such a condition is 'race and/as technology'.[12] Chun's formulation advocates understanding race not only as something that intersects with technology, but that functions as technology, that is, race as 'always already a mix of science, art, and culture'.[13] For Chun, race is not a static object (whether cultural or biological), but rather a tool that mediates bodies' relationships to other bodies. For 'race, like one's face, is not simply a private possession or technology . . . but rather exists at the cusp between the public and the private, the visible and the invisible'.[14] To return to Doane, through Zimmer, through Chun, the close-up of a face in cinema is an affective signifier of the technological apparatus, a potential site of identification or relation, and the means by which a subject is made.

By studying the face as a digital object away from its primary sites of recognition – online, in CCTV imagery, in identification documents – we encounter in narrative cinema the face as a story. In particular, the recent films of Scarlett Johansson tell stories about the face as made by and in relation to digital technology, but also in relation to discourses of celebrity, whiteness, and femininity. Johansson's face is a generative filmic object with which to interrogate the normative conditions of the face in contemporary digital culture. It is her face that becomes the computer in *Lucy* (Luc Besson, 2014), her face that is the alien black sheen of *Under the Skin* (Jonathan Glazer, 2013), and her face that is the absent signified in *her* (Spike Jonze, 2013). Focusing on Johansson's films enables us to think together the interface-object of celebrity in the contemporary, the technological face of digital cinema, and importantly, the face as primarily a gendered and raced technology in the making. As we will argue in the discussion below, to attend to the making of Johansson's face, or her face as technology, is to insist on this face's centrality to discourses not only of global face culture and digital cinema, but also Hollywood stardom and white femininity.

MAKING THE FACE

The recent appearance of Johansson as 'the face' of contemporary science fiction cinema might be explainable through her characteristic flat expression. This blank, or flattened style, can been traced back to her first 'adult' breakout roles in *Ghost World* (Terry Zwigoff, 2001), *Lost in Translation* (Sophia Coppola, 2003) and *Girl with the Pearl Earring* (Peter Webber, 2003). If this 'flat' performance or, in Lauren Berlant's words, 'underperformative', was pivotal to Johansson's earlier films, in her more recent films, Johansson's underperformance is mobilised as the performance of technological 'other'.[15] Her refusal of emotional codes in *Lucy*, for instance, is one of the ways that we know that she is becoming increasingly technological. Or, her learning of the human's emotional register in *her* is how we know she is becoming increasingly human-like. Similarly, in *Under the Skin*, her character is likened to a blank screen that, again, disturbs the normative expectations of emotional expression on screen. Crudely, Johansson's casting in these films appears to be about representing technology through her, by now, characteristic flattened emotionality. For us though, there is a more productive way of considering why Johansson is necessary for the films to work; this involves attending to the film's shared interests in digital subjectivity, surveillance technologies, and the face. It matters to these films that Johansson is a Hollywood star whose face is ubiquitous; it is this ubiquity which makes the films work, not only her performance style. The films play on the known quantity of her face. Through gestures of disguising, dissolving, breaking, making, ripping off and disappearing Johansson's face, the films challenge assumptions about recognition, revealing the face, her face, as technology – as something that is made by digital cinema, the Hollywood star system, and discourses of celebrity culture and new media. Much like facial recognition software must presume a stable, legible face, but more often reveals the impossibility of such a subject and the discriminatory ideologies encoded in acts of recognition, in recent science fiction films Johansson's face is represented as known, but gestures as well towards the processes through which this face comes to be known.

Under the Skin, an adaptation of a Michel Faber novel, follows an alien 'woman' who entraps human males in a black borderless mass. Scarlett Johansson plays the alien, listed as 'the woman' in the cast credits. In *Under the Skin*, alienness surfaces as the digital image – the film plays with and exploits the digital possibilities of cinema to produce alienness. In other words, the alien in *Under the Skin* is both a biological entity and digital image: a biometric being. Importantly, it is the face, Johansson's face, that is particularly central to the way that the film imagines conditions of surveillance. *Under the Skin* begins with the making of Johansson's character, 'the woman', imagined as a technological making, a cultural making and a process of self-making – this making is always both gendered and technological, a process of surveillance and of being watched. The film opens with the sound of her learning to make sounds, sounds that will eventually become language. We watch her eye being made; it, like language's introduction via sound, is introduced as a technological creation, referencing both vision as a technology and the face as a technological object. From the creation of this eye, the film cuts to a male motorcyclist retrieving an inert female body from the side of the road, and her face is presented for our observation. This face is likely to be initially taken for Johansson's; however, an initial reading of 'the dead woman' (Lynsey Taylor Mackay) as Johansson is disrupted when the camera pans back and Johansson is revealed to be naked, beside the body. Johansson proceeds to methodically undress the dead woman and put on her clothes.

In *Under the Skin*, Johansson's character, the woman, emerges from a computer-generated animation – the digital animation of her eye being formed. This digital animation draws our attention to this making of Johansson – the image-work – by the fact that the first face we see, which we think might be Johansson, is not. It is a lookalike who will be the person Johansson's alien looks like. Johansson then drives to a shopping mall, where she is filmed from behind. While Johansson is the ostensible subject of the camera gaze, it is the faces of the unknowing shoppers that are captured in this scene. Johansson is shown walking through a women's clothing store and then a cosmetics store, where the camera watches as women's faces are 'made'. The making-of-Johansson is complete when Johansson puts on lipstick, seen in the reflection of a compact mirror, producing a refracted image of Johansson's face. In these scenes, the making of 'the woman' is a process of mimicry and double-ness, a technological becoming, and a culturally coded 'making-up' of the face. *Under the Skin* brings together technologies of surveillance with technologies of gender, revealing the face as always also a gendered technology.

Yet, it is also interested in the process of surveillance in relation to celebrity and to the everyday. In *Under the Skin* Johansson plays against her media celebrity. As she walks through the centre of Glasgow, and drives around in a white van, her alienness there plays to the cinema audience's awareness that it is Scarlett Johansson doing those things. The uncanniness of a scene where Johansson walks through a Glaswegian shopping centre for instance, resides in the way a cinematic viewer, who knows that it is Johansson, watches a public who does not see her. They should be surveilling her, but because they are not, we surveil them. It is the Glaswegian public that we watch in these scenes, as cinematic cameras are likened to the probable CCTV cameras in the shopping centre. Here, the cinematic structures which usually produce Johansson's face as already known, become likened to surveillance structures which produce the general public as the site of observation. The sequence explodes what Garrett Stewart has referred to as the 'unique homology' that exists in cinema 'between agents in the world, unwittingly recorded, and characters in a film who act as if they weren't being'.[16] In *Under the Skin*, cinematic watching is likened to the scrutiny of surveillance in everyday life. Of course, this sequence, and the film as a whole, can only do this work because Johansson is a celebrity and her face is verified as such elsewhere, beyond cinema, by the surveillance technologies of celebrity culture. Because this is Johansson's face being misrecognised, we begin to see both that the apparatus of looking is something that can go awry, and that the face being watched is being made up as it is made visible.

In the final section of the film, 'the woman' is on the run. She escapes a sexual assault perpetrated by a forest ranger, only to be caught as she attempts to run away. She is thrown on the ground and he pulls at her underwear, but pulls too hard. The shot cuts to his point of view and we see her, her back, with two great gashes, two rips; her skin (the shell) has come away revealing black alien matter. The ranger runs away and the woman/alien bends back down to the ground; she grabs at her head and pulls off the human shell. The ranger comes back and douses the woman/alien with lighter fuel. He burns her/it alive. After the struggle, before the fire, is the most arresting scene of the film. The woman/alien pulls off her face revealing the bald black head and upper torso of an alien figure, with the faint facial features of Johansson; the alien holds the woman's face in her hands and these two Johanssons gaze at each other. The woman's face blinks. Here is the cinematic face as technology (Figure 18.1).

Figure 18.1   Woman holds her face, from *Under the Skin* (Jonathan Glazer, 2013).

The digital image manifests an 'impossible signifier' – the alien and human Johanssons – and the face is revealed (again) as technology, not a stable object but a tool that mediates one body's encounter with another. The white human celebrity woman's face is held in the look of the black alien woman (the other Johansson). The white human celebrity face is revealed as technology, as made. Simultaneously the black Johansson's face – the alien face – is subject to the audience gaze; it is 'revealed' to us and recognised by us as alien. As Lucas Hildebrand notes, 'The revelation of a black female body becomes the ultimate and absolute evidence of the character's non-humanity.'[17] As will be seen even more explicitly in *Lucy*, the alien black matter with which the film ends is not only a processual effect of the digital imaging software that makes the film and the cinematic face; it is also the production of technology – the biotechnical matter of advanced capitalist societies, the oil and plastics that make us. Johansson's face in this scene is not only an image in which mediated subjectivity is being made, and likewise, undone; her whiteness is seen to be made and undone by its proximity to blackness, a proximity which slips between technology and race as signifying difference.

THE FACE'S UNDOING

In *Lucy*, Johansson plays the title character who is forced into being a drug mule, involuntarily absorbs the synthetic drug CPH4, and releases 100 per cent of her brain capacity; Lucy becomes non-human because she exceeds the human. The naming of 'Lucy' implicitly allies her with the three-million-year-old female hominid fossil nicknamed 'Lucy' and the film explicitly works through a Darwinian narrative of evolutionary progress – Lucy becomes the best human but, in this process, also ceases to be human. Her cells, to preserve their own immortality, obliterate the human body that holds them back, and reform as a bio-machine. In particular, Lucy's human face is in various ways the site at which we can see her humanity at risk. By the end of the film, the human face is obliterated and what remains this time is definitely an interface: the knowledge Lucy has accrued is 'downloaded' as a black organic plastic mass – a computer that will have been.

The film has a lot of fun at undoing Johansson's face, playing with the value of this face. As with the play with Johansson's celebrity in *Under the Skin, Lucy* depends upon and plays with the value of Johansson's face and our attachment to it. The film has been described as ridiculous, 'idiotic' and over-the-top, an aspect that we would locate specifically in Johansson's performance of 'being machine'.[18] As more of her brain power is unlocked Lucy begins to talk monosyllabically, has a new clunkiness to her walk, and blankness to her expression. Pressing on the visual metaphors for becoming machine, the film is most spectacular in the colourful, dramatic, lengthy ways we watch Johansson's face dissolve. In a particularly notable scene, where her capacity is at 40 per cent, Johansson is on an aeroplane demonstrating her increased affinity to technology, through her relationship to laptops. Johansson's hands are shown typing on two laptops at once, sped-up, ostensibly to emphasise that the distinction between her ontological body and the machines she is using is disintegrating. Here, the technological as tool for the human subject dissolves into bio-technical assemblage. Johansson's hands attract the confused attention of a fellow passenger, who marvels at her improper use of technology. Johansson is approached by a cheery flight attendant who requests that she put her laptops away for landing. Johansson's inhuman-ness in this scene is a product of her relationship to the laptops, but also her affective difference to those around her. Unlike the man's astonished face, Johansson's registers nothing – she blinks awkwardly in time with the screen's flashing. Unlike the flight attendant's cheery disposition, Johansson is monosyllabic, not even lifting her head to communicate face to face with the attendant. She is past communicating with those around her and illegible to them. As she goes to drink her glass of champagne, this otherness becomes a disintegration. She loses a tooth in her champagne glass and her hand begins to dissolve in front of her eyes.

The digital special effects here make this scene, even as they are put to use to unmake Johansson's character. The digital play with undoing the body of Johansson is taken to the comedic extreme, as she runs towards the toilet and can barely muster enough ontological certainty to flip the 'occupied' latch. Once the painfully long scene of her trying to move the latch concludes, the shot cuts to Johansson's face reflected in the mirror, where she is trying to hold her dissolving face together with her similarly dissolving hands. In the fantastic

Figure 18.2   Lucy's face dissolves, from *Lucy* (Luc Besson, 2014).

realm of the film, Johansson devours CPH4 and her face seems to remake itself before she explodes (Figure 18.2). This immediately cuts to her passport photo in the hands of a Parisian police detective. In this cut, a link is made between Johansson's face being unmade in the aeroplane toilet and the biometric passport where her face is the site of governmental identification. There is a suggestion then, that without this face, or in the case of its undoing, Johansson's ability to be governed and surveilled by the law is similarly undone. The face's undoing is at once horrifying, freeing and technological (both in the diegesis of the film and in the digital technology that enables this scene). Johansson's underperformance is compared to the overperformance of the special effect. There are computer-generated effects throughout all three of these films, but the ones that register most effectively are the ones that decentre the certainty of Johansson's face, showing instead the variable ontology of the digital image.

The film gives away a final gesture of unease with the face as technology – as infinitely malleable, non-essential, of no origin – with its final two sequences that reaffirm the sanctity of the white female celebrity face and re-establish its import for the ongoing reproduction of humanity. Once Lucy realises that she cannot sustain her human form she is on a mission to impart all the wisdom her 100 per cent brain capacity has engendered, and to get this to a group of scientists led by Professor Samuel Norman (Morgan Freeman). In order to get as much from her power as possible, Lucy overdoses on CPH4 in a sequence even more spectacular than the aeroplane: we see what Lucy sees, the 'whole' of human history – Times Square throughout the ages, the formation of the solar system, the dinosaurs, the first mammals. This imaginary is intercut with Lucy becoming machine, finally: she turns into a black liquid supercomputer that eventually spits out a USB stick containing the sum total of human knowledge to be. We want to linger here on the similarities between *Under the Skin* and *Lucy* in their visualising of otherness through blackness. As Marc Francis notes, Johansson's 'repeated resignification' 'into blackness' poses a 'worrisome dilemma'.[19] As with *Under the Skin*, blackness indexes plasticity or technological matter. Yet, because *Lucy* explicitly situates itself within an evolutionary discourse, blackness here perhaps more than in *Under the Skin*, indexes the film's inability to develop or engage with racial politics. From the undifferentiated Asian 'baddies' to the Chinese prison graffiti that translates into English as the names of fruits, *Lucy* has been rightly critiqued for its racial politics. Perhaps most shocking is its clear message that human evolution reaches its pinnacle in white femininity. This is expressed through the relationship between the female hominid 'Lucy' and Johansson's character – during her time travels Lucy reaches out her hand in a Michelangelo-esque attempt to touch her distant relative. As Olivia Cole puts it, this scene, with no nuance whatsoever, represents 'humanity at its beginning, and then humanity at its end, at its most perfect. Blonde, white and blue-eyed'.[20]

Such an image of white supremacy makes the close-up scene of Johansson turning into black machinic matter all the more arresting. As the camera closes in on Johansson's face, with the blackness creeping up from her neck, the film attempts, similarly to *Under the Skin*, to keep this transformation from white to black separate from racialisation. As Andre Seewood notes, Johansson's 'becoming' racially marked as black is elided through the close-up cuts:

> Besson avoids emphasising the racial nature of this change by shooting the transfiguration in isolated close-up shots. We see a part of her leg, a part of her arm, a cheek and an eye socket, but not the entire wondrous change from White to Black [Figure 18.3].[21]

Johansson is never allowed to be black, even as she becomes machine. As with *Under the Skin*, the blackness that we are left with in both films is never a racially marked subject, but rather always the non-human. The narrative of technological becoming evident in both films is inseparable from race, yet race is the unspoken becoming that neither film can adequately incorporate. The making and unmaking of Johansson's face in these films determines the white privileged celebrity face to be the currency of new media face culture. Even as the subject here is whiteness, the blackness which takes over Johansson's face (specifically the black matter of digital media), inevitably recalls, without being able to account for, the ways that beyond the cinema it is people of colour that are disproportionately the subject of new media surveillance apparatus trained on faces.[22] Both films are full of missed opportunities to interrogate the links between race and technology, or, to return to Chun, the way that race is a technology, even as they are unable to visualise technology without reference to racial difference.

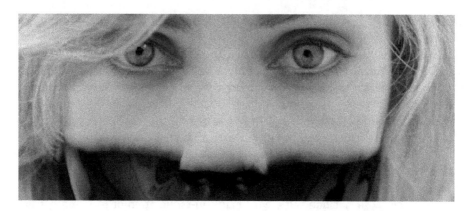

Figure 18.3   Lucy becomes a computer, from *Lucy* (Luc Besson, 2014).

THE ABSENT FACE

Lucy and *Under the Skin* represent the face as a dissolving object: unmade and remade by digital technology, which always makes the face, while also always potentially threatens to undo the promise of the face as site of identification. In Spike Jonze's film *her*, these questions once again play out, albeit this time through the absence of Johansson's face. The film follows a twee man, Theodore Twombly (Joaquin Phoenix), who falls in love with his new operating system, voiced by Johansson. The film opens by asking the audience to consider what the relationship is between the human face and a new media interface. The scene is a soft-focus close-up of Phoenix's face, a shot which lasts over a minute as Theodore narrates a letter that he produces in his job as a professional writer of other people's love notes. The shot of Theodore's face then becomes a shot of his computer screen, prompting from the first minutes of the film a juxtaposition between the human face and the interface of the screen, inviting a reading of both as technology. Theodore's exaggerated emotional performance, which in this scene and throughout the film is frequently shot as a close-up, invites scrutiny, and insists on the face as something 'that is made'. In the cut to the computer screen, we are invited to compare Theodore's made-up face with the explicitly technological interface of the screen. The screen displays a love letter giving us the opportunity to read this other surface as an emotional interface, another kind of face. While here the interface of the screen seems to provide a counterpoint to the human face, asking us to worry about the future of face-to-face relationships, *her*, as with *Lucy* and *Under the Skin*, also points towards the face as a technology.

her pushes the face-as-technology into more literal territory, turning Johansson's 'face' into a stylised operating system. The flat affective performance of Johansson's alien or dissolving-into-machinic subjectivity in *Under the Skin* and *Lucy* is here realised as a screen interface. This presents a problem for cinematic structures of feeling. As Jackie Stacey puts it, in the generic history of romance, 'conventionalised femininities have become legible through a repertoire of emotional intensities', or, in other words, emotional intensity registers femininity; in *her*, Theodore's face must do this work.[23] We see this from the opening shot and throughout the film – it is his face that must register the film's emotional content. It is his face we watch falling in love, it is his face we watch in bed, and it is his face that holds the camera's close-up shots. Moreover, we are never allowed to forget that there is something potentially feminine about this. In the opening scene, for instance, we learn that Theodore is writing a letter as a woman. Theodore's ability to signify as feminine is remarked upon numerous times in the film, in particular by his boss, Paul (notably played by the 'dudeish' Chris Pratt). In *her*, Theodore registers as feminine precisely because he holds/performs intense emotion, shot as close-ups. Theodore, throughout the film, is coded as hyperemotional, as perhaps too feminine. Here, we see a clear example of how the technologies of cinematic faces are also gendered technologies. The lack of the female face proves particularly troubling in the film's sex scenes. The female face is frequently (and in non-pornographic films) the site where we 'read' sex – in the close-up of the female face in pleasure.[24] The sex scene in *her* involves a minute and a half of black screen while we hear Theodore and Samantha's voices narrating what they would/are doing to each other. In this scene, it is Phoenix's face that dissolves into the black screen (where the past films have placed Johansson's face into proximity with blackness). His face meets hers, producing in the film another mode of technological blackness: the blank cinematic screen. The black-out screen is almost opposite to the cinematic close-up, is not 'a sign, a text, a surface that demands to be read'.[25] Instead, it is a surface that points towards that which cannot be represented – or perhaps to the desire that Phoenix's face cannot hold on its own.

That it is Johansson's face that is missing is particularly important and connects *her* to the previous films we've discussed. Similar to the way *Under the Skin* 'works' precisely through the uncanniness of Johansson as unrecognisable, *her* 'works' because Johansson's voice always reminds us of the absence of her face. This is perhaps why Samantha Morton, originally cast to voice Samantha, was replaced by Johansson at a very late stage in production. Johansson's voice, in ways that lesser-known stars cannot, calls to mind the face that is not there. The film further explores this when Samantha has another woman, Isabella (Portia Doubleday), act as a surrogate for her, act as her body in a sexual encounter with Theodore. While it is ostensibly the body that is important, it is the face that is primary throughout the scene. We watch Isabella arrive and, with the help of the camera and the earpiece (which is shot as a close-up), she makes her face (through the addition of technology) into Samantha's. Highlighting the centrality of the face to an affective performance, it is precisely through her face that

Isabella ruins the illusion – her body performs just fine. The illusion is disrupted, in Theodore's words, first because he does not know her, but more importantly, because 'her lip quivered'. In other words, we are brought back to the failure of the surrogate's face to be Samantha's (and doubly, the failure of Doubleday to be Johansson). This scene to some extent inverts the beginning of *Under the Skin* where Johansson becomes the girl at the side of the road. Both scenes work because audiences know Johansson and her absence disrupts processes of cinematic recognition.

In comparison to *Lucy* and *Under the Skin*, *her* contains a much stronger humanist lament for the face; rather than a play with its dissolution, *her* locates the pathos of a near technological future in the absence of the face. *her*, in ways that are not so much about digital play and manipulation, imagines what the absence of the female face means for cinematic codes of affect. As with *Under the Skin* and *Lucy*, we are brought back to the black expanse, the blank screen and the reconstruction of race and gender and/as technology through the face as technology. *her* is a white film which wills into view a white future for a city (LA) that is statistically unlikely to have one. Moreover, this future is one of complete homogeneity; as Edgar Rivera Colón points out, *her* is a film of 'elite whiteness'.[26] The casting of Johansson is once again key to maintaining the construction of whiteness: because her voice is recognisable the audience understands the 'neutral' software as white and female.[27] When the screen goes to black Johansson is once again visually 'resignified'. Reappropriating Hildebrand's description of moments of blackness in *Under the Skin*, we might consider the moments of cinematic blackness in *her* as such an about turn in the aesthetic schema – which is not just full of white bodies but tinted an Instagram-rose – that it appears as an 'embodiment of blackness . . . so blatant . . . it becomes difficult to understand the metaphor in any way other than as racialised, the embodiment of difference'.[28] Here the difference is marked by blackness as also an invitation to listen more closely, which ironically throws us back into the act of recognising the absent white celebrity face of Johansson. Once again, the face (here in its absence) is the technology by which we recognise the individual human as technologised and the difference of human and machine is upheld through a visual connection of the machine to a blackness that makes whiteness – technology and/as race.

In this essay, we have been interested in the particular relevance of the face for thinking through issues of identity as a technological mode. We insist, through our focus on Johansson's recent films, that Hollywood and new media celebrity culture are vital sites for exploring the politics of the face as technology. Indeed, the face in cinema is just as much a digital object as the face as produced by social media or biometric surveillance. In narrative cinema though, and in the recent films of Scarlett Johansson, the face is never just object, it is also always narrative. Here then, we are able to witness the face as an object in flux, as something that is made and remade in relation not only to its relationship to technology but also discourses of race and gender. The turn to narrative cinema enables us to account for not just the face as a technology, but also what faces signal about the presence of new technologies. The face is central to contemporary fantasies of digital media. Through our analyses of these films we identify a tension at the root of this fantasy, which proliferates through culture more broadly: a tension between a conservative impulse to understand the face as a privileged site of human encounter and, conversely, a desire to encounter the face as a radical site of instability in our technological present.

Postscript

In 2016, when we were first working on this article, Ricky Ma, a Hong Kong-based product and graphic designer, had recently unveiled his robot 'Mark 1'. News reporting on this achievement focused on the robot's uncanny likeness to Johansson. It was with this robot that the original article began – with us thinking about not only Johansson's as the face being replicated, but also the uncertainty about what it meant for a robot to have a face that was so similar to Johansson's, where the legality was unclear, and where the use of the replica was as yet undetermined. We used this robot as a way to begin to think about the value of Johansson's face and reflected on the articles about the robot that worried more generally over the emergent possibilities of technological facial replications. However, in preparing this chapter for this edited collection, the Mark 1 robot did not seem as appropriate a beginning or frame for the work.

What struck us both in reading the original published piece, was the way our everyday relationship to digital faces has changed dramatically. In the initial writing of the piece, we located Global Face Culture around surveillance and selfies. While we are sure there was much more we could have discussed originally, what seems notable now is our omission of faces as they are streamed via webcams. We are both aware of the changed context in which we now encounter our faces, everyone's faces, as primarily digital faces. In the moment in which we are revisiting this piece, in the midst of the COVID-19 pandemic, our own everyday encounters with the digitality of ours and our colleagues', friends' and families' faces seems like the frame through which to keep thinking critically about how faces are made by and through digital technologies. The issues that we raised in this piece initially still stand, we think, but now we would add the unavoidable ways that we are currently present for each other via our digital faces. The instability of the digital face, its plasticity and its persistent appearance as subject to and vector of racialised and gendered subjectivity, determines more than ever before how we can be with one another. How people are seen by/and/as technology is frequently, for the time being, how people are seen at all.

NOTES

1. This chapter is a shortened and revised version of the essay 'The Face as Technology', *New Formations: A Journal of Culture, Theory & Politics* 93 (2018), 122–37.

2. Karen Barad, *Meeting the Universe Halfway* (Durham, NC: Duke University Press, 2007), ix.

3. Sarah Kember, 'Face Recognition and the Emergence of Smart Photography', *Journal of Visual Culture* 13:2 (2014), 184.

4. Zach Blas, 'Escaping the Face: Biometric Facial Recognition and the Facial Weaponization Suite', *Media-N* 9:2 (2013). Available at: <http://median.newmediacaucus.org/caa-conference-edition-2013/escaping-the-face-biometric-facial-recognition-and-the-facial-weaponization-suite/> (last accessed 23 September 2021).

5. Ibid.

6. Mary Ann Doane, 'The Close-up: Scale and Detail in the Cinema', *differences: A Journal of Feminist Cultural Studies* 14:3 (2003), 96.

7. Ibid., 93.

8. Catherine Zimmer, 'Surveillance Cinema: Narrative between Technology and Politics', *Surveillance & Society* 8:4 (2011), 430. On the intersections of state surveillance and cinema, see also Tom Gunning, 'Tracing the Individual Body: Photography, Detectives, and Early Cinema', in L. Charney and V. R. Schwartz (eds), *Cinema and the Invention of Modern Life* (Berkeley: University of California Press, 1995), 15–45; Thomas Y. Levin, 'Rhetoric of the Temporal Index: Surveillant Narration and the Cinema of "Real Time"', in Thomas Y. Levin, Ursula Frohne and Peter Weibel (eds), *CRTL [SPACE]: Rhetorics of Surveillance from Bentham to Big Brother* (Cambridge, MA: MIT Press, 2002), 578–93; Garrett Stewart, *Closed Circuits: Screening Narrative Surveillance* (Chicago: University of Chicago Press, 2015).

9. Zimmer, 'Surveillance Cinema', 428.

10. Ibid., 430. See also See Simone Browne, *Dark Matters: On the Surveillance of Blackness* (Durham, NC: Duke University Press), 2015.

11. Zimmer, 'Surveillance Cinema', 430.

12. Wendy Hui Kyong Chun, 'Race and/as Technology; or, How to Do Things to Race', *Camera Obscura* 24:1 (70) (2009), 7–35.

13. Ibid., 8.

14. Ibid., 23.

15. Lauren Berlant, 'Structures of Unfeeling: *Mysterious Skin*', *International Journal of Politics, Culture, and Society* 28:3 (2015), 191–213.

16. Stewart, *Closed Circuits*, 2.

17. Lucas Hildebrand, 'On the Matter of Blackness in *Under the Skin*', *Jump Cut: A Review of Contemporary Media* 57 (2016). Available at <https://www.ejumpcut.org/archive/jc57.2016/-HilderbrandUnderSkin/index.html> (last accessed 7 October 2021).

18. Christopher Orr, '*Lucy*: The Dumbest Movie Ever Made about Brain Capacity', *The Atlantic*, 25 July 2014. Available at <http://www.theatlantic.com/entertainment/archive/2014/07/life-is-futile-so-heres-what-to-do-with-it-according-to-lucy-a-spoilereview/375006/> (last accessed 7 October 2021).

19. Mark Francis, 'Splitting the Difference: On the Queer-Feminist Divide in Scarlett Johansson's Recent Body Politics', *Jump Cut: A Review of Contemporary Media* 57

(2016). Available at <https://www.ejumpcut.org/archive/jc57.2016/-FrancisSkin/index.html> (last accessed 7 October 2021).

20. Olivia Cole, 'Lucy: Why I'm Tired of Seeing White People on the Big Screen', *Huff Post*, 28 July 2014. Available at <http://www.huffingtonpost.com/olivia-cole/lucy-why-im-tired-of-seei_b_5627318.html> (last accessed 7 October 2021).

21. Andre Seewood, '*Lucy* and the Absence of the Black Race in Origin of Humanity Theories', *IndieWire*, 7 January 2015. Available at <http://www.indiewire.com/2015/01/sa-2014-highlights-lucy-and-the-absence-of-the-black-race-in-origin-of-humanity-theories-235471/> (last accessed 7 October 2021).

22. See Simone Browne, *Dark Matters: On the Surveillance of Blackness* (Durham, NC: Duke University Press, 2015); and Rachel E. Dubrofsky and Shoshana Amielle Magnet (eds), *Feminist Surveillance Studies* (Durham, NC: Duke University Press, 2015).

23. Jackie Stacey, 'Crossing over with Tilda Swinton – the Mistress of "Flat Affect"', *International Journal of Politics, Culture, and Society* 28:3 (2015), 224.

24. Annamarie Jagose, *Orgasmology* (Durham, NC: Duke University Press), 2012.

25. Doane, 'The Close-up', 94.

26. Edgar Rivera Colón, 'Spike Jonze's Her: Loneliness, Race, & Digital Polyamory', *The Feminist Wire*, 3 March 2014. Available at <http://www.thefeministwire.com/2014/03/her-film-loneliness-race-spike-jonze/> (last accessed 7 October 2021).

27. It is notable that Scarlett Johansson's role as the Japanese character Major Kusanagi in the live action remake of *Ghost in the Shell*, has been criticised as whitewashing and imagines again whiteness as technological neutrality.

28. Hildebrand, 'On the Matter of Blackness'.

19. FROM HOLY GRAIL TO DEEPFAKE: THE EVOLVING DIGITAL FACE ON SCREEN

Lisa Bode

In the final third of *Blade Runner 2049* (Villeneuve, 2017) Harrison Ford's aged and haggard Deckard encounters an eternally youthful replica of Sean Young's Rachael, the replicant with whom he fell in love in Ridley Scott's original 1982 movie. Rachael is long dead, but Jared Leto's villain CEO, Wallace, offers Deckard this copy, 'an angel remade anew', as a bribe for information. The film seems to hold its breath with Deckard as she comes into view – first as a silhouette, recognisable by her sleek pompadour, the exaggerated Noir shoulders of her suit, and the assured click-clack of her heels on the floor – giving us a moment of anticipation for the sight of her face. Those of us familiar with the iconic character are invited to wonder: how will this Rachael be achieved, and how persuasive will she be? Emerging from the sulphurous gloom, the figure glides slowly towards us, her face immobile and doll-like as its details – the mascara-ringed doe eyes and the glossy painted lips in relief against unmarked porcelain – loom into increased clarity. Finally, in close-up, presented for scrutiny, Rachael's copy asks, 'Did you miss me? Don't you love me?' Deckard's response urges us to believe that in visual terms, the illusion is perfect. His face sags, mouth agape, trying to process the figure before him. Finally, grasping through his memory, he rejects her with a phony excuse: 'Her eyes were green,' he growls, before wrenching himself away.[1] While for Deckard she is a copy of what he has lost and longed for, for us she is a digital replica of a younger version of a human actress and, accordingly, her face is offered to us as a spectacular visual effect – a complex assemblage of labour, skill, time, money, software, performances, and anatomical observation and knowledge. As the film's publicity tells us, visual effects (VFX) supervisor John Nelson worked on her for a year and cited her as the biggest challenge of his career, saying, 'Digital humans are sort of like the holy grail — they're *really* hard.'[2]

Since the 1980s, 'holy grail' has been a common term for a persistent goal in digital visual effects: that of crafting a fully expressive photorealistic digital human for cinema, indistinguishable from a living actor. Since the mid-1990s, each new cinematic digital human face has been positioned by VFX artists and journalists as moving closer towards this goal in some way, although, as Dan North points out, the holy grail analogy 'might also inadvertently hint that such a goal is essentially elusive'.[3] Stephen Prince and Barbara Flueckiger have explained the historical evolution of digital bodies (bodies, more generally, rather than the human face, specifically) on screen as one driven by ever increasing processing power and quantum leaps in visual effects software and techniques.[4]

This view suggests that realism in animated digital human faces is a fixed known quantity: enough detailed modelling and rendering, enough processing power, and the goal can be reached. Yes, faster processing speeds have enabled computer graphics systems to handle exponentially larger amounts of data, which in turn have supported the development of various tools and software for more naturalistic and efficient modelling, animation, rendering, lighting, algorithms for realistic hair movement, and so on. But modelling, animation, rendering and algorithms are derived from data, research, and understandings about human anatomy, physics, human behaviour and perception. At the same time, some of this research has been driven by the desire to understand and approximate the visual and expressive dimensions of human faces as they look on screen.[5] Some has been shaped by the affordances of technology at particular times, and what it is of human faces and facial expressions that either can or can't be digitised, visualised or programmed. As Angela Ndalianis argues of Jeff Bridges's digital face in *Tron: Legacy*, the digital human face allows us to ponder 'the slippery nature of what it means to be human as a result of technological mediation'.[6] It is the evolution of this slipperiness that I want to trace in this essay.

I ask, then, what kinds of understandings about facial anatomy, the face's expressions, individuality and humanness have been drawn upon, or emerged at different times, through the quest to create photorealistic digital human faces, and to what extent does the recent emergence of machine learning generated deepfake videos indicate a continuity or break with older understandings? In attempting to answer these questions, I focus on a selection of what have been widely considered 'milestone' digital faces in the cinema, and examine making of materials, journalistic discourse, interviews with VFX artists, and research reports. Such materials provide useful insights, as John Thornton Caldwell argues into 'film's production of culture' and 'the general framing paradigms' used by those working in image-making to conceptualise, reflect upon, and communicate what they do both with each other, and to the viewing audience.[7]

THE FACE AS DATA

To represent and animate a human face requires conceiving the face as units of information, each described separately and brought into interaction with others. The two most basic units of the face, appearance and expression, in turn are divided into further information units. In early 1970s face animation projects, such as that of Fred Parke, these units were minimal: the key features of the face, such as the shape and relative position of eyes, eyebrows and mouth, were described geometrically as polygons, and expressions described as different iterations and parameters of this geometry.[8] But as the quest to create a photorealistic, as opposed to a stylised, expressive human face emerged in the late 1970s, much more complex informational models developed. These have aimed for a progressively complete virtualisation of the face's visual materiality. We see perhaps the beginnings of this in 1976's *Futureworld*, the poorly received sequel to Michael Crichton's *Westworld* (1973).

Futureworld has been often framed as a 'milestone' in histories of computer graphics and digital visual effects, as it gives us the first digital human face in cinema: that of actor Peter Fonda.[9] Peter Fonda plays a journalist, Chuck, investigating Delos's android populated theme park. As he has become too curious, the corporation decides he must be killed off and replaced by a compliant clone. Computers are presented as central to the cloning process, as machines to store, analyse and visualise different kinds of body data. In the cloning sequence, we see a laboratory of impassive technicians pressing buttons and watching a bank of monitors, while we hear a flat machine-like woman's voice reeling off measurements of facial anatomy, such as the thickness of the subject's eyelids, and the distance from his nose to his mouth. The camera inspects these data displays. One shows lines of text about blood type and other biological markers, another shows computer graphics visualising DNA structures. Next, dual monitors display graphical representations of body parts and kinetic mimesis, including a 3D wire-frame animation of a hand clenching and extending its fingers and spinning. We close in on a display of an animated 3D generic humanoid face, dummy-like in its smooth raster planes. It opens its eyes and mouth, raising its eyebrows and revealing teeth as it seems to speak.[10] Finally, our view settles on a monitor showing a face that is both recognisably Fonda, and recognisably computer-generated. As the camera zooms in, we are given forty seconds of what appears to be a virtual Peter Fonda death mask, hollow and inanimate, its eyes closed as it spins and turns in a black void. Fonda's angular and slightly feminine visage, with its hooded eyelids, wedge nose and small mouth, are rendered in grey polygons which smooth out into liquid silver curves as the shot proceeds, and the face continues to spin, filling the screen, spectacularising its dimensions and resemblance to an actual face, as ominous violins trill on the soundtrack.

In this way, *Futureworld* establishes the imaginary slippages between science fictional motifs (such as clones and androids) and the digital representation of human beings that have vibrated through the pervasive discourse around the photorealistic digital human as the 'holy grail' of the computer graphics and animation industries. But it also showcases various forms of then state-of-the art computer graphic representations of human faces and bodies, each focusing on a different aspect: biodata and the visualisation of 3D anatomical structures; the transcription of kinetic and facial expression; and the digitised topography of an actual face. Apart from Fonda's face, which was created specifically for the film by Gary Demos and John Whitney Jr of Triple I, these other kinds of research and development emerged out of different fields, steered initially towards other not necessarily cinematic goals. As Oliver Gaycken has observed, the development of digital visual effects for cinema has had 'profound and manifold links' to science visualisation.[11] In the following section I examine some of the important research foundations on which the digital human face and its expressions have been built, and I try to convey a sense of the knowledge exchange between science visualisation and digital visual effects.

FACE FOUNDATIONS: MUSCULAR EXPRESSIONS

At their core, animated digital faces aiming for photorealism, from Aki Ross in *Final Fantasy: The Spirits Within* (Sakaguchi, 2001) to Will Smith's clone in *Gemini Man* (Lee, 2019), are built on the foundations of 'muscle action models', which simulate the mechanical interactions of bone structure, muscles, connective tissue and skin.[12] Stripped back functional versions of these models first emerged in computer animation experiments of the early 1980s for plastic and reconstructive surgery simulation, and animated facial expressions and phonemes for an American Sign Language tool.[13] This model conceives the face in biomechanical terms, with virtual muscles activated as an interconnected system of levers to pull and squeeze beneath the tissue and skin, moving jaw bones, and deforming the skin mesh into expression and speech configurations.

From the early 1980s, the muscle actions for expressions were derived from Paul Ekman's and W. V. Friesen's Facial Action Coding System (FACS). FACS is a cognitive-emotional model of facial expression that, according to affect theorist and historian Ruth Leys, was designed to 'provide an atheoretical, anatomically based, standardised scoring system of the movements of the face that researchers could use to test their hypotheses about the relationship between emotion and facial expression'.[14] FACS, Leys shows, emerged out of a rise of affect research in the 1960s which combined cybernetics and Darwinian thinking about behaviour as adaptive responses to contexts, and posited the co-development of physiological responses such as facial expressions with 'affect programs' in the brain. Ekman's claims, however – that facial expressions are universal, modulated only by cultural expression rules – are based on assumptions and research methods that have been challenged for decades by other scholars in the field.[15] Yet, for complex industrial, technological and institutional reasons, Ekman's arguments and FACS have become the culturally dominant model for categorising and analysing facial expressions, and for explaining the relation between facial expressions and emotion. FACS underpins facial expression recognition training programmes that have been taken up by law enforcement and counter-terrorism agencies.

Moreover, what was designed as a tool for research into how we understand facial expressions was quickly adopted as a key supporting template for producing facial animation. Why though, specifically, was FACS adopted for computer animation of facial expressions? Stephen Platt and Norman Badler explained in their paper that one of the primary reasons they used FACS was because, of the available ways of describing facial expressions, FACS had the greatest 'ease of (computer) adaptation'. While other expression notation systems were pictorial or symbolic, FACS describes expressions as combinations of 'action units', each with its own description of the relevant muscle action, making it suitable for computer programming and storage.[16]

The adoption of FACS due to its pre-existing procedural format highlights the ways that the process of digitising material and social information may reconfigure our understandings and interpretations of the face to align with the affordances and limitations of our technologies. But of course, even as this process may shape our self-understanding down particular pathways, it can also provoke a consideration of what it is about us that may escape the grasp of the technology and its epistemology. Notably, journalistic reportage on each development in the terrain of digital humans has been run through with an anxious fantasy of human replacement by synthespians. This has prompted the question of what it is of humanness that may elude attempts to simulate it through technological means.

MYSTERIOUS SOULS, LIFE FORCES

An early version of this synthespian speculation appears in a 1983 article which optimistically predicted that 'within five years video images generated by computers will be indistinguishable from images of live performers'. Would actors be replaced? Author John Goodell reassured us that actors would still be required to dub in the voices, and 'guide' the behaviour of these 'video images'.

For, even if a computer can simulate human appearance, he reasoned, creative human behaviour such as acting, is a very different matter, as it is 'mysterious and wonderful'.[17] Through the 1980s and 1990s variations on this theme of the mysterious specialness of human actors are repeated in news reports and media commentary on progress towards the 'holy grail' of the photorealistic digital human. The line is always moving, and the very idea that human actors could be 'replicated' has led to deeper and more precise consideration of what acting is as an embodied endeavour. For instance, in 2011 David Cohen wrote: 'People imagine the future of movies as something like the holodeck in "Star Trek", want Marilyn Monroe in your scene? Tell the computer "add Marilyn" and voila! You're directing Marilyn Monroe.' However, he says: 'Computers can't yet and won't soon reverse-engineer the thinking that led to an artists' choices . . . What's more, a performance isn't just the actor's conscious choices. It's how the body reacts unconsciously.'[18] In this way the project to create a photorealistic expressive human face has continuities with the Enlightenment era automata projects, which, according to Jessica Riskin were driven by two contradictory forces 'the impulse to simulate and the conviction that simulation was ultimately impossible'.[19] In the early 2000s, however, in the wake of the poor reception of *Final Fantasy: The Spirits Within* (2001), the first feature-length animated film designed on photorealistic principles, a shift took place – a walking back from the idea of a fully autonomous digital human actor.

FINAL FANTASY, SKIN, HAIR AND UNCANNY VALLEYS

If the cloning sequence in *Futureworld* spectacularised dimensionality and the digitised topography of a recognisable individuated face, *Final Fantasy* placed visual emphasis on the surface textures of humanness: skin, eyes, hair. The digital faces of the film were promoted in trailers and press reportage as astonishing achievements. Lead character Aki Ross was singled out for special attention, with US$50 million reportedly spent on developing the algorithm for her hair, which swung almost hypnotically and blew lightly around her face in a smooth flowing bob. Images of Aki in a high-cut bikini and 'interviews' with her appeared in the press, positioning her as a virtual star.[20] In addition, as Jessica Aldred notes, the film's extended close-ups 'invite the viewer to marvel at the latest innovations in texture mapping; eyes, hair, beads of sweat and liver spots have never merited so much screen time'.[21] Aki and her digital co-stars were clad in skin that was lovingly rendered with pores, freckles, wrinkles and tiny pimples. This emphasis was motivated by the belief that organic human skin could be signified with textural imperfections to differentiate it from the smooth plastic skin of mannequins or dolls.

However, despite, or perhaps because of these surface markers of humanness (in combination with the promotion of her autonomy), Aki and her digital co-stars invited a heightened attention to the ways in which they did not look human or alive. Their skin is undifferentiated in colour. It looks dull, rubbery, and bloodless. Their eyes seem to reflect light – they gleam, widen, narrow and blink. But their pupils are static, unresponsive to shifts in light or emotion. In visual terms, the film marks a milestone in terms of the digital face's construction, providing visible markers upon which subsequent VFX artists and rendering software developers could seek to improve. The film's poor reception also marks the beginning of a turning point in Anglophone promotion and reception of digital bodies and faces on screen. This entailed a moving away from the idea of a fully AI rule-driven human to a promotional discourse that at times has positioned performance capture as transferring an actor's soul to a digital body.[22]

At the same time, in the early 2000s, the term 'uncanny valley' began to appear in Anglophone journalistic discourse. This term refers to a hypothesis developed in the context of 1970s Japanese robotics research to explain viewer aversion to the simulation of human likeness in robots.[23] As journalists and VFX artists in the early 2000s sought to understand why audiences tended to find digital human faces creepy and unsettling, the uncanny valley explanation became popularised in the news and entertainment media commentary on digital humans.[24] Consequently, numerous empirical studies published in the 2000s and 2010s, have tested viewer responses to replica human images of different kinds. Such studies have sought to find out what factors of facial appearance or expression most amplify or decrease the uncanny effect, to determine whether or not it is a universal experience, and to understand its underlying cognitive roots or evolutionary purpose.[25] In parallel, VFX artists working on human faces continually refer to the uncanny valley or related ideas about viewer cognition and attention to digital human faces. They strive to work out which informational units of the face's appearance and expressions need to be most developed in order to make that face seem alive and sentient and not trigger the uncanny valley cognitive reflex. This project has driven research to produce ever more intricate models of the face and its layers, and ever more detailed observations of human performance.

FACIAL ANATOMY FOR HD CINEMA

Facial anatomy research and modelling has been pushed into dizzying levels of detail to serve the visual requirements of cinema and overcome the uncanny valley response. Functional biomechanical models of the face are moving towards a complete material virtualisation. For instance, Mark Sagar began his research career building anatomically accurate models of the human eye for surgical training but pivoted to building anatomical models for digital cinematography. Discussing his work on virtual anatomy for WETA in 2011, he said:

No one's 100 percent sure which muscles are activated during speech . . . the muscles and fibers around the mouth have extremely complex structures and cross over each other, and are linked to each other and to many other structures in the mouth, such as ligaments . . . We're building this model and trying to work [the anatomy] out at the same time . . . Visual effects are getting to the point where we're doing research that's comparable to actual medical research.[26]

So too, skin has come to be understood as more than a surface on which to paint imperfections such as pores, freckles, wrinkles and stubble. It is now conceived as a multilayered structure alive with information: about surface topography, texture and colour variations, subsurface light reflectance and diffusion, melanin, hair dynamics and grooming, and blood flow displacement, as muscles squeeze capillaries in a frown or smile. Because actual human skin is visible and photographable, the move has been to gather the visual data required from specific actual faces themselves through high resolution photography. Skin has shifted from an object of pure data modelling to an object of direct data capture with the development of various technologies, such as Paul Debevec et al.'s Light Stage X. This spherical device, which was awarded a Sci-Tech Oscar in 2017, can apparently acquire the 3D visual data for shape, skin texture, colour and reflectance of an actual human face in ultra-high resolution in a matter of seconds.[27] Nonetheless, VFX supervisor for 2019's *Gemini Man*, Sheldon Stopsack, claims that this scan data was insufficient, and that for the digital young clone of Will Smith, they developed procedural ways of building up a model of pore structures at the microscopic level as well as 'the little ribbons and folds that fall between them'.[28]

Since the creation of a detailed and aged digital likeness of Brad Pitt for *The Curious Case of Benjamin Button* (2008), eyes have been singled out for separate detailed modelling and rendering. Digital Domain's Eric Barba enthused: 'As windows to Benjamin's soul, the eyes . . . required complex renders, designed to silence the frequent – and largely accurate – criticism of digital human eyes as being lifeless and empty.' A year's work was required on the eyes to make 'sure every nuance of look and movement was there: how they moved, how they teared up, the details around the conjunctive area'.[29] Each iteration of the digital human face must claim in some way to build on what has come before. As with the skin, the discussion of eye anatomy ten years later for *Gemini Man* discovers ever more details in need of modelling:

[A] huge component that had been neglected previously is the conjunctiva, which is a soft tissue that runs across the sclera, and folds back into the eyelids. We had observed what almost looks like a soft gradient in

Will Smith's eyes, which translated into motion when his eyes opened wide or squeezed shut – and that was this fairly transparent, but somewhat milky conjunctiva.[30]

The increasing completeness of these models suggests a trajectory that, if it continues, will eventually drill down into molecules and DNA. It bears out Vivian Sobchack's prescient argument in 2006 that the rhetoric of 'unlimited development' that runs through the projects of digital photorealism cannot sustain indefinite movement in one direction.[31] New foci for further development must always be located so the project – the search for the 'holy grail' – can continue. Indeed, in parallel with this increased attention to anatomical structures and the minutiae of the face's visible surfaces and movements, we can see that other directions have opened up for the demonstration of progress. These directions have focused on questions of facial performance and viewer perception.

The Eye of the Human Animator

With performance capture, the transference of performance data to a digital face has relied on FACS as the basis of what is called the 'face solve'. Essentially this means that the computer matches the kinetic data (derived from the movement of markers attached to an actor's face) to configurations or key poses in a FACS library. These FACS poses, and the blends between them, have been the foundational animation source for the facial expression of digital characters, such as those we see in *Beowulf* (Zemeckis, 2007) and the digital Peter Cushing in *Rogue One: A Star Wars Story* (Edwards, 2016).

There has been a common perception that something of the original performance seems to escape the grasp of technology in the performance capture process. It may be something about the limitations of capture technologies, or the limitations of FACS as a way of understanding and encoding expressions, but VFX artists have often claimed that something is lost between what could be seen on the actor's face on set and how the kinetic data from that performance reads on their character's digital face. For instance, Peter Plantec observed the differences between Anthony Hopkins's performance as caught on video and what remained of it in his digital facsimile in *Beowulf*:

Several layers of nuance were added by hand, but something was still missing. We're talking very subtle. For example, he had a subtle, nasty little smile that held so much meaning and some of it is missing in the final print. That tiny bit of smile apparently held a lot of emotional information, because I could feel the difference.[32]

Plantec's reference to the 'layers of nuance' added by hand speaks to the pains-taking work digital face animators in the 2000s and 2010s have been required to do to assist the transference of actor expression to digital face. It requires close observation of video reference of an actor's performance, noting the tiniest of details (a twitch at the corner of a mouth, a micro-expression, an infinitesimal saccadic eye movement) that may in some way communicate a character's thought, motivation, masked emotions. These tiny performance details are then hand animated into the digital face. It requires time, good reference footage, and a keen eye. The expressions of Peter Cushing's digital face in *Rogue One: A Star Wars Story* (2016), for example, were overseen by an ILM Digital Human Look supervisor and built on performance-captured impersonation by actor Guy Henry. Animators performed detailed observations of Cushing's original performance as Moff Tarkin in *Star Wars: A New Hope* (Lucas, 1977) and manually added barely noticeable tics from his idiolect. VFX Supervisor Hal Hickel explains too that random 'micro-motions' of the eyes were needed to make the character appear to have a complex working mind. At the same time, too much random micromotion could read to the viewer as 'noise' and seem unnatural.[33] The emphasis here, and indeed in the discussions of behavioural nuances of Rachael for *Blade Runner 2049* and young Will Smith for *Gemini Man*, is that the human eye of the animator is required to notice and include those tiny details of human communication: that almost imperceptible tilt of a head, the ephemeral flickering of an iris or pupil, a transparent but milky conjunctiva, and the ways dried saliva on lips might make them stick together for a fraction of a second before a mouth opens to speak.[34] These details have only become worthy of notice, description and replication through the project of making an expressive digital human face. At the same time, the emphasis placed on the eye of the animator in this VFX industry discourse implies that something human still evades technological simulation. Now, humanness is bound up with a way of seeing, defined against that of machine vision and learning.

DEEPFAKES

In late 2017 (the year of *Blade Runner 2049*'s release), something else bled into the discourse around digital humans, with the emergence online of deepfake open-access AI which could quickly generate digital replicas of human faces and insert them into video. Deepfakes, a portmanteau of 'deep learning' and 'fake', were at this time created by training neural networks on hours of footage and hundreds of photographs of a 'target' face until they could generate the requisite visual data to reproduce a persuasive likeness. The most commonly discussed neural networks used for deepfake creation are generative adversarial networks or GANs. As Yisroel Mirsky and Wenke Lee explain, a GAN 'consists of two neural networks that work against each other: the generator (G) and the discriminator (D)'.[35] The generator creates images of the face until the discriminator can no longer distinguish between the generated and the original face on which it was trained. A 2019 online video by YouTube VFX channel Corridor, demonstrating the process of creating a deepfake of Keanu Reeves for a low-resolution cell-phone video, reveals how GANs 'see' and generate a face.

On a monitor in a production office, a blurry beige formless shape floats in a black void. The shape becomes vaguely face-like with dark islands of pixels suggesting eyes and mouth. Patches of amorphous dark and light sharpen into legible features: eyebrows, eyes, noise and mouth, and the planes of a face. Gradually a recognisable smiling and talking Keanu Reeves face comes into view. Corridor's creative director, Niko, explains that the AI was trained on a data set of Keanu Reeves's face images taken from all angles and in all lighting conditions for ten days straight. It generated 230,000 iterations of Reeves's face until both the discriminator and its human overseer deemed it good enough. 'Boy, it's nice watching those faces crisp up,' Niko enthuses over the generation process.[36] Here, the creation of a human face is not the work of a year and a massive team allocated separate facial information units, drawing different fields of research into their vortex. It is not a virtual materialisation of a 3D anatomical structure. It is a two-dimensional pattern emerging from a field of pixels. At that time, deepfakes were most persuasive in low-resolution online video, as the faces were small, muddy and prone to glitching. But this is rapidly changing. The pace of development, according to John Fletcher, means that soon these faces will outstrip those of the cinema with 'inhuman levels of perfection', as 'bridging the uncanny valley is just another boardgame for AI to learn'.[37]

This view gives the sense of pure automation and a trajectory towards a machine vision objectivity, reminiscent of older arguments in classical film writing about the camera that sees all before it, unencumbered by the partiality and subjectivity of human perception.

However, the process is not so entirely dumb and disinterested. Yes, on one level, generative adversarial neural networks 'see' and generate images of the human face like they 'see' and make everything else: patterns of light, shade and colour information to be recognised and replicated. However, like the 'holy grail' faces of cinema, the architecture that underpins deepfakes and their uses in face-swap videos extends upon technologies and ways of knowing the face that have been originally developed for other purposes. In this case, the relevant intersections are with machine vision facial recognition and facial emotion processing for security, marketing, and human–computer interaction. As Mirsky and Lee point out, like facial recognition technology, most deepfake architectures rely on an intermediate map of the face's key markers, such as eyes, eyebrows, hair, mouth. Such facial landmarks are required for the generation of face-swap videos to avoid nightmarish faces with unmoored eyes and mouths, and to map the translation of expression from one performer to another. As with the development of digital faces and expressions for cinema, FACS is the standard system used to 'to measure each of the face's taxonomised action units' for deepfakes.[38] In this case though, FACS is detached from a biomedical and anatomical epistemology that penetrates the face's material structures. It is connected instead to a biometric epistemology that identifies the face as a pattern of geometric surface coordinates. These ways of seeing and knowing faces have come, as Zara Dinnen and Sam McBean put it, to 'enmesh' us in 'ambient technological systems' of surveillance for security and marketing.[39]

At the same time, if the 'holy grail' faces of the cinema have been shaped by economic factors, industry and practitioner cultures, and the aesthetic requirements of the medium, deepfakes are renowned for being a type of image that can be produced by almost anyone for any purpose. Deepfakes and deepfake technologies have emerged from particular kinds of online communities. Olivia B. Newton and Mel Stanfill's 2020 analysis of deepfake online open-source software communities on coding platform, GitHub, and related discussions on social media platform, Reddit, characterises these spaces as overwhelmingly masculine, technocratic and 'toxic'. Developing and testing new deepfake apps, using deepfakes largely to produce non-consensual celebrity face-swap pornography, the participants in these communities vary from programmers and engineers, VFX professionals and self-taught hobbyists, as well as thousands of anonymous users with 'throwaway' accounts that conceal their identity.[40] The ways of seeing 'humanness' in such deepfake communities are not necessarily shaped by human anatomy, behaviour, psychology and communication disciplinary perspectives, but technological problem solving, or 'things to do with data'. Newton and Stanfill find that in these deepfake commmunities, 'participants abstract away the human' and characterise the 'face' as a data type rather than a 'property of a person'.[41]

CONCLUSION

It should be clear that in many ways, although deepfakes have some technological and aesthetic commonality with, and may merge with their cinematic counterparts, they also represent a shift in foundations of the digital human face. As I have shown, the cinematic digital faces of Will Smith's clone and of Rachael's replica are luminous visual manifestations of dense structures of anatomical and behavioural information, as well as close human observation from animators and VFX artists, alert to the ways human viewers evaluate synthetic human faces. They draw upon and extend ways of seeing and thinking about faces from biomedical science, physics, paralinguistics, cognitive psychology, and so on, with long strands running back to the Enlightenment. Markedly, these are human-centred categories of inquiry. This is not to say that the cinematic 'holy grail' face is necessarily a more true or valuable manifestation of our ideas of humanness than the machine vision generated deepfake. For the former are not neutral, although they are certainly normative in the ways they conceive facial anatomy and expression with regards to gender, race, culture and facial difference.[42]

This is also not to say that all deepfakes are intrinsically determined by their connections to ambient machine vision surveillance systems and toxic masculine geek culture. As the technology becomes ever more accessible, its uses are broadening, and the kinds of discussions it generates become more complex. Beyond porn, the uses of deepfakes can be pedagogical, expressive, playfully performative and ethical. Rather than the broader 'human versus machine' anxieties that have accompanied the evolution of the digital face of cinema, deepfakes stimulate more focused questions about individual identity, persona appropriation, authenticity and the digital face as mask for trying on different online selves, for deception, and for strategic protection of privacy.[43] As Dinnen and McBean have argued, the images we make and consume of faces are 'not so much the flip side to biometric surveillance culture as they are its more palatable extension'.[44] The emerging uses of and discussions around deepfakes may also remind us of the stakes involved for how the informational regimes of digital faciality are shaped, who benefits, and what or who may elude them.

NOTES

1. As Sean Young's eyes are dark brown, Deckard's reference to green eyes here may be refer to memory of his first encounter with Rachael in the 1982 film, when he interrogated her using the Voight-Kampf machine. In the enlarged image of her iris, the eye is indeed green.
2. Sara Vilkomerson, 'How *Blade Runner 2049* was Able to Pull off that One Incredible Cameo', *EW*, 19 October 2017. Available at <https://ew.com/movies/blade-runner-2049-rachael-sean-young-cameo/> (last accessed 24 March 2021).
3. Dan North, 'From Android to Synthespian: The Performance of Artificial Life', in John Plunkett and James Lyons (eds), *Multimedia Histories* (London: Wallflower, 2005), 88–9.
4. Stephen Prince, *Digital Visual Effects: The Seduction of Reality* (New Brunswick, NJ: Rutgers University Press, 2012); Barbara Flueckiger, 'Digital Bodies', extract from *Visual Effects. Filmbilder aus dem Computer* (Marburg: Schüren Verlag, 2008), trans. Mark Kyburz (2010), 7.
5. I am not focusing on digital human faces in video games. Until recently they have not had the same requirements of photorealism, as only the most high-end graphic display processing has been able to support it (see the lag and glitch problems with *Cyberpunk 2077*, for instance). The ludic, narrative and interactive aspects of

games have tended to be more central than photorealism to our engagement with their characters and worlds.

6. Angela Ndalianis, 'Baroque Facades: Jeff Bridges's Face and Tron Legacy', in Dan North, Bob Rehak and Michael S. Duffy (eds), *Special Effects: New Histories, Theories, Contexts* (London: BFI Palgrave, 2015), 156–65.

7. John Thornton Caldwell, *Production Culture: Industrial Reflexivity and Critical Practice in Film and Television* (Durham, NC: Duke University Press, 2008), 3–7.

8. Frederic Parke, 'Control Parameterization for Facial Animation', in Nadia Magnenat Thalmann and Daniel Thalmann (eds), *Computer Animation '91* (Tokyo: Springer Japan, 1991).

9. See Flueckiger, 'Digital Bodies', 7.

10. The digitised and animated hand had been created by Ed Catmull (co-founder of Pixar) at University of Utah in 1972. The modelled and animated face had been created by Frederic Parke that same year. See Tom Sito's *Moving Innovation: A History of Computer Animation* (Cambridge, MA: MIT Press, 2015), 62–7 on the University of Utah's importance to the development of computer graphics.

11. Oliver Gaycken, '"Don't You Mean Extinct?": On the Circulation of Knowledge in Jurassic Park', in Dan North, Bob Rehak and Michael S. Duffy (eds), *Special Effects: New Histories, Theories, Contexts* (London: BFI Palgrave, 2015), 247.

12. Parke, 'Control Parameterization', 4.

13. Stephen M. Platt and Norman I. Badler, 'Animating Facial Expressions', *Computer Graphics* 15:3 (August 1981), 245–52.

14. Ruth Leys, *The Ascent of Affect: Geneaology and Critique* (Chicago: University of Chicago Press, 2017), 109.

15. Ibid., 79–80.

16. Platt and Badler, 'Animating Facial Expressions', 246.

17. John Goodell, 'Is it Real or Is it a Video Image?' *Los Angeles Times*, 27 March 1983, S7.

18. David Cohen, 'Synthespians Replacing Thespians? Not Soon,' *Variety*, 15 September 2011, 4.

19. Jessica Riskin, 'The Defecating Duck, or, The Ambiguous Origins of Artificial Life', *Critical Inquiry* 29:4 (Summer 2003), 631.

20. It should be noted that *Final Fantasy* was a Japanese–American co-production, and in the Japanese media context, virtual idols, such as Kyoko Date were already commonplace.

21. Jessica Aldred, 'From Synthespian to Avatar: Re-framing the Digital Human in Final Fantasy and The Polar Express', *Mediascape* (Winter 2011), 4.

22. Aldred, 'From Synthespian to Avatar'.

23. Masahiro Mori, 'The Uncanny Valley' (1970) reprinted *IEEE Robotics & Automation Magazine*, June 2012.

24. The earliest appearance seems to be an interview with Stan Winston, John Seabrook, 'It Came from the Dept of Special Effects', *New Yorker* 79:37, 1 December 2003.

25. For an overview see Lisa Bode, 'The Uncanny Valley', in Nichola Dobson et al., *The Animation Studies Reader* (New York: Bloomsbury, 2019).

26. Glen Zorpette, 'Dream Jobs 2011 Meet Weta Digital's Master of Face Animation', *IEEE Spectrum*, 31 January 2011. Available at <https://spectrum.ieee.org/geek-life/profiles/dream-job-mark-sagar> (last accessed 30 March 2021).

27. Melanie A. Farmer, 'Sci-Tech Oscar Honors Revolutionary Facial Capture System', *ACMSIGGRAPH*, 25 June 2019. Available at <https://www.siggraph.org/sci-tech-oscar-honors-revolutionary-facial-capture-system/> (last accessed 10 April 2021).

28. Jody Duncan, 'Uncanny', *Cinefex* 167 (October 2019), 68.

29. Jody Duncan, 'The Unusual Birth of Benjamin Button', *Cinefex* 116 (January 2009), 88.

30. Duncan, 'Uncanny', 67.

31. Vivian Sobchack, 'Final Fantasies: Computer Graphic Animation and the [Dis]illusion of Life', in Suzanne Buchan (ed.), *Animated Worlds* (Eastleigh: John Libbey, 2006), 171–82.

32. Peter Plantec, 'Crossing the Great Uncanny Valley', VFXWorld, *Animaton World Network (AWN)*, 19 December 2007. Available at <https://www.awn.com/vfxworld/crossing-great-uncanny-valley> (last accessed 15 April 2021).

33. Joe Fordham, 'Sacred Ground', *Cinefex* 151 (February 2017), 78.

34. Duncan, 'Uncanny', 68.

35. Yisroel Mirsky and Wenke Lee, 'The Creation and Detection of Deepfakes: A Survey', *ACM Comput* 1:1 (April 2021), 1:6–1.7.

36. 'How We Faked Keanu Reeves Stopping a Robbery', *Corridor Crew*, July 2019. Available at <https://www.youtube.com/watch?v=IzEFnbZ0Zd4&list=PLwVUbPpIRn1QDM8LOibX9WJ34u G7X9Fu3&index=38> (last accessed 4 January 2021).

37. John Fletcher, 'Deepfakes, Artificial Intelligence, and Some Kind of Dystopia: The New Faces of Online Post-Fact Performance', *Theatre Journal* 70:4 (December 2018), 463.

38. Mirsky and Lee, 'The Creation and Detection of Deepfakes', 1:7.

39. Zara Dinnen and Sam McBean, 'The Face as Technology', *New Formations* 93 (Summer 2018), 124.

40. Olivia B. Newton and Mel Stanfill, 'My NSFW Video has Partial Occlusion: Deepfakes and the Technological Production of Nonconsensual Pornography', *Porn Studies* 7.4 (2020), 405.

41. Newton and Stanfill, 'My NSFW Video', 402.

42. For a discussion of the gendered dimensions of digital faces, see Dan Golding 'The Memory of Perfection: Digital Faces and Nostalgic Franchise Cinema', *Convergence* 27:4 (August 2021). For work on the racial dimensions of digital faces, see Tanine Allison, 'Race and the Digital Face: Facial (Mis)Recognition in *Gemini Man*', *Convergence* 27:4 (August 2021), 999–1017.

43. HBO documentary about persecuted LGBTQ people, *Welcome to Chechnya* (2020), for instance, uses deepfakes to protect the identity of its participants, while allowing them 'to retain their humanity'. Joshua Rothkopf, 'Deepfake Technology Enters the Documentary World', *The New York Times*, 1 July 2020.

44. Dinnen and McBean, 'The Face as Technology', 124.

REFERENCES

Abel, Richard, *The Ciné Goes to Town: French Cinema, 1896–1914* (Berkeley: University of California Press, 1998).

Agamben, Giorgio, *The Open: Man and Animal*, trans. Kevin Attell (Stanford: Stanford University Press, 2004).

Agnew, Frances, *Motion Picture Acting: How to Prepare for Photoplaying, What Qualifications Are Necessary, How to Secure an Engagement, Salaries Paid to Photoplayers* (New York: Reliance Newspaper Syndicate, 1913).

Ahmed, Sara, *Queer Phenomenology: Orientations, Objects, Others* (Durham, NC: Duke University Press, 2006).

—— *The Cultural Politics of Emotion* (Edinburgh: Edinburgh University Press, 2014).

Aldred, Jessica, 'From Synthespian to Avatar: Re-framing the Digital Human in Final Fantasy and The Polar Express', *Mediascape* (Winter 2011), n.p.

Allen, Jennifer, 'Critics' Picks: Candice Breitz, Galerie Max Hetzler', *Artforum*, 6 September–18 October 2003, <https://www.artforum.com/picks/candice-breitz-5448> (accessed 20 February 2021).

Allison, Tanine, 'More than a Man in a Monkey Suit: Andy Serkis, Motion Capture, and Digital Realism', *Quarterly Review of Film and Video* 28:4 (1 July 2011), 325–41, <https://doi.org/10.1080/10509208.2010.500947> (last accessed 6 October 2021).

Ambrosio, Ciara, 'Composite Photographs and the Quest for Generality: Themes from Peirce and Galton', *Critical Inquiry* 42:3 (Spring 2016), 547–79.

Angulu, Raphael, Jules R. Tapamo and Aderemi O. Adewumi, 'Age Estimation via Face Images: A Survey', *J Image Video Proc* 42 (2018), n.p., <https://doi.org/10.1186/s13640-018-0278-6> (last accessed 10 October 2021).

Annas, Alicia, 'The Photogenic Formula: Hairstyles and Makeup in Historical Films', in Edward Maeder (ed.), *Hollywood and History: Costume Design in Film* (Thames and Hudson/Los Angeles County Museum of Art, 1987), 52.–77.

Astor, Mary, *A Life on Film* (New York: Delacorte Press), 1971.

Augé, Marc, *Non-Places: An Introduction to Supermodernity* (London and New York: Verso, 2009).

Aumont, Jacques, 'The Face in Close-up', in Anita Dalle Vacche (ed.), *The Visual Turn: Classical Film Theory and Art History* (New Brunswick, NJ: Rutgers University Press, 2003), 127–51.

Azar, M., Algorithmic Facial Image: Regimes of Truth and Datafication, *A Peer-Reviewed Journal About APRJA* 7:1 (2018), 27–35, <https://aprja.net/article/view/115062> (last accessed 22 September 2021).

Balázs, Béla, *Theory of the Film: Character and Growth of a New Art*, trans. Edith Bone (London: Dennis Dobson, 1952).

—— *Béla Balázs: Early Film Theory: Visible Man and the Spirit of Film*, ed. Erica Carter, trans. Rodney Livingstone (New York: Berghahn Books, 2010).

Balsamo, Anne, *Technologies of the Gendered Body: Reading Cyborg Women* (Durham, NC: Duke University Press, 1995).

Balsom, Erika, *Exhibiting Cinema in Contemporary Art* (Amsterdam: Amsterdam University Press, 2013).

Banerjee, Koel, 'Commodity, Citizen, Copy: Bollywood and the Aesthetics of Consumption' (PhD thesis, University of Minnesota, 2018).

Barad, Karen, *Meeting the Universe Halfway* (Durham, NC, Duke University Press, 2007).

Barker, Jennifer M., *The Tactile Eye: Touch and the Cinematic Experience* (Berkeley: University of California Press, 2009).

Barthes, Roland, 'The Face of Garbo', *Mythologies*, trans. Annette Lavers (Hill and Wang, 1972), 56–7.

—— *Camera Lucida: Reflections on Photography*, trans. Richard Howard (New York: Hill and Wang, 1980).

—— 'Leaving the Movie Theatre,' in Roland Barthes, *The Rustle of Language*, trans. Richard Howard (New York: Hill and Wang, 1986), 345–50.

Baudry, Jean-Louis, 'Ideological Effects of the Basic Cinematographic Apparatus,' *Film Quarterly* 28:2 (Winter 1974–5), 39–47.

—— 'The Apparatus: Metapsychological Approaches to the Impression of Reality in Cinema', *Camera Obscura* 1 (Fall 1976), 104–28.

Baughan, Rosa, *Physiognomy: The Handbook* (London: George Redway, 1885).

Bauman, Zygmunt, *Work, Consumerism and the New Poor* (Maidenhead: McGraw-Hill Education, 2007).

Bazin, André, 'Le Journal d'un curé de campagne and the Stylistics of Robert Bresson', in André Bazin, *What is Cinema?* Vol. 1, trans. Hugh Gray (California and London: University of California Press, 1967), 125–43.

Béghin, Cyril, 'Écrin Total', *Cahiers Du Cinéma* (June 2016), 31–3.

Béghin, Cyril and Nicholas Elliott, 'Un film pour l'avenir: entretien avec Nicolas Winding Refn', *Cahiers Du Cinéma* (June 2016), 34–8.

Belting, Hans, *Face and Mask: A Double History*, trans. Thomas S. Hansen and Abby J. Hansen (Princeton: Princeton University Press, 2017 [2013]).

Benjamin, Ruha, *Race After Technology: Abolitionist Tools for the New Jim Code* (Cambridge and Malden, MA: Polity, 2019).

Benjamin, Walter, 'The Work of Art in the Age of Mechanical Reproduction', in Jessica Evans and Stuart Hall (eds), *Visual Culture: The Reader* (London: Thousand Oaks; New Delhi: SAGE Publications, 1999), 72–80.

—— 'Little History of Photography', in Walter Benjamin, *The Work of Art in the Age of Its Technological Reproducibility and Other Writings on Media*, eds Michael W. Jennings, Brigid Doherty and Thomas Y. Levin, trans. Edmund Jephcott, Rodney Livingstone and Howard Eiland (Cambridge, MA: Harvard University Press, 2008), 274–98.

Bergstrom, Carl and Jevin D. West, *Calling Bullshit: The Art of Skepticism in a Data-driven World* (New York: Random House, 2020).

Berlant, Lauren, *The Queen of America Goes to Washington City: Essays on Sex and Citizenship* (Durham, NC: Duke University Press, 1997).

—— *The Female Complaint: The Unfinished Business of Sentimentality in American Culture* (Durham: Duke University Press, 2008).

—— 'Structures of Unfeeling: *Mysterious Skin*', *International Journal of Politics, Culture, and Society* 28:3 (2015), 191–213.

Berridge, Susan, 'From the Woman Who "Had It All" to the Tragic, Ageing Spinster: The Shifting Star Persona of Jennifer Aniston', in Deborah Jermyn and Su Murray (eds), *Women, Celebrity, and Cultures of Ageing: Freeze Frame* (London: Palgrave Macmillan, 2015), 112–26.

Biddle, Mary, 'Beauty Advice [Tired of Looking at the Same Face? Then Change your Coiffure as Hollywood Does!]', *Modern Screen* (November 1935), 16–17, 94–5.

The Big Swallow, dir. James Williamson, Williamson Kinematograph Company, 1901.

Blackhurst, Alice, '"The Camera Glides but Never Settles" between Chantal Akerman's La chambre and Laura Mulvey's Riddles of the Sphinx', *A Nos Amours*, 25 September 2015, <https://anosamoursblog.weebly.com/blog/the-camera-glides-but-never-settles-between-chantal-akermans-la-chambre-and-laura-mulveys-riddles-of-the-sphinx-by-alice-blackhurst> (last accessed 7 October 2021).

Blas, Zach. 'Escaping the Face: Biometric Facial Recognition and the Facial Weaponization Suite', *Media-N* 9:2 (2013), <http://median.newmediacaucus.org/caa-conference-edition-2013/escaping-the-face-biometric-facial-recognition-and-the-facial-weaponization-suite/> (last accessed 23 September 2021).

Bode, Lisa, 'No Longer Themselves? Framing Digitally Enabled Posthumous "Performance"', *Cinema Journal* 49:4 (2010), 46–70.

—— *Making Believe: Screen Performance and Special Effects in Popular Cinema* (Techniques of the Moving Image) (New Brunswick, NJ: Rutgers University Press, 2017).

—— 'The Uncanny Valley', in Nichola Dobson, Annabelle Honess Roe, Amy Ratelle and Caroline Ruddell (eds), *The Animation Studies Handbook* (New York: Bloomsbury, 2019), 59–68.

Bollas, Christopher, *Cracking Up: The Work of Unconscious Experience* (London and New York: Routledge, 1995).

Bonitzer, Pascal, 'The Silences of the Voice', trans. Philip Rosen and Marcia Butzel, in Philip Rosen (ed.), *Narrative, Apparatus, Ideology: A Film Theory Reader* (New York: Columbia University Press, 1986), 319–34.

—— 'Hitchcockian Suspense', in Slavoj Žižek (ed.), *Everything You Wanted to Know about Lacan (But Were Afraid to Ask Hitchcock)* (London: Verso, 1992), 15–30.

Bordwell, David, 'Intensified Continuity', *Film Quarterly* 55:3 (Spring 2002), 16–28.

Bradley, Rizvana, 'Black Cinematic Gesture and the Aesthetics of Contagion', *TDR: The Drama Review* 62 (Spring 2018), 14–30.

Bradshaw, Peter, 'Haneke's House of Horrors', *The Guardian*, 30 April 2008, <https://www.theguardian.com/film/filmblog/2008/apr/30/hanekeshouseofhorrors> (last accessed 24 September 2021).

Braun, Johanna (ed.), *Performing Hysteria: Images and Imaginations of Hysteria* (Leuven: Leuven University Press, 2020).

Brewster, Eugene V., 'Expression of the Emotions (Part 2)', *Motion Picture Magazine* (August 1914), 101–9.

Brooks, Daphne A., *Bodies in Dissent: Spectacular Performances of Race and Freedom, 1850–1910* (Durham, NC: Duke University Press, 2006).

Browne, Simone, *Dark Matters: On the Surveillance of Blackness* (Durham, NC: Duke University Press, 2015).

Buolamwini, Joy, 'InCoding – In the Beginning Was the Coded Glaze', *Medium*, 16 May 2016, <https://medium.com/ mit-media-lab/incoding-in-the-beginning-4e2a5c51a45d> (last accessed 10 October 2021).

—— 'When the Robot Doesn't See Dark Skin', *The New York Times*, 21 June 2018, <https://www.nytimes.com/2018/06/21/opinion/facial-analysis-technology-bias.html> (last accessed 10 October 2021).

Buolamwini, Joy and Timnit Gerbu, 'Gender Shades: Intersectional Accuracy Disparities in Commercial Gender Classification', *Proceedings of Machine Learning Research* 81:1 (2018), 1–15.

Busse, Bettina M., 'The Cindy Sherman Effect: Identity and Transformation in Contemporary Art', in *The Cindy Sherman Effect: Identity and Transformation in Contemporary Art* (Munich: Schirmer/Mosel, 2020), 10–32.

Butler, Judith, 'Sex and Gender in Simone De Beauvoir's Second Sex', *Yale French Studies*, 72 (1986), 35–49.

—— *Precarious Life* (New York: Verso Books, 2006).

Cahill, James, 'A YouTube Bestiary', in Paul Flaig and Katherine Groo (eds), *New Silent Cinema* (New York: Routledge, 2016), 263–93.

—— *Zoological Surrealism: The Nonhuman Cinema of Jean Painlevé* (Minneapolis: University of Minnesota Press, 2019).

Caldwell, John Thornton, *Production Culture: Industrial Reflexivity and Critical Practice in Film and Television* (Durham, NC: Duke University Press, 2008).

Carr, Larry, *Four Fabulous Faces* (New York: Arlington House, 1970).

Carroll, Noel, 'Béla Balázs: The Face of Cinema', *October* 148 (2014), 53–62.

Chandrasekhar, C. P., and Jayati Ghosh, *The Market that Failed: Neoliberal Economic Reforms in India* (New Delhi: Leftword, 2009).

Chapkis, Wendy, *Beauty Secrets: Women and the Politics of Appearance* (London: South End Press, 1999).

Charney, Maurice and Hanna Charney, 'The Language of Madwomen in Shakespeare and His Fellow Dramatists', *Signs* 3:2 (1977), 451–60.

Chaudhury, Maitreyee, *Refashioning India: Gender, Media, and a Transformed Public Discourse* (Hyderabad: Orient BlackSwan, 2017).

Chion, Michel, *The Voice in Cinema*, trans. Claudia Gorbman (New York: Columbia University Press, 1999).

Cho, Michelle, 'Face Value: The Star as Genre in Bong Joon-ho's Mother', in Kyung Hyun Kim and Youngmin Choe (eds), *The Korean Popular Culture Reader* (Durham, NC: Duke University Press, 2013), 168–93.

Chun, Wendy Hui Kyong, 'Race and/as Technology; or, How to Do Things to Race', *Camera Obscura* 24:1 (70) (2009), 6–35.

Coates, Paul, *Screening the Face* (New York: Palgrave Macmillan, 2012).

Cohen, David, 'Synthespians Replacing Thespians? Not Soon', *Variety*, 15 September 2011, 4.

Cohen, Josh, *Not Working: Why We Have to Stop* (London: Granta, 2018).

Cook, Gus. '*Beyond: Two Souls*, Performance Capture, and the Negotiatory Nature of Control', *The Velvet Light Trap* 81 (March 2018), 18–28, <https://doi.org/10.7560/VLT8103> (last accessed 10 October 2021).

Copjec, Joan, 'The Object-Gaze: Shame, Hejab, Cinema', *Gramma* 14 (2006), 163–82.

Coulthard, Glen Sean, *Red Skins White Masks* (Minneapolis: University of Minnesota Press, 2014).

Cox, Julian and Colin Ford (eds), *Julia Margaret Cameron: The Complete Photographs* (Los Angeles: Getty Publications, 2003).

Crawford, Joan, with Jane Kesner Ardmore, *A Portrait of Joan* (New York: Doubleday, 1962).

Crawford, Kate and Trevor Paglen, 'Training Humans', *Quaderni Fondazione Parada* 26 (Milano: Fondazione Prada, 2019).

—— *Excavating AI: The Politics of Images in Machine Learning Training*, n.d., <https://www.excavating.ai.> (last accessed 22 September 2021).

Croce, Arlene, *The Fred Astaire and Ginger Rogers Book* (New York: Galahad Books, 1972).

Dabashi, Hamid, *Close-Up: Iranian Cinema, Past, Present, Future* (London: Verso, 2000).

Dahlquist, Marina, Doron Galili, Jan Olsson and Valentine Robert (eds), *Corporeality in Early Cinema: Viscera, Skin, and Physical Form* (Bloomington: Indiana University Press, 2018).

Darwin, Charles, *The Expression of the Emotions in Man and Animals* (London: John Murray, 1872).

Daston, Lorraine and Peter Galison, *Objectivity* (Brooklyn: Zone Books, 2007).

De Luca, Raymond, 'Dermatology as Screenology: The Films of Lynne Ramsay', *Film Criticism* 43:1 (2019), n.p., <http://dx.doi.org/10.3998/fc.13761232.0043.102> (last accessed 24 September 2021).

Deleuze, Gilles, *Cinema 1: The Movement-Image*, trans. Hugh Tomlinson and Barbara Habberjam (Minneapolis: University of Minnesota Press; London: Continuum, 1986).

—— *Cinema 2: The Time-Image*, trans. Hugh Tomlinson and Robert Galeta (Minneapolis: University of Minnesota Press, 1989).

—— 'Postscripts on the Societies of Control', *October* 59 (Winter 1992), 3–7.

—— *Difference and Repetition* (New York: Columbia University Press, 1995).

Deleuze, Gilles and Felix Guattari, *A Thousand Plateaus: Capitalism and Schizophrenia*, trans. Brian Massumi (Minneapolis: University of Minnesota Press, 1987 and 2002).

—— *What Is Philosophy?* trans. Hugh Tomlinson and Graham Burchell (New York: Columbia University Press, 1996).

Delorme, Stèphane, 'Moment Musicaux: Narcisse, The Neon Demon de Nicolas Winding Refn', *Cahiers Du Cinéma* (June 2016), 36–7.

Deng, Jia, Wei Dong, Richard Socher, Li-Jia Li, Kai Li and Li Fei-Fei, 'ImageNet: A large-scale hierarchical image database', *2009 IEEE Conference on Computer Vision and Pattern Recognition*, 248–55, doi: 10.1109/CVPR.2009.5206848. Retrieved from <https://ieeexplore.ieee.org/document/5206848> (last accessed 10 October 2021).

Denson, Shane and Julia Leyda, *Post-Cinema: Theorizing 21st-Century Film* (Falmer: REFRAME Books, 2016).

Derrida, Jacques, *The Animal That Therefore I Am*, ed. Marie-Louise Mallet, trans. David Wills (New York: Fordham University Press, 2008).

Deshpande, Sudhanva, 'The Consumable Hero of Globalised India', in R. Kaur and A. Sinha (eds), *Bollyworld: Popular Indian Cinema through a Transnational Lens* (London: Sage, 2005), 186–206.

Dickens, Homer *The Films of Ginger Rogers* (New York: Citadel, 1975).

Didi-Huberman, Georges, *Invention of Hysteria Charcot and the Photographic Iconography of the Salpêtrière*, trans. Alisa Hartz. Originally published as *Invention de l'hysterie* (Paris: Éditions Macula, 1982; Cambridge: MIT Press, 2003).

Dinnen, Zara and Sam McBean, 'The Face as Technology', *New Formations* 93 (Summer 2018), 122–37.

DiNucci, Darcy, 'Fragmented Future', *Print* 53:4 (April 1999), 32, 221–2.

Doane, Mary Ann, 'The Voice in the Cinema: The Articulation of Body and Space', in Philip Rosen (ed.), *Narrative, Apparatus, Ideology: A Film Theory Reader* (New York: Columbia University Press, 1986), 335–48.

—— *The Emergence of Cinematic Time: Modernity, Contingency, the Archive* (Cambridge, MA: Harvard University Press, 2002).

—— The Close-Up: Scale and Detail in the Cinema', *differences: A Journal of Feminist Cultural Studies* 14:3 (2003), 89–111.

—— 'Scale and the Negotiation of Real and Unreal Space in the Cinema', in Lúcia Nagib and Cecília Mello (eds), *Realism and the Audiovisual Media* (London: MacMillan, 2009), 63–81.

—— 'Facing a Universal Language', *New German Critique* 41:2 (Summer 2014), 111–24.

The Doctors, CBS Television Distribution, 2008 – present.

Doniger, Wendy, *The Woman Who Pretended to Be Who She Was: Myths of Self-Imitation* (Oxford: Oxford University Press, 2006).

Dubrofsky, Rachel E. and Shoshana Amielle Magnet (eds), *Feminist Surveillance Studies* (Durham, NC: Duke University Press, 2015).

Duchenne du Boulogne, G. B., *The Mechanism of Human Facial Expression*, trans. R. Andrew Cuthbertson (Cambridge: Cambridge University Press, 1990).

Duckett, Victoria, 'Acting', in Claudia Springer and Julie Levinson (eds), *The Silent Screen, 1895–1927* (New Brunswick, NJ: Rutgers University Press, 2015), 25–48.

Duncan, Jody, 'The Unusual Birth of Benjamin Button', *Cinefex* 116 (January 2009), 71–118.

—— 'Uncanny', *Cinefex* 167 (October 2019), 58–78.

—— 'Nothing Short of Witchcraft', *Cinefex* 168 (December 2019), 92–111.

Dyer, Richard, *Stars* (London: BFI, 1979).

—— *White: Essays on Race and Culture* (Abingdon and New York: Routledge, 1997).

—— *Heavenly Bodies: Film Stars and Society* (London: Routledge, 2011).

Edkins, Jenny, *Face Politics* (Abingdon and New York: Routledge, 2015).

Eliot, George, *Daniel Deronda* (New York: Penguin Classics, 1995).

Ellenbogen, Josh, *Reasoned and Unreasoned Images: The Photography of Bertillon, Galton, and Marey* (University Park, PA: Penn State University Press, 2012).

—— 'Educated Eyes and Impressed Images', *Art History* 33:3 (2010), 490–511.

Ellis, John, 'Stars as a Cinematic Phenomenon', in Leo Braudy and Marshall Cohen (eds), *Film Theory and Criticism* (Oxford: Oxford University Press, 2004), 598–605.

Elsaesser, Thomas and Malte Hagener, *Film Theory: An Introduction Through the Senses* (London and New York: Routledge, 2009).

Elsaesser, Thomas, 'The "Return" of 3-D: On Some of the Logics and Genealogies of the Image in the Twenty-first Century', *Critical Inquiry* 39:2 (2013), 217–46.

Elsey, Eileen, 'Her Stories: Lynne Ramsay Talks about Narrative Structure and the Gender of Storytelling', *Vertigo* 2:4 (Spring 2003), n.p., <https://www.closeup-filmcentre.com/vertigo_magazine/volume-2-issue-4-spring-2003/her-stories/> (last accessed 24 September 2021).

Eng, David and Shinhee Han, *Racial Melancholia, Racial Dissociation: On the Social and Psychic Lives of Asian Americans* (Durham, NC: Duke University Press, 2019).

Epstein, Jean, 'L'Ame au Ralenti', *Écrits sur le cinéma: tome 1* (Paris: Editions Seghers, 1974).

—— 'Magnification and Other Writings', trans. Stuart Liebman, *October* 3 (Spring, 1977), 9–25.

—— 'Magnification', *French Film Theory and Criticism: A History/Anthology*, Vol. 1, ed. Richard Abel (Princeton: Princeton University Press, 1988), 235–40.

—— 'On Certain Characteristics of Photogénie', *French Film Theory and Criticism: A History/Anthology*, Vol. 1, ed. Richard Abel (Princeton: Princeton University Press, 1988). 314–20.

—— 'Photogénie and the Imponderable', *French Film Theory and Criticism: A History/Anthology*, Vol. 2, ed. Richard Abel (Princeton: Princeton University Press, 1988), 188–92.

Farahmand, Azadeh, 'Perspectives on Recent (International Acclaim for) Iranian Cinema', in Richard Tapper (ed.), *The New Iranian Cinema: Politics, Representation and Identity* (London: I. B. Tauris, 2002), 86–108.

Faris, Jocelyn, *Ginger Rogers: A Bio-Bibliography* (Westport, CA: Greenwood, 1994).

Farmer, Melanie A., 'Sci-Tech Oscar Honors Revolutionary Facial Capture System', *ACMSIGGRAPH*, 25 June 2019, <https://www.siggraph.org/sci-tech-oscar-honors-revolutionary-facial-capture-system/> (last accessed 10 April 2021).

Faurholt, Gry, 'Self as Other: The Doppelgänger', *Double Dialogues* 10 (Summer 2009), <https://www.doubledialogues.com/article/self-as-other-the-doppelganger/> (last accessed 24 September 2021).

Feldman, Seth, '*Tiger Child*: IMAX and Donald Brittain Times Nine', in Zoë Druick and Gerda Cammaer (eds), *Cinephemera: Archives, Ephemeral Cinema, and New Screen Histories in Canada* (Montreal: McGill-Queen's University Press, 2014), 159–83.

Fernandes, Leela, *India's New Middle Class: Democratic Politics in an Era of Economic Reform* (Minneapolis: University of Minnesota Press, 2010).

Fineman, Mia. *Faking It: Manipulated Photography Before Photoshop*. New York: The Metropolitan Museum of Art, 2012.

Flatley, Jonathan, *Like Andy Warhol* (Chicago: University of Chicago Press, 2017).

Flaxman, Greg and Elena Oxman, 'Losing Face', in Ian Buchanan and Patricia MacCormack (eds), *Deleuze and the Schizoanalysis of Cinema* (London and New York: Bloomsbury Academic, 2008), 39–51.

Fletcher, John, 'Deepfakes, Artificial Intelligence, and Some Kind of Dystopia: The New Faces of Online Post-Fact Performance', *Theatre Journal* 70:4 (December 2018), 455–71.

Flueckiger, Barbara, 'Digital Bodies', extract from *Visual Effects. Filmbilder aus dem Computer* (Marburg, 2008), trans. Mark Kyburz, 2010, 1–52.

Fordham, Joe, 'Middle-Earth Strikes Back', *Cinefex* 92 (January 2003), 70–142.

—— 'Beneath the Barnacles', *Cinefex* 107 (October 2006), 67–89.

—— 'Sacred Ground', *Cinefex* 151 (February 2017), 50–78.

—— '2049 Foresight', *Cinefex* 155 (October 2017), 54–79.

Foster, Hal, 'Post-Critical', *October* (1 January 2012), 3–8.

Foucault, Michel, *Discipline and Punish: The Birth of the Prison* (New York: Vintage Books, 1995).

Francis, Mark, 'Splitting the Difference: On the Queer-feminist Divide in Scarlett Johansson's Recent Body Politics', *Jump Cut: A Review of Contemporary Media* 57 (2016), n.p., <https://www.ejumpcut.org/archive/jc57.2016/-FrancisSkin/index.html> (last accessed 25 February 2021).

Frasca, Gonzalo, 'Simulation versus Narrative: Introduction to Ludology', in *The Video Game Theory Reader* (London: Routledge, 2003), 221–36.

Fred Ott's Sneeze, dir. William K. L. Dickson, Edison Manufacturing Company, 1894.

Freud, Sigmund, 'The "Uncanny"', in Sigmund Freud, *The Standard Edition of the Complete Psychological Works of Sigmund Freud*, Vol. XVII, trans. James Strachey et al. (London: The Hogarth Press, 1919), 217–53.

Fry, Naomi, '"Fake Famous" and the Tedium of Influencer Culture', *The New Yorker*, 20 February 2021, <https://www.newyorker.com/culture/on-television/fake-famous-and-the-tedium-of-influencer-culture> (last accessed 26 February 2021).

Galloway, Alexander R. *The Interface Effect* (Cambridge and Malden, MA: Polity, 2012).

Galton, Francis, 'Composite Portraits', *Nature* (May 1878), 97–100.

—— 'Composite Portraits Made by Combining Those of Many Different Persons into a Single Resultant Figure', *Journal of the Anthropological Institute* 8 (1879), 132–44.

—— 'Generic Images', *Nineteenth Century* 6:29 (1879), 157–69.

—— 'On Generic Images', *Notices of the Proceedings at the Meetings of the Members of the Royal Institution of Great Britain* 9, 25 April 1879, 161–70.

—— 'Conventional Representation of the Horse in Motion', *Nature* (July 1882), 228–9.

—— 'Letter to Alphonse de Candolle', in *Researches of Middle Life*, Vol. II of *The Life, Letters and Labours of Sir Francis Galton* (3 vols) (Cambridge: Cambridge University Press, 1884), 209.

—— 'Photographic Composites', *The Photographic News*, 17 April 1885, 243–5.

Garvie, Clare, Alvaro M. Bedoya and Jonathan Frankle, 'The Perpetual Line-Up', *Georgetown Law Center on Privacy and Technology*, 18 October 2016, <https://www.perpetuallineup.org/> (last accessed 22 September 2021).

Garvie, Clare, 'Garbage In, Garbage Out', *Georgetown Law Center on Privacy and Technology*, 16 May 2019, <https://www.flawedfacedata.com/> (last accessed 22 September 2021).

Gasman, dir. Lynne Ramsay, Holy Cow Films, 1998.

Gates, Kelly, *Our Biometric Future* (New York: New York University Press, 2011).

Gaycken, Oliver, 'Don't You Mean Extinct?: On the Circulation of Knowledge in Jurassic Park', in Dan North, Bob Rehak and Michael S. Duffy (eds), *Special Effects: New Histories, Theories Contexts* (London: BFI Palgrave, 2015), 241–53.

Gilman, Sander, *Seeing the Insane* (Lincoln: University of Nebraska Press, 1982).

—— *Difference and Pathology: Stereotypes of Sexuality, Race, and Madness* (Ithaca: Cornell University Press, 1985).

Godfrey-Smith, Peter, *Other Minds: The Octopus, the Sea and the Deep Origins of Consciousness* (New York: Strauss, and Giroux Farrar, 2016).

Golding, Dan, 'The Memory of Perfection: Digital Faces and Nostalgic Franchise Cinema', *Convergence* 27:4 (August 2021), 855–67.

González, Jennifer, 'The Face and the Public: Race, Secrecy and Digital Art Practice', *Camera Obscura* 24:1 (70) (2009), 37–65.

Goodell, John, 'Is it Real or Is it a Video Image?' *Los Angeles Times*, 27 March 1983, S7.

Gordon, Rae Beth, 'From Charcot to Charlot: Unconscious Imitation and Spectatorship in French Cabaret and Early Cinema', *Critical Inquiry* 27:3 (Spring 2001), 515–49.

Gray, Frank, *The Brighton School and the Birth of British Film*, 1st edn, 2019 (Cham: Springer International Publishing, 2019), <https://doi.org/10.1007/978-3-030-17505-4> (last accessed 10 October 2021).

Guilbert, Georges-Claude, *Gay Icons: The (Mostly) Female Entertainers Gay Men Love* (Jefferson, NC: McFarland & Company, 2018).

Gunn, Jenny, 'Deleuze, Žižek, Spring Breakers and the Question of Ethics in Late Capitalism', *Film Philosophy* 22 (Winter 2018), 95–113.

Gunning, Tom, 'Tracing the Individual Body: Photography, Detectives, and Early Cinema', in L. Charney and V. R. Schwartz (eds), *Cinema and the Invention of Modern Life* (Berkeley: University of California Press, 1995), 15–45.

—— 'In Your Face: Physiognomy, Photography, and the Gnostic Mission of Early Film', *Modernism/Modernity* 4 (January 1997), 1–29.

—— 'The Cinema of Attraction[s]: Early Film, Its Spectator and the Avant-Garde', in Wanda Strauven (ed.), *The Cinema of Attractions Reloaded* (Amsterdam: Amsterdam University Press, 2006), 381–8.

—— 'The Impossible Body of Early Film', in Marina Dahlquist, Doron Galili, Jan Olsson and Valentine Robert (eds), *Corporeality in Early Cinema: Viscera, Skin, and Physical Form* (Bloomington: Indiana University Press, 2018), 13–24.

Hall, Leonard, 'The Glamor Factories of Hollywood', *Stage* (July 1936), 18–20.

Hamilton, Sara, 'Freedom Is Glorifying Ginger', *Photoplay* (September 1936), n.p.

Hansen, Mark, 'Affect as Medium, or the "Digital-Facial-Image"', *Journal of Visual Culture* 2:2 (2003), 205–28.

Hao, Karen, 'This Is How We Lost Control of Our Faces', *MIT Technology Review*, 5 February 2021, <https://www.technologyreview.com/2021/02/05/1017388/ai-deep-learning-facial-recognition-data-history> (last accessed 22 September 2021).

Haraway, Donna, *When Species Meet* (Minneapolis: University of Minnesota Press, 2007).

Hartley, Lucy, *Physiognomy and the Meaning of Expression in Nineteenth-century Culture* (Cambridge Studies in Nineteenth-century Culture 29) (Cambridge: Cambridge University Press, 2001).

Hartman, Saidiya V., *Scenes of Subjection: Terror, Slavery and Self-Making in Nineteenth-century America* (Oxford: Oxford University Press, 1997).

Haug, Wolfgang Fritz, *Commodity Aesthetics, Ideology and Culture* (Amsterdam: International General, 1987).

Hell, Richard, 'Consuming Passion: Bresson and *The Devil, Probably*', in Bert Cardullo (ed.), *The Films of Robert Bresson: A Casebook* (London and New York: Anthem Press, 2009), 169–74.

Hennefeld, Maggie, 'Death from Laughter, Female Hysteria, and Early Cinema', *differences* (December 2016), 45–92.

—— *Specters of Slapstick and Silent Film Comediennes* (New York: Columbia University Press, 2018).

Hildebrand, Lucas, 'On the Matter of Blackness in *Under the Skin*', *Jump Cut: A Review of Contemporary Media* 57 (2016), n.p., <https://www.ejumpcut.org/archive/jc57.2016/-HilderbrandUnderSkin/index.html> (last accessed 7 October 2021).

hooks, bell, 'The Oppositional Gaze: Black Female Spectators', in hooks bell, *Black Looks: Race and Representation* (Boston: South End Press, 1992), 115–31.

Horek, Tanya, '#ReneeZellweger's Face', *Celebrity Studies* 6:2 (2015), 261–4.

Hustvedt, Asti, *Medical Muses: Hysteria in Nineteenth-century Paris* (New York: W. W. Norton & Company, 2011).

Ibrahim, Yasmin, 'Coalescing the Mirror and the Screen: Consuming the "Self" Online', *Continuum* 31:1 (2017), 104–13.

IBUG data set, Department of Computing, Imperial College London, <https://ibug.doc. ic.ac.uk/ resources/facial-point-annotations/> (last accessed 19 February 2021).

Ickes, Charlotte, 'Radical Immersion in the Work of Melvin Van Peebles, Isaac Julien, and Steve McQueen' (PhD thesis, University of Pennsylvania, 2016).

Jacobs, Joseph, 'The Jewish Type and Galton's Composite Photographs', *Photographic News*, 24 April 1885, 268–9.

—— 'On the Racial Characteristics of Modern Jews', *The Journal of the Anthropological Institute of Great Britain and Ireland* 15 (Trübner & Co., 1885–6), 23–62.

Jagose, Annamarie, *Orgasmology* (Durham, NC, Duke University Press, 2012).

Jermyn, Deborah, 'Introduction: "Get a Life Ladies. Your Old One is Not Coming Back": Ageing, Ageism and the Lifespan of Female Celebrity', in Deborah Jermyn (ed.), *Female Celebrity and Ageing: Back in the Spotlight* (London: Routledge, 2013), 1–14.

Jones, Douglas A., 'Black Politics but Not Black People: Rethinking the Social and "Racial" History of Early Minstrelsy', *TDR* 57:2 (2013), 21–37.

Jones, Kent, *L'Argent* (London, BFI, 1999).

Jones, Nate and E. Alex Jung, 'A History of Everyone Freaking Out About Renée Zellweger's Face', *New York Magazine*, 1 July 2016, <https://www.vulture. com/2014/10/history-of-freakouts-over-renee-zellwegers-face.html> (last accessed 6 October 2021).

Kanade, Takeo, *Picture Processing System by Computer Complex and Recognition of Human Faces* (Department of Information Science, Kyoto University, 1973).

—— *Computer Recognition of Human Faces* (Basel and Stuttgart: Birkhauser Verlag, 1977).

—— 'Takeo Kanade: Computer Face Recognition in Its Beginning', *MITCBMM*, 22 April 2016, Video. 25:10, <https://www.youtube.com/watch?v=fY98kQWxJQc&t=5s> (last accessed 22 September 2021).

Keller, Sarah and Jason N. Paul (eds), *Jean Epstein: Critical Essays and New Translations* (Amsterdam: Amsterdam University Press, 2012).

Kember, Sarah, 'Face Recognition and the Emergence of Smart Photography', *Journal of Visual Culture* 13:2 (2014), 182–99.

Kendall, Tina, '"The In-between of Things": Intermediality in *Ratcatcher*', *New Review of Film and Television Studies* 8:2 (2010), 179–97.

King, Barry, 'Stardom, Celebrity, and the Money Form', *The Velvet Light Trap* 65 (2010), 7–19.

Koch, Gertrude, 'Béla Balázs: The Physiognomy of Things', trans. Miriam Hansen, *New German Critique* 40 (1987), 167–77.

Kolko, Beth E., 'Erasing @race: Going White in the (Inter)Face', in Beth E. Kolko, Lisa Nakamura, and Gilbert B. Rodman (eds), *Race in Cyberspace* (London: Routledge 2000), 213–32.

Kosinski, Michal, 'Facial Recognition Technology Can Expose Political Orientation from Naturalistic Facial Images', *Scientific Reports*, 11 January 2021, 11:100, <https://doi.org/10.1038/s41598-020-79310-1> (last accessed 10 October 2021).

Kristeva, Julia, *Powers of Horror: An Essay on Abjection*, trans. Leon S. Roudiez (New York: Columbia University Press, 1982).

—— *Black Sun: Depression and Melancholia*, trans. Leon S. Roudiez (New York: Columbia University Press, 1989).

Krützen, Michaela, *The Most Beautiful Woman on the Screen: The Fabrication of the Star Greta Garbo* (Berlin: Peter Lang, 1992).

Kuhn, Annette, *Ratcatcher* (London: BFI, 2008).

LaBelle, Brandon, *Lexicon of the Mouth: Poetics and Politics of Voice and the Oral Imaginary* (London: Bloomsbury Publishing, 2014).

Langford, Michelle, *Allegory in Iranian Cinema: The Aesthetics of Poetry and Resistance* (London: Bloomsbury, 2019).

Le Brun, Charles. 'Les expressions des passions de l'âme. Par Charles Le Brun, 1727', <http://www.histoiredelafolie.fr/psychiatrie-neurologie/les-expressions-des-passions-de-lame-par-charles-le-brun-1727> (last accessed 27 September 2021).

Lemmon, Fay, 'Makeup Box Is First Ordeal of the Film Aspirant in Hollywood', *Dallas Morning News* (c. March–April 1934).

Lessing, Gotthold Ephraim, *Laocoön: An Essay Upon the Limits of Painting and Poetry*, trans. Ellen Frothingham (Mineola, NY: Dover Publications, 2005).

Leunissen, Mariska, 'Physiognomy', in Paul T. Keyser and John Scarborough (eds), *Oxford Handbook of Science and Medicine in the Classical World* (New York: Oxford University Press, 2018), 743–64.

Levin, Thomas Y., 'Rhetoric of the Temporal Index: Surveillant Narration and the Cinema of "Real Time"', in Thomas Y. Levin, Ursula Frohne and Peter Weibel (eds), *CRTL [SPACE]: Rhetorics of Surveillance from Bentham to Big Brother* (Cambridge, MA: MIT Press, 2002), 578–93.

Leys, Ruth, *The Ascent of Affect: Geneaology and Critique* (Chicago: University of Chicago Press, 2017).

Lindqvist, John Ajvide, *Let the Old Dreams Die*, trans. Ebba Segerberg (New York: Thomas Dunne Books, 2013).

Lippit, Akira Mizuta, *Electric Animal* (Minneapolis: University of Minnesota Press, 2000).

—— *Atomic Light: Shadow Optics* (Minneapolis: University of Minnesota Press, 2005).

Liu, David Palumbo, *Asian/American: Historical Crossings of a Racial Frontier* (Palo Alto, CA: Stanford University Press, 1999).

Longolius, Sonja, *Performing Authorship: Strategies of 'Becoming an Author' in the Works of Paul Auster, Candice Breitz, Sophie Calle, and Jonathan Safran Foer* (Bielefeld: transcript-Verlag, 2016).

Lowe, Lisa, *Immigrant Acts: On Asian American Culture Politics* (Durham, NC: Duke University Press, 2012).

Majumdar, Neepa, 'Embodiment and Stardom in Shahrukh Khan's Fan', *Framework* 58:1–2 (2017), 144–60.

Massood, Paula J., *Black City Cinema: African American Urban Experiences in Film* (Philadelphia: Temple University Press, 2003).

—— 'To the Past and Beyond: African American History Films in Dialogue with the Present', *Film Quarterly* 71:2 (Winter 2017), 19–24.

Maurice, Alice, 'The Essence of Motion: Figure, Frame, and the Racial Body in Early Silent Cinema', *The Moving Image: The Journal of the Association of Moving Image Archivists* 1:2 (Fall 2001), 124–5.

—— *The Cinema and Its Shadow: Race and Technology in Early Cinema* (University of Minnesota Press, 2013).

—— 'Making Faces: Character and Makeup in Early Cinema', in Marina Dahlquist, Doron Galili, Jan Olsson and Valentine Robert (eds), *Corporeality in Early Cinema* (Bloomington: Indiana University Press, 2018), 206–18.

Maxwell, Anne, *Picture Imperfect: Photography and Eugenics 1870–1940* (Brighton: Sussex Academic Press, 2008).

Mazaj, Meta, 'Border Aesthetics and Catachresis in Ali Abbasi's *Grans/Border* (2018)', *Transnational Screens* 11:1 (2018), 34–47.

McLean, Adrienne (ed.), *Costume, Makeup and Hair* (New Brunswick, NJ: Rutgers University Press, 2016).

—— *All for Beauty: Makeup and Hairdressing in Hollywood's Studio Era* (Chicago: Rutgers University Press, forthcoming 2022).

Michelson, Annette, 'Reading Eisenstein Reading "Capital"', *October* 2 (Summer, 1976), 26–38.

Mihailova, Mihaela, 'Collaboration without Representation: Labor Issues in Motion and Performance Capture', *Animation: An Interdisciplinary Journal* 11:1 (2016), 40–58, <https://doi.org/10.1177/1746847715623691> (last accessed 6 October 2021).

Mirsky Yisroel and Wenke Lee, 'The Creation and detection of Deepfakes: a survey', *ACM Comput* 54.1 (April 2021).

Mirzoeff, Nicholas, *The Right to Look: A Counterhistory of Visuality* (Durham, NC: Duke University Press).

Moakley, Paul, 'Inside the Cinematography of *Moonlight*: The Images That Inspired James Laxton', <https://time.com/behind-the-visuals-of-moonlight/> (last accessed 24 September 2021).

Morin, Edgar, *The Stars* [*Les Stars*, 1957], trans. Richard Howard (Minneapolis: University of Minnesota Press, 2005).

Morris-Reich, Amos, 'Anthropology, Standardization, and Measurement: Rudolf Martin and Anthropometric Photography', *British Journal for the History of Science* 46 (2013), 487–516.

Morvern Callar, dir. Lynne Ramsay, Company Pictures, 2002.

Moten, Fred, *Black and Blur* (Durham, NC: Duke University Press, 2017).

Motion Pictures from The Library of Congress Paper Print Collection 1894–1912 (Berkeley: University of California Press, n.d.).

Mottahedeh, Negar, *Displaced Allegories: Post-revolutionary Iranian Cinema* (Durham, NC: Duke University Press, 2008).

Muammad, Khalil Gibran, *The Condemnation of Blackness: Race, Crime, and the Making of Modern Urban America* (Cambridge, MA: Harvard University Press, 2010).

Mulvey, Laura, 'Visual Pleasure and Narrative Cinema', *Screen* 16:3 (1975), 6–18.

Mumford, Stephen, *Dispositions* (Oxford: Oxford University Press, 2003).

Münsterberg, Hugo, *The Photoplay: A Psychological Study* (New York: D. Appleton and Company, 1916).

Musumeci, Emilia, 'Against the Rising Tide of Crime: Cesare Lombroso and Control of the "Dangerous Classes" in Italy, 1861–1940', *Crime, Histoire & Sociétés / Crime, History*

& Societies 22:2 (2018), 83–106, <http://www.jstor.org/stable/45215827> (last accessed 8 April 2021).

Nancy, Jean-Luc, *Ego Sum: Corpus, Anima, Fabula*, trans. Marie-Eve Morin (New York: Fordham University Press, 2016).

Naremore, James, *Acting in the Cinema* (Berkeley: University of California Press, 1988).

Ndalianis, Angela, 'Baroque Facades: Jeff Bridges's Face and Tron Legacy', in Dan North, Bob Rehak and Michael S. Duffy (eds), *Special Effects: New Histories, Theories, Contexts* (London: BFI Palgrave, 2015), 154–65.

Nesbet, Anne, *Savage Junctures: Sergei Eisenstein and the Shape of Thinking* (London: I. B. Tauris, 2007).

Newton, Olivia B. and Mel Stanfill, 'My NSFW Video Has Partial Occlusion: Deepfakes and the Technological Production of Nonconsensual Pornography', *Porn Studies* 7:4 (2020), 398–414.

Ng, Alfred and Steven Musil, 'Clearview AI Hit with Cease-and-Desist from Google, Facebook over Facial Recognition Collection', *CNET*, 5 February 2020, <https://www.cnet.com/news/clearview-ai-hit-with-cease-and-desist-from-google-over-facial-recognition-collection/> (last accessed 22 September 2021).

Nguyen Tan Hoang, *A View from the Bottom: Asian American Masculinity and Sexual Representation* (Durham, NC: Duke University Press, 2014).

North, Dan, 'From Android to Synthespian: The Performance of Artificial Life', in John Plunkett and James Lyons (eds), *Multimedia Histories: From the Magic Lantern to the Internet* (London: Wallflower, 2005), 85–97.

Novak, Daniel Akiva, *Realism, Photography, and Nineteenth-century Fiction* (Cambridge: Cambridge University Press, 2008).

O'Brien, Charles, 'Camera Distance and Acting in Griffith Biographs', in Kaveh Askari, Scott Curtis, Frank Gray, Louis Pelletier, Tami Williams and Joshua Yumibe (eds), *Performing New Media, 1890–1915* (Bloomington: Indiana University Press, 2015), 41–7.

Osterweil, Ara, 'Under the Skin: The Perils of Becoming Female', *Film Quarterly* 67:4 (June 2014), 44–51.

Park, Julie, 'Unheimlich Maneuvers: Enlightenment Dolls and Repetitions in Freud', *The Eighteenth Century* 44:1 (2003), 45–68.

Parke, Frederic, 'Control Parameterization for Facial Animation', in Nadia Magnenat Thalmann and Daniel Thalmann (eds), *Computer Animation '91* (Tokyo: Springer Japan, 1991), 3–14.

Pearson, Karl, *Researches of Middle Life*, Vol. II of *The Life, Letters and Labours of Sir Francis Galton* (3 vols) (Cambridge and New York: Cambridge University Press, 1924).

Pearson, Roberta E., *Eloquent Gestures: The Transformation of Performance Style in the Griffith Biograph Films* (Berkeley: University of California Press, 1992).

Perez, Gilberto, *The Material Ghost: Films and their Medium* (Baltimore: The Johns Hopkins University Press, 1998).

—— 'Where is the Director?' *Sight and Sound* 15:5 (2005), 18–22.

Pickens, Therí A., *Black Madness :: Mad Blackness* (Durham, NC: Duke University Press, 2019).

Pitts-Taylor, Victoria, *Surgery Junkies: Wellness and Pathology in Cosmetic Culture* (New Brunswick, NJ: Rutgers University Press, 2007).

Plantec, Peter, 'Crossing the Great Uncanny Valley', VFXWorld, *Animaton World Network (AWN)*, 19 December 2007, <https://www.awn.com/vfxworld/crossing-great-uncanny-valley> (last accessed 15 April 2021).

Platt, Agnes, *Practical Hints on Acting for the Cinema* (New York: E. P. Dutton, 1921).

Platt, Stephen M. and Norman I. Badler, 'Animating Facial Expressions', *Computer Graphics* 15:3 (August 1981), 245–52.

Porter, Theodore and Paul Fleming, 'Life on the Bell Curve: An Interview with Theodore Porter', *Cabinet Magazine* 15 (2004), <https://www.cabinetmagazine.org/issues/15/fleming_porter.php> (last accessed 20 September 2021).

Poster, Mark, 'Foucault and Databases', in *The Mode of Information: Poststructuralism and Social Context* (Chicago: University of Chicago Press, 1990).

Prince, Stephen, *Digital Visual Effects: The Seduction of Reality* (New Brunswick, NJ: Rutgers University Press, 2012).

Psycho, dir. Alfred Hitchcock, Paramount Pictures, 1960.

Pugliese, Joseph, *Biometrics: Bodies, Technologies, Biopolitics* (London: Routledge, 2010).

Purse, Lisa, *Digital Imaging in Popular Cinema* (Edinburgh: Edinburgh University Press, 2013).

Quandt, James, 'On *Au hasard, Balthasar*', in Bert Cardullo (ed.), *The Films of Robert Bresson: A Casebook* (London, New York: Anthem Press, 2009), 81–5.

Queen, John and Hughie L. Cannon, 'Just Because She Made Dem Goo-goo Eyes' (1900), New York Public Library Digital Collections, <https://digitalcollections.nypl.org/items/853b76bb-efb1-9410-e040-e00a180610c4> (last accessed 21 September 2021).

Questions and Answers with Bradford Young, 'Times of Strife', *The American Society of Cinematographers*, February 2015, <https://theasc.com/ac_magazine/February2015/QandAwithBradfordYoung/> (last accessed 24 September 2021).

Rajadhyaksha, Ashish, 'The "Bollywoodization" of the Indian Cinema: Cultural Nationalism in a Global Arena', *Inter-Asia Cultural Studies* 4:1 (2003), 25–39.

Rancière, Jacques, *Dissensus: On Politics and Aesthetics*, ed. and trans. Steven Corcoran (London: Continuum, 2010).

Ranjan, Rajeev, Vishal M. Patel, and Rama Chellappa, 'HyperFace: A Deep Multi-task Learning Framework for Face Detection, Landmark Localization, Pose Estimation, and Gender Recognition', in *IEEE Transactions on Pattern Analysis and Machine Intelligence* 41:1 (1 January 2019), 121–35, <doi:10.1109/TPAMI.2017.2781233> (last accessed 10 October 2021).

Rapold, Nicolas, 'NYFF Interview: Ali Abbasi', *Film Comment*, 21 September 2018, <https://www.filmcomment.com/blog/nyff-interview-ali-abbasi/> (last accessed 6 February 2021).

Ratcatcher, dir. Lynne Ramsay, Pathé Pictures and BBC Films, 1999.

RecruiterFlow Blog, <https://recruiterflow.com/blog/recruiting-memes/> (last accessed 12 September 2021).

Redfield, James W., *Comparative Physiognomy or Resemblances Between Men and Animals* (Clifton Hall, NY: Redfield, 1866).

Rifkin, Mark, 'Indigenizing Agamben: Rethinking Sovereignty in Light of the "Peculiar" Status of Native Peoples', *Cultural Critique* 73 (2009), 88–124.

Riskin, Jessica, 'The Defecating Duck, or, The Ambiguous Origins of Artificial Life', *Critical Inquiry* 29:4 (Summer 2003), 599–633.

Rivera Colón, Edgar, 'Spike Jonze's Her: Loneliness, Race, & Digital Polyamory', *The Feminist Wire*, 3 March 2014, <http://www.thefeministwire.com/2014/03/her-film-loneliness-race-spike-jonze/> (last accessed 7 October 2021).

Roach, Joseph R., *The Player's Passion: Studies in the Science of Acting* (Ann Arbor: University of Michigan Press, 1993).

Rogers, Ginger, *Ginger: My Story* (New York: HarperCollins, 1991).

Rony, Fatimah Tobing, *The Third Eye: Race, Cinema, and Ethnographic Spectacle* (Durham, NC: Duke University Press, 1996).

Rosen, Philip (ed.), *Narrative, Apparatus, Ideology: A Film Theory Reader* (New York: Columbia University Press, 1986).

Russell, Catherine, *Experimental Ethnography: The Work of Film in the Age of Video* (Durham, NC: Duke University Press, 1999).

Saljoughi, Sara, 'Seeing Iranian Style: Women and Collective Vision in Abbas Kiarostami's *Shirin*', *Iranian Studies* 45:4 (2012), 519–35.

Saxena, Anvita, Ashish Khanna and Deepak Gupta, 'Emotion Recognition and Detection Methods: A Comprehensive Survey', *Journal of Artificial Intelligence and Systems* 2 (2020), 53–79, <https://doi.org/10.33969/AIS.2020.21005> (last accessed 13 October 2021).

Schlappich, Sam, 'Expressing Emotions on the Screen', *Motion Picture Magazine* (August 1916), 46–8.

Seabrook, John, 'It Came from the Dept. of Special Effects', *New Yorker*, 1 December 2003, 54.

Sekula, Allan, *Photography Against the Grain: Essays and Photo Works 1973–1983* (Halifax, Nova Scotia: The Press of Nova Scotia College of Art and Design, 1984).

—— 'The Body and the Archive', *October* 39 (Winter 1986), 3–64.

The Seventh Continent, dir. Michael Haneke, WEGA Filmproduktion, 1989.

Shaftesbury, Edmund, *Lessons in the Art of Acting* (Washington, DC: Martyn College Press, 1889).

Sharrett, Christopher, '*The Seventh Continent*', *Senses of Cinema* 34 (February 2005), <https://www.sensesofcinema.com/2005/cteq/seventh_continent/> (last accessed 24 September 2021).

Shaviro, Steven, *Post Cinematic Affect* (Winchester: Zero Books, 2010).

Shimizu, Celine Parreñas, *The Hypersexuality of Race: Performing Asian/American Women on Screen and Scene* (Durham, NC: Duke University Press, 2007).

Showalter, Elaine, *Hystories: Hysterical Epidemics and Modern Culture* (New York: Columbia University Press, 1997).

Siddons, Henry, *Practical Illustrations of Rhetorical Gesture and Action; Adapted to the English Drama from a Work on the Subject by M. Engel* (London: Sherwood, Neely and Jones, 1822).

Silverman, Kaja, *Threshold of the Visible World* (London and New York: Routledge, 1996).

Simmel, Georg, 'The Aesthetic Significance of the Face', in Kurt Wolff (ed.), *Georg Simmel: 1858–1918: A Collection of Essays* (Columbus: Ohio State University Press, 1959), 276–81.

Singer, Gregory, 'The Two Towers: Face to Face with Gollum', *ANIMATIONWorld* (blog), 17 March 2003, <https://www.awn.com/animationworld/two-towers-face-face-gollum> (last accessed 6 October 2021).

Sito, Tom, *Moving Innovation: A History of Computer Animation* (MIT Press, 2015).

Small Deaths, dir. Lynne Ramsay, National Film and Television School, 1996.

Smith, Imogen Sara, 'In Our Time: Abbas Kiarostami's *24 Frames*', *Film Comment* (February 2018), <https://www.filmcomment.com/blog/24-frames/> (last accessed 29 September).

Smith, Michelle, 'Meg Ryan's Face and the Historical Battleground of Ageing', *The Conversation*, 16 June 2016, <http://dro.deakin.edu.au/eserv/DU:30090186/smith-megryansface-2016.pdf> (last accessed 6 October 2021).

Smith, Shawn Michelle, *At the Edge of Sight: Photography and the Unseen* (Durham, NC, and London: Duke University Press, 2013).

Smyth, Sarah Louise, 'Postfeminism, Ambivalence and the Mother in Lynne Ramsay's *We Need to Talk about Kevin* (2011)', *Film Criticism* 44:1 (2020), n.p., <http://dx.doi.org/10.3998/fc.13761232.0044.106> (last accessed 24 September 2021).

Sobchack, Vivian, 'Final Fantasies: Computer Graphic Animation and the [Dis]illusion of Life', in Suzanne Buchan (ed.), *Animated Worlds* (Eastleigh: John Libbey, 2006), 171–82.

—— 'The Scene of the Screen: Envisioning Photographic, Cinematic, and Electronic Presence', in Shane Denson and Julia Leyda (eds), *Post-Cinema: Theorizing 21st-century Film* (Falmer: REFRAME Books, 2016), 88–129.

Spitzack, Carole, 'The Confession Mirror: Plastic Images for Surgery', *Canadian Journal for Political and Social Theory* 12:1–2 (1988), 38–50.

—— Stacey, Jackie, *Star Gazing: Hollywood Cinema and Female Spectatorship* (London: Routledge, 1994).

—— 'Crossing over with Tilda Swinton – the Mistress of "Flat Affect"', *International Journal of Politics, Culture, and Society* 28:3 (2015), 243–71.

Stanton, Mary Olmstead, *A System of Practical and Scientific Physiognomy; Or, How to Read Faces* (Philadelphia: F. A. Davis, 1890).

—— *The Encyclopedia of Face and Form* (Philadelphia: F. A. Davis, 1900).

Stark, Luke and Jesse Hoey, 'The Ethics of Emotion in Artificial Intelligence Systems', FAccT '21: Proceedings of the 2021 ACM Conference on Fairness, Accountability, and Transparency, March 2021, 782–93, <https://dl.acm.org/doi/10.1145/3442188.3445939> (last accessed 22 September 2021).

Steimatsky, Noa, *The Face on Film* (New York: Oxford University Press, 2017).

Stewart, Garrett, *Closed Circuits: Screening Narrative Surveillance* (Chicago, University of Chicago Press, 2015).

Strauven, Wanda, 'Introduction to an Attractive Concept', in Wanda Straven (ed.), *The Cinema of Attractions Reloaded: Film Culture in Transition* (Amsterdam: Amsterdam University Press, 2006), 11–28.

Strochlic, Nina, 'Framed "Afghan Girl" Finally Gets a Home', *National Geographic*, 12 December 2017, <https://www.nationalgeographic.com/pages/article/afghan-girl-home-afghanistan> (last accessed 22 September 2021).

Stutsman, Drake, 'The Silent Screen, 1895–1927', in Adrienne McLean (ed.), *Costume, Makeup and Hair* (New Brunswick, NJ: Rutgers University Press, 2016), 21–46.

Swerts, Thomas and Stijn Oosterlynck, 'In Search of Recognition: The Political Ambiguities of Undocumented Migrants' Active Citizenship', *Journal of Ethnic and Migration Studies* 47:3 (2020), 668–85.

Tagg, John, *The Burden of Representation: Essays on Photography and Histories* (London: Palgrave Macmillan, 1988).

Talbot, Frederick, *Moving Pictures: How They Are Made and Worked* (London: William Heinemann, 1912).

Taylot, Diana, 'A Savage Performance: Guillermo Gómez-Peña and Coco Fusco's "Couple in the Cage"', *TDR* 42:2 (1998), 160–75.

Thornham, Sue, '"A Hatred So Intense . . .": *We Need to Talk about Kevin*, Postfeminism and Women's Cinema', *Sequence* 2:1 (2013): 1–38.

Todorov, Alexander, Christopher Y. Olivola, Ron Dotsch and Peter Mende-Siedlecki, 'Social Attributions from Faces: Determinants, Consequences, Accuracy, and Functional Significance', *Annual Review of Psychology* 66 (January 2015), 519–45, <https://doi.org/10.1146/annurev-psych-113011-143831> (last accessed 13 October 2021).

Tolentino, Jia, 'The Age of Instagram Face', *The New Yorker*, 12 December 2019, <https://www.newyorker.com/culture/decade-in-review/the-age-of-instagram-face> (last accessed 24 February 2021).

Trifonova, Temenuga, *Warped Minds: Cinema and Psychopathology* (Amsterdam: Amsterdam University Press, 2014).

Tyree, J. M., 'Anti-*Psycho*-Logical: Notes on Lynne Ramsay's *You Were Never Really Here*', *Bennington Review* 6 (2018), <https://www.benningtonreview.org/jm-tyree-anti-psycho-logical> (last accessed 24 September 2021).

Uddin, Md Zia, Mohammad M. Hassan, Ahmad Almogren, Mansour Zuair, Giancarlo Fortino and Jim Torresen, 'A Facial Expression Recognition System Using Robust Face Features from Depth Videos and Deep Learning', *Computers & Electrical Engineering* 63 (2017), 114–25.

UTKFace, <https://susanqq.github.io/UTKFace/> (last accessed 22 September 2021).

Vertov, Dziga, *Kino-Eye: The Writings of Dziga Vertov*, trans. Kevin O'Brien (Berkeley: Univeristy of California Press, 1985).

Wall-Romana, Christophe, 'Epstein's Photogénie as Corporeal Vision: Inner Sensation, Queer Embodiment, and Ethics', in Sarah Keller and Jason N. Paul (eds), *Jean Epstein: Critical Essays and New Translations* (Amsterdam: Amsterdam University Press, 2012), 51–73.

Wallis, Brian, 'Black Bodies, White Science: Louis Agassiz's Slave Daguerrotypes', *American Art* 9:2 (Summer 1995), 39–61.

Wang, Y. and M. Kosinski, 'Deep Neural Networks Are More Accurate than Humans at Detecting Sexual Orientation from Facial Images', *Journal of Personality and Social Psychology* 114:2 (2018), 246–57, <https://doi.org/10.1037/pspa0000098> (last accessed 13 October 2021).

Warman, Edward B., *Gestures and Attitudes: An Exposition of the Delsarte Philosophy of Expression* (Boston: Lee and Shepard, 1892).

Wassen, Stina Fredrika, 'Where Does Securitisation Begin? The Institutionalised Securitisation of Illegal Immigration in Sweden: REVA and the ICFs', *Contemporary Voices: St Andrews Journal of International Relations* 1:1 (2018), 78–103.

We Need to Talk About Kevin, dir. Lynne Ramsay, BBC Films and UK Film Council, 2011.

Weber, Brenda R, *Makeover TV: Selfhood, Citizenship, and Celebrity* (Durham, NC: Duke University Press, 2009).

—— 'The Incredible Invisible Woman: Age, Beauty, and the Specter of Identity', in Maxine Craig (ed.), *The Routledge Companion to Beauty Politics* (New York: Routledge, 2021), 365–76.

Welchman, John, 'Face(t)s: Notes on Faciality', *Artforum International* 27 (1998), 131–8.

West, Thomas J., III, 'A Star is Reborn: Embodiment, Empathy, and *Judy* (2019)', *Medium*, 17 February 2021, <https://medium.com/screenology/a-star-is-reborn-embodiment-empathy-and-judy-2018-54f8a0510f67> (last accessed 6 October 2021).

Westmore, Perc, 'Corrective Make-up', In John Paddy Carstairs (ed.), *Movie Merry-Go-Round* (London: Newnes, 1937), 115–25.

'Which Face is Real?' <https://www.whichfaceisreal.com/about.html> (last accessed 13 October 2021).

Williams, Linda. 'Film Bodies: Gender, Genre, and Excess', *Film Quarterly* 44:4 (Summer 1991), 2–13.

—— 'Surprised by Blackface: D. W. Griffith and One Exciting Night', in Stephen Johnson (ed.), *Burnt Cork: Traditions and Legacies of Blackface Minstrelsy* (Amherst: University of Massachusetts Press, 2012), 133–6.

Wilson, Lena, 'Rachel Morrison's Deeply Empathetic Cinematography', *Seventh Row*, 9 May 2018, <https://seventh-row.com/2018/05/09/rachel-morrison/> (last accessed 24 September 2021).

Wojcik, Pamela Robertson (ed.), *Movie Acting, The Film Reader* (New York: Routledge, 2004).

Wolfe, Cary, *Zoontologies: The Question of the Animal* (Minneapolis: University of Minnesota Press, 2003).

You Were Never Really Here, dir. Lynne Ramsay, Film4 Productions, British Film Institute and Why Not Productions, 2017.

Yu, Brandon, 'A Vision of Asian-American Cinema That Questions the Very Premise', *The New York Times*, 11 February 2021, <https://www.nytimes.com/2021/02/11/movies/asian-american-cinema.html> (last accessed 23 September 2021).

Ziarek, Ewa, 'The Uncanny Style of Kristeva's Critique of Nationalism', *Postmodern Culture* 5:2 (January 1995), <http://pmc.iath.virginia.edu/text-only/issue.195/ziarek.195> (last accessed 24 September 2021).

Zimmer, Catherine, 'Surveillance Cinema: Narrative between Technology and Politics', *Surveillance & Society* 8:4 (2011), 427–40.

Zuberi, Tukufu, *Thicker than Blood: How Racial Statistics Lie* (Minneapolis: University of Minnesota Press, 2001).

INDEX